MEMORY AND AFFECT IN DEVELOPMENT

The Minnesota Symposia on Child Psychology

Volume 26

MEMORY AND AFFECT IN DEVELOPMENT

The Minnesota Symposia on Child Psychology

Volume 26

edited by

CHARLES A. NELSON
University of Minnesota

LEA

1993

LAWRENCE ERLBAUM ASSOCIATES, PUBLISHERS

Hillsdale, New Jersey   Hove and London

Lawrence Erlbaum Associates Inc., Publishers
365 Broadway
Hillsdale, New Jersey 07642

Library of Congress Cataloging-in-Publication Data

Memory and affect in development / edited by Charles A. Nelson.
    p.   cm. — (The Minnesota symposia on child psychology ; v.
26)
  "Papers presented at the 26th Minnesota Symposium on Child
Psychology, held 24–26 October 1991"—Pref.
  Includes bibliographical references and index.
  ISBN 0-8058-1261-X
  1. Memory in children—Congresses. 2. Emotions in children—
Congresses. I. Nelson, Charles A. II. Minnesota Symposium on
Child Psychology (24th : 1989 : University of Minnesota)
III. Series: Minnesota symposium on child psychology (Series) ; v.
26.
BF723.M4M445   1993
155.4'1312—dc20   92-47010
                                                                    CIP

Printed in the United States of America
10 9 8 7 6 5 4 3 2 1

Contents

Preface

This volume represents the papers presented at the 26th Minnesota Symposium on Child Psychology, held 24–26 October 1991, at the University of Minnesota, Minneapolis. As has been true since the inception of the Minnesota Symposia series, the faculty of the Institute of Child Development invited an internationally renowned group of investigators to present their work and to consider problems of mutual concern.

Of the many changes that have occurred in recent years in developmental psychology, two have been particularly prominent. One has been how diverse this field has become, thus resulting in the need for cross fertilization among disciplines. A second has been a trend for greater communication between those conducting basic research and those conducting clinical research, or indeed, engaged in the practice of psychology itself.

There are a number of examples of both of these trends, some of which will be illustrated in subsequent volumes. However, one that is particularly noteworthy concerns the relation between memory and emotion. Those who study emotion and emotional development know how substantial a role memory can be in their studies; one need only consider Freud's contribution as but one example (for some discussion of this, see Bretherton's chapter in this volume). On the other hand, although many who study memory and memory development need pay little attention to the role of emotion, there are certain subfields of memory research where emotion plays a prominent role. One example concerns memory of affectively relevant material (e.g., witness to a crime); a second concerns memory of emotionally charged situations (e.g., trauma, abuse).

When this symposium was first conceived, my idea was to bring together individuals who studied memory, individuals who studied emotion, and finally, individuals who studied the relation between memory and emotion. A second aim was to bring together both basic and applied researchers. By all accounts the symposium was a success, and I am confident that this is reflected in the resulting volume.

The opening chapter by Katherine Nelson (*Events, Narratives, Memory: What Develops?*) provides an incisive review of an extended research program on memory development by one of the foremost researchers in this field. In many respects this chapter anchors the book, as it provides a detailed exposition of early memory, and in so doing sets the stage for the succeeding chapters. Nelson's work is critiqued and amplified by Patricia Bauer (*Identifying Subsystems of Autobiographical Memory: Commentary on Nelson*), who served as discussant of Nelson's paper at the symposium.

Following Nelson's exposition of early memory, Robyn Fivush (*Emotional Content of Parent-Child Conversations about the Past*) offers a splendid example of how memory and affect are interrelated. Drawing on research of her own and of others, Fivush interweaves the threads of work on memory and emotion to present a view of how memory and emotion mutually influence one another. She does so, in part, by adopting a method pioneered by Nelson: the in-depth study of a small sample of children and their parents. The result is as clear a mien on this subject as any that exist. A critique of this work, and of Nelson's, is then provided by Louise Hertsgaard and Alexandra Matthews (*The Ontogeny of Memory Revisited: Commentary on Nelson and Fivush*), who argue that recent research in cognitive neuroscience may help shed additional light on memory/affect relations.

Peggy Miller, Lisa Hoogstra, Judith Mintz, Heidi Fung, and Kimberly Williams (*Troubles in the Garden and How They Get Resolved: A Young Child's Transformation of his Favorite Story*) amplifies some of the points raised by Fivush, and focuses their paper on one child's memory and reconstruction of his favorite story: Peter Rabbit. Drawing on his (fascinating) retellings of this story, Miller et al. are able to offer some compelling insights into the child's affective life. This is expanded upon in Ganie DeHart's incisive critique of this work (*Placing Affect and Narrative in Developmental and Cultural Context: Comments on Miller et al.*).

In many respects the chapters by Nelson, Fivush, and Miller et al. lay the ground work for the final chapters and commentaries of this volume, all of which are concerned with applying research on memory and emotion to real-life situations. In Graham Davies's chapter, for example (*Children's Memory for Other People: An Integrative Review*), research on children as eyewitnesses is discussed. In this comprehensive review, Davies discusses children's eyewitness memory based on both laboratory and field research. In somewhat startling fashion, Davies notes that these seemingly related areas are often at odds with one another. As Davies discusses, this can often make more difficult (viz. expert witnesses) the task of prosecuting those who perpetrate crimes against children.

This theme is amplified by Steven Penrod (*The Child Witness, the Courts, and Psychological Research*), who comments on this issue from the perspective of both researcher and practioner (in this case, lawyer).

The final chapter in the volume represents yet another application of work on memory and affect. Here Margaret Steward (*Understanding Children's Memories of Medical Procedures: "He Didn't Touch Me and it Didn't Hurt!"*) discusses her own work and the work of others on children's understanding of medical procedures. Drawing on both basic and applied research on memory and on emotional development, Steward tackles the challenging problem of how children remember and understand the procedures that are performed on them in the hospital (some of which are highly invasive). If the clinical relevance of this research is not readily apparent, it is made all the more so by the commentary that follows, by Susan Phipps-Yonas (*A Case Example of Clinically Relevant Research: Commentary on Steward*).

In integrative symposia such as this, the challenge of tying loose ends together can be formidable. In the current case, this challenge does not go unmet. Here Inge Bretherton (*From Dialogue to Internal Working Models: The Co-Construction of Self in Relationships*), a pioneer in the study of memory/affect relations, brings together bits of her own research to expand on many of the themes discussed in the preceding chapters.

Collectively, the chapters comprising this volume represent an attempt at integrating across historically separate domains of study. It was my goal as editor to bring the excitement that was generated about the relation between memory and affect during the actual symposium to the published version.

The Minnesota Symposia on Child Psychology has a long and cherished history here at the Institute of Child Development. Many people are responsible for assisting me in making the symposium itself, and the resulting volume, a success. First and foremost, of course, I owe my thanks to the presenters and contributors. Not only did they rise to the challenge of preparing lengthy talks and lengthy chapters, they did so with great aplomb and nary a missed deadline. Second, the graduate students at the Institute of Child Development deserve thanks for attending to the many administrative details of the symposium. Third, to Helen Dickison and my secretary, LuJean Huffman-Nordberg, I owe my eternal gratitude. Without these individuals letters of invitation would not have been sent and speakers would not have been picked up at the airport. Fourth, I'd like to thank Jackie Goodnow for being a sounding board for the theme of this symposium. When I first conceived of this topic, it was very much a loose constellation of ideas, with no central core. Jackie, who was then in residence as a visiting faculty member, and I met on several occasions, where she did a splendid job of helping me articulate what it was I wanted to accomplish in the symposium. Finally, I would like to acknowledge the financial support for the Symposium from the Institute of Child Development (Richard Weinberg, Director) and the Center for Research in Learning, Perception, and Cognition (Albert

Yonas, Director), both of the University of Minnesota; the National Institutes of Child Health and Human Development (R13 HD21906; Megan Gunnar, Principal Investigator); and the General Mills Foundation.

Charles A. Nelson

1 Events, Narratives, Memory: What Develops?

Katherine Nelson
City University of New York Graduate Center

Students of memory have been faced with the persistent problem of what it is that they are studying, and whether it comes in different types or whether there is a single structure, process, or function called Memory. Developmentalists face this problem particularly when they try to determine when and if some memory capacity or function emerges in childhood. In recent years developmental researchers have focused attention on generic event memory or scripts, episodic memory for specific episodes of events, and autobiographical memory as a particular type of episodic memory that constitutes one's life story. In contrast to these types of event memory is semantic memory, as first identified by Tulving (1972), which is organized as a decontexted knowledge system. In this paper I trace the evolution of thinking about these types of memory, based on early work with my group of colleagues and students at Yale and CUNY, and then bring this thinking up-to-date, based on a broad range of studies from other labs as well as our own.

Tulving's (1972) distinction between semantic and episodic memory was influential in my initial approach to problems in memory development in early childhood, beginning in the mid-1970s. However, because memories for real-life experiences, especially those from the infancy and very early childhood period, do not seem well-characterized as *semantic* (because they might not have any verbal component), I preferred the term *generic* as a contrast to *episodic*. Yet as has become evident, there is more than one type of generic memory.

The developmental problem posed by this distinction at first appeared to me to be frameable simply in terms of the origins of episodic and generic (semantic) memory—might one precede the other in development? (See Nelson & Brown, 1979.) When we first began pursuit of this question, there was next to no research on memory in children younger than school-age. One of the reasons for this neglect seemed to be the kind of memory that developmental researchers were concerned with, primarily verbal memory tested with lists of words or pictures. Preschool children were shown to perform poorly on these kinds of laboratory-based tasks. As Donaldson (1978) demonstrated for many types of tasks, preschool children may perform in ways that better reflect their cognitive abilities when presented with situations that make "human sense" to them, that is, that resemble situations that they experience in their everyday lives. Following this line of work memory researchers began to ask, not whether children could remember the things we had devised for them to remember—usually words, pictures, or objects—but what they could remember about the things they did everyday.

Thus the situation with respect to pre-school memory has changed dramatically over the past 20 years as an emerging perspective on ecologically valid and ethnographically situated memory research took memory out of the laboratory and into homes and day care centers to focus on the activities that children are involved in in their everyday lives and the kinds of information that they must remember if they are to carry through those activities successfully. This has been our focus at CUNY from the beginning. We have studied children's memory for experienced events, involving people, places, and actions. We have viewed memory for words and objects not as decontexted items but in terms of how they fit into the child's schemas for knowing about events. (See Perlmutter, 1980 for a collection of papers on this early work.)

Our first studies primarily concerned children's general event memory, or scripts for familiar events (Nelson & Gruendel, 1981). We found that children as young as 3 years had quite good and reliable representations of familiar, routine events, and could present a verbal account of them. We characterized this knowledge as generic, because it was almost always formulated in very general terms. Because the same children seemed not to have very good representations of *specific* episodes in their lives (Hudson & Nelson, 1986), we tentatively concluded that generic memory preceded episodic in development. This seemed to be a somewhat radical conclusion in that it implied that children's memory was abstract before it was specific, the opposite to traditional assumptions about development.

The script model that Schank and Abelson (1977) developed to describe narrative understanding and plans in terms of action sequences organized around a goal seemed to fit these early data from young children quite well. Our studies showed that preschool children have good generic script-type knowledge enabling them to represent familiar events in canonical causal-temporal sequences of actions, organized in terms of central events or goals, embedding sets of objects that fill action-object slots, and roles that people play within the event script. This generic knowledge, in the form of general event representations or scripts, was further shown to play a role in children's understanding and use of complex language, interpretation of and memory for stories and dramatic play, production of fantasy stories, and even the organization of object categories (French & Nelson, 1985; Lucariello & Nelson, 1985; Nelson, 1986; Nelson & Gruendel, 1979).

We therefore proposed that children first constructed scripts for familiar events, and that only after having established a sufficient body of script knowledge, would they be able to use that knowledge as a background from which to remember or reconstruct memory for a specific *novel* event. This conclusion seemed to fit well with the apparent difficulty that young children had in remembering episodes without a great deal of cuing from adults (Nelson, Fivush, Hudson, & Lucariello, 1983; Nelson & Ross, 1980). It also suggested an explanation for the phenomenon of infantile amnesia, the inability to remember events from the early years of one's life (Nelson, 1990; in press).

As I have commented elsewhere (Nelson, in press), it is quite remarkable that developmental psychologists—even those studying memory in young children— have in general neglected the infantile amnesia phenomenon, despite its clear implication that some very dramatic development takes place in the early childhood years that either establishes a new memory system, or enables existing memories to persist, or represses those that do exist (Freud, 1963). (See Pillemer & White, 1989 for a review of these issues. See also Bachevalier, 1992 for an alternative, neurally based explanation of the phenomenon.) The explanation for this development that was suggested by our initial inquiry was that adults do not remember episodes from early childhood because young children do not have episodic memory, but only general script memory; everything that is remembered from an experience is entered into the general script system. Only after that system is well-established could specific episodes be seen as novel and memorable in their own right.

Note that script memory is highly functional. It enables a person to predict and plan for future encounters of a similar situation, as well as to guide action within a familiar event, and to interpret reports or stories told by other people about such an event. Indeed, from a functional perspective, scripts appear to have much greater value than episodic memories for one-time happenings (Nelson, 1989b; in press). Thus it seems that evolution might have developed script-type generic memory as the basic form of human (as well as of other mammalian) memory. This possibility raised the questions: Why should children (or adults) ever have episodic memories? When might episodic memories become part of a long-lasting autobiographical memory system?

Contrary to our earlier conclusion, however, subsequent investigations at CUNY (e.g., Hudson, 1986; Hudson & Nelson, 1986; Nelson, 1989a; Nelson & Hudson, 1988)—and a great deal of research that Robyn Fivush, Judith Hudson, and other researchers have carried out since—established that very young children—as young as 1 year of age—*do* have, not only general event representations, but also specific memories for particular episodes in their lives. Our initial supposition that generic memory was first established to the exclusion of specific memories appeared to be wrong. These conclusions are based on a variety of studies, including parental reports, experimenter interviews about specific naturally occurring experiences, taperecording children talking alone (see description that follows), and questioning children about staged experimental episodes.

There remains something elusive about these findings, however. Children often require extensive cuing to elicit any information about events that they have experienced. Asking children to report on events they have experienced is not always fruitful; it often seems that the adult's memory is not matched by the child's, although children may report elements that adults have not noticed or have forgotten. Perhaps the absence of adult memories for early childhood experiences is the result of differential interests or attention. Moreover, young children's memories do not usually seem to endure for longer than about 6 months, unlike the memories of older children and adults, which in some cases last for decades. (Fivush & Hamond, 1990 have found evidence of memories in 4 year olds from as long as 2 years in the past, but this time span may be exceptional. Further verification to determine the conditions under which long-lasting memories in the early childhood years may be established is clearly needed.)

The questions raised earlier remain unanswered, however. The establishment of clear evidence that children have some episodic memories suggests further questions that might provide the central clue: *What* episodes do children remember and *why?*

In what follows I seek answers to these questions through evidence of very early episodic memory accounts and generic memory in one child's talk to herself, inquiring as to what enters into that talk and why. I then consider evidence of the influence of adult talk on the development of episodic or autobiographical memory with respect to the past, the present activity, and the future, and consider how each of these types of talk may affect memory for an event. I then consider the psychological and social sources of episodic and autobiographical memory together and suggest issues that may be resolved in future research. Finally, I consider how what Tulving referred to as Semantic Memory may have its roots as well in parent-child talk.

CHILD TALK ABOUT THE PAST: MONOLOGUE AND DIALOGUE

In pursuit of the answer to the "what" question, in 1981 I enlisted the help of a very cooperative mother and father of a 21-month-old highly verbal little girl, Emily. They agreed to record her talk to herself at bedtime and naptime for the purpose of investigating the nature and form of early episodic memories. I hypothesized that talk to self, which many very young children engage in, might contain revealing references to aspects of memory for real life events from the child's own perspective that would not be apparent when prompted by adults, even by parents. The resulting transcripts of her talk yielded a rich collection of her memories, both specific and general. These have been subsequently reported in previous publications (Nelson, 1988, 1989a, 1989b), which provide details about the research methods.

The first transcripts that emerged from this study indicated that Emily at 21 months was recalling (alone in her crib) fragments of remembered experiences, such as going to the library with her grandmother. (Such memories were verified by her mother who reviewed the tapes prior to their transcription.) By 24 months a surprising development was observed. The transcripts still contained fragments, but also some recounts that were quite coherently organized as what appeared to be "proto-narratives," that is, they had the form of a sequence of actions connected temporally and causally within a bounded temporal space. An example of this type from 23 months is the following:

> When my slep and, and, Mormor came. Then Mommy coming,   (1)
> then get up, time to go ho-o-ome. Time to go home. Drink P-water [Perrrier].
> Yesterday did that. Now Emmy sleeping in regular bed.

This account of mommy getting her at her baby sitter's is certainly not very elaborate or unusual, and it scarcely would count as a full-fledged narrative or story, yet it does have a coherent temporally organized action line, complete with different actors and locations.

Accounts of autobiographical memory in children as well as adults often invoke the idea of memory as narrative. Finding evidence for aspects of narrativity in very early episodic memories is at least suggestive that an important role in establishing episodic memory may be played by the narrative form itself. In order to evaluate this proposal we must be clear as to what counts as a narrative, and what does not. At the most basic level, narratives consist of the report of a sequence of actions by actors that are connected in some way, usually because they are organized to achieve a goal or solve a problem. There is a point to the narrative, a reason for the telling (Labov, 1972; Peterson & McCabe, 1983). Skilled narrators, of course, organize their stories around the point; thus they may not simply lay out in sequence the actions as they happened, but provide causal statements, evaluative comments, and re-arrange the events to provide suspense.

Bruner and Lucariello (1989) based their analysis of Emily's monologues on Burke's (1945) proposals about the "grammar of motives." In particular, they proposed that any narrative is based on implicit assumptions about the way things usually happen—the canonical who, where, why, what, and how of an event. The canonical form is equivalent to the script or general event representation that Gruendel and I studied, and that Schank and Abelson (1977) based their script and story analysis on. Whereas a script may form the basis for a simple narrative, for example, a recount of what happened at school, a good story, as Bruner and Lucariello (1989) pointed out, is formulated around "trouble" in the canonical form of the expected event: "Actions do not reach goals, scenes and agents do not match, instruments and goals are out of kilter, and so on. The narrative is a vehicle for characterizing, exploring, preventing, brooding about, redressing, or recounting the consequences of 'trouble.' " (pp. 76–77).

Bruner and Lucariello's idea of stories emerging from canonical event schemas is consistent with Gruendel's (1980) analysis of children's stories formulated around familiar events. She found that, when asked to tell a story, 4-year-olds produced simple scripts, while older children first transformed the script with a simple deformation of canonical form (e.g., having a garden produce lollipops rather than flowers), and only later (beginning at 8 years) produced a full problem-solving story line.

We would not expect then, that Emily's memory recounts at 2 to 3 years would be full story-like narratives. But as the months went by Emily's proto-narratives became more elaborate, incorporating linguistic devices identified on *a priori* grounds as characteristic of mature narratives, marking sequence, canonicality, and perspective (Bruner & Lucariello, 1989). For example, a production at 32 months is the following:

> We *bought* a baby, cause, the well because, when she, well, we *thought* it was for (2)
> Christmas, but *when* we went to the s-s-store we didn't have our jacket on, but I
> saw some dolly, and I *yelled* at my mother and said I want one of those dolly. So
> after we were finished with the store, we went over to the dolly and she *bought* me
> one. So I have one.

Linguistic devices such as those marking intentionality ("we thought," "I want"), temporality ("when," "after"), and causality ("so") take the canonical form of an event and transform it into a story with a point, providing a "landscape of consciousness" as well as a "landscape of action" (Bruner, 1986). Productions such as (2) certainly suggest that acquisition of the narrative form itself may have influenced Emily's organization of episodic memories. But how did she acquire the narrative form?

> Did the narrative format effectively organize her memories (perhaps thereby transforming them into autobiographical memories), or alternatively, did the memory recounts simply provide the content for practicing the narrative format? Where does the narrative format come from?

Before considering possible answers to these questions, we should note at least one other type of event report in Emily's monologues, the general script. An early example of a general script is the following:

> I can't go down the basement with jamas on. I sleep with jamas. Okay sleep with (3)
> jamas. In the night time my only put big girl pants on. But in the morning we put

jamas on. But, and the morning gets up . . . of the room. But, afternoon my wake up and play. Play with Mommy, Daddy . . . (24 mo.)

Although this account is somewhat inaccurate, it reflects Emily's concern with how things go. Later in the third year her "scripts" became highly extended, one concerned with the day's routine contained over 50 separate propositions reporting events in their canonical order, with several repetitions of the same event sequence. It is notable that these were formulated in terms of what will happen tomorrow, that is, the script served as the basis for anticipation of familiar event sequences. Later we see that this relation has its basis in parental talk.

These two types of event recounts found in Emily's monologues—general script and specific past episode—may be seen to have different relations to memory—specifically to autobiographical memory—and to the narrative process by which they are produced. As previously noted, script reports establish the canonical form of events but have no *point* beyond understanding (and therefore to some extent controlling) how the world is and what one can expect to happen.

Specific episodic recounts might concern a specific experience of a routine event (such as being picked up at her baby sitter's), but more often are based on a variation of a routine—for Emily, seeing a tow truck, getting a new TV, buying a doll. A relevant question is whether these variations or *episodic memories* recalled in her crib talk might establish them as *autobiographical memories,* in the sense that adults have autobiographical memories, or whether they represent only evanescent memories similar to an adult's memory for an unremarkable recent meal. There is in fact no evidence that these were more than evanescent memories. There was no case in the transcripts of a memory that was recounted at say 2 or $2\frac{1}{2}$ years being repeated or re-remembered at $2\frac{1}{2}$ or 3 years. The relation between episodic memories and autobiographical memory is addressed at greater length in a later section. Here I note only that autobiographical memory is not only long-lasting, but is presumably long-lasting for a reason. Thus the basic question is why some memories persist while others do not.

Relatedly, we might ask: why did Emily repeat these memories to herself? It is interesting that most of her accounts of specific episodes were not of episodes that she had talked about with her parents, at least according to mother's report, nor were they the sort of things that her parents would have specifically prepared her for with anticipatory talk. For example, the doll buying episode (2) was not anticipated because it was not planned. Indeed, as I have noted frequently, Emily's crib memories were of the ordinary, quotidian things of her life, not of the truly novel (from an adult point of view) such as the birth of her brother, her first day at nursery school, or her trips to visit grandparents by plane.

In fact, in the parent-child pre-bed talk available in this study there is little talk with parents about specific episodes from the past, although from what we know of other studies it is virtually certain that Emily experienced such talk. Still, the unremarkable topics of her memories, and her mother's disclaimer, indicate that Emily was not basing her crib memory talk on what her parents had rehearsed with her. Thus her memories seemed to emerge solely from her organization of her direct event experience.

A clue to the question of *why* these episodes may be found in their sometimes repetitive character. The account of her mother fetching her from the babysitter's (1) was repeated five times with variations in the telling in the course of the evening's monologue, for example. A possible interpretation of these repetitions is that they served the same purpose as her script-building monologues did. That is, they were different ways in which she focused on the characteristics of an event and seemed to examine and reexamine its parts, with the function of entering it correctly into her general knowledge system. From this point of view memory within the episodic system at this point in development (2 to 3 years) has the same value as memory in the generic system, differing only in the extent to which it represents repeated or unique information about events; and perhaps also differing in the length of time it may be held in memory (Nelson, in press).

Thus, despite the specificity of much of Emily's discourse about her experience, I believe that it is quite defensible to suggest that both her memory talk and her script productions served similar functions—to add to her knowledge base, derived from her experiences in the real world. I suggest that she was building a "world model," and that her monologues aided in that enterprise. This enterprise differs from the construction of a personal past such as the memories that become part of one's personal or autobiographical memory system, but it may provide a base from which such a system develops. I consider next evidence about another source of information about early memories— parent-child talk about the past.

PARENT-CHILD TALK ABOUT THE PAST

There have been a number of studies in the past 10 years that have analyzed talk about the past between parents and their children (see Hudson, 1990 for a review). Susan Engel (1986) at CUNY undertook a study of parent-child memory talk in the latter part of the second year, visiting four mother-child dyads over a 6-month period when the children were between 18 and 24 months. She also carried out a cross-sectional study of 2-year-old children who were specifically prompted by their mothers to talk about three memories of recent experiences. Like other investigators, Engel found that mothers varied in the amount of memory talk they engaged in, and the kinds of questions they asked (Ratner, 1984). But she also found that the dyads varied in the *kinds* of memories they focused on and in the *manner* in which they formulated their talk. She identified two styles of memory talk, which she called pragmatic and elaborative. Pragmatic mothers not only tended to talk about practical matters, such as where a child had left a toy, but when they talked about experiences they had shared, they tended to focus on the *who* and *what* rather than the *where, when, how,* and *why*. Elaborative mothers made stories of their experiences and invited their children to participate in them. In the most successful cases, even at 2 years children "co-constructed" the narrative with their mothers.

In the following example a boy (24 months; 17 days) and mother have been recalling a visit from Aunt Judy, with no apparent relevance to what follows regarding an event from 2 months previous.

<table>
<tr><td>C:</td><td>Mommy, the Chrysler building</td><td>(4)</td></tr>
<tr><td>M:</td><td>The Chrysler building?</td><td></td></tr>
<tr><td>C:</td><td>The Chrysler building?</td><td></td></tr>
<tr><td>M:</td><td>Yeah, who works in the Chrysler building?</td><td></td></tr>
<tr><td>C:</td><td>Daddy</td><td></td></tr>
<tr><td>M:</td><td>Do you ever go there?</td><td></td></tr>
<tr><td>C:</td><td>Yes, I see the Chrysler building\ picture of the Chrysler building\</td><td></td></tr>
<tr><td>M:</td><td>I don't know if we have a picture of the Chrysler building. Do we?</td><td></td></tr>
<tr><td>C:</td><td>We went to . . . my Daddy went to work</td><td></td></tr>
<tr><td>M:</td><td>Remember when we went to visit daddy? Went in the elevator, way way up in the building so we could look down from the big window?</td><td></td></tr>
<tr><td>C:</td><td>big window</td><td></td></tr>
<tr><td>M:</td><td>mmhm</td><td></td></tr>
<tr><td>C:</td><td>( )
When . . . we did go on the big building</td><td></td></tr>
<tr><td>M:</td><td>mmhm, the big building. Was that fun? Would you like to do it again? Sometime.</td><td></td></tr>
<tr><td>C:</td><td>I want to go on the big building.</td><td></td></tr>
</table>

(Unpublished data from Engel, 1986, used with permission)

In this excerpt, the child introduces the topic, and provides some evidence of having a memory of going to visit Daddy, but the mother reconstructs the remembered episode, providing the action sequence of going up in the elevator and looking out the big window, as well as the evaluative comment that it was fun and the child might like to do it again.

Engel found that the children of elaborative mothers engaged in more episodes and more extensive episodes of memory talk at 2 years than did the children of pragmatic mothers. Fivush and Fromhoff (1988) found a similar relation between mothers' talk and children's memory. They distinguished between elaborative and repetitive mothers. As in example (4) from Engel's data, elaborative mothers provide a progressive story line, inviting the child to contribute bits to the story, while repetitive mothers focus on a single bit of information without providing further narrative framing. A telling example of a repetitive mother's memory talk is the following from a conversation between a mother and her $2\frac{1}{2}$ year old child about their recent trip to Florida (Fivush & Hammond, 1990, pp. 230–231):

<table>
<tr><td>M:</td><td>And where did we eat breakfast? Where did we go for breakfast?</td><td>(5)</td></tr>
</table>

> C: What?
> M: Where did we go for breakfast? Remember we went out, Daddy, you, and
>   I? What restaurant did we go to?
> C: Gasoline.
> M: Gasoline? No, what restaurant did we go have breakfast at?
> C: Ummm . . .
> M: Do you remember? It was Burger . . . ?
> C: King!

In contrast to the mother in (4) who leads on from the child's comment to build a story organized around his contribution, here the mother is intent on extracting a single bit of information, but provides no additional cues for the child to build on, no little story about what happened at the restaurant, for example. Rather— perhaps because in the mother's view going to Burger King for breakfast is a novel and memorable event—she repetitively urges the child to produce the *correct* answer to the question, and finally provides the associative link that enables him to succeed on her terms. Whether her cue accesses any actual memory of the event on the part of the child cannot be established from this evidence, but there is no reason to believe that the child has produced anything more than a verbal association between Burger and King. This kind of talk about the past is unlikely to establish narrative as a format for episodic memory. Might it establish a different kind of format that would also be successful in fostering memory?

Evidence from Fivush and Fromhoff (1988) suggests not. In their study, as in Engel's, children of elaborative mothers revealed better memory for episodes 6 months later. However, this kind of data is inherently ambiguous. Mother-child dyads are mutually influentiable, thus attributing causal relations is not possible. For example, mothers might be led to tell more elaborate narratives with children who are more verbal, more responsive to the telling, more interested in the kinds of details such narratives contain. Moreover, mothers inclined to story-telling about the child's past experience may tend to have children who display the cognitive style that Wolf and Gardner (1979) called dramatist, being inherently inclined to engage in similar narrative constructions, thus encouraging the mothers' efforts.

However, the suggestion of a causal relation remains viable when other factors (such as general language ability, number of memories discussed) appear equal at the first measurement, and when the lagged observation (more memory displayed by children whose mothers provided more encouragement of a seemingly appropriate kind) seems to make psychological sense. At the least such replicated observations suggest that more controlled studies of the effects of parental talk on children's memory are needed.

It should be emphasized that the effects found by Engel were not simply that children remembered *more*. Rather, the narrative format of the memories was apparent in the kinds of information that children contributed and in the organization and language used to present it. As we saw in Emily's proto-narratives, this format organizes the memory as a coherent whole, representing the perspective of consciousness as well as the perspective of action.[1] As Hudson (1990) noted with regard to her own child's acquisition of the memory talk format, "Rachel learned a lot about how to remember, that is, about how to participate and, finally, to initiate conversations about the past rather than rehearsing specific content" (p. 183). Children "are learning *how* to remember, not *what* to remember" (p. 194). But, as is apparent from these other studies, some children have less experience with the narrative model that shows *how* to remember effectively than do others. It should be emphasized, however, that, as with other kinds of *style* differences in language and cognition (Nelson, 1981) parental style of memory talk is not an all or none issue, but rather one of points along a continuum, with extremes where some parents cast a great deal of talk about the past in narrative form while others talk about memories very little and provide little scaffolding for the child to model.

TALK ABOUT THE PRESENT

Thus far we have seen that talk about the past may provide a model of how to organize and remember events. What about talk in the present? Minda Tessler (1986) undertook to study aspects of the social construction of memory by examining the effects of adult framing of an event *while it was being experienced* by the child. She took $3\frac{1}{2}$-year-old children and their mothers on a visit to the Natural History Museum. Half the mothers were instructed not to provide any input regarding the visit beyond answering the child's questions, while the other half were encouraged to talk with their children as they usually would on such a visit. A week later the investigator returned and obtained children's memory for the museum trip in both a free recall and probed interview.

There was a striking difference between the children whose mothers provided a frame for the experience and those whose mothers did not in the number of memories that children recalled of what they had seen. Moreover, Tessler observed that, even among the mothers who were encouraged to act naturally, there was a difference in the style in which they interacted with their children about the

---

[1]Emily's memories were organized in this way from the age of about 23 months, earlier than any other child reported in the literature. Emily was a highly verbal child, skilled in language forms. In addition, the private speech monologues may have revealed more about her capability for formulating narrative than concurrent dialogic speech (see discussion in Nelson, 1989a). It also seems likely that she received models of formulating narrative accounts, not only from parental talk about the past (not observed in the data gathered, but presumably present at other occasions) and from stories, which she heard from an early age. Her capabilities as a memorist call out for further studies of this kind. Although a bright, charming, and verbal child, we have no reason to believe that she is unique.

experience. This style difference was very similar to that described by Engel (1986) for mothers talking about the past. Tessler formulated the two styles according to Bruner's (1986) distinction between *paradigmatic* and *narrative* cognitive styles. Some of the specific characteristics of the paradigmatic style included naming and a focus on object characteristics (see Example 5), whereas characteristics of the narrative style included the perspectives identified by Bruner and Lucariello (1989)—of time, intentionality, causality, evaluation. Narrative mothers more frequently related what was on view to the child's own experience.

Children of narrative mothers remembered significantly more than children of paradigmatic mothers. An intriguing finding was that no child remembered anything from the experience that had not been talked about between mother and child. It was not sufficient for the mother to talk about an object nor for the child to draw mother's attention to it; rather there had to have been an interchange between the two for the topic to become memorable.

Tessler (1991) extended these findings in subsequent research. In this study she took 4 year-old children on a picture-taking expedition with their mothers in an unfamiliar neighborhood. She first divided mothers into groups on the basis of the way that they interacted with their children around a picture book containing urban scenes. Paradigmatic mothers were those who displayed the characteristics in their talk about the book that had been identified in the previous study. Narrative mothers were those who displayed the opposite style in that situation. The two styles were further verified by analyzing the dialogues they carried on with their children during the picture-taking event. At a subsequent session the investigator returned with the pictures and interviewed the child about his or her memory for the event. The interview was conducted in either a narrative or a paradigmatic style, based on the characteristics previously identified, crossed with the mother's style. Thus a child might be in a consistent (narrative-narrative or paradigmatic-paradigmatic) or inconsistent (narrative-paradigmatic or paradigmatic-narrative) questioning condition.

The results of this study are very striking. Mother's style had consistent and significant effects on the child's style of recalling the event, regardless of the interviewer's manipulation. Further, children of narrative mothers recalled more of the pictures they had taken, and reported more from the event. There were no differences between the groups in the number of pictures recognized, however.

The results of this study strongly suggest that style is a characteristic passed from mother to child and resistant to the efforts of an interlocutor to elicit a different style through a different mode of questioning. Further, they suggest that the narrative style of framing an event *while it is being experienced* is more effective in producing a subsequent memory of that event than is the paradigmatic style. Yet it also appears that this effect is specific to the episodic narrative structure. The recognition results suggest that the underlying memory for the event components may not have differed.

PARENTAL TALK ABOUT THE FUTURE

I am not aware of any studies of parental talk about the future and their effects on children's experience and memory comparable to those on talk about the past and the present. However, in the transcripts of Emily's bedtime talk there were many examples of parental descriptions of what would happen after nap, the next day, or the next few days, and there were ample cases of Emily's recalling and embellishing these in her subsequent monologues. An early example that has been well studied is the following, first the father's story about what would happen on Saturday (told three times), and then Emily's monologue which followed immediately after he left the room. At this point Emily was $23\frac{1}{2}$ months old.

> (i) We're gonna go . . . to Childworld . . . and we're gonna buy (6)
> some diapers for Stephen, and some diapers for Emily, and we're gonna buy an intercom system, so that we can hear Stephen in different parts of the house . . .
> (ii) we're goin to Childworld and buy diapers for Stephen, and diapers for Emily, and what is called an intercom system, that plug in . . . Stephen, into Stephen's room . . . and then we go downstairs and we plug it in . . . and we get to hear Stephen . . . we'll see who wakes up . . . we'll hear him cry . . . through the intercom system . . . It's a neat gadget.
> (iii) On Saturday . . . we're gonna go to Childworld and we're gonna buy diapers for Emily and diapers for Stephen and an intercom system so we can hear Stephen in different parts of the house.
>
> E: And Daddy said . . buy diapers for Stephen and Emmy, and buy something for Stephen plug in and say ahhh . . . and put the in . . . on Saturday go Childworld buy diaper for Emmy, and diaper for the baby . . . and then buy something for the . . and see, for that baby . . . plug in, and get diapers for *any*body.
> And buy more that day at Childworld . . . and buy croutes . . . and maybe Childworld . . . cause the one that broken at Tanta's. The one that's broken. The one that's broken here, the . . . the infant seat . . . Dada actually at home. (23;15)

This recount is closely based on her father's talk up to the line "and get diapers for anybody"—incorporating his intonation and rhythm—although she has not been able to remember what they would buy (an intercom "so that we can hear Stephen cry in different parts of the house"). Emily then adds to the story with the suggestion that they get more ("croutes?" and an infant seat), presumably based on her own prior experience of what one may buy at Childworld. (The punctuation of this monologue cannot unfortunately capture the character of Emily's production. Ellipses indicate slight pauses with sustained intonation, commas falling intonation, and period a full stop.)

As in this case, Emily's anticipatory reports were usually based on accounts that her parents provided before they left the room about what they would do later that day or the next. Emily seemed to find these accounts interesting, and often attempted to repeat them in her monologue, as in the Childworld example. Might this kind of planning talk provide a model for Emily's organization of the event and her memory of the event? To what extent does future talk—like past and present talk—reflect narrative form? Usually such talk has a canonical temporal structure, locating the events in time and ordering them into a sequence. Often it projects intentions, attitudes, and evaluations ("you're gonna like it"). Thus it contains both the landscape of action and the landscape of consciousness that Bruner sees as critical to narrative.

Yet because they are anticipated events, such productions do not contain the "trouble" or the problem around which good stories are formed. Although often her parents' anticipatory talk concerned events that were unfamiliar to Emily (for example, a trip to visit friends at the beach) they were generally about events familiar to the parent, and thus were presented in the canonical event form of "this is the way things are and will be." It is notable that there is nothing particularly salient about anticipating even an exciting event—one does not anticipate the "trouble" that makes for a good story. (Of course one may be anxious that the event go well, or feel anxious if one cannot anticipate unknown aspects of an expected event, or has reason to predict that something untoward may happen. However, these are not the sort of *fun* reports of coming events that parents are likely to convey to children at bedtime.)

On the other hand, Emily's anticipatory monologues often went beyond the parents' account, using her own event script as the basis for speculation about the specific case. For example, in the following monologue at 24 months she wondered "who's going to bring the book tomorrow" to her baby sitters, reflecting her established knowledge from her "babysitter script" that one of the children who regularly attended her day care home would bring a book that her caregiver would read to the group.

> I don't, I don't know what boy bring book tomorrow. (7)
> Maybe Lance. I don't know which boy bring book today. Maybe Danny or maybe Carl, maybe my, maybe Lance, maybe (too-wee). How about Lance bring book. (24 mo.)

On another occasion she posed the question of what would happen at the doctor's when they visited—whether the doctor would take off her pajamas and her diaper. Emily's general scripts were not always sufficient to enable her to predict correctly. For example, she did not visit the doctor in her pajamas but in day clothes. Nonetheless, her monologues provided good evidence that she was not only establishing canonical event representations but was beginning to note the "trouble" (Bruner & Lucariello, 1989) that presents the occasion for narrating about a specific episode of that event.

In summary, the Emily transcripts provide information not only about general schematic and specific episodic memory, but ways that those memories are used to project into the future, both in talk by and with parents, and in her own speculations based on general event knowledge and on parental talk. Might these anticipations have affected how Emily experienced events later, or how she remembered them, parallel to Tessler's findings about talk about ongoing events? This is an important question, but we have little data to apply to it. There is no evidence in the monologues that Emily ever recounted a memory of an episode that had been anticipated in presleep dialogue or monologue prior to its happening. Thus we have no basis for speculating as to whether or not the anticipatory talk affected the experience or the memory of the experience. What we do know is that even at 2 years-of-age Emily attended to and attempted to repeat, and to enter into her own knowledge system, through additions, speculations, and inferences, accounts that her parents provided of what would happen in not yet experienced events. Such talk about the future has been little studied, in contrast to parental talk with young children about the past.

NARRATIVE FRAMES AND
UNDERSTANDABLE EVENTS

The research just reviewed provides a strong case for believing in a social construction theory of understanding, knowledge organization, and memory, in contrast to the usual concentration by cognitive psychologists on memory as an individual trait or capacity. What these various studies have found can be summarized as follows: Adults provide narrative frames that make understandable events. We have seen that they do this for events before they happen in Emily's parents' talk about what will happen the next day or after her nap. They also do it quite naturally in the course of experiencing an event with a young child, as Tessler's research showed. And as Engel and others have documented, adults induct their children into talk about past experiences, in effect teaching them the forms for how to engage in memory talk.

While each of these temporally situated types of talk provides a kind of narrative frame for what may become the child's episodic memory, they differ somewhat, not only in their timing with respect to the event, but in the type and organization of information provided about it. In talk about expected happenings parents typically provide a skeletal framework of what is going to happen, although they may emphasize parts of the event that they believe the child will find interesting. (At least in Emily's case these estimates seemed sometimes to be misguided, as in the father's apparent expectation that Emily would like to hear her baby brother cry "all over the house.") We can usually not anticipate the details of an event; rather we rely on our scripts of previous experiences to project into the future, inserting different "slot-fillers" into the appropriate slots in the skeletal script representation. Thus future accounts tend to look more like the detailless, rather flat productions that characterize script recounts. Emily easily picked up this form in terms of what will happen "tomorrow morning when we wake up" and used it for her own anticipatory talk.

Talk about the *ongoing* event concentrates more on the details of what the child is experiencing, both in terms of the child's actions and in terms of perceptions and their interpretations. Explanations, pointing out aspects of the experience, minor anticipatory comments, and comments on what has just happened are the rule. Narrative type parents may also link what is happening with something the child has experienced in the past, or with something she thinks the child knows. Thus the present talk is less a narrative than an ongoing commentary, something like a sports commentator's spiel. Yet it may have the effect of determining what will become part of the subsequent narrative about the remembered experience, as Tessler's studies documented.

Talk about the event *after* it has occurred is most likely to take on the characteristics of a full-blown narrative. It is likely to emphasize the high points of the experience, the child's affective responses to different parts, the intentions of the participants, causal relations between actions, and any unusual, unexpected, or particularly salient happenings. Of course, as we have seen, parents differ in the degree to which they frame their talk during the experience, as well as after the experience, in these narrative styles, and they may be expected to employ different styles as well in talking about what the child may expect to happen in an anticipated event, although we do not now have that information.

SOCIAL CONSTRUCTION OF MEMORY AND THE CHILD'S MEMORY

A number of authors recently have suggested that autobiographical memory is the product of social construction in early childhood (Fivush, 1988; Hudson, 1990; Nelson, 1991, in press; Pillemer & White, 1989). The suggestion here is that autobiographical memory is a distinct form of episodic memory, a form that comes into being as the child is inducted into the shared forms of talking about shared experiences and comes to incorporate the adult values of talking about the experience. The perspective is drawn from Vygotsky's (1986) theory, as well as from Bakhtin (1986; Wertsch & Stone, 1985), and from other earlier theorists who focused on the social construction of mind and self (e.g., Mead, 1934). It is not suggested that learning to talk about the past is a simple matter of acquiring models transmitted from parent to child; rather, a dialectical process of co-construction of remembered events seems the best way of thinking about it.

The social-cultural proposal does not deny that the child herself brings distinctive episodic memories to the sharing. There is good evidence that children may remember episodes that their parents have forgotten (Fivush & Hamond, 1989). As noted earlier, Emily's memories were largely of events that were not remarked or were not known by the parents, and were not rehearsed with her parents, but rather were first recounted to herself as she prepared to sleep.

To draw these pieces together, I suggest that basic general event knowledge is the basis for understanding and therefore remembering episodes, as we first proposed, and as Emily's memories indicate. Without a good script, knowledge about what happens, based only on direct experience with the happenings, may be quite chaotic, as is evident in some of Emily's earliest monologues. For example, consider a fragment of a monologue at 21 months:

> That Daddy brings down basement washing, I can hold Emmy,   (8)
> so, Daddy brings down the, the washing on the basement, washing,
> so my can, so why, the, the, the, no-daddy brings washing.

One might question whether this is a fragment of a memory for an episode at all. Certainly it has no coherent structure, albeit it has a clear topic. As she approached 2 years-of-age, however, Emily began to produce quite coherent recounts of experienced events, which exhibited good temporal-causal sequencing and logical understanding, as illustrated earlier.

As we know from recent work by Bauer and Mandler (1990) children are able to reconstruct brief temporal action sequences late in the first and early in the second year. It seems likely that holding action sequences in mind as memories rather than performing them overtly requires more cognitive processing power, and therefore is a later development. As the fragment of Emily's monologue (8) suggests, some of her earliest productions seemed to be attempts to bring into focus many different actions on the part of her father and mother as well as herself—rather than a sequence of actions from a single event—and these attempts resulted in complexive strings. Sometime between 2 and 3 years children are able to hold in mind, not only brief overt action sequences, but the representation of extended event sequences which they can externally represent in play (action) or in language. This is the basic event knowledge system that must also support the specific episodic memories that emerge about that time.

In summary, what the young child brings to the social construction process is the capacity for holding in mind a sequence of events, involving self and others, temporally and causally arranged. This capacity is applied both to generic scripts and to specific episodes.

The social construction process then builds on these skeletal event sequences. Parents and others may talk about what is going to happen, what is happening, and what has happened in different ways. Parents seem to assume that the child will experience, is experiencing, or has experienced, the same event in the same way as the parent, and can interpret what the parent is telling her about it. Evidence from Emily and others indicates that children may try very hard to do this interpretive work (see earlier examples) and they may sometimes succeed, although they may also misinterpret or be confused by what parents tell them, either because they lack the requisite background knowledge or because they have not experienced the same event in the same way.

The different ways that parents frame an event prior to, during, and after it is experienced will build on the basic event knowledge (which we can assume all children share) to construct memories together that may then enter into the child's autobiographical memory system. Depending on the kinds of episodic accounts the child hears and contributes to, the system will tend to be more or less narrative-like, and will form the basis for constructing better or poorer narratives about experiences, stories, dramatic play, and such activities as Show and Tell. As a socially constructed system, one may expect social and cultural variation in the kinds of memories developed, as well as individual and family differences.

MEMORIES AND MEMORY

This chapter reviews what we know about the development of generic memory, episodic memory, and autobiographical memory for personally experienced events. Does any of this have any bearing on the development of Memory, strictly conceived? For example, do children who experience more narrative talk and thus remember more from their personal experiences also prove to be better at other memory tasks, in school for example? It is somewhat surprising that very little work has been done on the relation between different kinds of tasks that are all alleged to call on one particular kind of cognitive ability, for example, memory.

Weinert (1991) has reported from Germany that studies his group have carried out reveal considerable variation among tasks such as story memory and memory for word lists. This does not seem surprising. If we view memory as a cognitive function, rather than a capacity or ability, we can see that it will enter into different activities in different ways. In particular, the kinds of personal memories discussed in this chapter may form the foundation for understanding stories, dramatic play, and even histories. Narrative formats are important to all of these, and familiarity with narrative forms would make memory and understanding in these kinds of activities easier. It is unlikely, however, that they would support learning the multiplication table or other mechanical or rote forms of memory.

But is it possible that these other forms of memory are also social constructions? Throughout this chapter I have emphasized the contribution of the narrative form of remembering to the organization of episodic memories in early childhood and thus to their accessibility to later recall. (For a full account of the implications of this development see Nelson, in press.) But what about those children who experience primarily paradigmatic memory talk with parents? Are they doomed to have no autobiographical memories? Probably not. Recall that the paradigmatic children in Tessler's (1991) study recognized just as many of the pictures that they had taken on their walk as did the narrative children, although they spontaneously recalled fewer and talked about the experience and the pictures in different ways. The recognition results suggest that they may have similar underlying memories of the experience, but that their ways of verbalizing that underlying knowledge have not been honed in the same way as that of the narrative children, who have learned to bring the information to recall and to organize it in narrative fashion.

It is worth recalling that Bruner (1986) emphasized the narrative mode of cognitive organization to contrast with the paradigmatic, which he believed had been up to that point the primary—if not the only—focus of studies in cognitive psychology. But the emergent recognition of the narrative mode of thought should not deny the significance of the paradigmatic, which after all retains its preeminence in what Vygotsky (1986) referred to as scientific thought, and which is much valued by our educational system.

Much developmental research has been devoted to the study of paradigmatic knowledge structures. For example, children's understanding of taxonomic category structures at the basic, superordinate, and subordinate levels has been the topic of a great deal of research in recent decades (Anglin, 1977; Mervis & Crisafi, 1982; Rosch, Mervis, Gray, Johnson, & Boyes-Braem, 1976). This kind of semantic memory structure may also be derived from the social construction process documented for narrative event memory. In this regard, Lucariello and I proposed that taxonomic categories are based in children's script knowledge, specifically that they first form "slot-filler categories" around objects that complement actions in an event scheme (Lucariello & Nelson, 1985; Nelson, 1983, 1985). For example, they may form slot-filler categories of foods that can be eaten for breakfast, or clothes that can be put on in the morning. This slot-filler model has been tested in category production, recall, word association, and picture choice tasks (Lucariello, Kyratzis, & Nelson, 1992; Lucariello & Nelson, 1985), demonstrating that preschool children do rely on such categories when required to produce or remember category members.

There is suggestive evidence in talk between Emily and her father about breakfast foods that parental talk may provide the ground on which paradigmatic thinking, specifically taxonomic modes of organization of knowledge in memory, may develop, in addition to providing the model for narrative organization of episodic memories. In the pre-bed dialogues with her father there were many discussions of what Emily would like to eat for breakfast the next day. For example, when she was not quite 2 the following discussion took place:

    E: What we have on breakfast day? What we have?   (9)
    F: What will we have for breakfast? You know, tomorrow morning, you're going to have yoghurt, and bananas and wheat germ, like mommy gave you this morning, remember that? Instead of an egg tomorrow we're going to have yoghurt and bananas and wheat germ . . .

Here her father provides a partial list of the category of breakfast foods. Later, Emily entered into the dialog more actively, specifying what she wanted, as in the following dialog from almost 27 months:

F: We'll get up . . . and we'll go down and have breakfast,   (10)
   you can choose what type of egg you want,
E: I want. . . . a boiled egg.
F: Okay. And you can choose what type of cereal you want, you can have either
   shredded wheat or cheerios.
E: Shredded *wheat!*

A month and a half later ($28\frac{1}{2}$), she entered her own suggestions:

E: And, so now tell me about today!   (11)
F: Well, today you had a Tanta day also.
E: I *want* . . yoghurt.
F: And you want yoghurt. I know and I think I'll have some raspberries for
    you tomorrow.
E: And I. . . . cereal!
F: Today you had strawberries, tomorrow I think you'll have raspberries.
E: Cereal! Cereal!
F: You'll have cereal? Okay. Cereal and yogurt? You want bananas in yogurt,
    or raspberries in your cereal?
E: Yeah.
F: Okay. That'll be good.
E: And strawberries in my cereal.

In these discussions, her breakfast food category was highly constrained to the particular situation and did not stray from the alternatives specified by this particular family (e.g., yoghurt, cereal, fruit, eggs). It did not wander into domains of pizza, hamburgers or other items appropriate for dinner. That is, her category of alternatives for breakfast was specific to that event—it constituted a *slot-filler category* of breakfast foods. But note that the language that simultaneously expresses and shapes her representations is not the abstract language of categories but the concrete language of social experience. To be sure, her language includes category terms, but these are particularized to specific experience.

Lucariello and I (1986) examined the use of object labels at different levels of a taxonomic hierarchy—superordinate, basic, and subordinate—by mothers and their 2-year-old children in natural discourse in care-taking and play contexts. We found that in 75% of the cases where mothers introduced a subordinate term in routine contexts, they did so in either a performance/actional discourse frame or a discrimination frame. The performance/actional frame specifies category-specific actions or functions, for example, "*put on* your jeans" which specifies both the function that creates the slot, and an alternative "filler." When used with a superordinate (47% of the superordinate cases in routine contexts) it emphasizes the function that holds the general category together (e.g., "Let's go *put on* your clothes"). The discrimination frame also emphasizes alternative slot-fillers, as in "Do you want apple juice or orange juice?" Thus, particularly in routine care-taking contexts mothers were found to introduce category terms at nonbasic levels in ways that emphasized the slot-filler category formation process. Other recent studies (Callanan, 1985) have provided further documentation for parental provision of category knowledge.

Achievement of an abstract category language depends upon the further development of a differentiated—or abstracted—level of semantic representation in which linguistic terms are related to one another directly and are not embedded in the experientially derived conceptual representation. The development of that level makes possible the representation of a true semantic hierarchy—a taxonomy that is based on hierarchical inclusion relations and not simply on combinations of event-contexted slots. The construction of this level in collaboration with adult informants is a major development of the preschool and early school years.

Thus we can see that it is not only episodic memory that is subject to social-cultural construction through narrative language models, but also what is generally termed semantic memory—or in Vygotsky's terms scientific, or in Bruner's terms paradigmatic modes of thought. In the latter case, however, the language frames are pragmatic or paradigmatic rather than narrative, although there is a whiff of narrativity as well in the discussion of what Emily will have for breakfast tomorrow morning (e.g., "we'll go down and have breakfast"). As with any dichotomization of styles, it is very likely that most parents employ some of each kind of talk, narrative and paradigmatic, and that the differences among them are more matters of emphasis than of exclusive focus.[2]

CONCLUSION

Studies of general event schemas and episodic memory now clearly support the conclusion that even very young children have both kinds, but that autobiographical memory—equivalent to what adults report—does not begin until age 3 or later. Development of true autobiographical memory appears to be a function of social-cultural construction, especially of acquiring narrative forms for remembering. Many studies of parent-child talk about the past support this proposal. In addition, studies of talk in the present show that different ways of discussing ongoing events have differential effects on the way that event is

---

[2]It should be emphasized that these parental styles are not a reflection of social class differences. The studies reported from CUNY by Engel and Tessler involved almost exclusively uppermiddle class, well educated parents.

remembered. Further, talk about what will happen in the future has been relatively unstudied, but it seems likely that, like talk in the present, it may help to organize memory for events. Clearly more studies about future talk are called for.

In the last section, some effects on the organization of memory and knowledge of categories of objects from pragmatic or paradigmatic talk—as contrasted with narrative talk—were discussed. What social-cultural influences may be observed on the organization of memory for children who engage more in paradigmatic talk with parents also deserves further investigation.

REFERENCES

Anglin, J. (1977). *Word, object and conceptual development*. New York: Norton.

Bachevalier, J. (1992). Cortical versus limbic immaturity: Relationship to infantile amnesia. In M. R. Gunnar & C. A. Nelson (Eds.), *Developmental behavioral neuroscience* (pp. 129–153). Hillsdale, NJ: Lawrence Erlbaum Associates.

Bakhtin, M. (1986). *Speech genres and other late essays*. Austin: University of Texas Press.

Bauer, P. J., & Mandler, J. M. (1990). Remembering what happened next: Very young children's recall of event sequences. In R. Fivush & J. A. Hudson (Eds.), *Knowing and remembering in young children*. New York: Cambridge University Press.

Bruner, J. S. (1986). *Actual minds, possible worlds*. Cambridge MA: Harvard University Press.

Bruner, J. S., & Lucariello, J. (1989). Monologue as a narrative recreation of the world. In K. Nelson (Ed.), *Narratives from the crib*. Cambridge MA: Harvard University Press.

Burke, K. (1945). *Grammar of motives*. Englewood Cliffs, NJ: Prentice-Hall.

Callanan, M. A. (1985). How parents label objects for young children: The role of input in the acquisition of category hierarchies. *Child Development, 56,* 508–523.

Donaldson, M. (1978). *Children's minds*. Glasgow: William Collins & Sons.

Engel, S. (1986). *Learning to reminisce: A developmental study of how young children talk about the past*. Unpublished doctoral dissertation, City University of New York Graduate Center.

Fivush, R. (1988). The functions of event memory: Some comments on Nelson and Barsalou. In U. Neisser & E. Winograd (Eds.), *Remembering reconsidered: Ecological and traditional approaches to the study of memory* (pp. 277–282). New York: Cambridge University Press.

Fivush, R., & Fromhoff, F. A. (1988). Style and structure in mother-child conversations about the past. *Discourse Processes, 8,* 177–204.

Fivush, R., & Hamond, N. R. (1989). Time and again: Effects of repetition and retention interval on two year olds' event recall. *Journal of Experimental Child Psychology, 47,* 259–273.

Fivush, R., & Hamond, N. R. (1990). Autobiographical memory across the preschool years: Toward reconceptualizing childhood amnesia. In R. Fivush & J. A. Hudson (Eds.), *Knowing and remembering in young children* (pp. 223–248). New York: Cambridge University Press.

French, L. A., & Nelson, K. (1985). *Young children's understanding of relational terms: Some ifs, ors and buts*. New York: Springer-Verlag.

Freud, S. (1963). Three essays on the theory of sexuality. In J. Strachey (Ed.), *The standard edition of the complete works of Freud* (vol. 7). London: Hogarth Press.

Gruendel, J. M. (1980). *Scripts and stories: A Study of children's event narratives*. Unpublished doctoral dissertation, Yale University.

Hudson, J. A. (1986). Memories are made of this: General event knowledge and the development of autobiographic memory. In K. Nelson (Ed.), *Event knowledge: Structure and function in development* (pp. 97–118). Hillsdale, NJ: Lawrence Erlbaum Associates.

Hudson, J. A. (1990). The emergence of autobiographic memory in mother-child conversation. In R. Fivush & J. A. Hudson (Eds.), *Knowing and remembering in young children* (pp. 166–196). New York: Cambridge University Press.

Hudson, J., & Nelson, K. (1986). Repeated encounters of a similar kind: Effects of familiarity on children's autobiographical memory. *Cognitive Development, 1,* 253–271.

Labov, W. (1972). *Language in the inner city.* Philadelphia: University of Pennsylvania Press.

Lucariello, J., Kyratzis, A., & Nelson, K. (1992). Taxonomic knowledge: What kind and when. *Child Development, 63,* 978–998.

Lucariello, J., & Nelson, K. (1985). Slot-filler categories as memory organizers for young children. *Developmental Psychology, 21,* 272–282.

Lucariello, J., & Nelson, K. (1986). Context effects on lexical specificity in maternal and child discourse. *Journal of Child Language, 13,* 507–522.

Mead, G. H. (1934). *Mind, self, and society.* Chicago: Chicago University Press.

Mervis, C. B., & Crisafi, M. (1982). Order of acquisition of subordinate-, basic-, and superordinate-level categories. *Child Development, 53,* 258–266.

Nelson, K. (1981). Individual differences in language development: Implications for development and language. *Developmental Psychology, 17,* 170–187.

Nelson, K. (1983). The derivation of concepts and categories from event representations. In E. Scholnick (Ed.), *New trends in conceptual representation: Challenges to Piaget's theory?* Hillsdale, NJ: Lawrence Erlbaum Associates.

Nelson, K. (1985). *Making sense: The acquisition of shared meaning.* New York: Academic Press.

Nelson, K. (1986). *Event knowledge: Structure and function in development.* Hillsdale, NJ: Lawrence Erlbaum Associates.

Nelson, K. (1988). The ontogeny of memory for real events. In U. Neisser & E. Winograd (Eds.), *Remembering reconsidered: Ecological and traditional approaches to the study of memory* (pp. 244–276). New York: Cambridge University Press.

Nelson, K. (Ed.). (1989a). *Narratives from the crib.* Cambridge MA: Harvard University Press.

Nelson, K. (1989b). Remembering: A functional developmental perspective. In P. R. Solomon, G. R. Goethals, C. M. Kelley, & B. R. Stephens (Eds.), *Memory: Interdisciplinary approaches* (pp. 127–150). New York: Springer-Verlag.

Nelson, K. (1990). Remembering, forgetting, and childhood amnesia. In R. Fivush & J. A. Hudson (Eds.), *Knowing and remembering in young children.* New York: Cambridge University Press.

Nelson, K. (1991, April). *Representational change and the emergence of autobiographical memory* Paper presented at meetings of the Society for Research in Child Development. Seattle, WA.

Nelson, K. (in press). Towards a theory of the development of autobiographical memory. In A. Collins, M. Conway, S. Gathercole, & P. Morris (Eds.), *Theoretical advances in the psychology of memory.* Hillsdale, NJ: Lawrence Erlbaum Associates.

Nelson, K., & Brown, A. L. (1979). The semantic-episodic distinction in memory development. In P. Ornstein (Ed.), *Development of memory.* Hillsdale, NJ: Lawrence Erlbaum Associates.

Nelson, K., Fivush, R., Hudson, J., & Lucariello, J. (1983). Scripts and the development of memory. In M. T. H. Chi (Ed.), *Trends in memory development research* (vol. 9). Basel, Switzerland: S. Karger.

Nelson, K., & Gruendel, J. (1979). At morning it's lunchtime: A scriptal view of children's dialogue. *Discourse Processes, 2,* 73–94.

Nelson, K., & Gruendel, J. (1981). Generalized event representations: Basic building blocks of cognitive development. In M. Lamb & A. Brown (Eds.), *Advances in developmental psychology* (vol. 1). Hillsdale, NJ: Lawrence Erlbaum Associates.

Nelson, K., & Hudson, J. A. (1988). Scripts and memory: Interrelations in development. In F. Weinert & M. Perlmutter (Eds.), *Memory development.* Hillsdale, NJ: Lawrence Erlbaum Associates.

Nelson, K., & Ross, G. (1980). The generalities and specifics of long term memory in infants and young children. In M. Perlmutter (Ed.), *Children's memory: New directions for child development* (vol. 10, pp. 87–101). San Francisco: Jossey-Bass.

Perlmutter, M. (Ed.). (1980). *Children's memory*. San Francisco: Jossey-Bass.

Peterson, C., & McCabe, A. (1983). *Developmental psycholinguistics: Three ways of looking at a child's narrative*. New York: Plenum.

Pillemer, D. B., & White, S. H. (1989). Childhood events recalled by children and adults. In H. W. Reese (Ed.), *Advances in child development and behavior* (vol. 21, pp. 297–340). New York: Academic Press.

Ratner, H. H. (1984). Memory demands and the development of young children's memory. *Child Development, 55,* 2173–2191.

Rosch, E., Mervis, C., Gray, W., Johnson, D., & Boyes-Braem, P. (1976). Basic objects in natural categories. *Cognitive Psychology, 8,* 382–439.

Schank, R. C., & Abelson, R. P. (1977). *Scripts, Plans, goals, and understanding*. Hillsdale, NJ: Lawrence Erlbaum Associates.

Tessler, M. (1986). *Mother-child talk in a museum: The socialization of a memory*. Unpublished paper. City University of New York Graduate Center.

Tessler, M. (1991). *Making memories together: The influence of mother-child joint encoding on the development of autobiographical memory style*. Unpublished doctoral dissertation, City University of New York Graduate Center.

Tulving, E. (1972). Episodic and semantic memory. In E. Tulving & W. Donaldson (Eds.), *Organization of memory* (pp. 382–403). New York: Academic Press.

Vygotsky, L. (1986). *Thought and language*. Cambridge MA: MIT Press.

Weinert, F. (1991). *Stability in change of memory functions in childhood* Paper presented at the International Conference on Memory, Lancaster University. Lancaster, England.

Wertsch, J. V., & Stone, A. (1985). The concept of internalization in Vygotsky's account of the genesis of higher mental functions. In J. V. Wertsch (Ed.), *Culture, communication, and cognition: Vygotskian perspectives*. New York: Cambridge University Press.

Wolf, D., & Garner, H. (1979). Style and sequence in symbolic play. In M. Franklin & N. Smith (Eds.), *Early symbolization*. Hillsdale, NJ: Lawrence Erlbaum Associates.

2 Identifying Subsystems of Autobiographical Memory: Commentary on Nelson

Patricia J. Bauer
University of Minnesota

One measure of the success of a research program is the extent to which it generates further research. By this measure alone, Katherine Nelson's program of investigation into the development of event knowledge and memory has been one of the most successful in developmental psychology. Her recent work on the source of infantile or childhood amnesia, and the development of auto-biographical memory, is an exciting "further development" in this arena. My commentary on her chapter in this volume has two functions. The first function is to interpret her arguments about the development of autobiographical memory using some of the language and concepts from the dynamical systems perspective. The intent of this interpretation is to clarify necessary and sufficient contributions to the ontogeny of autobiographical memory. The second function of my commentary is to develop some theoretical and empirical questions which are generated through the translation of Nelson's arguments into the language of dynamical systems. My goal in this exercise is, in some small way, to perform the function that Katherine Nelson so often has performed for me in my development as a scholar and researcher. Specifically, I hope that my questions will encourage her to continue to pursue "what develops" in the course of development of events, narratives, and autobiographical memory.

THE DEVELOPMENT OF AUTOBIOGRAPHICAL MEMORY

A major focus of Nelson's chapter is the development of autobiographical memory. Autobiographical memory is a particular type of episodic memory (Tulving,

1972) that constitutes one's life story or personal past. For developmental psychologists, a central question in the study of autobiographical memory is "when does it first begin?" The question of onset occupies such a prominent place on the stage because of the phenomenon of infantile or childhood amnesia. As adults, most of us are unable to remember specific events that took place prior to our third or even our fourth birthdays (see Rubin, 1982, for a review). A variety of alternative theoretical explanations as to the source of this phenomenon exist (see Pillimer & White, 1989, for a review). However, as Nelson has here and elsewhere pointed out (Nelson, this volume, in press), there has been little empirical work on the source of infantile amnesia. In her chapter, Nelson uses the results of a decade-long research program to try to fill this empirical gap. In so doing, she has derived a sociocultural account of the development of autobiographical memory that deserves our attention.

To aid in understanding Nelson's perspective on why we lack autobiographical memories from our earliest years I have borrowed a tool from the dynamical systems approach. A tenet of this approach is that complex phenomenon are the product of simpler, more elementary parts or *subsystems*. An understanding of the development of the complex whole entails charting the development of each of the individual subsystems that comprise it. In developmental psychology, this approach is probably most readily associated with the work of Esther Thelen on the development of the ability to walk (e.g., Thelen, 1989).

Thelen identified several different components that she thought might or might not influence the ability to walk. Some of the factors, such as the ability to alternate steps, to keep the steps in relative phase (i.e., to begin the second step half-way through the first), and to maintain a planar orientation of the foot, are specific to walking. Others, such as the ability to adjust speed of movement, extensor muscle strength, and overall motor control, are related to more general motor development milestones. Still others, such as motivation to walk, fall outside the domain of motor skills proper. Once a good "crop" of candidate subsystems is identified, the developmental course of each is charted, in order to identify the "critical value" or threshold level that each of the components must reach in order to support the behavior of interest, which in Thelen's case, is walking.

Figure 2.1 is a schematic representation of the developmental course of some of the subsystems of walking. Keep in mind that this example is being used for illustrative purposes only; it is not intended as a faithful depiction of the findings of Thelen and her colleagues. As you can see from the figure, when you place even a young infant in an environment in which it is adaptive to walk, namely, on a treadmill, you see that some of the necessary component abilities of walking emerge very early, much earlier than does the full-blown ability. For example, alternate stepping develops very early and very rapidly: It crosses threshold level by about 3 months-of-age. The ability to keep steps in relative phase develops

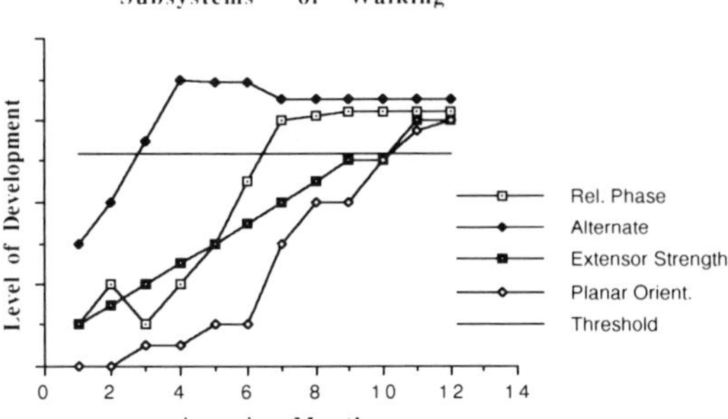

FIG. 2.1. A schematic representation of four subsystems of walking. The course of development of the pictured subsystems corresponds only roughly to that obtained.

not quite as early, but nevertheless, crosses the minimum threshold level by about 6 to 7 months. In contrast, a third component, extensor strength, develops much more slowly and gradually. Over the first 6 months of life flexor dominance wanes and the extensor muscles, particularly those that stabilize the foot, gain in strength. Children may not reach the threshold level of extensor strength until 10 or 11 months-of-age. Finally, planar orientation of the foot and leg, which enable the foot posture that is optimal for walking, undergoes yet a different developmental course, one that reaches threshold level at about 10 or 11 months. In summary, a new development, the ability to walk, emerges at the time that the different subsystems of the ability, each with a unique developmental course, reach a particular threshold level.

In a dynamical systems approach it is important that each of the components thought to contribute to an ability be tested to ensure that they do indeed contribute unique variance. The influence of any given component or ingredient can be tested in two ways. First, one can try to facilitate a particular subsystem, to see if the ability to which the subsystem is thought to contribute emerges. Second, one can try to surpress, or perturb, a subsystem to see if the whole system is disrupted. In the domain of walking, the critical role of extensor strength, for example, can be tested by alternately facilitating and perturbing that subsystem. Extensor strength can be "facilitated" by removing the impediment that it must overcome, namely, gravity. By putting babies in water, which relieves the effects of gravity, researchers were able to see if insufficient extensor strength was indeed "holding back" the entire walking system. Alternatively, to be certain of the importance of a particular subsystem one can perturb it, and see if the system is disrupted. By putting weights on babies, thereby increasing the resistance that the extensor muscles are required to overcome, researchers were able to directly test the importance of extensor strength (see Thelen, 1989).

At this point it is appropriate to ask how all this discussion of walking is helping us to understand the phenomenon of infantile amnesia or the development of autobiographical memory. I believe that it is appropriate to say that until not too long ago, the "picture" that Nelson and others (e.g., Hudson, 1986;

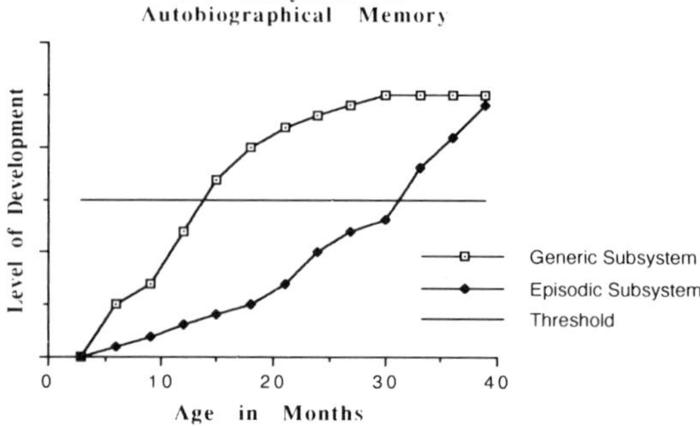

FIG. 2.2. An hypothetical course of development of the generic and episodic subsystems of autobiographical memory.

Nelson, 1990, in press) proposed as an explanation for why we did not have early autobiographical memories looked something like that in Fig. 2.2. Two subsystems of autobiographical memory were proposed: (a) a "generalized" or generic memories subsystem, and (b) a "specific" or episodic memories subsystem. The explanation for the phenomenon of infantile amnesia captured by this picture was that of two subsystems with different developmental courses. Autobiographical memory emerged relatively late in development, at the time that both subsystems crossed the necessary or threshold level. Like alternate stepping and relative phase, the memory subsystem responsible for forming generalized or generic representations of events developed early. In contrast, like extensor strength and planar orientation, the memory subsystem responsible for specific or episodic memories was thought to develop considerably later. In the language of dynamical systems, the generic memory subsystem crossed threshold early, but slower development of the episodic subsystem held back the autobiographical memory system.

As Nelson (this volume) has reviewed, there is a great deal of evidence to suggest that young children have generic memories of events. When you ask children as young as 3 years-of-age what happens in the course of everyday events or routines they provide temporally organized narratives, using impersonal pronouns and the timeless present tense. For example, in response to "what happens" when you go to the grocery, 3 year-olds will respond "You buy things and then you go home" (Hudson, Fivush, & Kuebli, in press). As Fivush (1984) and Hudson (1990) have demonstrated, preschool-age children use this narrative form to report on events after only a single experience of them. Even younger children show evidence of temporally organized memory for everyday events. Twenty-month-old children presented with a reverse-order model of a familiar event ("giving a teddy bear a bath" modeled as *dry the bear, wash the bear, put the bear in the tub*) will "correct" the sequence to its canonical order (Bauer & Thal, 1990). In a recent study, Hertsgaard and I demonstrated that children as young as 13 months-of-age have temporally organized memories of familiar events (Bauer & Hertsgaard, in press). These results strongly suggest that the generic subsystem of autobiographical memory crosses threshold level at an early age. In contrast, until quite recently, there was very little reason to believe that the episodic subsystem crossed threshold level until about the age of 3 (e.g., Hudson & Nelson, 1986). It seemed plausible then that as the latter ability crossed the threshold, autobiographical memory emerged.

The perspective that young children have only generic memory has since been revised, in light of recent evidence that even quite young children can remember specific episodes. One source of evidence that young children can remember specific episodes comes from the Emily data that Nelson (1988) provided. Between 21 and 36 months, Emily's prebed talk with her parents and to herself was recorded. In these presleep dialogues and monologues, Emily often recalled unique episodes that took place days to months before. Research by Fivush, Gray, and Fromhoff (1987) has shown that $2\frac{1}{2}$-year-old children are able to remember novel events that occurred as much as 6 months in the past. In addition, in our work we have shown that children under 2 years-of-age can remember instances of a novel event over periods of weeks (Bauer & Mandler, 1989) and even months (Bauer, Hertsgaard, & Dow, 1992). Data such as these make it difficult to argue that development of episodic memory lags so far behind that of generic. In fact, they have led to revision of the picture to reflect something more like the parallel development of the generic and episodic subsystems depicted in Fig. 2.3.

Recent work that Dow and I have done demonstrates the parallel developmental courses nicely. Using elicited imitation of action sequences we have tested 16- and 20-month-olds' ability to construct both generic and specific memories of events. The children participated in two testing sessions, separated by 1 week. At Session 1 the children imitated 6 modeled event sequences. At Session 2, the props used to enact half of the sequences were changed. The children spontaneously generalized their knowledge of the events, reproducing the change and no-change sequences at approximately equal levels. In a subsequent study we demonstrated that the children did indeed remember the specific props originally

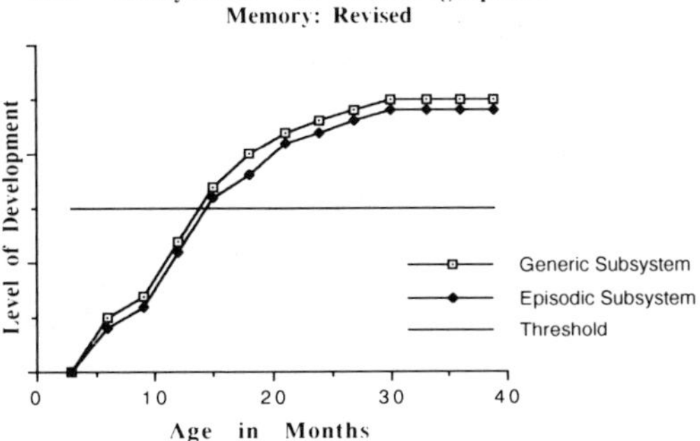

FIG. 2.3. A revised account of the hypothetical course of development of the generic and episodic subsystems of autobiographical memory.

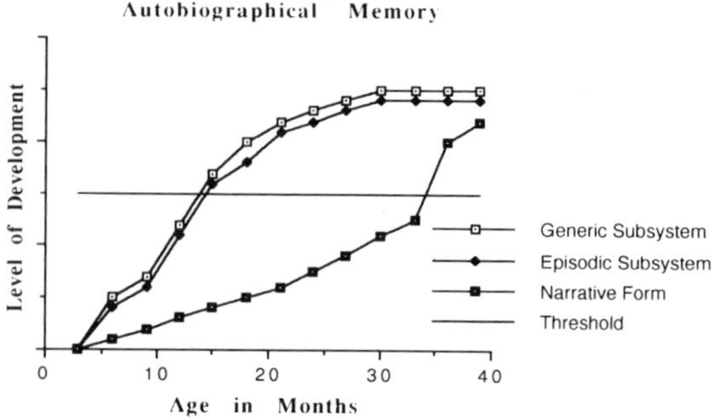

FIG. 2.4. An hypothetical course of development of the generic, episodic, and narrative form subsystems of auto-biographical memory.

used to enact the events. Thus, the children provided evidence of both a generic "script" for what usually occurred in the event sequence, as well as evidence of memory for a specific occurrence of the event (Dow & Bauer, 1991).

Given evidence of generic memories of events, as well as memory for specific aspects of those events, from an early age, why are there no autobiographical memories from the first few years of life? It seems that, in the language of the dynamical systems approach, generic and episodic memory constitute only two of the subsystems necessary for autobiographical memory. A third subsystem, implicated by Nelson (this volume), is the narrative-form subsystem. The narrative form enables the construction and maintenance of a *story* about your participation in a specific event. The narrative subsystem provides a means of organizing early episodic memories into a form which allows for memory of the *who, what, where, why,* and *how* that characterizes adult autobiographical memories. In other words, it is the advent of the narrative organization that allows one to begin to construct the personal history that is the hallmark of autobiographical memory. The reason that autobiographical memory is not in evidence until the age of 3 or later is because, as depicted in Fig. 2.4, this subsystem does not reach threshold level until then.

Another analogy with walking will hopefully serve to make the point. In the picture that Nelson is now painting, early episodic memory is analogous to the stepping movements that the baby makes before the other subsystems of walking are in place: The stepping movements are there, they are functional, but they are not useful to support walking until another subsystem, sufficient extensor strength, is attained. Analogously, episodic memory, like the stepping movements, is there, but it is not useful to support autobiographical memory until the third subsystem, the narrative form (the equivalent of sufficient extensor strength) is attained.

IMPLICATIONS OF THE "THREE SUBSYSTEMS" PERSPECTIVE ON AUTOBIOGRAPHICAL MEMORY

The view that the narrative form constitutes a third subsystem in the development of autobiographical memory resolves at least one issue, namely, the apparent lack of correlation between the onset of episodic memory and the onset of autobiographical memory. However, it raises several other issues. The balance of my remarks is devoted to development of some of those issues.

First, is there a qualitative difference between early episodic memory and early autobiographical memory? In other words, are we certain that they represent two distinct subsystems? If so, by what criteria do we distinguish between early episodic memories and early autobiographical ones? Nelson (Chapter 1) referred to two features that might differentiate early memories of specific episodes from true autobiographical memories. She noted that, unlike the memories of older children and adults, which can endure for long periods of time, early memories of specific episodes seem temporary or transitory. For example, in her crib talk, 21-month-old Emily mentioned specific episodes of events, and therefore, provided evidence of episodic memories (Nelson, 1988). However, because she did not refer to the episodes in her later crib talk, she provided no evidence that her early episodic memories endured for any significant period of time. There are data, however, that do suggest that young children remember some events over long periods of time. In one of the few studies of memory for distant past events in preschool-age children, Fivush and Hamond (1990) provided evidence of memories in 4-year-olds for events that they experienced 2 years in the past. As Nelson (this volume) notes, memory for specific events over this long time span may be exceptional. However, given that there are so few data of this nature, we really have no foundation for determination of how unusual a mnemonic feat this is among preschoolers.

Even if it were to be determined that verbal recounting of specific events from anything but the recent past is unusual for young children, it is not clear that this aspect can clearly differentiate early episodic from true autobiographical memory. It is true that out-loud repetition at a later point in time provides unequivocal evidence that a specific episode has been retained in memory over time. However, it does not follow from this that *absence* of out-loud repetition indicates that the event has been forgotten. I offer a personal anecdote to make this point. I have a very distinct memory of a specific trip to the toy department of a major department store. Due to moves that my family made when I was a young child, it is easy for me to date this trip as taking place sometime before my fourth birthday. On this trip I let my mother know, in no uncertain terms, that I desperately wanted a particular doll. In equally certain terms my mother advised me that I could not have said doll. My memory of this event is quite vivid; it includes an image of the lay-out of the store, the huge glass case in which the desired doll sat, and the long walk back to the car. To the best of my recollection, until the day that I spoke of this event at the symposium, I had never recounted this episode out loud. Yet certainly we would agree that I had retained this episode in memory over a very long period of time. Personal anecdotes aside, the point is that the data base on early memories of specific events is not large enough to support conclusions about whether or not such memories are evanescent, or endure over time.

A second feature that Nelson noted that might distinguish early episodic memories from true autobiographical ones is that extensive cuing is necessary to elicit evidence of the former (e.g., Fivush et al., 1987; Hamond & Fivush, 1991). Examples of the extent to which adults must go to extract evidence of memory from young children are readily available in the protocols included in Nelson's chapter. However, this feature of mnemonic performance may not be unique to very young children. Hudson and Fivush (1987) found that 6th graders had clear memories of an event that they had experienced as 6-year-olds. Their memories were only elicited, however, with a great deal of verbal prompting (e.g., "what else did you do?") and cuing (i.e., using pictures taken during the event as mnemonic aids). In addition, for young children, heavy reliance on cuing may be specific to eliciting *verbal* memories of past events. When children are able to show what they remember, rather than tell what they remember, they evidence accurate memories for past events with minimal cuing and prompting (e.g., Bauer & Mandler, 1989; Fivush, Kuebli, & Clubb, 1992; Price & Goodman, 1990). In sum, it is not clear that the length of time over which events are remembered, or the extent to which early memories are dependent upon cuing, differentiates young children's early memories for specific episodes from true autobiographical memory. If autobiographical memory is to be viewed as a distinct subsystem, criteria by which it can be differentiated from run-of-the-mill episodic memory must be clarified.

A second, yet clearly related question arises as to the status of the third subsystem, the narrative form. Does development of the narrative form represent the emergence of a *necessary* component of autobiographical memory? Alternatively, does it indicate that a reporting convention has been mastered or acquired? Another way of asking this question is whether the emergence of the narrative form truly signals the emergence of autobiographical memory, or whether it signals when autobiographical memory can be measured? By including the narrative form as a necessary subsystem, is autobiographical memory effectively operationalized in such a way as to render it impossible to find evidence of it *before* development of the narrative form? Reference to the dynamical systems perspective may once again prove useful in addressing this question. If the narrative form is in fact a necessary subsystem, then one ought to be able to "push around" the emergence of autobiographical memory by facilitating or perturbing the course of development of the narrative form. The other two necessary subsystems, generic and episodic memory, are in place quite early. If we were to provide the third subsystem, the narrative form, earlier, would we see evidence of autobiographical memory earlier as well? Alternatively, if we were to hold back its development, would we see that autobiographical memory did not emerge until even later?

It is obvious that we cannot conduct either of the experiments that would allow us to address directly these questions. We cannot significantly accelerate the development of the narrative form, nor can we deny children exposure to it. However, there are two types of "natural experiments" that we can pursue. First, Nelson (this volume) summarized two different styles of language that mothers exhibit when they talk with their children about the past. Mothers who make stories about past experiences and invite their children to "join in" on the construction of the stories are said to use an *elaborative* (Engel, 1986; Fivush & Fromhoff, 1988) or *narrative* (Tessler, 1986) style. In contrast, mothers using a *pragmatic* (Engel, 1986), *repetitive* (Fivush & Fromhoff, 1988), or *paradigmatic* (Tessler, 1986) style talk to their children about practical matters (e.g., Where did you leave your toy?) and try to extract particular bits of information about past experiences (e.g., What was the name of the restaurant where we had breakfast?). The elaborative or narrative style seems to represent the prototype of the narrative form. It is known that children learn a concept faster when they are trained on prototypical exemplars (e.g., Anglin, 1977). Exposure to the elaborative or narrative style does seem to influence memory for events in the short term. That is, children of mothers using the elaborative or narrative style recall more about past events than children of mothers using the repetitive or paradigmatic style (Fivush & Fromhoff, 1988; Tessler, 1986). Would exposure to the elaborative versus the paradigmatic style influence the course of development of the narrative form itself? If so, one might predict that children of mothers using the elaborative style would have autobiographical memories from earlier in their lives, relative to children of mothers using the paradigmatic style. Data necessary to test this prediction have, to date, not been obtained.

The type of natural experiment possible through examination of the development of autobiographical memory in children exposed to the elaborative as compared to the paradigmatic style also could be done cross culturally (see Rogoff & Mistry, 1990, for discussion of the utility of a cross-cultural perspective on the study of memory performance). Cultures differ with respect to the narrative form, and in the type and frequency of talk about the past. Do children in "child-centered" cultures such as ours, which talk to children about the past, about how they felt during the event, have autobiographical memories from earlier on, relative to cultures that do not engage in such memory talk with their young children? Natural experiments on the timing of exposure to the narrative form, and on the extent of experience with talking about oneself and the past, could provide valuable insight as to the status of the narrative form as a necessary subsystem of autobiographical memory.

Importantly, it is not clear that evidence that children of mothers using the elaborative style, or children of "elaborative cultures," had autobiographical memories from earlier in life would unequivocally establish the causal role of the narrative form in the development of autobiographical memory. Differences in the timing of emergence of autobiographical memory for children exposed to elaborative versus paradigmatic styles could still be explained in terms of greater depth of processing provided through the elaborative style. As an illustration, recall Nelson's description of Tessler's (1986) first study, that is, the study in which children visited the Natural History Museum with their mothers. Half of the mothers were asked to provide no input to their children, but simply to answer their children's questions. The other half of the mothers were asked to talk about the event as they usually would. When interviewed 1 week later, the children in the second group recalled more about the trip to the museum than did the children whose mothers only answered their questions. Although this finding can be interpreted as due to the supporting scaffolding provided by the mothers, it also can be interpreted in terms of an elaboration or spread of encoding model of memory (Craik & Tulving, 1975). That is, it could be argued that children who experienced more conversation surrounding the museum trip were more involved in the activity, and their greater involvement lead to greater elaboration of the experience, and thereby, better recall of it.

A typical finding in the elaboration or spread of encoding literature is that persons in the "elaboration" condition have better recall, but not necessarily better recognition, relative to persons in the "shallow processing" condition (see Wingfield & Byrnes, 1981). This is precisely the finding from Tessler's (1991) second study, as described by Nelson. In this study, Tessler had parents and children take a walk around an unfamiliar neighborhood. During the walk they took pictures and talked about the event either in an elaborative fashion (elaborative processing condition) or in a more paradigmatic fashion (shallow processing condition). In a subsequent interview the children in the elaborative processing condition *recalled* more about the walk, relative to the other children. However, there was no difference between the groups in the amount *recognized*. The question that these findings raise is whether the influence of a more elaborative style (i.e., a "good" narrative form) is exerted on memory, per se, or on reporting style or ability? Again, this relates back to the question of whether development of the narrative form is necessary or causal for the emergence of autobiographical memory.

Thinking about the narrative form as a necessary subsystem of autobiographical memory raises two final questions. Upon mastery of the narrative form, could early episodic memories conceivably be "turned into" autobiographical ones? In other words, could a particular event that happened before mastery of the narrative form later *become* an autobiographical memory? Or is it the case that, in the absence of components of the narrative form, aspects of events unique to autobiographical memory would simply not be encoded? Finally, one of the characteristics of adults' earliest memories about the past is their highly visual or imaginal, as compared to narrative or propositional, nature (Rubin, 1982). How can we reconcile this aspect of early autobiographical memory with an argument that the development of this memory system is necessarily dependent upon acquisition of a narrative form?

CONCLUSION

The riddle of the fate of our earliest memories has seemed intractable. Most of the accounts of the source of childhood or infantile amnesia have been unincumbered by data from children in the period actually covered by the amnesia. As data are becoming available, it is increasingly clear that even young children possess some of the component abilities critical to the formation of memories for specific events that happened in the past. Children under the age of 2 years remember both general and specific aspects of events. Nelson has argued that, at this young age, missing from the autobiographical "mix" is the ingredient that allows children to transform these early memories into ones that endure, and which have personal significance. That missing ingredient is the narrative form. A true evaluation of this proposal will await clear criteria for differentiation of early episodic from early autobiographical memories, and stringent tests of the extent to which the narrative form represents a necessary subsystem for autobiographical memory, as compared to the acquisition of a reporting style or convention. Regardless of the outcome of this evaluation, the research that promises to be generated by this proposal will inform our understanding of early memory, and of the process of construction of a personal past.

REFERENCES

Anglin, J. M. (1977). *Word, object, and conceptual development.* New York: Norton.

Bauer, P. J., & Hertsgaard, L. A. (in press). *Increasing steps in recall of events: Factors facilitating immediate and long-term memory in 13.5- and 16.5-month-old children. Child development.*

Bauer, P. J., Hertsgaard, L. A., & Dow, G. A. A. (1992, May). *After 8-months have passed: Memory for specific events by 1- to 2-year olds.* Paper presented at the biennial meetings of the International Society for Infant Studies, Miami, FL.

Bauer, P. J., & Mandler, J. M. (1989). One thing follows another: Effects of temporal structure on 1- to 2-year-olds' recall of events. *Developmental Psychology, 25,* 197–206.

Bauer, P. J., & Thal, D. J. (1990). Scripts or scraps: Reconsidering the development of sequential understanding. *Journal of Experimental Child Psychology, 50,* 287–304.

Craik, F. I. M., & Tulving, E. (1975). Depth of processing and the retention of words in episodic memory. *Journal of Experimental Psychology: General, 104,* 268–294.

Dow, G. A. A., & Bauer, P. J. (1991, April). *Very young children's event representations: Specifics are generalized, but not forgotten.* Paper presented to the Society for Research in Child Development, Seattle, WA.

Engel, S. (1986). *Learning to reminisce: A developmental study of how young children talk about the past.* Unpublished doctoral dissertation, City University of New York Graduate Center.

Fivush, R. (1984). Learning about school: The development of kindergartners' school scripts. *Child Development, 55,* 1697–1709.

Fivush, R., & Fromhoff, F. A. (1988). Style and structure in mother-child conversations about the past. *Discourse Processes, 8,* 177–204.

Fivush, R., Gray, J. T., & Fromhoff, F. A. (1987). Two year olds talk about the past. *Cognitive Development, 2,* 393–410.

Fivush, R., & Hamond, N. R. (1990). Autobiographical memory across the preschool years: Toward reconceptualizing childhood amnesia. In R. Fivush & J. A. Hudson (Eds.), *Knowing and remembering in young children* (pp. 223–248). New York: Cambridge University Press.

Fivush, R., Kuebli, J., & Clubb, P. A. (1992). The structure of events and event representations: A developmental analysis. *Child Development, 63,* 188–201.

Hamond, N. R., & Fivush, R. (1991). Memories of Mickey Mouse: Young children recount their trip to Disneyworld. *Cognitive Development, 6,* 433–448.

Hudson, J. A. (1986). Memories are made of this: General event knowledge and the development of autobiographical memory. In K. Nelson (Ed.), *Event knowledge: Structure and function in development* (pp. 97–118). Hillsdale, NJ: Lawrence Erlbaum Associates.

Hudson, J. A. (1990). Constructive processing in children's event memory. *Development Psychology, 26,* 180–187.

Hudson, J. A., & Fivush, R. (1987). As time goes by: Sixth graders remember a kindergarten experience. *Emory Cognition Project Report #13.* Emory University, Atlanta.

Hudson, J. A., Fivush, R., & Kuebli, J. (in press). Scripts and episodes: The development of event memory. *Applied Cognitive Psychology.*

Hudson, J. A., & Nelson, K. (1986). Repeated encounters of a similar kind: Effects of familiarity on children's autobiographical memory. *Cognitive Development, 1,* 253–271.

Nelson, K. (1988). The ontogeny of memory for real events. In U. Neisser & E. Winograd (Eds.), *Remembering reconsidered: Ecological and traditional approaches to the study of memory* (pp. 244–276). New York: Cambridge University Press.

Nelson, K. (1990). Remembering, forgetting, and childhood amnesia. In R. Fivush, & J. A. Hudson (Eds.), *Knowing and remembering in young children* (pp. 301–316). New York: Cambridge University Press.

Nelson, K. (in press). Towards a theory of the development of autobiographical memory. In A. Collins, M. Conway, S. Gathercole, & P. Morris (Eds.), *Theoretical advances in the psychology of memory.* Hillsdale, NJ: Lawrence Erlbaum Associates.

Pillimer, D. B., & White, S. H. (1989). Childhood events recalled by children and adults. In H. W. Reese (Ed.), *Advances in child development and behavior—Vol. 21* (pp. 297–340). New York: Academic Press.

Price, D. W. W., & Goodman, G. S. (1990). Visiting the wizard: Children's memory for a recurring event. *Child Development, 61,* 664–680.

Rogoff, B., & Mistry, J. (1990). The social and functional context of children's remembering. In R. Fivush & J. A. Hudson (Eds.), *Knowing and remembering in young children* (pp. 197–222). New York: Cambridge University Press.

Rubin, D. C. (1982). On the retention function for autobiographical memory. *Journal of Verbal Learning and Verbal Behavior, 21,* 21–38.

Tessler, M. (1986). *Mother-child talk in a museum: The socialization of a memory.* City University of New York Graduate Center.

Tessler, M. (1991). *Making memories together: The influence of mother-child joint encoding on the development of autobiographical memory style.* Unpublished doctoral dissertation, City University of New York Graduate Center.

Thelen, E. (1989). Self-organization in developmental processes: Can systems approaches work? In M. R. Gunnar & E. Thelen (Eds.), *Systems and development—The Minnesota Symposia on Child Psychology* (pp. 77–117). Hillsdale, NJ: Lawrence Erlbaum Associates.

Tulving, E. (1972). Episodic and semantic memory. In E. Tulving, & W. Donaldson (Eds.), *Organization of memory* (pp. 382–403). New York: Academic Press.
Wingfield, A., & Byrnes, D. L. (1981). *The psychology of human memory*. New York: Academic Press.

3 Emotional Content of Parent-Child Conversations About the Past

Robyn Fivush
Emory University

> *The past is beautiful because one never realizes an emotion at the time. It expands later; and thus we don't have complete emotions about the present, only the past.*
>
> —Virginia Woolf

Reminiscing is a quintessentially human activity. We talk about past experiences with friends and family and reflect on our past during quiet moments alone. We interpret present experience in light of previous experience and plan for our future by examining our past. Moreover, our past experiences are emotionally saturated; we recount and reminisce about particular events because they are personally significant and emotionally meaningful. Most provocative, as the opening quote from Virginia Woolf suggests, the emotional meaning of an event may only emerge in retrospect. From this perspective, emotions should be considered in a social interactional framework; as we recount events to others and ourselves, the emotional meaning of the past evolves.

In this chapter, I examine the ways in which parents discuss emotional aspects of past experiences with their young children. The basic assumption underlying this research program is that children are learning both the forms and the functions of personal narratives in social interaction. Because personal narratives are emotionally significant, children may also be learning how to think about and evaluate their emotional life through participating in early adult-guided conversations about the past. In the first section I outline the theoretical framework within which the research is conceptualized and discuss the evidence for the social construction of children's personal narratives. I then turn to a more detailed exposition of three research studies examining the emotional content of parent-child conversations about the past. To foreshadow, the research indicates consistent and intriguing differences in the ways that parents discuss past emotions with daughters and with sons. In the final section, I discuss the developing relationships among autobiographical memory, emotions, gender, and self-concept.

THEORETICAL FRAMEWORK

The idea that social interaction influences the emergence and organization of personal narratives stems from Vygotsky's dialectical model of development (Vygotsky, 1978; see also Wertsch, 1985). Vygotsky argued that cognition develops through participation in culturally structured interactions, rather than solely as a result of internal cognitive change. New skills emerge as cultures provide more powerful "tools" for thinking. Tools are conceptualized broadly as culturally provided means of solving problems and creating products for the maintenance and evolution of the culture. The most flexible and powerful tool that a culture provides is language. It is primarily through language that children learn new ways of organizing and operating on their world.

Although the culture as a whole provides the tools for cognitive growth, the developmental process obviously occurs at a more local level. By participating in adult-guided interactions, children learn the specific cognitive skills deemed important and necessary by their culture (Cole, 1985).[1] This process operates at two levels simultaneously. First, the adult engages the child in specific tasks that are considered appropriate. By placing children in particular activity contexts, adults are teaching children which activities are important for the child to participate in and learn about (see especially Rogoff & Gardner, 1984, for a full discussion). These activities will differ depending on the child's age (i.e., some activities are deemed more appropriate for young children whereas others are deemed more appropriate for older children), as well as other factors such as gender, mental ability, and proclivity.

Second, the adult structures the task such that the child learns through participation. At first, the adult provides the entire task structure and goal, and the child is an active onlooker. By being present as the task is accomplished and by being drawn into the activity by the adult, the child begins to learn about the task. Very soon, the child begins to participate more fully in the interaction. Although still dependent on the adult to provide the overall structure, the child is now able to perform various task components leading to goal attainment. Finally, through participating in adult-guided interactions, the child internalizes the entire task structure and the means for attaining the goal. The child is now able to complete the task independently. This process has been documented in such diverse areas

---

[1]Although the focus of this chapter is on adult-child interactions, Vygotsky's theory is both micro- and macro-developmental. The developmental process is the same for any novice learning about a new task domain from a more expert partner, whether the interactants are children or adults.

as book reading (Snow & Goldfield, 1983), language games (Bruner, 1983), problem-solving (Wertsch, McNamee, McLane, & Budwig, 1980) and strategic memory tasks (Paris, Newman, & Jacobs, 1985; Ratner, 1980).

Arguing from this perspective, the development of autobiographical memory is closely tied to children's developing ability to organize their memories into culturally conventionalized narrative forms (see Hudson, 1990, Pillemer & White, 1989, and Nelson, 1991, for related arguments). That is, the tools that Western culture provide for structuring memories of personal past experiences include canonical narrative forms. By participating in conversations about past events, children will come to internalize these narrative forms and use them in organizing their own personal memories. Before this idea is explored in more detail, several assumptions need to be stated explicitly.

First, I am not claiming that personal memories are absent before children have acquired the culturally provided narrative forms of organization. There is growing evidence that children as young as 20- to 24 months-of-age verbally recall a great deal of specific information about particular past experiences[2] (Fivush, Gray, & Fromhoff, 1987; Hudson, 1990; Nelson, 1988). Rather, these early memories are not organized as narratives. Quite possibly, early memories are represented in script-like formats (see especially Bauer & Mandler, 1989 and Bauer & Shore, 1987, for evidence on this point), with a script being defined as a spatially-temporally organized sequence of actions (Nelson, 1986). Although narratives may also follow a temporal order, a good narrative must go beyond a simple chronological sequence (e.g., Labov, 1982; Peterson & McCabe, 1983).

This brings us to the second assumption: Narratives provide a particular way of organizing experience. In canonical Western narratives, events have a beginning, a middle, and an end. Moreover, events occurring earlier in the narrative sequence are seen as leading up to and often causing events occurring later in the narrative sequence. Most important, narratives have a point, or a climax (e.g., Labov, 1982; Miller & Sperry, 1988; Peterson & McCabe, 1983). We tell particular stories because they are entertaining or educational or moral, and so on. In this way, the narrator stands in an emotional or evaluative relationship to the story. We tell stories about our past that are personally significant and emotionally meaningful. Canonical narrative forms provide both causal and emotional cohesion to events.

Perhaps most important for the arguments presented here, it is further assumed that the narrative tools provided by the culture are both externally and internally directed. Vygotsky argued quite cogently that it is not simply the case

---

[2]Note that I am referring here only to verbal recall. There is a great deal of evidence that even during the first year and a half of life, infants can recall past experiences using other measures of recall, such as reinstatement (e.g., Rovee-Collier, 1984) and re-enactment (e.g., Bauer & Shore, 1987). The issue of when and how the ability to recall information develops is well beyond the scope of this chapter, but obviously, certain basic memory skills are necessary for children to be able to engage in conversations about past experiences with adults, and these skills seem to develop during the first two years of life.

that culturally provided tools change the way in which we interact with the world; they also change the way in which we interact with ourselves. The narrative forms for organizing personal memories provide a coherent structure for recounting the past to others and also a coherent structure for representing the past to ourselves. As children learn the canonical forms for talking about past experiences in adult-guided conversations about the past, they are also learning to represent these experiences as more conventionalized narratives.

Note also that children are learning narrative forms through language. As mentioned earlier, Vygotsky claimed that language was the most flexible and powerful tool available for the socialization of cognition. Through participating in a particular language group, children are learning particular ways of processing experience and solving problems. In this sense, language comes to organize the way in which children interact with others. Further, as language is internalized, it also comes to direct how children interact with themselves in their private world. With development, language organizes and regulates one's own thought and behavior. Language is the medium through which children learn the canonical narrative forms (i.e., social conversations). Language simultaneously provides the structures for organizing personal memories (i.e., the narrative forms themselves). According to this view, then, language is a primary means through which adults socialize young children and the linguistic forms displayed in these early conversations serve both as the medium of socialization and, as they become internalized, also serve as the forms of internal organization.

The argument thus far, then, is that children's autobiographical memories become more and more narratively organized as children participate in adult-guided conversations about the past. Because adults are engaging children in conversations about their past experiences, children are learning that their personal past is an important topic of conversation and reminiscence. Further, the particular narrative forms displayed in these early conversations will come to be internalized by children, such that children will begin to recount and represent their past experiences in more conventionalized narrative forms. Narrative forms provide a particular type of cohesion to experiences. In learning the narrative forms, children are also learning how to make sense out of their past experiences and how to evaluate these experiences in terms of personal and emotional significance. Thus far, these claims have been theoretical; I now turn to the evidence that children are, indeed, learning the narrative forms for recounting the past in early adult-guided conversations.

PARENT-CHILD CONVERSATIONS ABOUT THE PAST

Developmental Course

Parents and children begin talking about past events virtually as soon as children begin talking (Eisenberg, 1985; Engel, 1986; Hudson, 1990; Nelson, 1988).

During this early phase, however, when children are about 18 months-of-age, the adult provides the entire content and structure of the conversation and the child participates minimally if at all. Essentially the adult asks questions and provides information about the event which the child simply repeats or confirms. At this point, children are contributing little to the recounting of the event. Within a few months, however, children become much more active participants in these conversations. They now recall a good bit of information about the event under discussion and may even begin to initiate conversations about a past event. But they are still dependent on the adult to place these bits of recalled information into a coherent story about what happened (Eisenberg, 1985; Sachs, 1983). Finally, sometime between 3- and 4-years-of-age, children become able to give a reasonably coherent account of a past experience with minimal adult support. The child is now able to narrate an event independently, although children's narrative skills obviously continue to develop throughout childhood (Hudson & Shapiro, 1991; Peterson & McCabe, 1983).

This developmental progression accords with a Vygotskian perspective. At first, the adult structures the task for the child. Gradually the child comes to take over more and more components of the task until she is able to accomplish the task on her own. But in order to claim that children are learning narrative forms in these early conversations, we need to be able to demonstrate that the specific narrative skills displayed in the early adult-child conversations are incorporated into the child's independent repertoire.

Recent research has begun to demonstrate just this. In particular, several studies have now documented that mothers vary in the way in which they discuss past experiences with their children (Engel, 1986; Fivush & Fromhoff, 1988; Hudson, 1990; McCabe & Peterson, 1991; Reese & Fivush, 1991). Some mothers show an elaborated narrative style, in which the event is described in richly embellished ways, other mothers show a less elaborated style, giving fewer details, and providing less information about the event under discussion, and especially less evaluative information. In a descriptive longitudinal study, McCabe and Peterson (1991) have shown that children of more elaborative parents become more competent narrators than children of parents who talk less about the past and display fewer of these narrative forms in their conversations. Even more specific, I have recently found that it is the particular narrative devices that mothers are displaying in early conversations about the past that children are using in their independent narratives later in development (Fivush, 1991). Mothers who provide a great deal of orienting information, information that places the event in spatial-temporal context, have children who subsequently provide this kind of information in their independent narratives. And mothers who tell complex temporal narratives that include information about causes and consequences of events, have children who later tell complex temporal narratives independently. Finally, mothers who provide a great deal of evaluative and emotional information in their narratives early in development have children who include this kind of information in their independent narratives later in development. These findings strongly suggest that children are learning specific narrative skills through participating in adult-guided conversations about the past.

The Role of Evaluation and Emotion in Narratives

As mentioned earlier, narratives are more than simple chronologies. In order to tell a good story, one must clearly relate what happened (i.e., referential information). One must also place the event in an appropriate context by informing the listener about the who, where and when of the event (i.e., orientation information). Finally, one must provide the listener with an evaluative or emotional framework for understanding the significance or the meaning of the event. Evaluation provides the emotional tone and texture of an experience. The evaluation informs both the listener and the self what the personal meaning of this particular event is.

Evaluations play a particularly important role in personal narratives (see especially Labov, 1982, for an extended discussion of the role of evaluation in personal narratives). Many theorists have argued that personal memories are intricately related to the self-concept (Brewer, 1986; Fivush, 1988; Neisser, 1988). Memories of the past provide us with information about the kinds of people we are (e.g., Markus, 1977; Neimeyer & Rareshide, 1991), as well as providing a sense of continuity of self over time (e.g., Chandler, Boyes, Ball, & Hala, 1987; Neisser, 1988). I argue that it is the emotional and evaluative aspect of personal memories that provide the critical link between personal memories and self-concept. The emotional evaluation of a past event provides the personal significance of particular events and informs the self about what kinds of events are important and for what reason. In this way, the emotional evaluation we place on our personal experiences contributes to our evolving self-concept.

Given the theoretical approach outlined here, it becomes important to examine how emotional aspects of past events are discussed in early parent-child conversations. If children are learning the canonical narrative forms for recounting and representing their past in early adult-guided conversations, they may also be learning the emotional framework for evaluating events in these conversations. The fact the mothers who make more evaluative and emotional comments when discussing the past with their children early in development have children who explicitly include emotional information in their personal narratives later in development (Fivush, 1991) supports this idea. But the critical questions are what kinds of emotions are talked about and how are they integrated into the understanding of the event. Only by answering these questions can we address the ways in which children are learning to evaluate their past in early adult-guided conversations. Before turning to the research aimed at answering these questions, however, it is necessary to place the research in the context of what we already know about how parents and children talk about emotion.

The Socialization of Emotions

Over the past few years, there has been an abundance of research on emotional development (see, e.g., Harris, 1989, and Saarni & Harris, 1989, for reviews). Although different theorists emphasize different aspects of emotions, there is growing consensus that emotional experience and expression result from a complex interplay between biology and culture. Whereas biology may provide the physiological substrate for emotions, culture provides the rules for which emotions are considered appropriate in particular situations and how these emotions should be displayed (Gordon, 1989; Lutz & White, 1986). Moreover, these cultural rules are communicated through language (Lewis & Michalson, 1982). It thus becomes imperative to examine the ways in which parents talk about emotions with their young children.

Recent research has documented that mothers and children begin talking about emotions extremely early in development (see Bretherton, Fritz, Zahn-Waxler, & Ridgeway, 1986, for a review). By 18 months-of-age, most children have at least a few emotion words in their working vocabulary. By 24 months-of-age children are able to talk about their own emotions, others' emotions, and to comment on the causes and consequences of emotions. Most interesting, several studies have shown that children's use of emotion language is related to mother's use of emotion language (Beeghly, Bretherton, & Mervis, 1986; Dunn, Bretherton, & Munn, 1987; Usher, Ridgeway, Barrett, Nitz, & Wagner, 1988). For example, Dunn et al. (1987) found that mothers' talk about emotions when their children were 18 months-of-age predicted the children's use of emotional language at 24 months-of-age. Usher et al. (1988) also found a relationship between mothers' talk about the causes and consequences of emotions and their children's ability to explain emotions. These findings suggest that children are learning how to talk about emotions in early adult-guided conversations.

Some intriguing gender differences have also been found in this literature. Mothers talk more about emotions with daughters than with sons, and by 24 months-of-age, girls are talking more about emotions than are boys (Dunn et al., 1987; Zahn-Waxler & Ridgeway, in press). This pattern suggests that girls are socialized to be attuned to emotions beginning very early in development. What make these findings particularly noteworthy is that, as adults, females talk more about emotions, and value emotional expressiveness more than males (Allen & Hacoun, 1976; Balswick & Avertt, 1977). Adult females are also better able to perceive and understand other's emotional expressions than are males (see Block, 1983, for a review).

In addition, mothers may talk more about anger with sons than with daughters, although references to anger are relatively rare overall (Greif, Alvarez, & Ulman, as cited in Lewis & Michalson, 1982). Again, there is some suggestion in the literature that adult females may have more difficulty expressing anger than do adult males (Zahn-Waxler, Cole, & Barrett, in press). Thus, early patterns of emotion talk between parents and children seem related in intriguing ways to gender differences in adult's processing of emotion.

It should be borne in mind, however, that virtually all of this research has examined Western, White middle-class mothers and children. It is entirely possible that emotional socialization might differ as a function of culture and/or class. In fact, Miller and Sperry (1987) found that White working-class mothers emphasized anger and aggression with their young daughters. However, these researchers did not include any male children in their study; it is possible that anger and aggression would have been even more greatly emphasized with sons than with daughters in this population as well. Still, we need to be sensitive to the possibility of cultural differences in emotional socialization.

Emotions About the Past

Talking about emotional aspects of the past differs in fundamental ways from talking about present emotions. Most obvious, when discussing a past emotion, the child is not currently experiencing the emotional state. Rather, the emotional state is being recreated and represented through language. In this situation, the child may be better able to reflect on particular kinds of emotional states and reactions. Similarly, talking about past emotions might provide a way for adults to inform children about which emotional reactions are appropriate or inappropriate and why. That is, both the adult and the child, in discussing a past emotion, are simultaneously interpreting that emotional reaction. Moreover, by focusing on particular emotions, adults may be informing children about the kinds of emotions that are, or "should be," prevalent in that child's emotional life. And by talking about particular emotions in the context of particular kinds of events, adults may further be informing children about what kinds of events are associated with, or cause, specific emotions. Thus, discussing emotional aspects of past events seems an ideal situation in which to study the socialization of emotions.

Moreover, as argued earlier, emotions provide a critical link between the past and the self-concept. Particular past events become important because they inform both the listener and the self something about who we are. Interestingly, Miller and Sperry (1988) found that children include emotional and evaluative information in their recounts of the past as early as age $2\frac{1}{2}$. This finding strongly supports the argument that evaluations are a critical aspect of personal narratives. But if adults are helping to reconstruct the past event with the child, and part of that reconstruction involves an emotional framework, then the way in which adults are helping to structure the emotional framework with their children will influence how the child ultimately comes to view those events, and themselves. By helping to provide an emotional framework for understanding the past, adults may be helping to form their children's developing personal narratives, and their children's developing concept of self.

Given these arguments, it becomes important to examine the ways in which adults discuss the emotional aspects of past events with their young children. In the remainder of this chapter, I discuss three studies that have begun to examine this issue. Because no previous empirical work had been conducted on this issue, the research should be viewed as exploratory. However, as will be seen, the pattern of findings across the three studies are reasonably consistent and begin to provide some good evidence for the ways in which parents are socializing their children's emotional lives. Most intriguing, gender differences emerged in all three studies, suggesting that females and males may be learning very different emotional self-concepts.

STUDY 1: EMOTIONAL CONTENT OF MOTHER-CHILD CONVERSATIONS ABOUT THE PAST

The first study was a preliminary investigation of the emotional content of mother-child conversations about the past (Fivush, 1989). Eighteen mothers and their 30- to 35-month-old children participated. In this, and in all three studies, the dyads were White middle-class college-educated residents of a large urban area. I return to this limitation later. Mothers were informed that we were interested in their children's memory and were asked to discuss special novel events, such as a trip on an airplane or an outing to the circus. Interviews were conducted in the home. The parent and child sat comfortably together; a research assistant sat to the side monitoring the tape recorder and taking notes on the nonverbal context. The parent decided which events to discuss and for how long. No mention was made that we were interested in emotion. It should also be noted that in the following discussion, I focus exclusively on parental contributions to the conversations. I return to the issue of children's contributions to these conversations in discussing the overall pattern of findings across the three studies.

Analyses focused on: (1) how many and what kinds of emotion words mothers used in these conversations, and (2) how emotions were integrated into the ongoing conversation about the past event. All emotion words mothers used were counted and categorized as positive (e.g., happy, like, fun) or negative (e.g., sad, angry, scared). Further, the conversations in which the emotion words were embedded were categorized as single utterances (i.e., the mother mentions an emotion but the child does not respond to this reference), or as extended conversations. Extended conversations were further divided into:

1. Confirmations, in which the mother attributes an emotional state to the child and the child confirms this attribution. For example:

    M: You were so happy
    C: Yeah

2. Elaborations, in which the mother attributes an emotional state to the child, the child confirms it and the mother continues to expand or elaborate on this attribution. For example:

M: Were you scared?
C: Yeah
M: Yeah, I had never seen you so scared.

Or:

M: (we saw) motor boats. And do you remember when people ride behind them?
C: Yes
M: That looks like fun, doesn't it?
C: Yeah, I like to ride in boats
M: You would? I would too.

3. Explanations, in which the causes or consequences of an emotional state are discussed. For example:

M: What makes you scared?
C: A raccoon
M: A raccoon? Why does a raccoon make you scared?
C: That, that brown eyes
M: Those brown eyes
C: Yeah (makes hissing sound)

Or:

M: Why was Big Bird angry? Do you remember why Big Bird was angry?
C: It was his birthday
M: It was his birthday. And what happened? Why was he angry?. . . . Who was he angry with?
C: Oscar
M: He was angry at Oscar, right. And why was he angry at Oscar? He thought they forget his —?
C: Birthday
M: Right.

The first question concerned the number and type of emotion words used. Figure 3.1 shows the mean number of positive and negative emotion words used with daughters and with sons in each of the studies to be discussed. As can be seen in

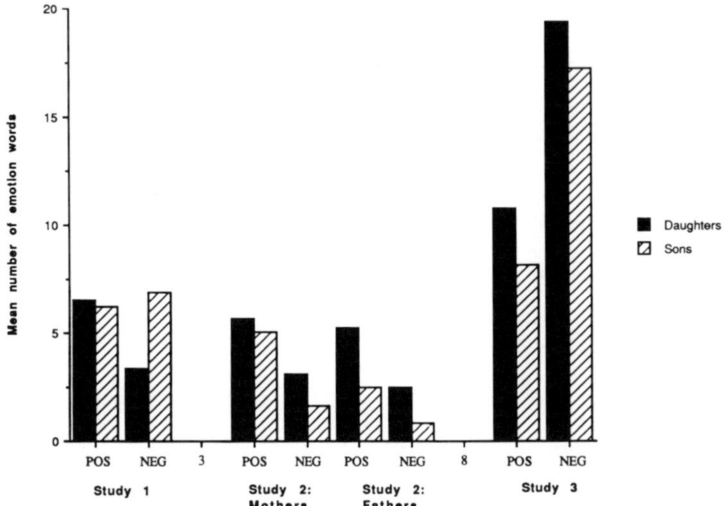

FIG. 3.1.   Mean number of positive and negative emotion words used by parents in Studies 1, 2 and 3.

the first panel of this figure, mothers in this study used approximately equal numbers of positive and negative emotion words with daughters and with sons. However, a closer look at who the emotion was attributed to revealed an interesting difference. All emotions were categorized as either referring to the child's emotional state or to another's emotional state. Of all the positive emotion words the mothers used, 87% referred to the child's emotional state for sons, and 86% referred to the child's emotional state for daughters. However, for negative words, 70% referred to their son's negative emotional state, but only 27% referred to their daughter's negative emotional state. Thus, mothers were equally likely to attribute positive emotions to daughters and to sons, but significantly more likely to attribute negative emotions to sons than to daughters.

Given this finding, a closer look at exactly which emotion words mothers were using seemed warranted. Table 3.1 shows the frequency of usage of specific emotion words with sons and with daughters in this study. As can be seen, mothers used a limited number of different emotion words. This may be because of the limited emotional vocabulary of children this young, but as will be discussed, a greater variety of emotion words were used in the subsequent studies reported in this chapter. More interesting, while there were few differences in the types of positive emotion words used with daughters and with sons, there were differences in negative emotion words used. Specifically, mothers talked about sadness more with daughters than with sons, and more about fear and anger with sons than with daughters. Strikingly, mothers in this data set never talked about anger with daughters but did talk about anger with sons relatively frequently.

TABLE 3.1
Frequency of Mention of Specific Emotion Words by Mothers in Study 1

Emotion Word	With Daughters	With Sons
Positive:		
Like	25	27
Fun/Good	21	13
Happy	3	4
Other (excited, favorite, proud)	3	5
Negative		
Sad/Cry	14	8
Scared/Afraid	11	28
Angry/Mad	0	12
Other (upset, don't like)	2	7

The next question concerned the way in which emotions were integrated into ongoing conversations. In total, 121 conversational units about emotions were coded (see Fig. 3.2 for number of conversations falling into each category.[3] Of these, 52 (43%) were single utterances and 69 (57%) were extended conversations. Single utterances more often referred to positive emotions (79%) than to negative emotions (21%), but there were no differences due to gender. Some interesting patterns emerged for the extended conversations, however. Thirty (43%) of these conversations were about positive emotions, and these conversations were almost exclusively confirmations with sons. With daughters, mothers were equally likely to confirm or elaborate. Thus it seems that mothers tend to elaborate on positive emotions more with daughters than with sons. For negative emotions, the patter was quite different. Mothers did not confirm and rarely elaborated on negative emotions with daughters, but frequently confirmed and elaborated on negative emotions with sons. Further, 10 of the extended conversations about negative emotions with sons (36%) focused on explaining the causes and consequences of emotions, but only 1 of the 11 conversations with daughters (9%) was explanatory.

Overall, the pattern of results suggest that mothers are more accepting of negative emotions from sons than from daughters. Although the actual number of positive and negative emotion words used did not differ by gender of child, mothers were more likely to attribute negative emotions to sons than to daughters, and they were more likely to confirm and elaborate on negative emotions with sons than with daughters. Perhaps most striking, mothers in this data set never discussed anger with daughters but did with sons. The exception to

---

[3]The numbers on Fig.3.1 do not add up to 121 because an additional coding category, negotiations, were dropped from discussion for purposes of this chapter. For more details on this category, see Fivush (1989).

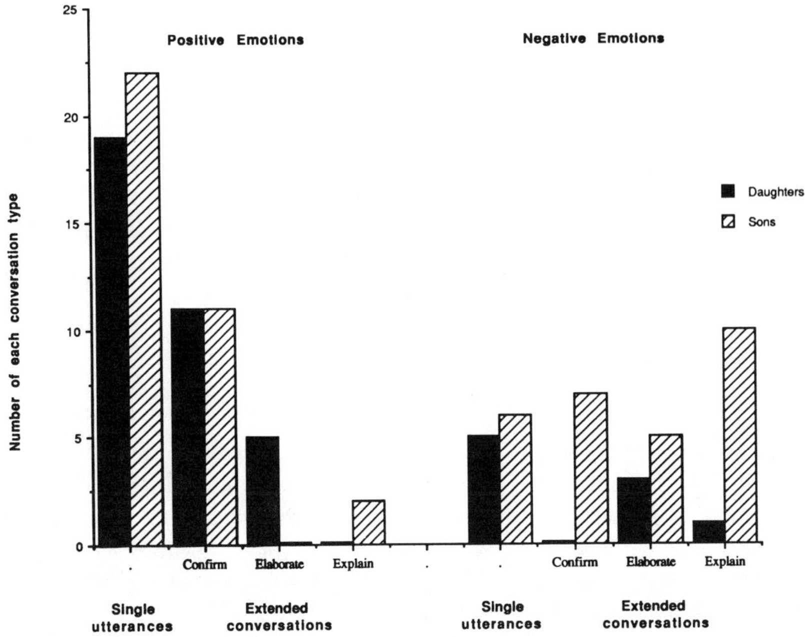

FIG. 3.2.   Mean number of each conversation type in Study 1.

this pattern is the emotion of sadness, which was discussed more frequently with daughters than with sons. Finally, there is some suggestion in these data that mothers are more likely to discuss the causes and consequences of emotions, especially negative emotions, with sons than with daughters.

STUDY 2:MOTHER-CHILD AND FATHER-CHILD CONVERSATIONS ABOUT THE EMOTIONAL ASPECTS OF PAST EVENTS

In some sense, the first study raised more questions than it answered. Although the gender differences in the emotional content of conversations about past events were intriguing, they clearly needed to be replicated. Further, the question arose as to how other important socializing agents, especially fathers, might perform in this type of task. It seemed particularly important to study fathers for two reasons. First, there is a great deal of evidence that, as adults, females and males show different patterns of emotional language. In general, females talk more about emotions than do males (Wheeler & Nezlick, 1977), females value emotions more than males (Allen & Haccoun, 1976), and females are better able to decode others' emotions than are males (Block, 1983). These differences might suggest that, as parents, females will be more likely to talk about emotions with their children than are males.

Second, fathers tend to gender-type their children to a greater extent than do mothers. That is, across many different measures of gender-typing behavior, including discipline, toy choice, and interactional patterns, fathers are more likely to make distinctions between daughters and sons than are mothers, and these distinctions fall along traditional gender lines (see Siegal, 1987, for a review). This might suggest that fathers, even more than mothers, would exhibit differences in the ways in which they structure conversations about past emotions with daughters and sons. Together, these lines of research suggest that mothers should talk more about emotions overall than do fathers, but that when fathers do talk about emotions, they should show even greater differences due to the gender of the child than do mothers.

In order to examine these possibilities, Janet Kuebli and I (Kuebli & Fivush, 1991) compared mother-child and father-child conversations about the emotional aspects of past events. Twenty-four two-parent families with a 40-month-old child participated. Instructions were virtually identical to Study 1, except that parents were asked to discuss three past events with their children and there was no research assistant present during the parent-child conversations. Each parent independently conversed with their child about three special, one-time events, and again, no mention was made of our interest in emotion. Order of mother-child and father-child conversations was counterbalanced across families.

As in Study 1, we were interested in the number and type of emotion words parents used in these conversations, and these means are displayed in the middle panel of Fig. 3.1. Overall, parents used more emotion words in conversations with daughters than with sons. Contrary to our expectations, however, there were no significant differences between mothers' and fathers' frequency of emotional language, although the means are in the expected direction. Of the total number of parents' emotional attributions, 43% referred to the child's own emotional state. Further, mothers and fathers did not differ in their pattern of positive and negative emotional attributions to their children. Of emotions attributed to sons, 53% were positive and 47% were negative, and of emotions attributed to daughters, 41% were positive and 59% were negative, which do not represent significant differences. However, looking at emotions attributed to others, both mothers and fathers attributed a higher percentage of positive emotions to others in conversations with daughters (57% of emotions attributed to others were positive) than in conversations with sons (37% of emotions attributed to others were positive). Thus, although parents did not differ in attributing positive or negative emotions to their children in this study, they did attribute more positive emotions to others in conversations with daughters than with sons.

Related to this, parents were significantly more likely to attribute emotions to a communal group (e.g., "We had so much fun") than to an individual (e.g.,

TABLE 3.2
Frequency of Mention of Negative Emotions by Mothers and Fathers in Study 2

	Negative Emotion Category		
	Sad	*Scared*	*Angry*
Mothers			
with daughters	14	9	4
with sons	2	12	3
Fathers			
with daughters	15	8	2
with sons	2	2	0

"You had so much fun") with daughters than with sons. With daughters, 28% of all emotional attributions were communal in nature, whereas with sons, only 19% of emotional attributions were communal. This pattern suggests that parents are placing emotions in a more social interactive framework with daughters than with sons.

Examining the actual emotion words that parents used also revealed some interesting gender differences. First of all, both mothers and fathers used a greater variety of emotion words with daughters (a mean of 4.87 different emotion words per event) than with sons (a mean of 2.87 different emotion words per event). Thus, parents are expressing a wider range of emotional experience with daughters than with sons. Further, parents seemed to discuss negative emotions differently with daughters than with sons. Table 3.2 displays the mean number of emotion words parents used with daughters and with sons referring to the three negative emotions of sadness, anger and fear (e.g., the words "sad," "cry," and "unhappy" for sadness, the words "angry" and "mad" for anger, and so on). As can be seen in the table, in contrast to Study 1, parents in this study rarely talked about anger with either daughters or sons. However, once again we see that parents are talking overwhelmingly more about sadness with daughters than sons, and this is true for both mothers and fathers. Finally, fear seems to be mentioned less frequently in father-son conversations than in any of the other three types of dyads.

These results indicate that fathers talk about emotional aspects of past events about as frequently as mothers do with their young children. Current conceptions of individual differences in emotional expressivity suggest that expressivity may vary as a function of the situation as well as gender (Dosser, Balswick, & Halverson, 1983). The present findings indicate that adult males can be as emotionally expressive as females in conversations with their young children. However, these conversations did differ as a function of the gender of the child. Both mothers and fathers talk more about emotions with daughters than with sons, they talk about a greater variety of emotions with daughters than with sons, they attribute more positive emotions to others in conversations with daughters than with sons, and they attribute emotions to a communal group rather than an individual more often with daughters than with sons. This pattern suggests that parents are emphasizing emotions more with daughters than with sons. More provocatively, parents seem to be emphasizing interactional aspects of emotions with daughters more so than with sons.

These results both confirm and clarify the findings of the first study. First, in both studies, parents tended to emphasize positive emotions with daughters more than with sons, although in the first study these emotions were attributed to the child and in the second study they were attributed to others. Second, the finding in this study that parents talk more about emotions with daughters than with sons is in accord with the finding from the first study that mothers elaborate on emotions more with daughters than with sons. Both findings indicate that emotions are emphasized more with daughters than sons. Further, in both studies parents discussed sadness more with daughters than with sons. In the first study, mothers never talked about anger with daughters but did so with sons; in this study, mothers and fathers rarely talked about anger with either sons or daughters. Finally, although mothers in the first study discussed fear more with sons than with daughters, this pattern did not hold in the second study. However, mothers in this study did seem to discuss fear with their children more often than did fathers, especially with sons.

STUDY 3: MOTHER-CHILD CONVERSATIONS ABOUT SPECIFIC EMOTIONAL EVENTS

The first two studies, examining the spontaneous discussion of emotion during parent-child conversations about the past events, revealed many intriguing gender differences. However, because of the methodology, it was not always possible to do more fine-grained analyses of the way in which emotions were integrated into ongoing conversations, and, more important, not all parents discussed the same emotions with their children, making certain types of comparisons difficult. For example, although parents seem to differ in the frequency with which they discuss sadness and possibly anger and fear with sons and with daughters, it is not clear whether they might also discuss these emotions in qualitatively different ways. Therefore, in the third study, 15 mothers with 32- to 35-month-old daughters and 15 mothers with 32- to 35-month-old sons were explicitly asked to discuss particular types of emotional events with their children (Fivush, 1991).

As in the first two studies, mothers were told that we were interested in how much children could remember about particular types of events. We then asked mothers to discuss four specific past events with their children, one event in which the child experienced happiness, one in which the child experienced sadness, one for anger and one for fear. These four emotions were selected because these were the most frequently discussed emotions in the spontaneous conversations. Order of emotional event discussed was randomized across children. Although emotions were an obvious part of instructions to mothers, we did not inform mothers that we were interested in discussion of the emotion itself.

Several things should be noted about this methodology. First, mothers were asked to discuss three negative emotional events (sadness, anger, and fear) and only one positive emotional event (happiness). Thus, by definition, mothers would be expected to talk more about negative emotions in this study than in the previous studies. Second, mothers were asked to select events during which their children experienced a specific emotion. Therefore, most emotional attributions would be expected to focus on the child. In fact, this is what was found and the few emotional attributions to people other than the child were eliminated from analysis. Finally, mothers were choosing events associated with each of these emotions. Thus we could examine the kinds of events that mothers select as illustrative of specific emotions, and determine whether different kinds of events are associated with the same emotion for daughters and sons.

As can be seen in the last panel of Fig. 3.1, mothers did, indeed, use many more negative emotion words in these conversations than positive emotion words, but there were no differences due to gender of child. Also note that mothers are talking more about emotions overall in this study than in the previous two studies. This is most likely due to differences in the task instructions.

A more interesting question concerned the way in which these emotions were integrated into the ongoing conversations. Preliminary analysis of the protocols indicated that the majority of mothers' utterances about emotions (74%) fell into one of two mutually exclusive categories:[4] (1) Attributions, in which the mother attributes an emotional state to the child, (e.g., "You were so sad"); and (2) Explanations, in which the mother focused on the cause or consequence of an emotional state (e.g., "That loud noise scared you.", and "What did Aaron do that made you angry?"). The mean number of each of these utterance types for each emotional event discussed are shown in Table 3.3.

Conversations about sadness contained more utterances focusing on emotion with daughters than with sons. Moreover, mothers gave more explanations about sadness in conversations with daughters than with sons. In contrast, mothers talked more about anger with sons than with daughters. There were no gender differences in conversations about fear or happiness, although mothers generally focused on explanations about fear with both daughters and sons.

Examination of the conversations further suggested that mothers and children

---

[4]Two additional categories, denials and general emotion questions, were included in the original coding scheme but these occurred so rarely that they were dropped from analysis (see Fivush, 1991, for details of data reduction and coding).

TABLE 3.3
Mean Number and Type of Mothers' Conversational Utterances About Emotions for Each Event in Study 3

Gender	Event Type			
	Sad	Angry	Scared	Happy
Females				
Attributions	4.73	2.27	4.73	3.00
Explanations	10.27	4.60	9.60	2.73
Males				
Attributions	3.40	3.73	5.33	2.67
Explanations	5.80	7.27	10.13	3.20

often engaged in a three-utterance sequence in discussing emotions: The mother would attribute an emotion to the child, the child would confirm the attribution and the mother would then reconfirm this emotional reaction. For example, the mother might say, "Were you angry when Aaron bit you?", to which the child responds, "Yeah," and the mother reconfirms that reaction by again saying, "Yeah." In reconfirming an attribution, the mother is implicitly accepting the particular emotional response as appropriate. In reconfirming an explanation, the mother is concurring that particular kinds of events cause particular kinds of emotional reactions. The mean number of mothers' reconfirmations following children's confirmations of attributions and explanations is shown in Table 3.4. Analysis on the frequency of mothers' reconfirmations revealed that mothers reconfirmed attributions and explanations of anger more frequently with sons than with daughters, suggesting that anger is a more acceptable reaction for sons than daughters. There were no gender differences for the other three events.

Related to this aspect of the conversations, it was also the case that many

TABLE 3.4
Mean Number of Reconfirmations by Mothers for Each Event Following Children's Confirmations of Attributions or Explanations in Study 3

Gender	Event Type			
	Sad	Angry	Scared	Happy
Females				
Attributions	.87	.33	.13	.47
Explanations	1.87	.47	1.60	.67
Males				
Attributions	.33	.60	.47	.33
Explanations	1.47	1.40	1.73	.27

TABLE 3.5
Number of Conversations Including Each Type of Resolution for Each Event Type in Study 3

	Assures/ Comforts	Reestablishes Relation	Retaliation	None
Scared				
Females	8	1	0	5
Males	8	0	0	5
Sad				
Females	6	0	1	8
Males	1	0	1	12
Angry				
Females	2	4	1	4
Males	0	1	6	4
Happy				
Females	0	0	0	12
Males	1	0	0	10

conversations ended with some kind of emotional resolution. For example, in discussing a fearful event, mothers often ended the conversation by comforting or reassuring children. Forty-one of all the conversations (41% of the total number of conversations) contained some kind of resolution, as displayed in Table 3.5.

Looking at each emotion independently, only one conversation about a happy event contained any type of resolution, most likely because happiness is not an emotion that needs to be resolved. Of the 17 conversations about fearful events containing a resolution, 94% focused on the adult comforting or reassuring the child, and this was equally likely to occur in conversation with a daughter as with a son. An example of this type of conversation will help illustrate. In this excerpt, a mother and daughter are discussing an experience during which the child's friend pretended to be a monster (in these examples, ". . ." stands for some words or utterances deleted for clarity):

M: Do you remember when we went to (name of park)? And Michael was there? What happened?

C: He got me, and play with me

M: . . . But what happened? What did Michael do?

C: He got, he scared me

M: He scared you. How did he scare you? He was pretending to be a monster, wasn't he?

C: Yeah

M: And he was coming toward you, clumpedty-clump. And what did you do?

C: I was getting out of the way

M: (You) went the other way. Did you run for Mommy?

C: He was scaring me

M: He was scaring you? He didn't mean to though. He was just pretending. He was just playing with you. Yeah, and ever since then, we've had to say Michael was really sorry he did that. He was just pretending and he really is sorry he did that. 'Cause it took a long time to get over, didn't it?

This mother does several things that were quite typical during conversations with both sons and daughters about scary events. First, she focuses on the cause of the child's fear ("How did he scare you?"). Second, she confirms that fear was a reasonable reaction in this situation by repeating the child's emotional attribution. But rather than dwelling on the emotion itself, she quickly turns to how the fear was resolved ("And what did you do?"). Finally, she ends the conversation by reassuring the child that Michael was "just pretending" and that the child need not feel afraid. We see this same concern with resolution in a second example of a mother and daughter discussing a scary event:

M: You came downstairs crying

C: Yeah

M: Why were you crying?

C: 'Cause Trent said he was gonna kill me

M: Were you scared?

C: Yeah

M: Very scared?

C: Yeah

M: What do you do when you're scared?

C: (unintelligible)

M: But did you cry?

C: No

M: Yes you did. But then we talked about it, right, and you were okay.

Again, we see the focus on resolving the child's emotion through adult reassurance. It is interesting to note that mother-child conversations about fear were more likely to include emotional resolutions than conversations about any other emotion, suggesting that mothers may be particularly concerned with dissipating children's fear and with reassuring children that everything is all right.

For sad events, 7 conversations with daughters contained a resolution, and 86% of these resolutions were again an adult comforting or reassuring the child that everything was all right. Here is an example of a mother and daughter talking about a minor injury:

M: What happened to your finger?

C: I pinched it

M: You pinched it. Oh boy, I bet that really made you feel sad.

C: Yeah . . . it hurts

M: Yeah, it did hurt. A pinched finger is no fun . . . But who came in and made you feel better?

C: Daddy!

Note that the mother first attributes an emotional reaction to her daughter, which her daughter confirms. The mother then reconfirms the emotional reaction and then almost immediately provides a resolution by asking who came and made the injury better. In contrast, only 2 conversations about sadness with sons contained any resolution at all, and one of these concerned comfort and reassurance; the other concerned retaliation against the person who made the child sad.

For angry events, 7 conversations with daughters and 7 conversations with sons contained a resolution. However, with daughters, 57% of these resolutions involved reestablishing harmonious relations with the person who caused the anger. For example, in the following conversation, a mother and daughter are discussing a time when the child's playmate took all of her toys away from her:

M: Did you play with Niklaus a little bit yesterday?

C: Yeah

M: Did he make you angry?

C: Yeah

M: What did he do?

C: He, I was yelling at him

M: Um-hmmm

C: And Yolanda came

M: Yolanda came, that's right. She said you were fighting. What was wrong? What was Niklaus doing?

C: He took away my toys

M: Yeah. What toys did he take away?

C: My elephant

M: . . . What else did Niklaus do?

C: He played with me

M: Um-hmm. Was that fun when he played with you?

C: Yeah

M: Um-hmmm. He only made you angry when he took away (your elephant)?

C: Yeah

Several things should be noted about this conversation. First, the mother does attribute anger to her daughter. But notice that when the daughter confirms that she was angry, the mother does not reconfirm this emotion. Most interesting, after discussing how the playmate took away the child's toys, the mother switches the emotional tone of the conversation and asks, "Was that fun when he played with you?", and further resolves the angry episode by stating, "He only made you angry when he took away (your elephant)." In this way, the mother ends the conversation by reestablishing a harmonious relationship between the child and her playmate. A second example concerns a mother and daughter discussing an incident that morning when the older sister took the child's crayons away:

    M: How did you feel?
    C: ummm, FINE (shouted)
    M: You cried?
    C: NO, FINE
    M: Oh fine (laughs). You felt fine. Were you upset when Catherine took your crayon?
    C: Yeah
    M: Umm-hmm. What did you say to her?
    C: To not take it!
    M: Right. Don't you take it. That's my crayon. Do you love Catherine?
    C: ummm, let's see, YEAH
    M: Good, I'm glad you said that. Good answer.

This is an extremely interesting example for several reasons. First, the child begins by denying that she was upset when her sister took her crayon, but her mother does not accept this response and pursues until the child confirms this attribution. (Note that we cannot know whether or not the child was actually upset at the time of the experience, but we can assume that the child's behavior indicated to her mother that she was, in fact, upset. I will return to the issue of the veridicality of emotional attributions later on.) This mother even reconfirms her daughter's negative response, but then after working to get her daughter to admit being upset, the mother completely switches the emotional tone and asks her daughter if she loves her sister, and then praises her highly for saying yes. In this way, the mother ends the conversation by reestablishing a loving relationship between the child and her sister.

Only one conversation about anger with a son ended with this kind of resolution. The remaining 86% of the conversations resolved anger through a discussion of retaliation. Again, an example will help illustrate:

    M: Who bites (you)?
    C: Uh, ummm, Johnny bites me
    M: Yeah, and what do you think when Johnny bites you?
    C: That I will shoot him

M: You're gonna shoot him?

C: (nods yes)

M: When he bites you?

C: Yes

M: Yeah, where did he bite you?

C: He bite me on the cheek

M: That's right, he did.

C: Yeah and (unintelligible) I got a gun, I'm gonna shoot him

M: You're gonna shoot Johnny?

C: Yeah, and Johnny's got in my gun

M: Oh, OK.

At three points in this short excerpt, this child mentions physical retaliation against his aggressor, and each time the mother either implicitly or explicitly accepts this response. One might argue that the child is only mentioning aggression in fantasy, but in several conversations, the child mentions a real retaliatory act. For example, here is one mother and son discussing another child taking away his toys:

M: What did you do?

C: I got angry

M: You did. And what did you do to Michael?

C: I hit him

M: You hit him

C: (unintelligible)

M: 'Cause Michael comes and takes away your toys. . . (the mother now tries to switch the conversation to another incident with Michael, but the child continues the first conversation)

M: What happened when you made Michael a cake?

C: I hit him

M: You hit him. Did he cry?

C: Yep

M: And what happened? Did you cry too?

C: Yeah

M: Why did you cry?

C: 'Cause he bothered my toy

M: 'Cause he bothered your toy and it made you sad and angry, didn't it?

Several things should be noted about this conversation. First, the child mentions twice that he hit his friend, and neither time does the mother suggest that this might not have been an appropriate reaction. At the end of the conversation, it almost seems like the mother might turn the conversation around and talk about her son feeling sad about hitting his friend. But when the child claims he cried because his friend bothered his toy and not because he hit his friend, the mother explicitly accepts this as appropriate by reconfirming the emotional reaction.

It must be emphasized that mothers did not initiate discussion of retaliation. In every single instance in which retaliation was discussed with sons, it was the child who brought it up. However, it was also the case that in all of these conversations, the mother accepted retaliation as a reasonable resolution of anger. In the entire corpus, there was only one instance in which the mother did suggest retaliation as a possible resolution for anger, and this conversation occurred with a daughter. The interchange is striking:

> M: Let me think of a time you were angry. Umm, well, when Jason bit you, did it make you angry?
>
> C: (nods yes)
>
> M: Did you hit him?
>
> C: (nods no)
>
> M: Did you try to bite him back?
>
> C: No
>
> M: No, 'cause you're a sweet little girl.

Overall, then, mothers are providing very different kinds of resolutions about different kinds of emotional events. For scary events, mothers seem particularly concerned with comforting and reassuring children. Both the frequency and the consistency of type of resolution for scary events indicates that mothers are concerned with dissipating their children's fear. For sad events, mothers rarely provide any kind of resolution with sons but frequently comfort and reassure daughters. This suggests that mothers are more focused on discussing and resolving sadness with daughters than with sons. Angry events show quite a different pattern. Here, mothers are concerned with reestablishing a harmonious relationship with daughters but not with sons. Instead, mothers accept retaliation as a reasonable response to anger when their sons suggest it. Because daughters never suggested retaliation in these conversations (which is an interesting finding in its own right), it is not clear how mothers would have responded in this situation. Still, the focus on harmony with daughters seems somewhat incompatible with retaliation. Finally, and not surprisingly, mothers do not provide resolutions for happy events, because happy events do not need to be resolved.

A final question concerned the types of events mothers selected to illustrate particular emotions. Recall that mothers were instructed to ask their children about events during which the child experienced each of these four emotions. The kinds of events that mothers selected to discuss provide evidence for the kinds of events mothers think are related to particular kinds of emotions. Inspec-

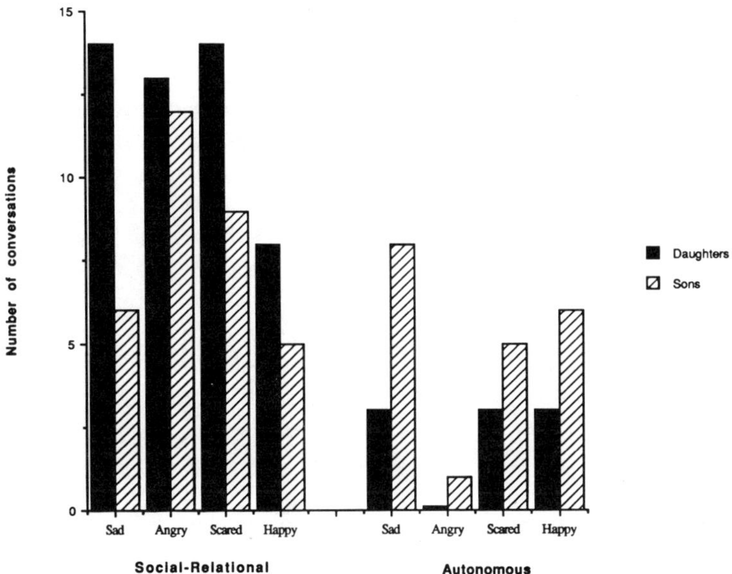

FIG. 3.3.   Number of social-relational and autonomous events discussed for each emotion in Study 3.

tion of the various themes that mothers chose indicated that events could be divided into two broad categories: social-relational themes and autonomous themes. Social-relational themes focus on other people being involved in or causing a particular emotional state or reaction. For example, in discussing happy events, many mothers talked about visiting friends or relatives. Autonomous themes focus on something the child experienced alone as causing the emotion. For example, for sad events, several mothers discussed the child losing a toy. The number of conversations focusing on social-relational themes and on autonomous themes for each event is shown in Fig. 3.3.

Overall, mothers discussed social-relational themes more with daughters than with sons, and autonomous themes more with sons than with daughters. More specifically, for sad events, mothers often discussed events in which the daughter's sadness was caused by someone else's misfortune. In fact, one third of the conversations about sadness with daughters were about someone's illness or death. This theme never occurred in a mother-son conversation. Instead, mother-son conversations about sadness tended to focus on lost toys and the child not getting his own way. For scary events, mothers discussed events in which their daughters were scared by friends or by animate characters such as the wicked witch in "The Wizard of Oz." This theme occurred with sons as well, but not to the same extent. Mother-son conversations about fear were more often about the child being scared when alone, usually by thunder or the dark. This gender difference also emerged in discussions of happy events. With daughters, mothers discussed family gatherings and playing with friends; with sons, they also discussed family outings but only talked about the activities children engaged in and did not discuss the other people present. Only for angry events were there no gender differences: here, virtually all the conversations concerned another child's aggression.

Taken together, the pattern of findings in this study point to striking gender differences in mother-child conversations about past events, especially for the emotions of sadness and anger. Mothers talk more about sadness with daughters than with sons, they emphasize explanations of sadness more with daughters than with sons, and they are concerned with resolving sadness to a greater extent with daughters than with sons. In contrast, mothers talk more about anger with sons than with daughters, they accept anger as a reasonable emotional reaction to a greater extent with sons than with daughters, and they accept retaliation as an appropriate reaction to anger with sons. Moreover, the fact that mothers resolve anger with daughters by trying to reestablish the damaged relationship is in accord with the general tendency for mothers to place emotions in a more social-relational framework with daughters than with sons.

Across the three studies, then, several consistent patterns emerge. Before discussing the implications of the empirical findings, however, some limitations of the research are outlined.

SOME LIMITATIONS OF THE RESEARCH

The Role of the Child

In reviewing the research findings, I have focused exclusively on parental contributions to these conversations. It seems legitimate to focus on parents, at least in these initial exploratory studies, for several reasons. First, it is overwhelmingly the parent who initiated discussion of emotion. Across all three studies, children rarely brought up an emotional state or reaction before the parent introduced this topic. Moreover, although not discussed in this chapter, children in these studies actually used few emotion words overall, and there were no differences between male and female children in the number or type of emotion words used in any of the three studies. Finally, whenever children did discuss emotions in these conversations, parents almost always responded to the child's utterance. It was rarely the case that a child would mention an emotion and the parent would not follow-in on this topic. In this way, parents are playing an important role in taking the child's contribution and interpreting and evaluating the child's emotional experience. As discussed earlier, it is through language that parents and children are reflecting on and evaluating the emotional meaning of their past experiences. By constructing these experiences with their children, parents are providing information about the interpretation and appropriateness of particular emotions in particular situations.

But clearly, conversations are bidirectional and the child most likely has some influence in directing the parent to discussing specific emotions in particular ways. The most obvious example of this influence is in the discussion of retaliation by sons but not by daughters in the third study. It is not the case that mothers resolve anger through retaliation in conversations with sons. Rather, males tend to suggest retaliation against their aggressor and mothers accept this response. As mentioned earlier, it is not clear how mothers would react if daughters suggested retaliation. The point is that the child is having an important influence on the way in which the mother discusses specific emotions. In future research, the role of the child in recreating the past emotional experience in these conversations needs to be explicated.

The Veridicality of Emotional Attributions

By focusing on parents, we are also focusing on the parent's attribution of the child's emotional reaction or state. One might question how accurate parents are in attributing emotions to their children. Although this is an important question, I believe that it is not relevant for the issue of emotional socialization. Again, a critical assumption underlying this research is that the ways in which parents help children to recreate their emotional experiences influences children's developing understanding and evaluation of their past experiences. Thus, it is not so much a question of accuracy as one of interpretation of emotional experience.

However, even given this argument, it should be noted that across all three studies, children generally agreed with their parent's emotional attributions. In coding the transcripts, we always included categories for denials and negotiations of emotional reactions, and although these did occur, they were infrequent (but see Stein, Trabasso, & Liwag, 1991). One reason for this is that parents may be generally accurate at interpreting their children's emotional reactions. A second possibility is that children have difficulty recalling their emotional experience and therefore are willing to accept whatever emotional attributions their parents make. This seems unlikely, as there is evidence from other research that young children spontaneously discuss emotions of both themselves and others in other situations (see Bretherton et al., 1986, for a review). A final possibility is that children disagreed with their parents' attributions but, for whatever reason, chose not to discuss the disagreement. Although these possibilities cannot be disentangled from the present data, it is the case that there was remarkable agreement in these conversations between parents and children in emotional attributions.

A related question concerns the events that mothers selected to illustrate particular emotions in the third study. Recall that it was the mother who selected events for discussion. Thus the focus on social-relational themes with daughters and autonomous themes with sons is a difference which can only be attributed to mothers, and not necessarily to children. If asked to discuss events in which they experienced these various emotions, it is not clear whether girls would have discussed social-relational themes and males would have discussed autonomous themes (see Hudson, Gebelt, Haviland, & Bentivegna, 1991, and Stein & Levine, 1987, for some relevant data). This is certainly an interesting question for future research. But, again, the theoretical perspective outlined here would suggest that the important question is one of how parents help children to understand and evaluate their experience. The themes parents chose to illustrate particular emotions are part of that emotional socialization.

Generalizability to Other Populations

As mentioned earlier, in all three studies, only White middle-class urban residents participated. We need to be extremely cautious in generalizing these findings to other populations. A basic tenet underlying the idea of emotional socialization is that different cultures provide different ways of interpreting and evaluating emotional experience (Lutz & White, 1986). Thus it is not only possible, but theoretically predicted that children growing up in different cultural contexts would participate in different kinds of conversations about past emotions and, subsequently would develop different kinds of emotional self-concepts.

Miller, Potts, Fung, Hoogstra, and Mintz (1990) have examined some aspects of emotional socialization through narratives about the past in a White working class inner-city population. Unfortunately for the arguments presented here, they only examined mothers and daughters. But interestingly, they found that mothers in this culture valued anger as an emotional response from their daughters (see also Miller & Sperry, 1987). Miller and her colleagues argue that these mothers are socializing their daughters to the harsh realities of their lives, and an important aspect of this socialization is teaching their daughters to stand up for their rights. Although limited, these results support the notion that the socialization of emotion is culturally influenced. Thus, in discussing the implications of the studies presented here, it is important to keep in mind that the conclusions may only apply to the particular cultural group studied.

SUMMARY OF RESEARCH FINDINGS

Across the three studies presented, examining both spontaneous and more directed discussion of emotional aspects of the past, parents displayed different patterns of emotional socialization with daughters than with sons. In general, parents talked about emotions more and elaborated about emotional states and reactions more with daughters than with sons. Further, parents seemed to place emotions in a social-relational framework to a greater extent with daughters than with sons. In the second study, mothers and fathers stressed the communal aspects of emotions more with daughters than with sons, and in the third study, mothers selected social events as illustrative of emotions to a greater extent with daughters than with sons. In addition to these general differences, parents also discussed specific emotions differently with daughters and with sons.

Sadness

In all three studies, parents talked about sadness more with daughters than with sons. In the first study, mothers mentioned sadness more frequently, and elaborated more on the emotional state of sadness with daughters than with sons. In the second study, both mothers and fathers talked about sadness more with daughters than with sons. In the third study, mothers talked more about sadness, and focused more on explaining sadness, with daughters than with sons. They were also more concerned with resolving sadness through adult comfort and reassurance with daughters than with sons, suggesting that mothers may be especially concerned about how their daughters deal with feeling sad. Finally, as seen in the third study, mothers focus on others being a cause of the child's sadness more so with daughters than with sons.

Anger

Although conversations about anger were rare with either sons or daughters in the second study, in both the first and third studies, mothers talked about anger more with sons than with daughters. Although anger seems to be caused by other children's aggressive acts for both sons and daughters, it was also the case that mothers accepted anger as an appropriate emotional response more often with sons than with daughters, and mothers accepted retaliation as an appropriate reaction to anger with sons. The fact that mothers often focused on resolving anger through re-establishing the damaged relationship with daughters further suggests that anger was not viewed as an appropriate emotion for daughters.

Happiness

There is some suggestion in these data that parents focus more on positive emotions with daughters than with sons. In the first study, mothers were significantly more likely to attribute positive emotions than negative emotions to daughters but showed no differential pattern of attribution with sons. Similarly, in the second study, parents talked about the positive emotions of other people to a greater extent with daughters than with sons. And the focus on resolving anger through reestablishing harmony in the third study further suggests that parents are focusing on keeping interpersonal relationships happy and positive with daughters more so than with sons. And as with the other emotions discussed in the third study, mothers place happiness in a more social-relational context with daughters than with sons.

Fear

Parent-child discussions of fear showed somewhat inconsistent patterns across the three studies. In the first study, mothers talked about fear more with sons than with daughters, but this was not true in the second study. However, in the second study, mothers did seem to talk about fear with sons more than did fathers. This pattern suggests that mothers may attribute more fear, and accept fear as a more appropriate emotional reaction with sons than do fathers. Interestingly, in the third study, mothers seemed quite concerned with resolving their children's fearful reactions, and provided adult comfort and reassurance frequently and equally often with daughters and with sons. However, there was some indication that fear is caused by people and the social world for daughters more so than for sons.

IMPLICATIONS: RELATIONSHIPS AMONG MEMORY, EMOTION, GENDER AND SELF-CONCEPT

The pattern of results across the three studies clearly indicate that parents are discussing the emotional aspects of past events differently with daughters than with sons. In this section, I consider how these differences might be related to children's developing autobiographical memory, their understanding of their emotional lives, and their developing self-concept. I first discuss the specific emotions of sadness and anger, and then turn to a more general discussion of emotional socialization.

The fact that parents focus on the emotion of sadness with daughters suggests that females may be learning that sadness is a frequently occurring and important emotional state. Previous research has demonstrated that mothers who talk a great deal about emotions in general, foster talk about emotions in their children (Dunn et al., 1987; Usher et al., 1988). Given this finding, it seems possible that parental discussion of a particular emotion might lead children to focus on that specific emotion. Further, focusing on a particular emotion may not only lead the child to talk about that particular emotion more often, but also, as argued in the earlier part of this chapter, may lead the child to think about that particular emotion more often. In this way, because parents talk about sadness so much with daughters, females may come to talk about and think about sad events to a greater extent than do males. This is an extremely interesting possibility given the fact that females are more prone to depression than males beginning in adolescence. Recent theory and research have postulated that females may become depressed because females tend to ruminate on feeling sad whereas males tend to avoid sad feelings (Conway, Giannopoulos, & Stiefenhofer, 1990; Nolen-Hoeksema, 1987). Beginning in middle childhood, females already report feeling sadness more frequently than males (Brody, 1984; Stapley & Haviland, 1989). The present results provide some evidence about the ways in which rumination on sad feelings may develop.

Yet mothers also seem more concerned with comforting their daughters about sadness than their sons. This might suggest that mothers are teaching daughters how to cope with sadness. Ironically, however, the resolution provided daughters for feeling sad comes from other people's comfort and reassurance. That is, females may be learning that they are unable to cope with sad feelings themselves, but rather need another, perhaps stronger person to help comfort them. Even the fact that mothers are more likely to provide resolutions to sad events for daughters than for sons suggests that mothers may believe their daughters have more difficulty coping with sadness than do their sons. Further, by emphasizing comfort and reassurance as a coping strategy, mothers may be encouraging their daughters to talk to others when feeling sad, again emphasizing interactive reflection and rumination on the emotion itself as a way of dealing with sadness.[5]

Finally, other people are a potent cause of sadness for females but not for males. This provides evidence for how parents place emotions in a social-relational framework with daughters more so than with sons. In this way, females may be learning how emotions are regulated by social interactions. Notably, by early adolescence, females report feeling sad in social situations more often than when alone, whereas males report the reverse (Stapley & Haviland, 1989).

Anger shows a very different pattern. Parents tend not to dwell on angry emotions with daughters. Anger is not an acceptable emotional reaction in most situations; even when anger is acceptable, parents focus on not acting on the anger, but rather on reestablishing harmony. In this way, females may be learning that they should not feel anger, and when they do, they certainly should not express it. Moreover, females may be learning that they are responsible for keeping relationships smooth and harmonious. When anger threatens to disrupt a relationship, the appropriate response is to resolve the situation by reestablishing a positive interpersonal connection. Thus, females may be socialized as "peacekeepers" (see Zahn-Waxler et al., in press, for related arguments). In contrast, parents seem to be teaching males that anger is acceptable and that retaliation may be appropriate. Certainly, there was no indication in any of these studies that males were discouraged from expressing their anger in the interest of keeping a relationship harmonious.

There are many ways to interpret these findings. One could argue that females

---

[5]Discussion of disturbing and sad events may also be therapeutic, and certainly many clinical interventions involve deep, prolonged exploration of sad feelings. However, successful intervention usually focuses on reinterpreting and moving beyond these sad feelings rather than simply ruminating on them.

are being taught to deny their anger and to care more about the aggressor's emotional state than their own. Males, on the other hand, are being taught that anger is a healthy response in particular situations. Yet at the same time, the only response that males have to anger is retaliation. Males may be taught to stand up for their rights, but it may very well be at the cost of the relationship. By contrast, females are being taught that anger does not necessarily mean the dissolution of a relationship. They can feel angry and still care about the other person. Thus, there are both positive and negative aspects to the ways in which males and females are being socialized to understand and deal with anger. Moreover, it seems quite possible that the way in which parents talk about emotions will change as a function of their child's age. In particular, it seems unlikely that parents will continue to accept retaliation as an appropriate response from their sons as their sons grow older. This is an important issue for future research.

In addition to differences in the ways in which specific emotions are talked about, there are two general differences in the ways in which parents discuss past emotions with daughters and with sons. First, parents discuss emotional aspects of the past more with daughters than with sons, and, second, parents place emotions in a more social-interactional framework with daughters than with sons.

By talking more about emotions overall, parents may be teaching daughters to focus on emotions as an important part of thinking about the past. Previous research has established that parents who talk frequently about emotions have children who subsequently talk a great deal about emotions (Beeghly et al., 1986; Usher et al., 1988). Further, as mentioned earlier, parents talk more about emotions with daughters than with sons, and by 24 months-of-age, girls are talking more about emotions than are boys (Dunn et al., 1987). The present research extends these findings to conversations about past emotions, and suggests that females may come to incorporate emotions into their personal memories to a greater extent than do males. Given the parental patterns documented here, we might expect females to have more emotionally saturated memories of the past than do males. Interestingly, the little research that has examined differences in emotional memories has found that adult females recall more emotionally laden memories than do adult males (Davis, 1991).

Parents not only talk more about emotions with daughters than with sons; they also elaborate more about emotions and use a greater variety of emotion words with daughters than with sons. Because females have a greater vocabulary for talking about and thinking about emotional aspects of past experiences, females may come to have a more differentiated understanding of emotions. Both their own emotional life and the emotional lives of others may be seen as richer and more complex by females than by males.

Finally, parents are emphasizing the social-relational aspects of emotions more with daughters than with sons. For females, emotions are caused by other people to a greater extent than for males, emotions are more communal for females than for males, and females are more responsible for maintaining positive interactions than are males. Taken together, this pattern suggests that females will come to understand emotional life as an integral part of social interaction. Females will be more attuned both to their own emotions and to the emotions of those around them. Research with adults clearly indicates that females are more sensitive to the emotional states of others than are males (see Block, 1983, for a review). The present results suggest this may be due to females coming to understand emotions as regulating social interactions to a greater extent than do males. Females are socialized to understand themselves in terms of their emotional connections with others.

The argument that females are more relationally oriented than males is similar to current theorizing about gender differences in self-concept development proposed by Chodorow (1978) and Gilligan (1982). However, these theorists argue from a psychoanalytic perspective that these gender differences arise from the early mother-child bond. Briefly, both males and females begin life in close relation to the mother. But males need to separate from the mother in order to form an appropriate gender identity. In so doing, males break the relation and become independent. They further deny all feminine aspects of themselves and denigrate feminine traits in others. In this way, males become emotionally closed and independently oriented. Females, in contrast, do not have to separate from the mother in order to form an appropriate gender identity. Thus females remain emotionally bonded to their mother and, by extension, come to define themselves in relation to others.

The present findings support the idea that females become relationally oriented and males become independently oriented, but suggest an alternative developmental pathway to this outcome. What we are seeing in these early parent-child conversations about past emotions is a possible mechanism by which children are learning the culturally accepted roles for their gender. Because parents stress the social-relational aspects of emotional life with daughters, females may come to be relationally oriented. Males, in contrast, are not getting this message. Emotions are discussed as more autonomous entities with sons, and males may therefore be learning that emotional life is internal and self-contained.

Overall, these results indicate that females and males may be learning very different emotional self-concepts. Females are learning that emotions are an important and integral part of their past experiences. Females are further learning that emotions are a part of social interaction, and, more specifically, that one's own and others emotions are intertwined. Females are responsible for others' emotional well-being and their own emotional well-being is dependent on others' emotional states. At the same time, females are learning to focus on feelings of sadness. But recall that even sadness is often caused by others' illness and misfortune, again stressing the social relational aspects of emotional life. Males, on the other hand, are not learning to focus on the emotional aspects of past experiences to the same extent. For them, the past is not as emotionally saturated nor as emotionally differentiated as it is for females. Moreover, emotions are internal and self-contained. Emotions are not part of the glue that keeps interactions running smoothly.

However, we need to be extremely cautious in arguing about possible adult gender differences from these findings. The gender differences in these early parent-child conversations certainly relate in intriguing ways to gender differences in adult's emotional processing. But it is also the case that there were few differences between mothers and fathers in the ways in which they structured conversations about past emotions with their children. These findings suggest that under certain situations, males are as emotionally expressive as females. The ability and the inclination to talk about emotional aspects of past events may be a function of the context and the conversational partner (Dosser et al., 1986). When discussing shared personal experiences with their daughters, both mothers and fathers talk a great deal about emotions. But with sons, both mothers and fathers talk less about emotions. These findings suggest, first, that males are capable of emotional expressivity in certain situations, and, second, that even those gender differences which seem to be robust in the empirical literature may only be apparent in some situations.

One reason why parents may be emotionally expressive with their young daughters is because they are implicitly (and most likely unconsciously) socializing their children into the accepted cultural role. Because females are expected to be more emotionally expressive than males, parents may assume their young daughters will be more interested in and more able to discuss emotions. This expectation would lead parents to discuss emotions more with daughters than with sons, which would, in turn, lead to daughters coming to talk more about the emotional aspects of the past than do sons, thus fulfilling the parental expectations. Some support for this interpretation comes from the finding that mothers are more emotionally expressive with daughters than with sons beginning during the very first weeks of life, well before there are gender differences in infants' emotional expression (Malatesta, Culver, Tesman, & Shepard, 1989).

Another possibility is that parents are emotionally expressive with daughters because daughters are more likely to elicit this kind of discussion. Although we cannot dismiss this possibility, recall that in these conversations, it was almost always the parent who initiated discussions about emotions. Moreover, there were no quantitative differences in how daughters and sons talked about emotions in these conversations. Thus it seems more likely that the high frequency of emotional talk is due to the parental contribution to the conversations. In either case, it is important to keep in mind that males as well as females are capable of emotional expressivity and do discuss emotional aspects of their past experiences in certain situations. What remains a paradox is how males learn these skills if they are not being displayed in early parent-child conversations.

Finally, it is important to emphasize that, in this chapter, I have focused on the ways in which parents differentially interact with sons and with daughters, and these differences are significant. But it is also the case that there is a great deal of variability within each gender group. Some parents talk quite frequently about emotions with their sons, and some parents rarely talk about emotions with their daughters. Thus it is important to keep in mind that gender is only one factor among many possible factors affecting the ways in which parents structure conversations about the past.

DIRECTIONS FOR FUTURE RESEARCH

The research reported in this chapter is clearly exploratory. We are just beginning to understand how parents structure conversations about past emotions with their young children, and many more questions are raised by these results than are answered. Three critical issues must be addressed in future research.

First, we need to examine how and what children are contributing to these conversations. Is it the case that parents talk more about emotions overall with daughters than with sons because daughters are somehow more receptive to these discussions? Similarly, are anger and sadness discussed differently with daughters than with sons because females and males are somehow experiencing and/or expressing these emotions differently to begin with? For example, the fact that males bring up retaliation in response to anger whereas females do not is an unexpected and intriguing finding. It is well documented that males engage in more aggressive play than do females at least by age 2 (see Smith, 1987, for a review). Do males emphasize retaliation because they do, in fact, retaliate more often than females, and thus have a very different experience of anger than females? And is this difference a product of earlier emotional socialization? Emotional socialization begins extremely early in development (e.g., Malatesta et al., 1989). By the time children are engaging in conversations about past emotions, they already have a long history of learning how to interpret and evaluate their emotional life. A challenge facing future research is to try to examine the concurrent and reciprocal roles that parents and children are playing in constructing emotional evaluations of the past.

A second critical issue is to extend this research to other cultural groups. As already discussed, the theoretical perspective developed here leads to the prediction of differences among cultural groups depending on the values and standards accepted within the culture for emotional expression. Especially in the case of gender, which is highly culturally defined, it is important to delineate similarities and differences in emotional socialization.

Finally, we must examine the long term effects of early parent-child conversations on children's developing autobiographical memory and emotional self-concept. At this point, there is no direct evidence that the differences documented here influence developmental outcome. Still, the research conducted thus far indicates consistent and tantalizing differences in the ways in which parents discuss past emotions with daughters and with sons. Some of the differences are startling and some are quite subtle. But these differences exist and, in all probability, have a profound influence on the way in which children come to understand their past and themselves.

ACKNOWLEDGMENTS

Parts of this research were supported by a grant from the Spencer Foundation. Many people were of invaluable assistance in collecting, transcribing and coding data. I would especially like to thank Winifred Diggs, Liza Dondonan, Nicole Harsch, Catherine Johnson, Elyse Kreiger, Elaine Reese, Naomi Singer and Stephen Souffer. I would also like to thank Janet Kuebli and Elaine Reese for comments on an earlier version of this chapter.

REFERENCES

Allen, J. G., & Haccoun, D. M. (1976). Sex differences in emotionality: A multidimensional approach. *Human Relations, 29,* 711–722.

Balswick, J., & Avertt, C. P. (1977). Differences in expressiveness: Gender, interpersonal orientation, and perceived parental expressiveness as contributing factors. *Journal of Marriage and the Family, 38,* 121–127.

Bauer, P. J., & Mandler, J. M. (1989). One thing follows another: Effect of temporal structure on 1 to 2 year olds' recall of events. *Developmental Psychology, 25,* 197–206.

Bauer, P. J., & Shore, C. M. (1987). Making a memorable event: Effects of familiarity and organization on young children's recall of action sequences. *Cognitive Development, 2,* 327–338.

Beeghly, M., Bretherton, I., & Mervis, C. (1986). Mothers' internal state language to toddlers. *British Journal of Developmental Psychology, 4,* 247–261.

Block, J. (1983). Differential premises arising from differential socialization of the sexes: Some conjecture. *Child Development, 54,* 1335–1354.

Bretherton, I., Fritz, J., Zahn-Waxler, C., & Ridgeway, D. (1986). Learning to talk about emotions: A functionalist perspective. *Child Development, 55,* 529–548.

Brewer, W. F. (1986). What is autobiographical memory? In D. C. Rubin (Ed.), *Autobiographical memory* (pp. 25–49). New York: Cambridge University Press.

Brody, L. R. (1984). Sex and age variations in the quality and intensity of children's emotional attributions to hypothetical situations. *Sex Roles, 11,* 51–59.

Bruner, J. (1983). *Children's talk: Learning to use language.* New York: Norton.

Chandler, M., Boyes, M., Ball, L., & Hala, S. (1987). The conservation of selfhood: A developmental analysis of children's changing conceptions of self-continuity. In T. Honess & K. Yardley (Eds.), *Self and identity* (pp. 108–120). London: Routledge & Kegan Paul.

Chodorow, N. (1978). *The reproduction of mothering.* Berkeley: University of California Press.

Cole, M. (1985). The zone of proximal development: Where culture and cognition create each other. In J. V. Wertsch (Ed.), *Culture communication and cognition* (pp. 146–161). New York: Cambridge University Press.

Conway, M., Giannopoulos, C., & Stiefenhofer, K. (1990). Response styles to sadness are related to sex and sex-role orientation. *Sex Roles, 22,* 579–587.

Davis, P. (1991, July). *Gender differences in autobiographical memory.* Paper presented at the

NATO Advanced Research Conference: Theoretical perspectives on autobiographical memory. Grange, England.

Dosser, D. A., Jr., Balswick, J. O., & Halverson, C. F., Jr. (1983). Situational context of emotional expressiveness. *Journal of Counseling Psychology, 30,* 375–387.

Dunn, J., Bretherton, I., & Munn, P. (1987). Conversations about feeling states between mothers and their young children. *Developmental Psychology, 23,* 132–139.

Eisenberg, A. R. (1985). Learning to describe past experience in conversation. *Discourse Processes, 8,* 177–204.

Engel, S. (1986, April). The role of mother-child interaction in autobiographical recall. In J. A. Hudson (Chair), *Learning to talk about the past.* Symposium conducted at the Southeastern Conference on Human Development, Nashville.

Fivush, R. (1988). The functions of event memory. In U. Neisser & E. Winograd (Eds.), *Remembering reconsidered: Ecological and traditional approaches to the study of memory* (pp. 277–282). New York: Cambridge University Press.

Fivush, R. (1989). Exploring sex differences in the emotional content of mother-child conversations about the past. *Sex Roles, 20,* 675–691.

Fivush, R. (1991). The social construction of personal narratives. *Merrill-Palmer Quarterly, 37,* 59–82.

Fivush, R. (1991). Gender and emotion in mother-child conversations about the past. *Journal of Narrative and Life History, 1,* 325–341.

Fivush, R., & Fromhoff, F. A. (1988). Style and structure in mother-child conversations about the past. *Discourse Processes, 11,* 337–355.

Fivush, R., Gray, J. T., & Fromhoff, F. A. (1987). Two year olds talk about the past. *Cognitive Development, 2,* 393–410.

Gilligan, C. (1982). *In a different voice.* Cambridge, MA: Harvard University Press.

Gordon, S. L. (1989). The socialization of children's emotions: Emotional culture, competence, and exposure. In C. Saarni & P. L. Harris (Eds.), *Children's understanding of emotion* (pp. 319–349). New York: Cambridge University Press.

Harris, P. L. (1989). *Children and emotion.* Oxford: Basil Blackwood.

Hudson, J. A. (1990). The emergence of autobiographic memory in mother-child conversation. In R. Fivush & J. A. Hudson (Eds.), *Knowing and remembering in young children* (pp. 166–196). New York: Cambridge University Press.

Hudson, J. A., Gebelt, J., Haviland, J., & Bentivegna, C. (1991). *Emotion in children's narratives.* Submitted.

Hudson, J. A., & Shapiro, L. (1991). Effects of task and topic on children's narratives. In A. McCabe & C. Peterson (Eds.)., *New directions in developing narrative structure* (pp. 89–136). Hillsdale, NJ: Lawrence Erlbaum Associates.

Kuebli, J., & Fivush, R. (1991). *Gender differences in parent-child conversations about past emotions.* Submitted.

Labov, U. (1982). Speech actions and reactions in personal narrative. In D. Tannen (Ed.), *Analyzing discourse: Text and talk* (pp. 219–247). Washington, D.C.: Georgetown University Press.

Lewis, M., & Michalson, L. (1982). The socialization of emotions. In T. Field & A. Fogel (Eds.), *Emotion and early interaction,* (pp. 189–212). Hillsdale, NJ: Lawrence Erlbaum Associates.

Lutz, C., & White, G. M. (1986). The anthropology of emotions. *Annual Review of Anthropology, 15,* 405–436.

Malatesta, C. Z., Culver, C., Tesman, J. R., & Shepard, B. (1989). The development of emotional expression during the first two years of life. *Monographs of the Society for Research in Child Development,* No. 219.

Markus, H. (1977). Self-schemata and processing of information about the self. *Journal of Personality and Social Psychology, 35,* 636–678.

McCabe, A., & Peterson, C. (1991). Getting the story: A longitudinal study of parental styles in eliciting narratives and developing narrative skill. In A. McCabe & C. Peterson (Eds.), *Developing narrative structure* (pp. 217–253). Hillsdale, NJ: Lawrence Erlbaum Associates.

Miller, P. J., & Sperry, L. L. (1987). The socialization of anger and aggression. *Merrill Palmer Quarterly, 33,* 1–31.

Miller, P. J., & Sperry, L. L. (1988). Early talk about the past: The origins of conversational stories of personal experience. *Journal of Child Language, 15,* 292–315.

Miller, P. J., Potts, R., Fung, H., Hoogstra, L., & Mintz, J. (1990). Narrative practices and the social construction of self in childhood. *American Ethnologist, 17*(2), 292–311.

Neimeyer, G. J., & Rareshide, M. B. (1991). *Personal memories and personal identity: The impact of ego identity development on autobiographical memory recall.* Unpublished manuscript. University of Florida, Gainesville.

Neisser, U. (1988). Five kinds of self-knowledge. *Philosophical Psychology, 1,* 35–59.

Nelson, K. (1986). *Event knowledge: Structure and function in development.* Hillsdale, NJ: Lawrence Erlbaum Associates.

Nelson, K. (1988). The ontogeny of memory for real world events. In U. Neisser & E. Winograd (Eds.), *Remembering reconsidered: Ecological and traditional approaches to memory* (pp. 277–282). New York: Cambridge University Press.

Nelson, K. (1991, April). *Emergence of autobiographical memory at age 4.* Paper presented at the Biennial meeting of the Society for Research in Child Development, Seattle, WA.

Nolen-Hoeksema, S. (1987). Sex differences in unipolar depression: Evidence and theory. *Psychological Bulletin, 101,* 259–282.

Paris, S. G., Newman, R. S., & Jacobs, J. E. (1985). Social contexts and functions of children's remembering. In C. J. Brainerd & M. Pressley (Eds.) *The cognitive side of memory development* (pp. 81–115). New York: Springer-Verlag.

Peterson, C., & McCabe, A. (1983). *Developmental psycholinguistics: Three ways of looking at a child's narrative.* New York: Plenum.

Pillemer, D., & White, S. H. (1989). Childhood events recalled by adults and children. In H. W. Reese (Ed.), *Advances in child development and behavior: Vol. 22* (pp. 297–346). New York: Academic Press.

Ratner, H. H. (1980). The role of social context in memory development. In M. Perlmutter (Ed.), *New directions for child development, No 10: Children's memory* (pp. 49–68). San Francisco: Jossey-Bass.

Reese, E., & Fivush, R. (1991). *Parental styles for talking about the past.* Submitted.

Rogoff, B., & Gardner, W. (1984). Adult guidance of cognitive development. In B. Rogoff & J. Lave (Eds.), *Everyday cognition: Its development in social context.* Cambridge, MA: Harvard University Press.

Rovee-Collier, C. K. (1984). The ontogeny of learning and memory in human infancy. In R. Kail & N. Spear (Eds.), *Comparative perspectives on the development of memory* (pp. 103–134). Hillsdale, NJ: Lawrence Erlbaum Associates.

Saarni, C., & Harris, P. L. (Eds.). (1989). *Children's understanding of emotion.* New York: Cambridge University Press.

Sachs, J. (1983). Talking about the there and then: The emergence of displaced reference in parent-child discourse. In K. E. Nelson (Ed.), *Children's language, Vol. IV* (pp. 1-27). New York: Gardner Press.

Siegal, M. (1987). Are sons and daughters treated more differently by fathers than by mothers? *Developmental Review, 7,* 193–209.

Smith, P. (1987). Exploration, play and social development in boys and girls. In D. J. Hargreaves & A. M. Colley (Eds.), *The psychology of sex roles* (pp. 118–141). London: Hemisphere.

Snow, C. E., & Goldfield, B. A. (1983). Turn the page please: Situation-specific language acquisition. *Journal of Child Language, 10,* 551–569.

Stapley, J. C., & Haviland, J. M. (1989). Beyond depression: Gender differences in normal adolescents' emotional experiences. *Sex Roles, 20,* 295–308.

Stein, N. L., & Levine, L. J. (1987). Thinking about feelings: The development and organization of emotional knowledge. In R. E. Snow & M. J. Farr (eds.). *Aptitude, learning and instruction, Vol 3: Connative and affective process analysis* (pp. 165–197). Hillsdale, NJ: Lawrence Erlbaum Associates.

Stein, N. L., Trabasso, T., & Liwag, M. (1991, April). Children's and parents' memory for real life emotional events: Conditions for convergence or polarization. In N. L. Stein (Chair). *Children's memory for emotional and stressful events.* Symposium conducted at the meetings of the Society for Research in Child Development, Seattle.

Usher, B., Ridgeway, D., Barrett, K., Nitz, K., & Wagner, E. (1988, April). *Maternal correlates of children's communication about emotion.* Paper presented at the meetings of the International Conference on Infant Studies, Washington, DC.

Vygotsky, L. S. (1978). *Mind in society: The development of higher psychological processes.* Cambridge, MA: Harvard University Press.

Wertsch, J. (1985). *Vygotsky and the social formation of mind.* Cambridge, MA: Harvard University Press.

Wertsch, J., McNamee, G. D., McLane, J. B., & Budwig, N. (1980). The adult-child dyad as a problem solving system. *Child Development, 51,* 1215–1221.

Wheeler, L., & Nezleck, J. (1977). Sex differences in social participation. *Journal of personality and social psychology, 35,* 742–754.

Zahn-Waxler, C., Cole, P., & Barrett, K. (in press). Guilt and empathy: Sex differences and implications for the development of depression. In K. Dodge & J. Garber (Eds.), *Emotion regulation and disregulation.* New York: Cambridge University Press.

Zahn-Waxler, C., & Ridgeway, D. (in press). Research strategies for assessing mothers' interpretations of infant emotions. In R. Emde, J. Osofsky, & P. Butterfield (Eds.), *Parental perception of infant emotions.*

4 The Ontogeny of Memory Revisited: Commentary on Nelson and Fivush

Louise Hertsgaard
Alexandra Matthews
University of Minnesota

The issues surrounding memory and the role that emotional experience plays in forming and maintaining early memories have important implications for the field of developmental psychology. Traditionally, cognitive and affective development have been studied separately. New research, such as that presented by Nelson (this volume) and Fivush (this volume), has begun to explore some of the ways in which these areas might overlap and influence one another. This commentary first addresses some issues and questions raised by Katherine Nelson in her chapter, followed by those issues raised by Robyn Fivush (chapter 3). Finally, we ask how these two approaches might be combined to further increase our understanding of the intersection of memory and affect.

The question of how emotion and memory might interact has both practical and theoretical importance. It is of crucial importance in the context of children's testimony about traumatic life events such as emotional and physical abuse (see Davies, chapter 7), while on a more theoretical level, it may be able to inform our understanding of the phenomenon of infantile amnesia. Why do adults have so few specific memories of their early years? How does the ability to establish a personal or autobiographical memory system develop?

INFANTILE AMNESIA AND THE ONTOGENY OF AUTOBIOGRAPHICAL MEMORY

In answer to these questions, Nelson distinguishes among three types of memory: generic memory for familiar, canonical events; episodic memory for specific, often novel, events; and autobiographical memory for the particular type of episodic memory that becomes incorporated into a personal "life story". In previous work, Nelson has argued that infantile amnesia may result from the lack of episodic memory in early life. Episodic memory grows out of a background of generic knowledge; infants begin with only generic memory, and do not develop episodic memory capabilities until they have established a sufficient body of general script knowledge (Nelson, 1990). Because script-based memory appears to be extremely functional for young children, Nelson asks what advantage is conferred by the ability to remember specific episodes in addition to scripts. "Why should children (or adults) ever have episodic memory?" (see p. 3). According to Nelson, true autobiographical memory goes beyond even this ability to recall a single episode. Through acquisition of the narrative form, memories for specific events become a part of a long-lasting personal memory system by becoming embedded in an ongoing story about the *self*. It seems equally reasonable to ask "why do we have *autobiographical* memory?"

All individuals have personal memories of themselves from the past, and people often enjoy sharing their earliest recollections. However, as noted by Graham Davies (chapter 7) and Steven Penrod (chapter 8), the veracity and the reliability of such early memories is often questionable. Individuals often report difficulties in differentiating between knowing stories about themselves in an event in family history and actually remembering the event itself. For example, they may have heard a given narrative so many times that it may seem they have a memory for the event, when all they really have is a memory for the story. Even Piaget reported having fabricated a "memory" of an event that never took place (Piaget, 1962). Memory may not always be a faithful representation of the past. Could the acquisition of the narrative form be important primarily for giving children the ability to reconstruct and possibly revise past events?

Although generic memory has such high utility for infants, it has been shown that children under the age of three can also exhibit memories for specific past episodes (Fivush, Gray, & Fromhoff, 1987; Fivush, Hudson, & Nelson, 1984; Hudson & Nelson, 1986). Other researchers using different methods have found these abilities even earlier (see for example, Bauer & Mandler, 1989). Why is it that these memories do not persist? Why are they so evanescent? Adult's episodic memories are also frequently evanescent: We can remember what we had for breakfast today, but probably not what we had for breakfast on the first Tuesday in August. We may have better memories for significant autobiographical events such as birthdays, but can we remember all of them? The narrative form is well established by the age of 9 or 10, but are we able to specifically remember our 10th birthday? Does this inability to remember imply that the memory was never established? Was it once established but since forgotten, or is the memory still there, but somehow inaccessible? How might the narrative form provide a mechanism for establishing long-lasting individual memories?

Cognitive and memory theorists have disagreed as to whether or not a lack of the ability to remember represents only the loss of access to a memory that is still preserved, or whether forgetting is a true loss of previously stored information. According to Larry Squire's neurophysiological perspective on memory (Squire, 1987), the belief that memory is permanent is popular and widespread. But just because special circumstances can often elicit recall of memories that were previously unavailable, this does not prove that all past experiences are permanently stored. It only proves that the brain stores more memories than are readily accessible. Forgetting thus represents a true loss of information through morphological changes in the brain and decreases or reversals of synaptic connectivity (Squire, 1987). Infant's and very young children's brains have more synapses and connections than do the brains of adults. Synaptic pruning and selective neuronal loss take place throughout the first years of life (Goldman-Rakic, 1987). This process could conceivably provide a biological basis for rapid forgetting in very young children.

Another mechanism that might account for remembering and forgetting is *rehearsal*. Rehearsal can involve reenactment, verbal retelling or silent, nonverbal repetition. Consider the role of rehearsal in the development of generic, episodic, and autobiographical memory. Might it be reasonable to suppose that generic or script memory is based on memory for specific episodes which are rehearsed through frequent reenactment, but from which details have been omitted, perhaps by an active forgetting process? Similarly, memory for novel episodes might not be retained for more than a few months by very young children because they are not reenacted and because children lack both the verbal skills and the nonverbal strategies for rehearsal. Parents help children to acquire the narrative form, and through discussions about past events, give children the opportunity to rehearse those events.

But some episodes from children's past experience do not get included in conversations with parents, and thus do not get rehearsed. As both Nelson and Fivush note, parents do most of the guiding of these conversations, and references made by children may not be understood or recalled by adults. Also, early in development, children may be interested in and pay attention to different aspects of events than do adults (Nelson, chapter 1). The eventual acquisition of the narrative form may for the first time give children the capacity for both shared and independent rehearsal of past events, which allows them to consolidate and preserve narrative accounts of past events.

Nelson further argues that children acquire the narrative form necessary for autobiographical memory as a result of the influence of parental talk and parent-child conversations about the past. The style of parental talk can be shown to have differential effects on the way that children remember events. Children of parents with elaborative or narrative styles appear to be better at recalling past events than do children whose parents use a pragmatic or paradigmatic style (see pp. 8–12). This explanation is very similar to that proposed by an elaborative or depth of processing model of memory. As noted by many cognitive and memory theorists, elaboration facilitates recall by enriching the episodic representation and providing additional routes to stored information at the time of reinstatement or retrieval (Anderson & Reder, 1979; Graf, 1982; Mandler, 1988). Are parents who use a elaborative narrative style in their conversations with children about past events merely sharing with their children an effective rehearsal strategy? Can autobiographical memories be seen as episodic memories that have persisted because of multiple access routes created through elaborative processing? Are there any differences between generic, episodic, and autobiographical memories that cannot be explained in terms of opportunity for rehearsal, consolidation, and elaboration? Is language the fundamental requirement for these strategies to be effective?

THE EMOTIONAL CONTENT OF EARLY MEMORY

The role of language in relation to the narrative form and autobiographical memory is also discussed by Fivush in her chapter on the emotional content of parent-child conversations (Fivush, chapter 3). Fivush notes that children learn the narrative form through language. She argues that language serves to organize both how children interact with others and how they interact with themselves in private thought and behavior. Language thus provides the basic structures necessary for organizing personal memories. Adult-guided conversations about the past help children to create increasingly organized narrative memories (see p. 42).

Given this basic theoretical foundation, Fivush goes on to examine the emotional content of parent-child conversations about the past. What role do emotions play in organizing memory? How might conversation between parents and children provide an emotional framework for evaluating past events? How does the emotional content of such conversations affect memory for those events? The research findings reviewed by Fivush offer some intriguing insights into these issues, but they also raise a number of important and, as yet, unanswered questions.

Among the most interesting of these insights is the finding that parents include more emotional content in their conversations with daughters than they do with sons. And, with regard to specific emotions, parents talk more about sadness with daughters and more about anger with sons. Gender differences in sex-stereotyped activities as well as in emotional expressions and memory for emotions appears to emerge very early (Bauer, in press; Fivush, chapter 3). What might be the basis for such gender differences?

Results of a PET (Positron Emission Tomography) study conducted at the University of Minnesota by Jose Pardo (personal communication, October, 1991) suggest that, in adults, there may be gender differences in the brain bases for processing certain emotions. Male and female subjects were directed to think of something sad. PET scans were taken while subjects were feeling the emotion of sadness. Pardo found that when females were feeling sad, a large portion of their right prefrontal cortex was active. In contrast, when males were feeling sad, a smaller portion of their left prefrontal cortex was active and they showed virtually no activation of the right prefrontal cortex. The distribution of cortical activity was different; the area of cortical activation for females was not only larger but was also situated in the opposite hemisphere from that of the males. When men and women were experiencing the emotion of sadness, there were gender differences not only in the amount of cortical activation, but also in the distribution of that activation (J. Pardo, personal communication). This pattern of brain activation, although based on preliminary data, suggests that men process sadness in the left hemisphere, which has been linked to analytic processing, while women process sadness in the right hemisphere, which has been linked to intuitive, holistic thinking and to feelings of depression.

The data Fivush presents in her chapter suggest that parents treat sadness in sons and anger in daughters in similar ways (see pp. 49–51). There is anecdotal evidence of experiential parallels between sadness in men and anger in women. Women often report that they can't really experience anger, that they don't know what to *do* with their anger, and men often report that this is their experience of sadness. Pardo's PET study suggests that at least for adults there may be gender differences in the neural substrate for the same emotions. Is it possible that these brain differences are the result of cultural conditioning alone, or might these differences be due to innate sex differences in brain structure? Alternatively, might there be some interaction of culture and biology that could produce the kinds of differences we see so early in children and which appear to be at the physiological level in adults?

In addition to gender differences in emotional processing, researchers in the area of temperament have shown that there are individual differences between young children on such dimensions as activity level, positive and negative emotional expressivity, fear of novelty, distress to limitations, and in the ability to use attention to regulate distress and other behaviors (e.g., Rothbart, 1989). Research by Gunnar and Nelson (submitted) has shown a correlation between emotional behavior and brain response to novelty. Their study showed that 12-month-old children who exhibited the most emotional distress to a brief separation from mother also showed a larger brain response to infrequently presented stimuli as measured by the event-related potential (ERP). What role might such individual differences play in affecting the way that parents talk to children about past events? Might it affect the emotional content of such conversations? Apart from any influence on the parents, might such child characteristics also affect the types of events, or particular aspects of events that children consider to be interesting and that might become a part of their autobiographical memories? The parents in Fivush's study talked to children about emotions in similar ways; however, could individual differences among *parents* additionally have an effect on the content of their conversations with children such that it could be expected to affect the children's subsequent memory? How might we study these aspects of individual differences as they relate to the development of children's emotions and their ability to remember emotional events?

The questions of how gender and individual differences in emotional experience might arise are important ones, but they may provide only partial answers to the larger question concerning the effect of emotional experience on memory for a specific event. By focusing exclusively on parental contributions to emotional conversations, Fivush's current studies also do not address this issue. However, in previous work, Fivush has stated that children reported past events that were "frightening" or "exciting" (Fivush et al., 1987, Hammond & Fivush, 1991). Are emotional events that children consider to be important more likely to become a part of autobiographical memory? How can we begin to investigate this relation between emotion and memory?

Recent neurophysiological research has shown that structures in the limbic system of the brain are linked both to the emotional evaluation of events and to the ability to remember specific past episodes (Mishkin & Appenzeller, 1987; Squire, 1986). Research with animals has further shown that physiological reactions triggered by a stress induced change in emotional state can have long-lasting effects on the animal's ability to store information—actually promoting the storage and recall of adaptive behaviors (de Kloet, 1991). Although related work with human children and adults has shown some relation between emotional arousal and performance on specific laboratory tests of learning and memory (see Davies, chapter 7), little research has been done to investigate directly the effects of emotion on human episodic or autobiographical memory. Because our brains appear to be organized in a way that allows us to process emotion and memory together, it would seem to be even more important to find ways to examine how emotional experience might affect the development of auto-biographical memory.

INTERACTIONS BETWEEN NARRATIVE STYLE AND EMOTIONAL CONTENT

Both Nelson and Fivush stress that adult-guided conversations about the past are necessary for children's acquisition of the narrative form and for their organization of autobiographical memories. In addition, they both stress important differences in the ways adults interact with children. Nelson has concentrated on differences in the style of parental talk—pragmatic or paradigmatic versus narrative or elaborative, while Fivush has concentrated on the different ways in which parents talk to sons and daughters about emotions. What kinds of *interactions* might we expect to find between emotional content and pragmatic versus elaborative styles? Are these dimensions orthogonal, or might we expect additive or synergistic effects among them? Might the emotional contents of personal memories be altered through the acquisition of the narrative form? Are there gender differences in the use of elaborative vs. pragmatic styles? Might parents who use an elaborative style be more likely to also include discussions of emotions when talking about the past? Would they be more or less likely than parents who use a pragmatic style to differentiate between daughters and sons when discussing emotional aspects of past experience? And finally, what effects might these interactions between conversational styles and emotional content have on children's autobiographic memories?

The research by Nelson and Fivush present thought-provoking approaches to questions concerning the ontogeny of memory and the relation of memory and emotion. Both authors emphasize the exploratory nature of their work and the need for additional research in order to further investigate these compelling issues. They both stress that there is a need to understand more completely what the child brings to the process of acquiring the narrative form and to the process of evaluating the emotional significance of personal experience. Studies that take into consideration such child characteristics as gender and temperament may add a needed dimension. Research that includes perspectives from the adult cognitive literature may also be helpful in understanding the processes involved in children's developing memory systems. Finally and perhaps most importantly, future research that complements the recent evidence from studies of the neural substrate of memory may result in significant progress toward the goal of understanding how the brain contributes to the experience of emotion, the development of autobiographical memory, and the interactions between them.

ACKNOWLEDGMENTS

This paper was supported by a National Institute of Health and Human Services training grant (5-T32-HD01751-13) for both authors.

REFERENCES

Anderson, J. R., & Reder, L. M. (1979). An elaborative processing explanation of depth of processing. In L. S. Cermak & F. I. M. Craik (Eds.), *Levels of processing in human memory*. Hillsdale, NJ: Lawrence Erlbaum Associates.

Bauer, P. J. (in press). Memory for gender-consistent and gender-inconsistent event sequences by 25-month-old children. *Child Development*.

Bauer, P. J., & Mandler, J. M. (1989). One thing follows another: Effects of temporal structure on one- to two-year olds' recall of events. *Developmental Psychology, 25*, 197–206.

de Kloet, E. R. (1991). Brain corticosteroid receptor balance homeostatic control. *Frontiers in Neuroendocrinology, 12*(2), 95–164.

Fivush, R., Gray, J. T., & Fromhoff, F. A. (1987). Two year olds talk about the past. *Cognitive Development, 2*, 393-410.

Fivush, R., Hudson, J., & Nelson, K. (1984). Children's long-term memory for a novel event: An exploratory study. *Merill-Palmer Quarterly, 30,* 303–316.

Goldman-Rakic, P. (1987). Circuitry of the prefrontal cortex: Short-term memory and the regulation of behavior by representational knowledge. In F. Blum (Ed.), *Handbook of physiology: Higher functions of the nervous system.* Bethesda, MD: American Physiological Society.

Graf, P. (1982). The memorial consequences of generation and transfer. *Journal of Verbal Learning and Verbal Behavior, 21,* 539–548.

Gunnar, M. R., & Nelson, C. A. (1992). *Event-related potentials in year-old infants predict negative emotionality and hormonal responses to separation.* Submitted.

Hammond, N. R., & Fivush, R. (1991). Memories of Mickey Mouse: Young children recount their trip to Disneyworld. *Cognitive Development, 6,* 433–448.

Hudson, J. A., & Nelson, K. (1986). Repeated encounters of a similar kind: Effects of familiarity on children's autobiographic memory. *Cognitive Development, 1,* 253–271.

Mandler, G. (1988). Memory: Conscious and unconscious. In P. R. Solomon, G. R. Goethals, C. M. Kelley, & B. R. Stephens (Eds.), *Memory: Interdisciplinary approaches* (pp. 84–106). New York: Springer-Verlag.

Mishkin, M., & Appenzeller, T. (1987). The anatomy of memory. *Scientific American, 256,* 80–89.

Nelson, K. (1990). Remembering, forgetting, and childhood amnesia. In R. Fivush & J. A. Hudson (Eds.), *Knowing and remembering in young children.* New York: Cambridge University Press.

Piaget, J. (1962). *Play, dreams, and imitation in childhood.* New York: Norton.

Rothbart, M. K. (1989). Temperament in childhood: A framework. In G. A. Kohnstam, J. E. Bates, & M. K. Rothbart (Eds.), *Temperament in childhood* (pp. 59–76). New York: Wiley.

Squire, L. R. (1986). Mechanisms of memory. *Science, 232,* 1612–1619.

Squire, L. R. (1987). *Memory and Brain.* New York: Oxford University Press.

5

Troubles in the Garden and How They Get Resolved: A Young Child's Transformation of His Favorite Story

Peggy J. Miller
University of Illinois at Urbana–Champaign

Lisa Hoogstra
Judith Mintz
Heidi Fung
Kimberly Williams
University of Chicago

One of the enduring legacies of William Wells Newell, the compiler of the classic 19th-century collection of children's folklore, is his insight into children's complex relationship to cultural resources. According to "Newell's paradox" (Fine, 1980), children are both conservative and innovative toward traditional lore. They treat the formulas of play "as Scripture, of which no jot or tittle is to be repealed" (Newell, 1883/1963, p. 22), yet delight in modifying traditions and inventing languages, legends, and games. This paradox applies not only to children's folklore but to other cultural texts, including narratives. Stories of personal experience, family stories, stories from children's literature—all evoke contradictory impulses to conserve and to innovate. Underlying this paradox is the child's intense involvement in particular texts, an involvement which is evident in repeated listenings and spontaneous retellings. The child can't stop telling the story; the parent can't tell or read it to her often enough.

Although children's passionate engagement in stories is recognized by teachers (Paley, 1981; Rosen, 1988) and students of children's literature (Hearne, 1990), developmental researchers have tended to neglect this problem in favor of other aspects of narrative (but see Favat, 1977 and Tucker, 1981). For example, in recent years there has been a strong interest in the developmental origins of narrative talk, and it is now well established that even very young children are able to recount past experiences in conversation (e.g., Eisenberg, 1985; Engel, 1986; Fivush, Gray, & Fromhoff, 1987; Fivush & Fromhoff, 1988; Miller & Sperry, 1988; Sachs, 1983; Sperry, 1991). However, the emphasis has been on the content, structure, and social conduct of incipient narratives. How young children invest narratives with meaning, how they use and reuse stories, has received less attention. The present chapter intends to redress this imbalance. We show how one young child appropriated, used, and reused a story during a 4-week period of intense involvement. The story, in this case, is a classic of children's literature, "The Tale of Peter Rabbit" by Beatrix Potter. We document systematic changes across the retellings in how the plot was configured and advance the interpretation that a chief function of the retellings was to resolve the disturbances posed by the written story, disturbances that were personally meaningful to the 2-year-old narrator. Drawing on concepts from Vygotsky and Bakhtin, we propose some explanations for how these changes came about.

PAST RESEARCH ON PERSONAL STORYTELLING

Because the current study evolved out of past research on personal storytelling, this related work is briefly described. A personal story is a story, told in ordinary conversation, in which the narrator recounts a remembered experience from his or her own life. It is a temporally ordered, evaluated account in which the narrator casts himself or herself as protagonist. For several years our research has been concerned with the role that this type of storytelling plays in early childhood socialization. The larger theoretical project has been to develop a discourse model of the socialization and meaning-creation processes. The model that we favor derives from Vygotskian theory (1978, 1987) and from practice approaches to narrative. According to this model, (a) families are organized so as to bring young children and caregivers together recurrently for particular activities, which are mediated by particular forms of discourse; and (b) the social and psychological consequences for the child of routine participation in socializing practices depend on how messages are packaged in discourse. When messages are packaged in self-relevant ways—as they are in personal storytelling—the consequences for the child include not only the acquisition of discursive skills but the creation of self or identity. (See Miller, in press; Miller et al., 1990; Miller et al., 1992 for a fuller explication of this model.)

For present purposes it is important to highlight the fact that the model rests on a practice approach to stories. That is, in keeping with recent developments in narrative theory in anthropology, folklore, and sociolinguistics (Bauman, 1986; Bauman & Briggs, 1990; Hymes, 1975; Kirshenblatt-Gimblett, 1975; Polanyi, 1985; Robinson, 1981), the model requires that stories be treated not as disembodied texts but as integrated performances, embedded in their immediate contexts of use. In this view, personal storytelling, like literacy, is not monolithic; rather, stories defined in particular ways are told for particular purposes in particular contexts of use. As applied to the socialization of young children, this perspective raises the following questions: Do different cultural groups routinely engage in personal storytelling in the everyday settings that young children inhabit? How is personal storytelling conducted vis à vis children? At what age do children begin to participate in storytelling? What uses do they make of stories? Does personal storytelling, which is explicitly self-referential, play a privileged role in self construction?

This practice-oriented discourse model has led us to several insights about how stories of personal experience function in the socialization and self-constructive processes, insights that would not otherwise have emerged. Although these insights concern stories of personal experience, whereas "The Tale of Peter Rabbit" is a different narrative genre, it was by this route that we came to appreciate the importance of retellings, to wonder whether the phenomenon applied to other narrative genres, and to begin to see that personal stories and written stories could function similarly in the child's life.

The first discovery has to do with the widespread and recurrent nature of narrative practices. In studies of White, working-class children in South Baltimore (Miller & Moore, 1989; Miller & Sperry, 1988) and of culturally diverse children (low-income African American, working-class White, and middle-class White in Chicago and middle-class Chinese in Taipei), personal storytelling occurred routinely as part of everyday family life, forming an important part of the naturally-occurring verbal environment that young children inhabited (Miller, in press). In addition, the children in these studies were exposed to personal storytelling in three related ways: stories were told *around* young children as copresent others,[1] *about* young children as ratified participants, and *with* young children as conarrators. The latter occurred in ordinary family interaction at median rates of 2.4 per hour for $2\frac{1}{2}$ year olds and 4.7 per hour for 5 year olds in the culturally diverse sample (Miller et al., 1992). Studies by Heath (1983), Sperry (1991), and Scollon and Scollon (1981) provide further evidence that young children from a variety of cultural backgrounds are routinely exposed to and participate early in personal storytelling practices.

The second insight that followed from the practice-oriented discourse model is that the narrated self is a relational self. This is evident at multiple levels of analysis (Miller et al., 1992). When young children conarrated or told personal stories with another person, they located the self in a social nexus. In other words, the child portrayed himself or herself as "being with" another person in some past event. At the same time the child was "being with" another person in the present, that is, in the very act of conarrating the past event. Moreover, these levels of relatedness were connected. This was evident, for example, in the use of social comparison as a means of linking self and other: not only did the majority of social comparisons of self and other occur when a sibling or peer

---

[1]By "co-present other" we mean that the child was present while a story was being told to another person. Although the child was not the addressee, he or she was a potential onlooker and overhearer of the story.

participated in the conarration but the focal child was overwhelmingly compared with siblings or peers in the recounted event. A link is thereby established between the event of narration (who participated in the conarration) and the narrated event (what was talked about). In addition, at times the narrator altered her account of her own past experience, depending on what the conarrator said about the past event.

This brings us to the third insight that follows from the model, namely the dynamic nature of narrative practices. The finding that personal stories recur, hour by hour, in children's everyday home environments, in conjunction with the finding that the version of personal experience that the child creates may change, depending on who is present in the narrating event and what they say, suggests that personal storytelling is an important means by which young children reconstruct and revise their experiences of self in relation to other.

The dynamic nature of narrative practices is most apparent when a narrator spontaneously retells a particular story. Our corpus of naturally-occurring personal stories includes spontaneous retellings by children from each of the communities we have studied (working-class White, low income African American, middle-class White, and middle-class Chinese). Although these retellings undoubtedly serve multiple functions, sometimes children seemed to retell stories as a means of gaining relief from or resolution to some distressing past experience. For example, a 30-month-old child from the low-income African-American community told three versions of her experience of being frightened by a movie. In the first she fled from the scene, in the second she sought comfort from her parents, and in the third she was no longer scared. These revisions of narrated experience speak to the issue of the emotional content of early autobiographical memories (Pillemer & White, 1989; White & Pillemer, 1979) and raise the possibility that such contents change across repeated tellings. By recounting or reenacting a troubling experience from the past, the young narrator seemed to regain her equilibrium through a reintegration of experience (Bruner & Lucariello, 1989). In such cases retellings function in a manner that is similar to the heuristic use of stories in adolescent and adult conversation (Ochs, Smith, & Taylor, 1988; Robinson, 1981) and to the therapeutic use of stories in psychoanalysis (Nye, 1988; Spence, 1982).

In addition, children sometimes used stories of vicarious experience in this manner. Instead of retelling a story of self-experience, they retold a story about someone else's experience. For example, a 32-month-old child from South Baltimore retold a story in which her uncle punched her grandfather. A 31-month-old middle-class child appropriated his mother's story about falling down and hurting herself and recast it as a first-person account, repeating it several times. Both of these retellings were told with marked affect. Vicarious retellings raise some fascinating and puzzling issues that revolve around the Bakhtinian question, whose story is it? Stories in which a child recounts his or her experience are obviously personal stories: the child has recreated in the here-and-now an event that he or she directly experienced in the past. But there is a broader sense in which a story could be *personal,* that is, in the sense that a child might appropriate and use for his or her own purposes someone else's experience, someone else's story. Framed in this way, any story has the potential to be a *personalized* story, a story that is personally meaningful or useful to the narrator. As we shall see, "The Tale of Peter Rabbit" is personalized in just this way by the 2-year-old narrator.

In sum, our past research on personal storytelling from within a practice-oriented discourse model led us to see that narrative retellings are embedded in and continuous with a complex and dynamic network of narrative practices that mediate family-child relations on a daily basis and that define and redefine the child's experiences of self in relation to other. It also led us to see that retellings may function to resolve or reintegrate distressing past experiences and that vicarious stories can get used and personalized in this way.

THE PETER RABBIT RETELLINGS

The examples cited earlier suggest that retellings are not confined to any of the several communities under study. However, owing to relatively long intervals between longitudinal data points, it was not possible to trace out sustained uses of particular stories. This is precisely the value of the Peter Rabbit retellings, which were collected from the privileged vantage point of a family member. These retellings were produced by the first author's son during a 4-week period of intense involvement with "The Tale of Peter Rabbit." Many of the classic works in the study of child language have been conducted by linguist or psychologist parents who could not resist the temptation to observe the language development of their own offspring. The first author followed in this tradition in that she made video tapes of her son Kurt interacting at home at regular intervals during the second year of his life. She also supplemented these observations with more extensive audio-recorded or hand-written sampling of his play behavior.

Kurt was first introduced to "The Tale of Peter Rabbit" during a 2-week visit with his paternal grandparents. He was 23;05 when his grandmother gave him the collection of Beatrix Potter's (1980) stories. Listening to written stories read aloud was at this point a taken-for-granted part of his everyday life. "Peter Rabbit" immediately became his favorite story and he repeatedly requested that it be read to him over the next several weeks. His family accommodated his interest, reading it daily, sometimes several times a day. In these readings his parent or grandparent read the story while he listened attentively and looked at the pictures. Thus, Kurt's retellings of the stories coincided with fairly constant exposure to the written story. Although the changes that occur across the retellings are reminiscent of the reconstructive and personally-flavored processes of remembering described by Bartlett (1932), the task was not a memory task of the usual sort in which recall is tested after a single exposure to the stimulus materials.

DESCRIPTION OF THE SPEECH CORPUS

The corpus of Peter Rabbit talk consists of five retellings produced on five different days. The collection of these texts predated and perhaps helped to inspire the first author's interest in narrative: At the time of recording she assimilated them to her then current interest in children's play, thinking of them as fantasies, which, in a sense, they are. The first, third, and fourth retellings were audio-recorded; the second and fifth were hand-written, with accompanying notes about context. Any sustained talk about Peter Rabbit that Kurt produced with his mother was recorded. She was not prepared for Kurt's first retelling and hence the opening segment of that retelling, initiated by him, was not recorded. Once Kurt's intense interest in Peter Rabbit became evident she occasionally introduced the topic of Peter Rabbit at a time when she was already recording his talk. There is no way to know what, if anything, Kurt said about Peter Rabbit in her absence.

There was a discernible temporal patterning to the retellings. The interval between Kurt's first exposure to the story and his first retelling was 1 week; between retellings 1 and 2, another week; between retellings 2, 3, and 4 only a day or two; and between retellings 4 and 5, a week. In other words, the retellings were not spaced evenly over the 4 weeks but formed a temporal cluster at the point at which Kurt had had about 2 weeks of exposure to the written story.

The Peter Rabbit retellings were sandwiched between two of the regular video recordings of Kurt's speech. These occurred 8 days before the first retelling and 14 days after the final retelling. The first half hour of each of these video recordings involved everyday interaction between Kurt and his mother, thus providing a baseline comparison with the retellings. Basic descriptive information about the video-recorded baseline samples and the retellings is provided in Table 5.1.

Mean length of utterance (MLU) in morphemes, a widely used measure of language level, was computed according to Brown's (1973) guidelines. Kurt's language level, as assessed in the baseline speech samples, was in the advanced normal range, although not as advanced as Nelson's (1989) Emily.[2] The MLU

---

[2]The MLU values for Kurt are roughly comparable to those for Eve, the most advanced of Brown's (1973) three subjects; Bloom and Lahey's (1978) subjects had an average MLU of 2.54, with a range of 2.30–2.83, at 25 months, whereas Kurt's MLU was 4.0 at $24\frac{1}{2}$ months; Nelson (1989) reports that Emily's MLU was 3.61 in dialogues and 5.40 in monologues during the period from 21 to $22\frac{1}{2}$ months; Kurt's MLU was 2.8 in the baseline sample at 23 months and 4.0 in the first retelling at $23\frac{1}{2}$ months.

TABLE 5.1
Description of Speech Samples

Samples	Age	MLU[a]	Utterances		Turns	
			Child	Adult	Child	Adult
Baseline Sample I	23;04	2.8	240	278	144	149
Retelling 1	23;12	4.2	62	60	41	47
Retelling 2	23;21	6.4	60	2	1	2
Retelling 3	23;23	6.5	20	28	13	14
Retelling 4	23;24	4.8	142	123	77	79
Retelling 5	24;02	6.1[b]	30[b]	5[b]	6[b]	4[b]
Baseline Sample II	24;16	4.0	212	261	136	145
			Total 766	757	419	440

[a]Mean length of utterance in morphenes.
[b]Excludes digressions.

values also indicate that the Peter Rabbit retellings occurred during a period of rapid language development, with Kurt's MLU increasing more than a point over the 6-week interval between the two baseline speech samples.

What is more interesting is that the MLU values for the 5 retellings were considerably higher than for the baseline speech samples. Kurt operated at a more advanced linguistic level within the context of narrating the Peter Rabbit story than he did at other times within the same developmental interval. Nelson (1989) found a marked discrepancy in length between Emily's dialogic versus monologic speech in favor of the monologic. The corpus of Kurt's speech included no direct parallel to Emily's monologic crib speech, that is, speech that occurred in the absence of an interlocutor. Yet there was considerable variation across the retellings in the extent to which Kurt's talk was structured monologically versus dialogically in the presence of an interlocutor. Retellings 2 and 5 were highly monologic, with Kurt holding the floor for long stretches of uninterrupted talk. (Properly speaking, these monologic retellings are soliloquys, a term that more accurately captures their complicated addressivity, which is discussed more fully below.) By contrast, retellings 1, 3, and 4 were dialogically organized, as Kurt and his interlocutor exchanged multiple brief turns. The average MLU in the monologic retellings was 6.4, compared with 4.8 in the dialogic retellings, thereby confirming Nelson's finding for Emily.

Another possible factor contributing to longer utterance length in the retellings was the narrative form of the retellings. In order to explore this possibility further, narrative utterances were compared with nonnarrative utterances in the baseline speech samples (see Table 5.2). For this analysis, all utterances that occurred within stretches of temporally-ordered discourse that was displaced from the here-and-now (in the past, hypothetical, or future) were treated as narrative utterances. All other utterances were counted as nonnarrative utter-

TABLE 5.2
Length (MLU) of Narrative Vs. Nonnarrative Child Utterances

Samples	Narrative	Nonnarrative
Baseline Samples		
I	4.1 (41)	2.6 (199)
II	6.1 (28)	3.7 (184)
Retellings		
1	4.2 (62)	–
2	6.4 (60)	–
3	6.5 (20)	–
4	4.8 (142)	–
5	6.1 (30)	–
	M = 5.4 (383)	M = 3.1 (383)

ances. Narrative utterances were longer on average than were nonnarrative utterances within both baseline speech samples.[3]

These analyses, thus, suggest that the monologic mode and the narrative form contributed to longer utterance length in the retellings. It is likely that interest in particular topics motivated Kurt's use of both the monologic mode and narrative speech—two tools for thinking about and reordering experience. As mentioned earlier, Kurt's interest in Peter Rabbit was expressed not only in his repeated tellings of the story but in his repeated requests to listen to the story. This raises the question, Why was he so interested in this story? Let us table this question for the moment and turn to the story that inspired the retellings (Potter, 1980).

THE TALE OF PETER RABBIT

Once upon a time there were four little Rabbits, and their names were—Flopsy, Mopsy, Cotton-tail, and Peter. They lived with their Mother in a sand-bank, underneath the root of a very big fir-tree.

'Now my dears,' said old Mrs. Rabbit one morning, 'you may go into the fields or down the lane, but don't go into Mr. McGregor's garden: your Father had an accident there; he was put in a pie by Mrs. McGregor (p. 8).

Mrs. Rabbit then leaves to go to the baker's and Peter, who is "very naughty," (p. 9) runs directly to Mr. McGregor's garden. There he proceeds to stuff himself

---

[3]This finding echoes research on writing that shows that narrative is mastered earlier and more easily than other discourse genres (Crowhurst, 1991; Perera, 1984).

on lettuces, French beans, and radishes until discovered by the fearsome Mr. McGregor, who gives chase. Peter gets caught in a gooseberry net, hides in a watering can, and narrowly avoids being stomped by Mr. McGregor. Mr. McGregor goes back to work but Peter finds that he is lost. ". . . (H)e was out of breath and trembling with fright, and he had not the least idea which way to go" (p. 13). Eventually, after an unsettling encounter with a white cat, he spies the gate, escapes through it, and doesn't stop running until he gets home to the big fir-tree. Peter is not very well that evening and his mother doses him with camomile tea. But his siblings—Flopsy, Mopsy, and Cottontail—have bread, milk, and blackberries for supper.

This story is told in pictures as well as words, and it has had enormous appeal to children and their parents since its first publication in 1901. The "Tale of Peter Rabbit" has been rated the bestselling children's book of all time in the United States (Smith, 1990). Beatrix Potter herself explained the story's appeal in terms of its origins, the story having been written originally as a picture-letter to a 5-year-old boy (Linder, 1971). She said, "It is much more satisfactory to address a real live child; I often think that that was the secret of the success of Peter Rabbit, it was written to a child—not made to order" (p. 110).

Critics have commented on the tension in the story between social conformity and individual freedom (Nikola-Lisa, 1990). According to Taylor, Whalley, Hobbs, and Battrick (1987), "It is the classic tale of the naughty child, flying in the face of authority, deliberately disobeying instructions—and getting his just deserts" (p. 99). The story thus exemplifies one of the basic properties of narrative, namely that it poses some departure from a canonical cultural pattern, leading to conflicts and difficulties that need to be resolved (Bruner, 1990; Burke, 1945; Goffman, 1959). The first departure from the canonical—Peter's flouting of his mother's prohibition—is followed by another: Upon entering the garden, Peter proceeds to indulge his oral desires to the point of sickness. As a consequence of these mischievous deeds, he finds himself in a series of life-threatening predicaments involving Mr. McGregor, human enemy of the rabbit family. Moreover, his misbehavior not only separates him physically and morally from his mother but dramatizes how different he is from his good siblings. Deviation from the moral code leads to mortal danger and to disruption of familial relationships.

On the face of it, the little rabbit as chief protagonist caught up in this particular plot would seem to have a great deal of resonance for a 2 year old. Issues of orality, security, attachment, obedience, and independence come into play, issues that one or another developmental theory regards as basic to early development. This makes the story a good candidate for emotional investment by a young child. Returning to the question raised earlier, one factor that may contribute to Kurt's interest in the story is its thematic relevance to his developmental level.

But there is another factor worth considering. There is evidence that the particular embodiment of these issues, especially the fact that the story is set in a garden, is congruent with Kurt's idiosyncratic experience, knowledge, and interests. He had spent many enjoyable hours in his grandparents' gardens. In the preceding month his maternal grandparents had told him about the mother rabbit who had a nest of babies in their garden, and his paternal grandmother had written him a small book about the woodchucks who ate the flowers in her garden. In addition, in the first baseline speech sample, Kurt produced two linked stories of personal experience about her garden. The first was a story about a past event in which Kurt helped his grandmother to plant the garden. The second was a hypothetical narrative in which Kurt excitedly imagined what kinds of flowers and plants he might see in his grandmother's garden when he visits her the following day. (On the following day she herself gives Kurt the Peter Rabbit storybook, and his first retelling, a week later, occurs in proximity to her garden.) Thus, Kurt's familiarity with and keen interest in gardens predated and perhaps primed his interest in Peter Rabbit's adventures in Mr. McGregor's garden.

ANALYSIS OF THE RETELLINGS: STORY CONTENT AND PLOT

Some of the most obvious features of Kurt's retellings and of changes in the retellings occur at the level of story content and plot. These are described first, followed by micro-level analysis of how Kurt deployed communicative resources to narrate and renarrate the story.

As in the written story, the retellings are set in a garden. Plants are growing or getting stepped on or planted or watered, and, invariably something gets eaten. Some walking or running in, to, or from the garden occurs in every retelling. In addition, three of the retellings (1, 2, and 5) occur in close proximity to a garden; the real garden provides a stage on which the story is projected.

Fictional characters are also appropriated from "The Tale of Peter Rabbit." There is one obligatory character—Peter Rabbit himself. Mother Rabbit is the only other character who appears repeatedly (in 2, 4, and 5). There is a gradual increase across the retellings in the number of characters invoked, from one (Peter Rabbit) in the first retelling to the full cast of main characters (Peter, Mother Rabbit, Flopsy, Mopsy, Cottontail, and Mr. McGregor) in the final retelling. Not surprisingly, given Kurt's repeated exposure to the written story, his memory for the characters becomes more complete across the retellings. Despite these changes, however, the centrality of Peter Rabbit and of his relationship to Mother Rabbit remains fairly constant and is further supported by the fact that Kurt refers to the retellings as "talk about Peter Rabbit" or "talk(ed) about Peter Rabbit and the mother."

TABLE 5.3
Troubles and Their Resolution in the Retellings

	Retellings				
Trouble	1	2	3	4	5
P. R. violates rules of garden	X	X		R	R
Conflict between P. R. and Mother Rabbit		X,R		R	R
Conflict between rabbit and human worlds		X	X	X	R
P. R. afraid of natural world			X	R	R

Note. P. R. = Peter Rabbitt; X = trouble was invoked; R = trouble was resolved.

In addition to the continuities between the written story and the successive retellings, there are also striking successive alterations of the written story, culminating in a remarkable reconfiguration of the plot. As can be seen in Table 5.3, Kurt appropriates from the written story four "troubles" (Bruner, 1990) or deviations from the canonical: Peter Rabbit's violation of rules of the garden, conflict between Peter Rabbit and Mother Rabbit, conflict between the rabbit and human worlds, and Peter Rabbit's fear of the natural world. Each of these troubles is systematically posed, reposed, and resolved across the retellings. Once a trouble is resolved, it remains resolved. In the final retelling an inclusive resolution is achieved.

In the first retelling Kurt describes Peter Rabbit as "naughty" (the same word that is used in the written story), indicating that Peter Rabbit has violated certain conventions for being in the garden.[4] Specifically, he eats plants (e.g., iris, marigolds) that should not be eaten. In retelling 2 Peter Rabbit continues to violate rules of the garden by stepping on stalks. But it is the resulting conflict between Peter Rabbit and his mother that gets foregrounded in this retelling: It is elaborated and replayed at length and eventually resolved. In contrast to the written story, this resolution is achieved by bringing Mother Rabbit into the garden with Peter. Conflict between the rabbit and human worlds is also invoked in retelling 2 in a brief episode in which Peter Rabbit and his mother are killed by a car. Retelling 3 forefronts dangers in the garden: Peter Rabbit is afraid of a wheelbarrow and a blue jay, and scutters under the bushes to sleep.

Whereas the introduction of troubles takes precedence in retellings 1 through 3, the process of resolution is most apparent in retellings 4 and 5. In retelling 4 Peter Rabbit and his mother are aligned with one another from the start. Mother Rabbit holds the hands of the little rabbits as they water the plants, and mother

---

[4]A concern with the way in which the garden "works," a canonical representation of what gardens in general are like, provides the background against which Peter Rabbit acts upon the garden. For example, in the course of narrating Peter Rabbit's actions, Kurt asserts various "facts" about gardens, "pine trees get all sticky/," and "broccoli's green/."

and the "bunnies" plant seeds together. This is the first retelling in which the bunnies behave constructively in the garden. In addition, although Peter Rabbit encounters potential dangers in the garden (e.g., a buzzing bee), he is not frightened. By retelling 4, then, three of the four troubles have been resolved: Peter is abiding by the rules of the garden, amiable relations between Peter and Mother Rabbit have been restored, and Peter is no longer afraid in the garden. However, conflict between the rabbit and human worlds is still evident as the bunnies stomp granddaddy's car. In the final retelling the processes of resolution, already in play, are brought to completion. Harmony is achieved not only among the rabbits but with their former enemy, as Mr. McGregor joins the rabbits in planting parsley in the garden.

ANALYSIS OF THE RETELLINGS: HOW THE RETELLINGS WERE NARRATED

Thus, dramatic changes in plot occur across the retellings, culminating in an original resolution to the disruptions appropriated from the written story. The chief theoretical challenge is to provide an explanation for how these changes came about. We believe that one factor that facilitated Kurt's reworking of the story was his familiarity with it. It is unlikely, however, that increased familiarity alone could account for the kinds of changes that occurred across the retellings. Were familiarity the only factor, one would expect to see progression toward a more complete, detailed, and veridical account of the story actions. We believe that at least two other factors were involved, both of which have to do with how the retellings were narrated.

The analytic tools that we draw upon derive from a Bakhtinian framework (Bakhtin, 1981; Wertsch, 1991). Bakhtin was a Soviet literary scholar, philosopher, and discourse theorist. He is perhaps best known for his analyses of novelistic discourse, but his conceptualization of language as culturally shaped and socially situated has much broader application. Unlike traditional linguistic conceptions of language, Bakhtin took the utterance, rather than the sentence, as his unit of analysis. Every utterance involves the invocation of a speech genre, a form of social speech associated with a particular situation (e.g., dinner table conversation, military commands, bookreading with a young child). Although speech is never free from generic constraints, Bakhtin indicates that speakers can achieve some individuality of expression by creatively appropriating and reaccenting existing genres, and by orchestrating particular voices.

Kurt's retellings thus exemplify a fundamental property of speech genres, namely that they are prepackaged ways of organizing speech, which simultaneously offer a set of resources for creating emergent performances. Any particular performance involves both the voice type of the speech genre and of a concrete individual. In Bakhtinian terms, Kurt appropriates "The Tale of Peter

Rabbit" and uses it to create a series of unique performances; he populates it with his own intention.

The retellings also exemplify another key Bakhtinian concept, namely the inherent dialogicality or multivoicedness of speech. According to Bakhtin, every utterance is not only expressed from the perspective of a particular voice or speaking personality, but it is addressed to another particular voice. In addition, every utterance has a history of ownership by previous voices. Bakhtin thus emphasized the multiple ways in which voices come into contact with other voices. One way in which this happens is called "ventriloquation," the process by which one voice speaks through another voice or voice type.

These perspectives led us to organize the analysis of narrating talk in terms of two questions. First, who is Kurt talking to in these tellings? This requires an analysis of the circumstances of the telling, including who the interlocutor is and how she responds to Kurt's narrations. Second, what stance does Kurt, as narrator, take toward the narrated event? These questions are addressed in turn.

The Dialogic Context of the Retellings: Who is Kurt Talking to?

On first glance, the question of who Kurt is talking to seems quite straightforward. In all of the retellings his mother is present as interlocutor and, for the most part, she is the only interlocutor. Kurt is thus talking almost exclusively to his mother in a private context in which they are unlikely to be interrupted. However, a closer look reveals that the issue of who Kurt is addressing is more complicated. As described earlier, retellings 2 and 5 were structured as soliloquys, rather than dialogic exchanges. Kurt seems to be talking not so much to his mother as to himself in her presence. He thus commands a high degree of control or authorship of the retellings.

Even the retellings (1, 3, 4) that are organized dialogically share this quality. Although Kurt's mother launches two of these retellings by introducing the topic of Peter Rabbit, Kurt quickly volunteers new information about Peter and elaborates on his actions. Although his mother is attentive and responsive to what he says, she takes a nondirective role, mirroring back to Kurt what he has just said, either in the form of confirmation queries or repetitions of his contributions. This mode of interaction is reminiscent of the contingent responding that characterizes American middle-class mothers' participation in pretend play with young children (Haight & Miller, 1992; Kavanaugh, Whittington, & Cerbone, 1983). Kurt is thus allowed to retain control of the narrative topic.

In Vygotskian terms, the retellings qualify as egocentric speech in the sense that they function simultaneously as speech for others and speech for oneself (Vygotsky, 1934/1987). Wertsch (1985) describes the transitional and undifferentiated nature of egocentric speech as follows,

> The appearance of egocentric speech, roughly at the age of three, reflects the emergence of a new self-regulative function similar to that of inner speech. Its external form reflects the fact that the child has not fully differentiated this new speech function from the function of social contact and social interaction. (p. 111)

Wertsch goes on to cite evidence that the presence of a supportive listener is especially conducive to the use of egocentric speech.

However, in contrast to much of the research in which egocentric speech accompanies and assists the child to solve a problem or cope with a cognitive task that has some physical representation in the here-and-now, Kurt used egocentric speech to resolve the troubles posed by the Peter Rabbit story itself. In Watson's (1989) terms, his problem solving was more representational than enactive. Nelson (1989) argued that Vygotsky's conception of egocentric speech did not accurately characterize Emily's presleep monologues, either functionally or formally. By contrast, Kurt's retellings seem to provide a good fit with Vygotsky's account of the functions of egocentric speech. From a formal standpoint, however, our findings are consistent with Nelson's: Kurt's speech in the retellings was more complex and explicit than his ordinary talk, rather than more abbreviated as Vygotskian theory predicts. This suggests that what Vygotsky called *egocentric* speech emerges earlier in linguistic development than he believed. But more importantly, it points to the inadequacy of Vygotsky's formulation of the emergence of inner speech in light of contemporary evidence that children are able to use displaced speech, including incipient narrative, from an early age (e.g., Eisenberg, 1985; Fivush, Gray, & Fromhoff, 1987; Miller & Sperry, 1988; Sachs, 1983; Sperry, 1991). The theoretical challenge, then, is to integrate Vygotsky's account of the differentiation of speech functions with an account of the development of narrative and of other verbal genres.

In sum, the dialogic context remains constant across the five retellings of Peter Rabbit. Kurt speaks both to his mother and to himself in her presence in a manner characteristic of egocentric speech. In addition, the self-regulative function of egocentric speech is evident in his use of narrative speech to resolve the disturbances and conflicts posed by the Peter Rabbit story. The more general "problem" that Kurt attempts to solve across the retellings is to create a coherent mapping between his own experiences and the written story, a mapping in which the experiences of Peter Rabbit and the other characters line up with his experiences of gardens and relationships. The interested but nondirective mode of his interlocutor permits him maximal latitude to concentrate on his train of thought and to author the narrations himself. Under these circumstances, Kurt was able, at barely 2 years-of-age, to successfully use a story heuristically, and, indeed, to work with that story repeatedly over a sustained period of time.

The Narrator's Stance: Whose Voice Is It?

Let us turn now to the problem of the narrator's stance toward the narrated event. By stance we mean not just the narrator's perspective on the story but the degree of his affective involvement or commitment to that perspective. For example, does Kurt, as narrator, see the story from the standpoint of an observer and if so, is the observer a neutral or interested observer? Does he insert himself into the story, enacting the voice of a character or speaking directly to the characters? Does he step out of the story entirely and comment on it at a meta-level? To answer these questions requires micro-analysis of how specific communicative devices are deployed in the retellings, included first-, second-, and third-person person point-of-view; affective marking (e.g., explicit emotion terms, paralinguistics, repetition) to create vicarious participation in the story; quoted speech and other means for enacting or envoicing the story in the here-and-now; importation of real-world persons into the story; and explicit metalinguistic references to the telling itself. Wolf (1990) has recently argued that during the second year of life children become able to adopt a range of stances toward events and to articulate and mark them linguistically. The following analysis of the retellings supports this claim. Further, we suggest that Kurt's ability to inhabit multiple stances toward the story enabled him to take control of the plot, thereby restoring canonical order.

In the analysis that follows, each retelling is considered in turn. Owing to space restrictions, only retelling 2 will be analyzed at length. Retelling 2 was selected for this purpose because it is a highly complex and affectively marked retelling and because Kurt alternates among several stances in the course of this single retelling. See Appendix A for a verbatim transcript of retelling 2.

Retelling #1

Kurt's first retelling occurred while he was seated in a highchair gazing out at his paternal grandmother's flower-filled garden. The talk is dialogically organized, and the content is simple and straightforward: Kurt appropriates the character of Peter Rabbit, projects him into the real-world garden, and attributes to him two classes of actions that are central to the written story: eating prodigiously and walking from the woods into the garden.

The retelling is structured in terms of a series of parallel episodes each of which describes a different plant that Peter devoured (e.g., iris, little pine tree, broccoli, flowers, plants hanging on the sycamore tree). Although Kurt takes an observer or spectator's stance toward Peter's actions (Wolf, 1990), he, like the narrator of the written story, is not a neutral observer. Early in the retelling he characterizes Peter as "naughty/" and later he exclaims "uh oh!/" and "THAT Peter Rabbit!/", and yet his manner of delivery conveys not censure but excitement about Peter's mischievous deeds: many of his utterances are marked by excited intonation ("Peter Rabbit ate the iris!"), emphatic stress ("Peter Rabbit ate the IRIS/"), and evaluative intensifiers ("ate them *all* up/"). Throughout this retelling Kurt seems to side subtly with Peter Rabbit, to enter into Peter's experience vicariously, while preserving some distance between himself and Peter through third-person, past tense narration.

Retelling #2

The second retelling also took place in proximity to a garden. Kurt is standing on his maternal grandparents' front porch next to the flower garden. He has been fantasizing that a crow built a nest in the marigolds. The topic of Peter Rabbit is introduced by his mother, who says, "I wonder if Peter Rabbit ate any of these marigolds last night? (1).[5] This overture triggers an outpouring of soliloquized talk to which his mother contributes only one additional utterance.

Although the interactive mode differs dramatically, retelling 2 begins in a manner that is similar to the first retelling. Kurt projects Peter Rabbit into the real-world garden and describes his actions from an observer's perspective. Early in this retelling, however, Kurt appropriates a second character from the written story, namely Peter's mother. In contrast to the written story, he brings Mother Rabbit into the garden with Peter, and it is the conflict between these two characters that provides the central problematic. This conflict is occasioned by Peter Rabbit's violation of the rules of the garden—stepping on a stalk (9)—and is conveyed primarily through enacted speech, which is discussed shortly. However, the first mention of Mother Rabbit establishes the conflict from an observer's perspective ("his mother didn't help him/" 10), and it is followed immediately by a contradictory statement ("his mother helped him/" 11). This inconsistency is carried through the first half of the retelling: At times Peter Rabbit and his mother are in overt conflict; at other times they are aligned with one another. Complicating matters further, they encounter danger from the human world ("some cars came and killed them/" 28). Thus the first half of retelling 2 establishes the three related troubles described earlier (Table 5.3): that Peter Rabbit violated the rules of the garden, that he and his mother are in conflict, and that the human and rabbit worlds are in conflict.

In this highly complex and emotionally charged retelling, the conflict between Peter Rabbit and his mother is forefronted and elaborated as Kurt takes multiple stances toward the conflict. Beginning in line 12, this conflict is enacted or replayed in the here-and-now via the device of quoted speech. Kurt as narrator aligns himself with the voice of rabbit authority by rendering in direct quotation Mother Rabbit's prohibition to Peter, " 'don't step on this little stalk,' mother said/" (12). He repeats and varies this prohibition five times (14–17). Kurt thus takes a participant's stance toward the past event by animating or envoicing the character of Mother Rabbit. Moreover, there is a shift across the quoted prohibitions from past to historical present tense in the framing verb of saying (*said* in 12 and 14 to *says* in 15). Such tense shifts are characteristic of oral narrative genres of personal experience (Bauman, 1986) and mark movement toward an even more participatory stance toward the past event. In this case, the shift to the

---

[5]Numbers in parentheses refer to the corresponding lines in the transcript of retelling 2 in Appendix A.

present tense collapses Kurt's voice as narrator and Mother Rabbit's voice. The two voices, in effect, merge.

Interwoven with the quoted prohibitions are threads from Kurt's real-world personal experience, rendered in the third person. First, people who ordinarily populate the actual garden, namely Grandma (18, 19) and Kurt himself (20) are incorporated into the narration and brought into contact with the fictional characters. Specifically, Grandma's and Kurt's actions of planting flowers in the garden are offered as explanation for Mother Rabbit's prohibition: "Don't go in there/ Grandma planted some flowers in there/ Grandma planted some flowers in there/ Kurt did help/" (17–20). The blending of Kurt's voice as narrator with Mother Rabbit's voice thus becomes even more apparent. The boundary between the quoted prohibition and the subsequent explanation is not clearly marked: It could be spoken by Mother Rabbit or by Kurt himself. Kurt's concern that Peter Rabbit not trample the newly planted flowers is ventriloquated through the voice of Mother Rabbit (Bakhtin, 1981).

Second, real-life events that Kurt had experienced the evening before in the company of his mother and grandmother (going to see the boats, going in the grocery store cart, buying oranges and cat food, 30–32) are attributed to Peter Rabbit and his mother. In other words, Kurt's identification with Peter Rabbit is expressed by casting Peter Rabbit as the subject of Kurt's own past actions. Thus, in these two ways Kurt has brought his real-world experience together with the storyworld of Peter Rabbit; he has personalized the story of Peter Rabbit by incorporating into it bits and pieces of his experience. More specifically, he has used his personal experience—of amicable relations between himself and a mother/grandmother figure—to create a particular voicing of the narration, one in which the perspectives of Peter Rabbit and Mother Rabbit are brought closer together. This is accomplished by invoking Kurt and Grandma's joint actions in support of Mother Rabbit's prohibitions and by attributing directly to Peter Rabbit and Mother Rabbit the shared activities of Kurt and his mother and grandmother.

Later in the retelling the conflict between Peter Rabbit and his mother intensifies ("mother smacks Peter/" 45) as Kurt replays again and again Mother Rabbit's prohibition (37, 39, 40, 42, 44, 46, 48), framing each repetition in the historical present tense. The pivotal moment in the retelling occurs immediately after the final quoted prohibition. Kurt says, "mother's a rabbit/ mother jumps in there with Peter/" (49–50). With these two utterances the narrator brings Mother Rabbit and Peter together, acknowledging Mother Rabbit's identity as a rabbit, like Peter, and reversing her prohibition by having her jump in with Peter. Kurt as narrator then does something very interesting: he steps into the frame of the story and directly addresses the characters, "no, no, get out mother, get out Peter/" (51). His concerns are not ventriloquated through the voice of Mother Rabbit but are claimed as his own.

That is, there is a microgenetic shift across this soliloquy in the narrator's participant stance toward the characters, and, concomitantly in the characters' relationship to one another. Kurt initially aligns himself with Mother Rabbit's point-of-view, against Peter, literally speaking in her voice. Having done so a dozen times—while invoking, in repeated juxtaposition, the amicable relations between Kurt and his mother/grandmother—he makes her voice his own and at the same time brings the formerly estranged characters together. It appears that his participation in the story in the character of Mother Rabbit has enabled him to appropriate the voice of rabbit authority and to thereby gain control over the characters by means of the same participatory mode, that is, by stepping into the story itself.

Immediately after these developments Kurt's father and then his grandmother fortuitously appear on the porch, and Kurt turns to each and provides a concise summary of the central action of the story. In this summary Peter Rabbit and Mother Rabbit enter the garden together. Having resolved the conflict between Peter Rabbit and Mother Rabbit, he does not replay the conflict for his new audience. In contrast to the earlier part of the retelling in which Kurt's stance alternated between interested observer and participant in the story action, Kurt now takes what Wolf (1990) has called an executive stance toward the past event: He explains at a meta-level what he did ("Kurt *talked about* Peter Rabbit and the mother/," 52; "*talkin about* Peter Rabbit and the mother/" 59), explicitly noting his role as narrator and recapping the resolution ("mother did help Peter/ and the mother got out too/" 61–62). In other words, after intervening in the story and appropriating the voice of authority, he steps out of the story entirely and reflects back upon it. His resolution of the conflict appears to have given him some distance on the events in the garden.

Retelling #3

The third retelling, unlike the first and second, took place indoors at Kurt's home, not in proximity to a garden. It was preceded by discussion with mother about a letter from Kurt's paternal grandmother in which she recounted how the woodchucks had eaten her marigolds.

Retelling 3 is structured as two parallel episodes in which something in the garden frightens Peter Rabbit, and he hides in the bushes. In the first episode it is the wheelbarrow that scares him, in the second, the blue jay. In both cases Kurt explicitly characterizes Peter's mental state as "scared." It is as though he is narrating within the consciousness of Peter Rabbit. Like retelling 1, Kurt consistently assumes a stance of interested, involved observer, but unlike retelling 1, he now has access to Peter's internal state. Kurt's affective engagement with the frightened Peter is indicated by the manner in which the relevant utterances are delivered: they are marked by emphatic stress ("and the wheelbarrow SCARED Peter/") and stuttering ("and the and the and the and the blue jay scared Peter/"). In addition the frightening blue jay is not only described but envoiced "and the blue jay flew in the tree and 'caw' said him/."

In the written story Peter Rabbit's prevailing emotion is fear once he is discovered by Mr. McGregor, and this feeling is explicitly acknowledged twice—immediately after Mr. McGregor starts to chase Peter ("Peter was most dreadfully frightened . . ." p. 11) and immediately after the chase ends ("Peter sat down to rest; he was out of breath and trembling with fright." p. 13) Thus, there is a strong parallel between retelling 3 and the written story in terms of Peter Rabbit's feelings and in terms of the narrator's access to those feelings. However, the sources of fear differ. In this connection it is interesting to note that a wheelbarrow and some blackbirds are mentioned and depicted on page 15 of the written story. On this same page Peter Rabbit's reaction to the sound of Mr. McGregor's hoe is described, "Peter scuttered underneath the bushes." Note the similarity in Kurt's account of Peter's reaction to the blue jay, "he scuttered right under a bushes to take a nap/."

Retelling #4

The fourth retelling began in Kurt's bedroom and continued in the bathroom as he got ready to take a bath. It is occasioned by a toy rabbit, which his mother refers to as "Peter Rabbit." The shift from one room to the other is marked by intervening talk unrelated to Peter Rabbit, thereby providing a natural division of the retelling into two segments.

In the first segment Kurt takes an observer's perspective toward the actions of the "little rabbits." This segment of the retelling is bounded by parallel episodes in which it is explicitly established, through third-person, past-tense narration that Mother Rabbit helped the little rabbits, first, to water plants and second, to plant seeds. There is only one moment of conflict, namely when the rabbits stomp grandaddy's car. In general, Kurt's narrating stance is that of a more neutral observer than he has been in the previous retellings: This is evident in the lack of explicit references to emotions, emotion-charged verbs, or affectively marked paralinguistics.

The second segment of retelling 4 begins with a shift in narrative stance, as Kurt announces his intention to talk about Peter Rabbit ("want to talk in bath, Peter Rabbit in bathroom/" "want to talk about Peter Rabbit/"). As in retelling 2, Kurt makes explicit metalinguistic reference to the retellings from outside the storyworld. Kurt then shifts back to an observer's stance, narrating the actions of Peter Rabbit and the mother, namely that they were walking or coming some-where. Then, for the first time in any of the retellings, Kurt explicitly refers to himself as observer, "Kurt saw them coming/." Several turns later, he recycles again through the walking of Peter Rabbit and his mother, again explicitly describing himself as observer, "Kurt was peeking out the front door/ . . . (saw) Peter Rabbit and the mother/."

Retelling #5

The setting of the final retelling was the same as that of retelling 2, namely Kurt's maternal grandparents' garden. The retelling is immediately preceded by pretend play with a toy tractor on the theme of baling hay.

The interactive form also resembles retelling 2 in that it is organized as a soliloquy to which Kurt's interlocutor contributes only four turns. However, this retelling does not have the driven quality of retelling 2. Kurt digresses twice to comment on happenings in the here-and-now garden (e.g., he sees a dove perched on the wire, notices when it flies). It is as though his vision has expanded to encompass the real garden for its own sake—not just as a stage for Peter Rabbit.

The retelling is structured in terms of a series of actions by Peter Rabbit and the other story characters. They appear and re-appear in different combinations, all amicable. No sooner is Peter Rabbit introduced than Flopsy, Mopsy, Cotton-tail, and Peter's mother appear. They walk around the garden. Mr. McGregor joins the little bunnies. Mother Rabbit and Mr. McGregor plant parsley. Mother Rabbit and Mr. McGregor and the three little bunnies plant parsley. Thus, the one disturbance that remained in retelling 4, namely the conflict between the rabbits and the human world, is resolved. A harmony more inclusive than that offered at the conclusion of the written story has been achieved.

Moreover, the behavior of the rabbits is, in other respects, beyond reproach. The first action attributed to Peter is one of obedience, "Peter not stepped in this stuff right here/." Note that the wording here is virtually identical to the prohibition attributed to mother rabbit in retelling 2 (see lines 37, 46). Kurt as narrator is speaking through the voice of Mother Rabbit in a process of ventriloquation (Bakhtin, 1981). He has adopted the perspective of the rule-enforcing Mother Rabbit, a perspective that is carried through this retelling. The rabbits sniff the strawberries but do not eat them. When Peter does eat something, it is parsley, an appropriate food for a rabbit, and there is no suggestion that he eats immoderately.

Thus, although Kurt as narrator does not take a neutral observer's perspective toward the characters, he seems less affectively engaged. Retelling 5 continues the pattern noted in retelling 4 in that it is devoid of explicit affective content. (Unfortunately, the recording of retelling 5 did not include paralinguistic information.)

There is another revealing omission in the final retelling. In contrast to retellings 2, 3, and 4 Kurt does not incorporate himself or any other persons from his real world experience into the storyworld. In this respect retelling 5 resembles the first retelling. Having succeeded in reconfiguring the story line in a way that restores canonical order, he has receded into the observer-author's role.

In sum, three patterns can be discerned from this analysis of narrative stance. First, Kurt inhabited multiple stances toward the story world, including vicarious observer, participant in the story action, and commentator about the story. Second, there was a gradual differentiation and elaboration across the retellings within given stances. Within the vicarious observer stance, Kurt eventually gained access to Peter Rabbit's internal states; as commentator, Kurt eventually differentiated author and observer roles. And finally, there seemed to be a gradual *cooling* of affect in the later retellings, evident in a more consistently distanced stance toward the story.

CONCLUSION

In conclusion, we shall bring together the major results of these several analyses. The Peter Rabbit retellings seem to have been motivated by Kurt's intense interest and involvement in the "Tale of Peter Rabbit." This interest was evident both in the retellings and the relistenings. The characters and plot of the written story, insofar as they parallel the ordinary emotional experience of a 2-year-old and the idiosyncratic gardening experience of this particular 2-year-old, posed for Kurt multiple threats of disruption to the canonical order of *his* world—that he might disobey his mother, that he might behave destructively in the garden, that secure relations with his grandmother might be disturbed, that he might encounter dangers in the garden. It is these highly personalized problems that fueled Kurt's repeated use of the story—his persistent efforts at formulating, reformulating, and resolving—and enabled him to muster linguistic resources that exceeded his usual linguistic level.

In a recent paper on the Inuit of the Canadian Arctic, Briggs (1991) describes how one 3-year-old child was socialized through participation in recurrent *dramas* in which a caregiver teased or challenged the child about personally relevant, affectively charged issues. Although the Inuit dramas do not originate in a written source and the caregiver's role is much more prodding and directive, Briggs' account, like the current one, points to the child's involvement with cultural texts as a major mechanism of meaning creation:

> My notion is that the kernal questions, [posed in the dramas], frequently repeated and often dangerous from the point of view of the child, will be perceived by the child as important problems to be solved. The child will focus on questions when they occur, and they will act like magnets, drawing his or her attention to any events that might provide clues to their meanings, and to appropriate ways of dealing with the problem. The plots, themselves often dangerous, constitute such events, and I suggest that every time the question occurs, it will resonate with other occurrences, so that each plot will provide additional clues to how to deal with the problem. Meanings will cumulate, and in this way, little by little, children will create for themselves worlds that contain variants of the plots of their parents' worlds. (p. 147)

The analyses of the Peter Rabbit retellings reveals a high degree of systematicity in the creation of variant plots. Four troubles were posed in the early retellings, and each was resolved in turn; the order in which the troubles were taken up paralleled the order in which they were introduced in the written story; and an ever more inclusive resolution was achieved.

Moreover, with the multiple resolutions attained in retelling 5, the retellings ceased to occur. In baseline speech sample two, which occurred 2 weeks after the last retelling, the topic of Peter Rabbit was introduced into the conversation twice by Kurt's mother. First, when Kurt talked about a real rabbit that he had seen, she asked whether it was Peter and he said, "no/ . . . it was a cottontail/." Later, she asked whether he had seen Peter Rabbit lately. He answered affirmatively but, upon further questioning, did not pursue the topic.

The cessation of the retellings, in conjunction with the temporal patterning described earlier, indicate that the retellings peaked at 2 weeks of exposure to the written story—with retellings 2, 3, and 4 occurring in rapid succession—and then declined to zero. This pattern corresponds with the emotional trajectory of the retellings, in that the peak of affective marking occurred within the temporal peak. Retelling 2 was the most affectively marked retelling and the only retelling in which the narrator inhabited a sustained participatory stance. Retelling 3 was the only retelling in which Peter Rabbit's emotional state of fear was articulated. Affective marking began to decline in retelling 4 and continued in retelling 5. This pattern raises the possibility that in repeatedly telling the story, Kurt recreated the emotional experience associated with the written story—the build-up to a peak of suspense and its diminution. Were this pattern corroborated with other children, it would suggest that the narrative form itself provides a tool for emotion regulation.

In attempting to explain how the changes in plot came about, we proposed three factors that are plausibly involved. The first factor was Kurt's familiarity with the story. The second centered on the social circumstances and interactive mode of the retellings, which supported Kurt's heuristic use of narrative. A sympathetic interlocutor was always present; Kurt's concentration was not disturbed; and he was allowed to exercise authorship of the narrations.

The third factor was more complex and required micro-level analysis of how linguistic resources were used to create narrative stances. We found that despite his limited linguistic resources, Kurt was able to establish multiple narrative stances by aligning himself as narrator with the interests of various fictional characters whom he had appropriated from the written story. He accomplished this in several ways: by using words and affective markings that betrayed his vicarious participation in the actions that he recounted, by enacting the voices of particular characters, and by incorporating himself and other persons from his real life into the story and bringing them into contact with the fictional characters. In addition, in two of the retellings, he stepped out of the story entirely to reflect back on what he had just said. In both cases, this meta-commentary occurred after he had inhabited and reinhabited various intrastory stances. Our claim is that Kurt's ability to inhabit multiple stances toward the storyworld enabled him to take control of the story characters, thereby transforming the plot and creating a coherent mapping between his own experiences and the Beatrix Potter story.

Although this claim may seem to overstate the cognitive capabilities of such a young child, it is consistent with Wolf's (1990) description of young children's growing ability to adopt a variety of stances toward events during the second year. It is also compatible with Dunn's (1988) account of the social awareness and decided lack of egocentricity that young children show within the complex emotional world of the family. Dunn reports, for example, that in the third year children were more likely to reason in disputes that had earlier caused them most distress and anger. She argues that there may be special learning potential in "emotionally urgent situations that occur within the family" (p. 180). What our study adds is that young children may also be highly motivated to apply their reasoning powers to stories, especially those that invoke emotionally urgent family situations.

Any study of a single case, particularly a study of the author's own child, is subject to obvious limitations of generalizability. Without investigating other cases in the same detail, we cannot know whether the processes of narrative appropriation and transformation that we have identified apply to other 2-year-olds. However, the several examples cited earlier from culturally diverse children suggest that narrative retellings are not unique to Kurt.

There are two other limitations of these data that ought to be acknowledged. First, there is no way to check whether the corpus of Peter Rabbit retellings is comprehensive. Perhaps Kurt produced other retellings, which his researcher-mother simply did not notice. Second, there is a significant omission in the data in that the repeated readings of the written story were not recorded. Were we to undertake another case study, we would remedy this omission, so as to be able to track correspondences between the rereadings and the retellings. Of course, that would lead to an even more overwhelming quantity of data. The greatest strength of the in-depth study of single cases, namely the wealth of detailed material for analysis and interpretation, is also the greatest obstacle to its more widespread use (Nelson, 1989). In the present case, we are aware that there are many other analyses, especially of specific linguistic features, that could be fruitfully undertaken.[6] Despite the difficulties involved, we believe that additional studies of this sort are worth doing, for there is no better way to reveal the actual process by which children recreate and improvise meaning out of cultural resources. This is socialization from the child's perspective.

ACKNOWLEDGMENTS

Preparation for this article was supported, in part, by a grant from the Spencer Foundation, awarded to the first author.

---

[6]For example, Hoogstra (1992) has conducted an analysis of the way in which repetition of words and phrases functions within the retellings to convey affective tone and temporal/spatial movement.

We wish to thank Kristin Alexander, Nancy Baym, Lois Bloom, Jean Briggs, Cindy Clark, Betsy Hearne, Barbara O'Keefe, and James Wertsch for stimulating discussions and constructive criticisms of earlier drafts. We also appreciate Charles Nelson's thoughtful editing. We are grateful to Cindy Clark for help with transcription.

REFERENCES

Bakhtin, M. (1981). *The dialogic imagination: Four essays.* Austin: University of Texas Press.

Bartlett, F. C. (1932). *Remembering.* Cambridge, England: Cambridge University Press.

Bauman, R. (1986). *Story, performance and event: Contextual studies of oral narrative.* New York: Cambridge University Press.

Bauman, R., & Briggs, C. L. (1990). Poetics and performance as critical perspectives on language and social life. *Annual Review of Anthropology, 19,* 59–88.

Bloom, L., & Lahey, M. (1978). *Language development and language disorders.* New York: Wiley.

Briggs, J. L. (1991). Mazes of meaning: The exploration of individuality in culture and of culture through individual constructs. *The Psychoanalytic Study of Society, 16,* 111–153.

Brown, R. (1973). *A first language: The early stages.* Cambridge, MA: Cambridge University Press.

Bruner, J. (1990). *Acts of meaning.* Cambridge, MA: Harvard University Press.

Bruner, J., & Lucariello, J. (1989). Monologue as narrative recreation of the world. In K. Nelson (Ed.), *Narratives from the crib* (pp. 73–97). Cambridge, MA: Harvard University Press.

Burke, K. (1945). *A grammar of motives.* New York: Prentice-Hall.

Crowhurst, M. (1991). Interrelationships between reading and writing persuasive discourse. *Research in the Teaching of English, 25,* 314–338.

Dunn, J. (1988). *The beginnings of social understanding.* Cambridge, MA: Harvard University Press.

Eisenberg, A. R. (1985). Learning to describe past experiences in conversation. *Discourse Processes, 8,* 177–204.

Engel, S. (1986). *Learning to reminisce: A developmental study of how young children talk about the past.* Unpublished doctoral dissertation, The City University of New York.

Favat, F. A. (1977). *Child and tale: The origins of interest.* Urbana, IL: National Council of Teachers of English.

Fine, G. A. (1980). Children and their culture: Exploring Newell's paradox. *Western Folklore, 39*(3), 170–183.

Fivush, R., & Fromhoff, F. A. (1988). Style and structure in mother-child conversations about the past. *Discourse Processes, 11,* 337–355.

Fivush, R., Gray, J. T., & Fromhoff, F. A. (1987). Two-year-olds talk about the past. *Cognitive Development, 2,* 393–409.

Goffman, E. (1959). *The presentation of self in everyday life.* New York: Doubleday.

Haight, W., & Miller, P. J. (1992). The social nature of early pretend play: Middle-class mothers' participation in everyday pretending. *Merrill-Palmer Quarterly, 38,* 331–349.

Hearne, B. (1990). *Choosing books for children* (2nd Ed.). New York: Delacourte Press.

Heath, S. B. (1983). *Ways with words: Language, life, and work in communities and classrooms.* Cambridge, England: Cambridge University Press.

Hoogstra, L. (1992). *Cognitive and affective functions of repetition in a 2-year-old's narrations of 'Peter Rabbit.'* Paper presented at the annual meeting of the Speech Communication Association, Chicago.

Hymes, D. (1975). Breakthrough into performance. In D. Ben-Amos & K. S. Goldstein (Eds.), *Folklore: Performance and communication* (pp. 11–74). The Hague: Mouton.

Kavanaugh, R. D., Whittington, S., & Cerbone, M. J. (1983). Mothers' use of fantasy in speech to young children. *Journal of Child Language, 10*, 45–55.

Kirshenblatt-Gimblett, B. (1975). A parable in context: A social interactional analysis of story-telling performance. In D. Ben-Amos & K. S. Goldstein (Eds.), *Folklore: Performance and communication* (pp. 105–130). The Hague: Mouton.

Linder, L. (1971). *A history of the writings of Beatrix Potter*. London: Frederick Warne.

Miller, P. J. (in press). Narrative practices: Their role in socialization and self-construction. In U. Neisser & R. Fivush (Eds.), *The remembering self: Construction and accuracy in the self-narrative*. Cambridge, England: Cambridge University Press.

Miller, P. J., Mintz, J., Hoogstra, L., Fung, H., & Potts, R. (1992). The narrated self: Young children's construction of self in relation to others in conversational stories of personal experience. *Merrill Palmer Quarterly, 38*(1), 45–67.

Miller, P. J., & Moore, B. B. (1989). Narrative conjunctions of caregiver and child: A comparative perspective on socialization through stories. *Ethos, 17*, 43–64.

Miller, P. J., Potts, R., Fung, H., Hoogstra, L., & Mintz, J. (1990). Narrative practices and the social construction of self in childhood. *American Ethnologist, 17*(2), 292–311.

Miller, P. J., & Sperry, L. L. (1988). Early talk about the past: The origins of conversational stories of personal experience. *Journal of Child Language, 15*, 293–315.

Nelson, K. (Ed.). (1989). *Narratives from the crib* Cambridge, MA: Harvard University Press.

Newell, W. W. (1963). *Games and songs of American children*. New York: Dover. (Original published in 1883).

Nikola-Lisa, W. (1990, March). *The cult of Peter Rabbit: A Barthesian analysis*. Paper presented at a meeting of the Society for Popular Culture, Toronto.

Nye, C. H. (1988). *Psychoanalytic narratives: the formulation of meaning*. Unpublished doctoral dissertation, The University of Chicago, Chicago.

Ochs, E., Smith, R., & Taylor, C. (1989). Detective stories at dinnertime: Problem-solving through co-narration. *Cultural Dynamics, 2*, 238–257.

Paley, V. G. (1981). *Wally's stories: Conversations in the kindergarten*. Cambridge, MA: Harvard University Press.

Perera, K. (1984). *Children's writing and reading*. London: Basil Blackwell.

Pillemer, D., & White, S. H. (1989). Childhood events recalled by adults and children. In H. W. Reese (Ed.), *Advances in child development and behavior* (Vol. 22, pp. 297–340). New York: Academic Press.

Polanyi, L. (1985). *Telling the American Story*. Norwood, NJ: Ablex.

Potter, B. (1980). *The tale of Peter Rabbit*. London: Warne. (Original published in 1901).

Robinson, J. A. (1981). Personal narratives reconsidered. *Journal of American Folklore, 94*(371), 58–85.

Rosen, B. (1988). *And none of it was nonsense: The power of storytelling in school*. Portsmouth, NH: Heinemann.

Sachs, J. (1983). Talking about the there and then: The emergence of displaced reference in parent-child discourse. In K. E. Nelson (Ed.), *Children's language* (Vol. 4, pp. 1–28). New York: Gardner Press.

Scollon R., & Scollon, S. B. K. (1981). *Narrative, literacy, and face in interethnic communication*. Norwood, NJ: Ablex.

Smith, J. A. (1990, June 14). Life after squirrel nutkin: Review of Beatrix Potter's letters and of the journal of Beatrix Potter 1881–1897. *New York Review of Books*, pp. 19–22.

Spence, D. P. (1982). *Narrative truth and historical truth: Meaning and interpretation in psychoanalysis*. New York: W. W. Norton.

Sperry, L. L. (1991). *The emergence and development of narrative competence among African-*

American toddlers in a rural Alabama community. Unpublished doctoral dissertation, The University of Chicago, Chicago.

Taylor, J., Whalley, J. I., Hobbs, A. S., & Battrick, E. M. (1987). *Beatrix Potter 1866–1943: The artist and her world*. London: Warne with the National Trust.

Tucker, N. (1981). *The child and the book*. Cambridge, England: Cambridge University Press.

Vygotsky, L. S. (1978). *Mind in society*. Cambridge, MA: Harvard University Press.

Vygotsky, L. S. (1987). Thinking and speech. In R. W. Rieber & A. S. Carton (Eds., N. Minick, Trans.). *The collected works of L. S. Vygotsky* (Vol. 1, pp. 39–285). New York: Plenum. (Original published in 1934).

Watson, R. (1989). Monologue, dialogue, and regulation. In K. Nelson (Ed.), *Narratives from the crib* (pp. 263–283). Cambridge, MA. Harvard University Press.

Wertsch, J. V. (1985). *Vygotsky and the social formation of mind*. Cambridge, MA: Harvard University Press.

Wertsch, J. V. (1991). *Voices of the mind: A sociocultural approach to mediated action*. Cambridge, MA: Harvard University Press.

White, S. H., & Pillemer, D. B. (1979). Childhood amnesia and the development of a socially accessible memory system. In J. F. Kihlstrom & F. J. Evans (Eds.), *Functional disorders of memory*. (pp. 29–73) Hillsdale, NJ: Lawrence Erlbaum Associates.

Wolf, D. P. (1990). Being of several minds: Voices and versions of the self in early childhood. In D. Cicchetti & M. Beeghly (Eds.), *The self in transition* (pp. 183–212). Chicago: The University of Chicago Press.

APPENDIX A

Retelling 2

001   *Mother:* I wonder if Peter Rabbit ate any of these marigolds last night?
002   *Kurt:* ate that one/ (points to marigold)
003   Peter Rabbit came around the path/ (gestures toward walk)
004   Peter Rabbit came around the walk/
005   ate this marigold right there/
006   he came up on the porch/
007   he came around the bend/
008   he walked/
009   he stepped on that stalk right there/ (gestures toward garden on left side of porch)
010   his mother didn't help him/
011   his mother helped him/
012   "don't step on this little stalk," mother said/
013   mother helped him/
014   mother said, "don't step on this pile"/
015   "don't walk in there, don't step in there," mother says/
016   "don't go in there"/
017   "don't go in there"/
018   Grandma planted some flowers in there/
019   Grandma planted some flowers in there/

020   Kurt did help/
021   Peter did run/
022   Peter did walk/
023   Mother and Peter did walk/
024   them came in this grass/
025   them were some where/
026   them were down this road/
027   them were way down the street/
028   some cars came and killed them/
029   Peter Rabbit and mother went in the yellow car/
030   went in the car to see the boats/ (Kurt did the previous evening)
031   Peter Rabbit went in the grocery store cart to get groceries (Kurt did the
        previous evening)
032   Peter Rabbit and mother went to grocery store to get oranges and cat food/
        (Kurt did the previous evening)
033   *Mother:* They went to get food for the kitty cat?
034   *Kurt:* them walked way down the street to get kitty cat food/
035   them walked down the street/
036   mother caught a rabbit/
037   mama says, "don't step in that stuff right there"/ (gestures toward garden
        on right of path)
038   right there sitting at the corner/
039   mother says, "no, no, don't step in that"/
040   mother says, "Peter, don't step in that"/
041   starting get a green flower in it/ (refers to plant in garden)
042   mother says, "no, no don't step in that, Grandma planted that stuff right
        there"/
043   Grandma used a trowel/
044   mother says, "no, no, don't step in that"/
045   mother smacks Peter/
046   mother says, "no, no, don't step in this stuff right here"/
047   Grandma planted other stuff/
048   mother says, "no, no, don't step in there, Peter"/
049   mother's a rabbit/
050   mother jumps in there with Peter/
051   no, no, get out mother, get out Peter/

(Kurt's father appears on the porch)

052   *Kurt to Father:* Kurt talked about Peter Rabbit and the mother/
053   came around the path/
054   up to the porch/
055   up to the house/

056   they came/
057   step in that stuff/ (refers to flower box)
058   Grandma planted flower/

(Kurt's grandmother appears on porch)

059   *Kurt to Grandmother:* talkin about Peter Rabbit and the mother/
060   Peter Rabbit and the mother/
061   mother did help Peter/
062   and the mother got out too/

6 Placing Affect and Narrative in Developmental and Cultural Context: Comments on Miller et al.

Ganie B. DeHart
SUNY at Geneseo

Children's narratives can provide the substance for research into a wide variety of developmental issues. Narrative can be studied as a developing skill in its own right, as an indicator of other developing skills, as a sociocultural form to be acquired by children as part of their socialization, or as a tool an individual child applies to developmental issues. Until recently, psychologists have focused much of their research dealing with children's narrative on the cognitive and linguistic skills developed and demonstrated in the ways children talk about the past (e.g., Eisenberg, 1985; McCabe & Peterson, 1991; Pratt & MacKenzie-Keating, 1985; Sachs, 1983). Recent work by Peggy Miller and others, including Katherine Nelson (1989), moves our understanding of children's storytelling and of the issues to be considered in connection with their developing narrative skills beyond the cognitive and linguistic realm and into the realm of social and affective functions. Although this is familiar territory for anthropologists, for many psychologists it places narrative into new contexts, both socially and developmentally.

One aspect of the analysis by Miller and her colleagues that sets it apart from earlier work on narrative is its focus on "socialization from the child's perspective," its emphasis on the child's perception of and involvement with the story. This focus is quite different from the treatment of stories as disembedded texts to be remembered—accurately or not so accurately—that is typical of some cognitively-oriented research on children's narrative. Yet I suspect that children's fascination with hearing and telling stories stems not from the objective memory challenges the stories pose, but rather from the subjective affective experiences they offer.[1]

Peggy Miller's program of research focuses our attention on two related issues. The first issue concerns the role played by storytelling in socialization—that is, the functions that storytelling may serve at the cultural or societal level. The second issue involves the role of storytelling in individual meaning creation, especially in the emerging understanding of the self—the possible functions of storytelling for the individual child. Some of Miller's previous research (Miller & Moore, 1989; Miller & Sperry, 1988) is concerned with the first issue; the *Peter Rabbit* study focuses on the second, giving us a clear sense of what one individual child was doing in his retellings of a particular story.

However, the developmental functions of storytelling for individual children in any sense beyond the purely idiosyncratic can only be understood with reference to the broader socialization issues. In the case of the *Peter Rabbit* study, we can form generalizable hypotheses about the affective functions of narrative for children only if we put Kurt's particular experience into a clearer developmental, interpersonal, and cultural context.

NARRATIVE AND AFFECT IN DEVELOPMENTAL CONTEXT

In line with the symposium theme of memory and affect, one of the first developmentally oriented questions to be asked is how affect and narrative might be related to each other. In connection with the research by Miller and her colleagues, this question is clearly bidirectional. On the one hand, how does affective engagement with stories and their subject matter influence the narratives that children produce? On the other hand, what role does narrative, especially the retelling of significant stories, play in the resolution of affective issues for children?

In answer to the first question, Miller et al. argue that emotional identification with the characters and conflicts in *Peter Rabbit* "fueled Kurt's repeated use of the story. . . and enabled him to muster linguistic resources that exceeded his usual linguistic level" (p. 107). Kurt's affective engagement with *Peter Rabbit* can be seen most clearly in his personal identification with Peter. Miller et al.

---

[1]Like Kurt, I was given a copy of *Peter Rabbit* as a preschooler, and it became one of my favorite books for a time. There are certain phrases from the book that impressed themselves on my memory—the wonderful repetition of "Flopsy, Mopsy, Cottontail. . . and Peter," for example, and the mysterious-sounding "camomile tea," which I mistakenly assumed must be caramel-flavored. Far more vivid to this day, however, are the feelings the book evoked in me—apprehension when Peter ventured into the garden, uneasiness elicited by the sinister creepiness of the white cat watching the goldfish, relief when Peter was finally safely at home. I loved *Peter Rabbit*, but it was not a benign, innocent book to me; instead, it brought forth powerful emotions, many of them unpleasant.

point out that this identification is apparent in Kurt's attributing to Peter some of his own past actions, such as going to the grocery store and planting flowers with his grandmother. However, it is also apparent in the prohibitions Kurt places on Peter Rabbit in his retellings and in a certain ambiguity in Kurt's references to mothers. When Kurt repeatedly tells Peter not to step on the newly planted garden, the identities of both the speaker and the recipient of the prohibitions are ambiguous. The prohibitions Kurt includes in his retellings of the story seem closer to garden-related prohibitions Kurt himself might have received in the past than to prohibitions given to Peter Rabbit in Beatrix Potter's original story. In the same vein, it is not always clear when Kurt mentions "Mother" or "the mother" in his retellings whether he is referring to Mother Rabbit or to his own mother.

It is clear that the story of Peter Rabbit has great emotional resonance for Kurt, and it seems reasonable that Kurt's identification with Peter and the conflicts Peter becomes involved in does indeed drive his repeated retelling and reworking of the story. In fact, it is noteworthy that he does not simply repeat the story word-for-word as it would have been read to him, as might be expected if the sound or specific phrasing of the story were the major source of its appeal. Instead, he reworks and transforms the story, indicating a more personal involvement in its issues.

It is less clear that it is Kurt's affective engagement with the story *per se* that produces the longer than usual utterances in his retellings. It is possible that the conversational and social context of the retellings allows Kurt to display his linguistic competence more fully than dialogues with adults do, rather than that the affective content of the retellings somehow pushes him to a higher linguistic level. In fact, Kurt showed elevated MLU's during monologues and narrative speech in general, as did Katherine Nelson's Emily (Nelson, 1989). Some of my data on sibling conversations (DeHart, 1990) yielded similar finding for $2\frac{1}{2}$- and $4\frac{1}{2}$-year-olds, who consistently produced longer utterances during monologues than during dialogues with their siblings. Together, these results support the notion that conversational structure, rather than affective content, is the key factor in the elevated MLU's, since it is unlikely that all of these situations involved intense affective engagement.

In answer to the second question about the relationship between affect and narrative, Miller et al. apply Vygotsky's concept of egocentric speech to affective problem-solving, arguing that the self-regulative function of egocentric speech can apply as well to resolving an affective issue as to solving a physical or cognitive problem. This represents an interesting extension of Vygotsky's notion into the affective realm, providing a specific theoretical underpinning for the idea that children sometimes work through emotional issues by talking about them.

Existing research evidence does not reveal how widely these analyses of the connections between affect and narrative may apply. Miller et al. have analyzed some results of affective engagement with a story and some functions of narrative for one particular child. They have revealed to us some things that *can* happen in a child's development—one way that a child can react to an affectively charged story, one way that a child can resolve affective issues, and one potential use of narrative. However, a number of developmental questions remain to be answered, concerning both the generalizability of Miller et al.'s analysis to other children and the centrality of the processes they have identified to children's affective development.

First of all, to what extent is Kurt's reaction to an affectively charged story *typical* of children at his level of development? Does intense affective engagement always produce overt retellings and performance at a linguistically advanced level? Or does it have the opposite effect for some children under some circumstances or at very high levels of intensity? And how common are Kurt's appropriation of a literary story and his use of narrative to resolve affective issues?

Second, to what extent is the reworking of experience found in Kurt's narratives a *critical* factor in children's emotional development? In what other settings and activities might this reworking take place? Miller et al. suggest that children sometimes retell stories as a means of resolving a distressing past experience; by what other means might children accomplish this goal?

Miller et al. propose that if Kurt's pattern were "corroborated with other children, it would suggest that the narrative form itself provides a tool for emotion regulation" (p. 108). Does the narrative form have a privileged function in this regard? Is there something specific about narrative that fosters the regulation of emotions? To what extend does language *in general* play this role?

A final set of questions concerns the relative frequency with which narrative serves the function it appears to serve for Kurt in the *Peter Rabbit* study, compared to other possible functions of narrative. How commonly do repeated retellings of a story involve the processing of emotional issues? For what other purposes are stories repeated by children? For example, in some settings children's narratives seem to serve primarily as entertainment for self or others (e.g., Heath, 1983). At times, storytelling may primarily reflect imitation of a socially modeled cultural form. Of course, all of these functions are interrelated and often simultaneously present. Kurt's stories, for example, seemed to be highly entertaining to his family. In addition, they reflect a narrative blending of real and fantasy elements that is both modeled and encouraged by educated, middle-class, American parents. This blending is reflected in the question from his mother that starts one of his retellings—"Did Peter Rabbit eat some of these marigolds last night?"

NARRATIVE AND AFFECT IN INTERPERSONAL
AND CULTURAL CONTEXT

A full understanding of the significance of the *Peter Rabbit* study also requires that it be placed more clearly in cultural context, as Miller has done in her work with working-class children in South Baltimore (Miller & Moore, 1989) and with culturally diverse children in Chicago and Taiwan. Miller et al. provide examples from several cultural settings that suggest Kurt's narrative retellings are not unique to him. However, while storytelling by, for, and about children is present across cultures, the interpersonal settings, forms, functions, and affective impacts of that storytelling vary. Cultural issues that are important to an understanding of the affective significance of narrative include variability in how adults and children interact, in how narratives are constructed and used, and in how the self is conceptualized.

One issue related to cultural variability in adult-child interaction is the role of the interlocutor in eliciting, shaping, and constructing the stories a child tells. As Miller et al. point out, Kurt's mother had a particular style of interacting with him that was nondirective, accepting, noninterfering—and typical of middle-class American mothers. She encouraged his reworkings of *Peter Rabbit* and seemed to delight in his use of fantasy. This interaction style and stance toward fantasy in children's storytelling may be rather culture-specific. For example, Heath (1983) found that middle-class parents in Piedmont Carolina encouraged children to tell fantasy stories in much the same way that Miller encouraged Kurt's narratives. In contrast, lower-class White parents emphasized factual recounting of events and regarded fantasy stories as lying, whereas lower-class Black parents encouraged a different sort of fictionalized narrative expanding on real-life events. Thus, the opportunity to personalize a narrative in the way that Kurt did is likely to exist only in certain cultural settings.

While a supportive interlocutor is necessary for the production of dialogic narratives, monologic narratives—which in Kurt's case seemed more affectively intense—are another matter. In my data on mother-child and sibling conversations (DeHart, 1990), dialogic storytelling interactions similar to those in Kurt's first, third, and fourth retellings were fairly common between mothers and their $2\frac{1}{2}$- or $4\frac{1}{2}$-year-old children. Such interactions never occurred between the same children and their older siblings. However, the children sometimes produced monologic narratives in the presence of their siblings that resembled Kurt's second and fifth retellings. This type of monologic narrative was virtually absent from the mother-child sessions.

It would be interesting to know the extent to which children who have not been encouraged to produce dialogic narratives make use of monologic narratives as a means of resolving affective issues. Monologic narratives may appear as an outgrowth of dialogic narratives with caregivers, in which case they would be seen mainly in cultural settings where such dialogic narratives occur. Or, they may emerge independently, in response to issues in children's affective development.

A relevant cultural question about narrative construction and use is the extent to which varying story elicitation techniques influence the functions a story can serve for a child. Does it make a difference, for example, if the child spontaneously tells the story in response to something in the environment (as Kurt often seemed to do), if the child tells a particular story with explicit urging from a parent (as the children in Miller's South Baltimore study often did), or if the parent uses a more indirect method to elicit a story, such as the story-starting questions that were common in the black community studied by Heath (1983)? There must be both individual and cultural differences in the story elicitation techniques children are exposed to, and it also seems reasonable that there would be individual and cultural differences in the affective functions that the elicited stories could serve for children.

There may also be subtle differences in the affective functions served by narratives of personal experience and retelling of literary stories. Telling and retelling a personal story allows a child to replay and process the meaning of an actual personal experience. In contrast, retelling a literary story allows a child to replay and process general issues and concerns raised by elements of the story (though it may also remind a child of *specific* experiences and create opportunities to replay and process *them*, as Kurt seems to have done with several gardening incidents). In the process, a child appropriates and shapes the story, making it his or her own, but even a retold literary story is still not exactly the same as a personal experience that has been turned into a story. The initial process of turning a personal experience into a story would seem to provide a particularly rich opportunity for involvement with affective issues.

Different cultural settings may favor either personal narratives or retellings of literary stories, with potentially different consequences for children. Though Miller et al. cite examples of storytelling from several cultural settings, these examples do not represent one kind of narrative. Instead, there seems to be cultural variation in the form, genre, content, and participant structure of the stories being told, as well as in the extent to which individual children are encouraged to tell stories and the form of stories that are encouraged. For example, both the adults and children in Miller's South Baltimore study produced vivid stories of personal experiences, some appropriated from other narrators. In my study of middle-class families (DeHart, 1990), the mothers produced and elicited numerous retellings of classic children's stories (for example, *The Little Engine That Could* while playing with a train set and *Make Way for Ducklings* while playing with ducks on a pond in a village set). In both cases, children are hearing and being encouraged to tell stories, but the stories differ greatly in their immediacy and presumably also in their affective connection to personal experience. It may be that the affective differences between the two experiences are more pronounced for stories that are requested or elicited by an adult than for stories that are spontaneously produced and reworked by a child.

The final set of cultural issues I wish to consider has to do with the use of narrative in self-construction—an issue that Miller et al. refer to briefly in connection with the *Peter Rabbit* study but have treated more extensively elsewhere (Miller, Potts, Fung, Hoogstra, & Mintz, 1990). Recently, several writers

(Markus & Kitayama, 1991; Triandis, 1989) have suggested that there are major cultural differences in how the self is conceptualized, with some cultures (such as middle-class American culture) placing greater emphasis on the independent, private, individual self, and other cultures (such as Japanese culture) placing greater emphasis on the interdependent, public, relational self.

Presumably, the process of self-construction is different for children growing up in these two types of cultures, and thus the role of narrative in that process would also be different. Cultural differences in conceptualization of the self might be associated with cultural differences in the forms of storytelling in which children participate. For example, perhaps cultures that emphasize the private, independent self are more likely to encourage individual story-telling and fantasizing by children, whereas cultures that emphasize the public, interdependent self are more likely to encourage group storytelling or the retelling of traditional or family stories. The emphasis on personal meaning creation like that seen in Kurt's stories could also be an outgrowth of his culture's assumptions about the self. In this case, Kurt's mother's "interested but nondirective mode" that "permits him maximal latitude to concentrate on his train of thought and to author the narrations himself" (p. 100) would reflect a whole set of cultural assumptions not only about mother-child interaction and narrative but also about the self.

In the *Peter Rabbit* study, Miller and her colleagues have presented a compelling analysis of the affective dimensions of one child's retellings of a particular narrative. Their work raises a host of interesting questions about the significance of narrative to affective development and the role that culture may play in determining that significance. Answers to those questions obviously depend on further study—not large-scale, cross-sectional studies of groups of children, but additional intensive case studies of individual children from a variety of cultural backgrounds, as the nature of the research question demands.

REFERENCES

DeHart, G. (1990). Young children's linguistic interaction with mothers and siblings. Doctoral dissertation, University of Minnesota, 1990. *Dissertation Abstracts International, 51,* 3156B.

Eisenberg, A. R. (1985). Learning to describe past experiences in conversation. *Discourse Processes, 8,* 177–204.

Heath, S. B. (1983). *Ways with words: Language, life, and work in communities and classrooms.* New York: Cambridge University Press.

Markus, H. R., & Kitayama, S. (1991). Culture and the self: Implications for cognition, emotion, and motivation. *Psychological Review, 98,* 224–253.

McCabe, A., & Peterson, C. (Eds.). (1991). *Developing narrative structure.* Hillsdale, NJ: Lawrence Erlbaum Associates.

Miller, P. J., & Moore, B. B. (1989). Narrative conjunctions of caregiver and child: A comparative perspective on socialization through stories. *Ethos, 17,* 43–64.

Miller, P. J., Potts, R., Fung, H., Hoogstra, L., & Mintz, J. (1990). Narrative practices and the social construction of self in childhood. *American Ethologist, 17,* 292–311.

Miller, P. J., & Sperry, L. L. (1988). Early talk about the past: The origins of conversational stories of personal experience. *Journal of Child Language, 15,* 293–315.

Nelson, K. (Ed.). (1989). *Narratives from the crib.* Cambridge, MA: Harvard University Press.

Pratt, M. W., & MacKenzie-Keating, S. (1985). Organizing stories: Effects of development and task difficulty on referential cohesion in narrative. *Developmental Psychology, 21,* 350–356.

Sachs, J. (1983). Talking about the there and then: The emergence of displaced reference in parent-child discourse. In K. E. Nelson (Ed.), *Children's language* (Vol. 4, pp. 1–28). New York: Gardner Press.

Triandis, H. C. (1989). The self and social behavior in differing cultural contexts. *Psychological Review, 96,* 506–520.

7 Children's Memory for Other People: An Integrative Review

Graham M. Davies
University of Leicester

On February 4th 1990, 7-year-old Julie was roller skating back to her home on the outskirts of Brighton, England. As she passed a red car parked at the side of the road, she was seized from behind by a man who forced her into the trunk and then drove off. In the darkness of the trunk, Julie found a hammer which she used to bang on the door. The man told her to "shut up." Later she was to recall, "I heard gravel from the road hitting the car. There was music, I can't remember what kind, coming from inside the car. I hit on the door with the hammer. I took the roller boots off because if he opened the trunk I could get away quicker."

The man drove Julie to a remote spot on the Sussex Downs before sexually assaulting her, strangling her and leaving her for dead. Julie was found wandering, naked and dazed, by a couple who fetched the police. At the time of Julie's disappearance police were already on the trail of a man for child abduction after a young girl of eight had noted down the registration plate of a car which had tailed her and a friend as they walked home. Police traced the plate to a red Ford Cortina driven by Russell Bishop, a 24-year-old local man.

Julie had described the man who attacked her as being "a man in his 30s or 40s, dressed in blue with a moustache." She had little chance to see his face when she was attacked, but had the presence of mind to notice the gold wristwatch and strap on his arm as he clutched at her. Apart from the discrepancy of age, the description was consistent with Bishop's known appearance and 3 days after the attack he was placed on a line-up which Julie, still recovering from her injuries, attended. She had no hesitation in picking out Bishop who was then arrested and charged with attempted murder, indecent assault, and kidnapping.

At Bishop's trial in December 1990, Julie testified from behind a screen in the courtroom concerning her memory of the incident and reaffirmed her identification. In addition to Julie's evidence, the police had forensic evidence linking Bishop to semen stains on the child's tracksuit and tire marks at the attack site matched Bishop's car. Bishop chose to plead not guilty, but faced with such overwhelming evidence the jury had little hesitation in bringing in a guilty verdict. Bishop received a life sentence. Julie is making a good recovery. Subsequently, police confirmed that Bishop was the same man who had been unsuccessfully prosecuted for the murder of two young girls just 3 years previously (London *Times* 16.11.90; 14.12.90).

In England and Wales, as in many State legislatures in the US, identification evidence alone is sufficient to mount a successful prosecution in a criminal trial. Despite the horrifying nature of her attack, Julie was able to accurately select the man responsible and her choice was amply confirmed by the forensic evidence linking him to the crime.

But how representative is Julie of the prowess of children in general at recognizing strangers? And how, if at all, do children's competencies at such everyday tasks develop and mature with age? To answer such questions demands scrutiny of two contrasting literatures; studies of the development of face processing on the one hand and research on juvenile eyewitness testimony on the other. In general, researchers in these two camps have pursued very different agendas and, not surprisingly, have on occasion emerged with rather different conclusions.

Students of face processing have studied children for the clues the ontogeny of the process provides for models of face recognition in mature adults. Researchers into juvenile testimony have been concerned with such practical issues as the likely reliability of witnesses of different ages in courts of law. As I have argued elsewhere (Davies, in press) such *pure* and *applied* research has different goals and different priorities. Laboratory research tends to be driven by theory, to emphasize elucidation of basic mechanisms and to be judged by the rigor of control and precision of measurement. Applied research, by contrast, tends to be problem oriented and is judged by the degree to which the paradigms employed capture the real world events that they seek to simulate.

It is argued that neither approach can in itself provide an ecologically sound description of children's ability to recognize others. The more traditional theory-driven research ignores the affective and social dimension of person recognition and divorces it from the everyday context in which the process occurs. The more practically oriented applied research tends to produce results which are situation-specific and frequently ignores the broader cognitive developmental issues underlying performance. Contrasting these two research traditions will be useful for the study of memory in general and memory and affect in particular.

DEVELOPMENTAL STUDIES OF FACE PROCESSING

This section surveys the major methods and findings from experimental studies on face recognition and considers the strengths—and limitations—of such an approach.

Basic Paradigm and Findings

In contrast to the literature on face perception in infancy (see, for instance, Nelson & Ludemann (1989) for a review) the study of face recognition in children has developed few novel research techniques. Like early research on children's memory in general (Goulet, 1968) it has been generally content to adapt techniques originally developed for adults. Although such a procedure has advantages in terms of direct comparisons of normative data between adults and children, it can only proscribe the range of issues that are explored.

Thus, the most frequently employed paradigm involves the sequential exposure of children to a set of photographs of unfamiliar faces (the study set), each exposed for between 5 and 20 seconds, which must then be recognized either as a serial task where the study faces are intermixed with novel distracters (test set) or by means of a two-alternative, forced-choice task. Measures of performance begin with the simplicity of counting items correct and move on to more sophisticated measures based on signal detection theory (Banks, 1970) such as d' or A'. Typically, such experiments utilize large numbers of target faces in the study set (between 15 and 20) and minimal delay (no more than 5–20 minutes). Data derived from them has been taken to provide some global assessment of the strengths and weaknesses of children's face recognition competencies and as a starting point for theory.

Such studies demonstrate a general improvement in accuracy within an age range from 5- to 10-years-of-age whether measured by serial (Cross, Cross, & Daly, 1971) or forced choice (Goldstein & Chance, 1964, 1965) methods. As Flin and Dziurawiec (1989) observe, this technique does not lend itself to studies of preschool children; there is a dearth of research on the perceptual processing competencies of toddlers. The picture from age 10 to 14 years yields more studies but somewhat confusing results. A number of researchers, beginning with Carey, Diamond, and Woods (1980) and Flin (1980) have reported a regression in performance in early adolescence, though the form of the regression and its age of onset seems to vary quite widely between studies.

In Carey et al.'s (1980) original study this dip in performance occurred between 12- and 14-years-of-age, while for Flin (1980) it was somewhat earlier at 11–12 years. A number of subsequent studies have reported similar declines in performance on faces, though there is little consistency in the precise age of onset or magnitude of the effect: Sometimes the drop is statistically insignificant, whereas on other occasions performance of effected adolescents has fallen below the norms for 10-year-olds (see Flin, 1985a for a review). Although occasional failures to replicate have been reported (Chance, Turner, & Goldstein, 1982; Thomson 1984), the ubiquity of the finding suggests this is a true finding rather than a sampling artifact of a cross-sectional design. Some researchers have seen this regression as specific to faces but similar dips have been reported for other homogeneous stimulus sets such as faces or flags (Flin, 1985b). Beyond this period of turbulence, performance rapidly asymptotes to adult levels (Ellis, Shepherd, & Bruce, 1973).

A range of other subject factors have been explored using variations on this paradigm. As with adults (Ellis & Deregowski, 1981) children perform better at recognizing faces of their own race compared to another (Cross, Cross, & Daily 1971; Feinman & Entwisle, 1976). The 'other race' effect appears to increase with age (Chance et al., 1982) though with cross-sectional designs it is difficult to rule out the possibility that any widening discrepancy in performance is an artifact of a general growth in competence at this particular face recognition task. Again, as with the adult literature (Shepherd, 1981), there are few indications of any overall differences in competency between males and females, nor, within the limited range tested, has mental age been found to predict face recognition accuracy (Chance & Goldstein, 1984).

Apart from race of face, there are few stimulus variables that have been explored systematically from a developmental perspective. Ellis and Flin (1990) report that increases in exposure time lead to higher accuracy for 10-year-olds but not 7-year-olds which they interpret in terms of a metacognitive deficiency in their younger children. A recent study by Davies and Robertson (in press) explored the role of interest factors which have been shown to have potent effects on young children's recall (Chi, 1978). This study compared the ability of boys and girls aged 7, 9, and 11 years and adults to recognize sets of faces and popular cars. Cars were less accurately recognized than faces for the 11-year-old and adult groups. Moreover, all subjects applied a more lax criterion to their recognition of the vehicles: They were more ready to respond positively that they had seen a car before, irrespective of whether it was a target or foil. Unusually, sex of observer contributed to the results: Males outperformed females on cars while females enjoyed a modest advantage over males on faces. The latter result may owe something to the use of exclusively female faces as target material. The superiority of the males on cars can plausibly be linked to interest factors which was reflected in their greater ability to label the vehicles and recognize them in an altered view.

One area that has received considerable attention has been the impact of disguise and fragmentary viewing on face recognition, factors of potentially practical as well as theoretical importance. Such studies were originally undertaken to assess the relative contribution of different parts or features of the face to successful recognition (Shepherd, Davies, & Ellis, 1981). Much of the data collected from children showed striking similarities to that from adults. Thus, children found upper features more informative than lower and the eye area proved a better clue than the mouth, with front views of noses proving least informative of all (Goldstein & Mackenberg, 1966). When assessed by the ability to identify school mates from such fragmentary data, a clear developmental improvement was present from age 4 to age 10.

Whether the ability to recognize fragmentary parts of faces sheds real light on the way faces are processed is debatable (Shepherd et al., 1981). Research (and newspaper competitions!) support the view that conventional faces are recognized as much by the relation between features as on the basis of the features themselves (Davies & Christie, 1982). Such a conclusion is supported by studies that have examined the factors the determine the basis of judgments of similarity for pairs of novel faces by observers of different ages. Pedelty, Levine, and Shevell (1985) asked groups of subjects from age 7 to adulthood to make such pairwise similarity judgments on a small population of faces. Multidimensional scaling revealed that the basis for these judgments remained surprisingly invariant over age and while some isolated features (e.g., hair) were important, relational measures (face width, distance between nose and lip) were also significant.

This stability in dimensional saliency was challenged by Carey (1978, 1981) in her studies of the impact of disguise on facial recognition. Diamond and Carey (1977) asked subjects aged 6- to 16-years to observe a number of novel faces which were then identified among a triad of alternatives. The foils consisted of models wearing the same paraphernalia (identical clothing, hairstyles, or glasses) as the target. Carey found that children below 10-years-of-age performed poorly on this task compared to older subjects, a result she interpreted in terms of a change in the way the faces were processed with age. Children below 10 years, argued Carey, relied on "piecemeal" information (isolated features) rather than the "configurational " cues (relationships between facial features) that typify the mature face processor. Not only is this view inconsistent with the saliency and multidimensional scaling data, there are also difficulties in accepting Carey's interpretation of her data.

First, the effects that Carey reported were exclusive to novel faces; children exposed to the faces of friends failed to show the effect. Second, Flin (1985a) has demonstrated that the effect is lost if faces that are discrepant in appearance are used as foils; Carey employed stand-ins who were physiogenically similar to the targets. Finally, Ellis (1990) demonstrated that the effect need not be based on the processing of discrete features but could be accomplished by quite gross transformations: Simply shrinking the size of the target face from study to test and introducing a foil that is the same physical size as the stimulus will induce large numbers of errors in 6-year-olds.

Ellis concludes that such studies demonstrate that preschoolers are generally just less skilled than their older compatriots at extracting invariant features from faces and that all transformations (clothing, disguise, expression changes) are uniformly detrimental to subsequent recognition accuracy.

In sum, research that has utilized the classic study-test paradigm portrays the recognition of a stranger's face as a gradually acquired skill that improves markedly between 5- and 10-years-of-age but pursues an erratic course thereafter. It is influenced by familiarity: Faces of different sex are equally well recognized but not those of a different race. Changes, such as masking or disguise severely limit recognition accuracy for those below 10-years-of-age, particularly where they effect areas of high density information such as the eyes or hair. There is no compelling evidence that the particular strategies for encoding information change qualitatively with age, any change being in the general proficiency of encoding skills.

Face processing methodology is a simple technique that has led to the economic generation of much useful and intriguing data about how faces are recognized by children and adults under a range of conditions. It has spawned a number of very powerful theories in which the various components of the recognition processes have been isolated and identified and face processing has been clearly differentiated from the processing of words and objects (Bruce & Young, 1986; Valentine, 1991).

The "modal model" of face processing incorporates three major components. The central feature is some form of face recognition unit which fires in response to a familiar face and recruits new units when confronted with novel faces. This in turn is connected to a processing device on the input side which detects and analyses facial stimuli. Face recognition units in turn are interfaced with a third system that contains other information about the person concerned. According to the modal model, face recognition always proceeds from detection, through stimulation of units, to access to the relevant sematic information, such as name, occupation and so on. Such models were derived from experimental data and case studies of brain injured patients (Ellis, Jeaves, Newcombe, & Young, 1986). The developmental implications of such models are only now being explored (Carey, 1992; Ellis, 1992).

However, the presence of orderly data and useful theories should not obscure the inevitable limitations of a purely laboratory-based approach. Not only are there indications that results may be over sensitive to small changes in procedure but the paradigm itself neglects many potentially powerful influences roaming through the real world of face recognition.

Methodological Sensitivities

The most influential of contemporary face processing theories, that of Bruce and Young (1986) distinguishes between a surface representation of faces derived from the specific picture observed and structural codes extracted from the picture which enable the observer to recognize the person from a variety of viewpoints.

Studies, like most of the developmental literature, which rely extensively on representing the same stimulus at test as is used at study run the risk of confounding picture processing skills with more fundamental face processing abilities.

Two examples underline the fragility of some of the laboratory data. Flin and Dziurawiec (1989) reproduce the results of an unpublished study of face processing in 7- and 10-year-old children where the nature of the pose of the face changed between study and test or was maintained. When pose was maintained from study to test, the normal superiority of the 10-year-olds was observed. However, changing the pose at test eliminated the age effect. Likewise, Ellis and Flin (1990) examined the impact of extending the delays between study and test from the usual few minutes to up to 1 week. They report that the usual superiority of 10-year-olds over 7-year-olds was present at immediate testing—but disappeared entirely when 1 week separated study and test, a result that was replicated and did not result from basement or ceiling effects.

Such findings appear to indicate that the face processing paradigm is sensitive to relatively small changes in procedure when employed with children. No doubt these fascinating results will be explored further with profit to the generalizability of face recognition theory (Ellis, 1992). However, they caution against the too ready extrapolation of laboratory findings to the real world of the child witness. Results from face processing experiments are routinely invoked to estimate children's eyewitness performance (e.g. Goldstein & Chance, 1964) when the conditions and factors operating in the real world may be very different to those in the laboratory. Some of these potentially confounding factors are briefly outlined next.

Ecological Validity

Face processing studies have a number of obvious and not so obvious differences to eyewitnesses in the real world. Two of these differences, the typically brief delays and the use of multiple targets have already been described. Others include the use of static, neutrally posed pictures which cut out potential body, clothing and movement cues that can be important for identification purposes (Davies, 1989). There may also be differences in mental set and level of affect, particularly if the witness is also a victim (Cole & Loftus, 1987). Further, faces are rarely glimpsed in isolation in the laboratory but rather in a physical context (Chance & Goldstein, 1984). In everyday life the use of such contextual cues has a powerful impact upon whether a face will be identified (Young, Hay, & Ellis, 1985). Not surprisingly perhaps, if contexts in the form of scenic backgrounds are introduced into the slides of faces used in laboratory studies, their removal or reinstatement strongly influences whether the face will be recognized subsequently (Davies & Milne, 1982; Markham, Ellis, & Ellis, 1991).

All of these factors make face processing studies, at best, an incomplete guide to the performance of children recognizing other people in applied settings. This uncertainty is underlined by the results of a study by Soppe (1986), which appears to be the only one so far to examine directly the predictive power of face processing studies. He reported no systematic relation for children aged 8–13 years between their ability to recognize one of two strangers who entered their classroom and performance on an orthodox face processing task. Clearly, single experiments of this kind may have low generalizability; in statistical terms it is the equivalent of a two item test (Shavelson & Webb, 1981). However, if replicated, such negative findings underline the importance of widening the data base of developmental studies of face processing before making strong inferences as to the likely levels of competence of children at different ages at eyewitness tasks.

EYEWITNESS TESTIMONY STUDIES

As indicated earlier the great majority of eyewitness studies have been motivated by concerns to ascertain the general competency of child witnesses of differing ages. Such practical concerns are of direct relevance to issues over the age at which children may safely be permitted to give testimony at trial and/or whether such testimony should be subject to a special caution to the jury from the judge during the summing up (Spencer & Flin, 1990). Much early research tended to take as its model, the witness as bystander. However, many recent studies have been conducted in the light of the continuing debate over the reliability of children's evidence in child abuse trials (Doris, 1991) and there have been increasing studies in which children interact directly with a stranger, as part either of a contrived incident or a naturally stressful event in the child's life. These three types of experiment have sometimes provided contrasting outcomes.

In areas of child physical and sexual abuse it has been frequently highlighted that the alleged abuser is a close relative, caretaker or neighbor whose identity is known to the child (Finkelhor, 1979). Given that children as young as 5 years of age are capable of recognizing their friends even when part of their face or hair is obscured (Goldstein & Mackenberg, 1966), such studies might be thought superfluous. However, recent analysis of actual sexual abuse cases coming before the courts in England and Wales suggest that there is a much greater tendency to prosecute in cases involving strangers. In a recent survey 22% of all cases coming before Courts in England and Wales involved an accused who was unknown to the child prior to the offense (Davies & Noon, 1991). Moreover, in some jurisdictions where rules concerning the appearance of children are more liberal, children are called as witnesses in a variety of other contexts. Flin, Bull, Boon, and Knox (1990) analyzing court citations in Glasgow, Scotland found that the most frequent appearances of juveniles were in cases in which children observed violent or unruly incidents in the street (52%). Clearly in such cases questions of identity and disputed identity are likely to figure strongly.

Paradigms and Findings

Given the forensic significance of identification evidence, it is surprising that so much of the existing literature has focused purely on one potential phase of the procedure: the identification of the accused from photographs. Typically, children observe a stranger, either as a result of a contrived incident or natural event; after an interval, they will be called up to select the stranger from an array of photographs. The prevalence of such studies probably says more about their logistical ease than the forensic prevalence of the process.

In the British legal system, most children who are witnesses to the actions of strangers will be interviewed by detectives who will take a written statement that contains a *verbal description* of the suspect. Subsequently, children may be asked to cooperate with a police technician to produce a *composite portrait,* either an artist's impression or a "face" assembled from a kit of features (an "Identikit" or "Photofit" picture). Lately such methods have been supplemented by computerized systems such as "E fit" or "Mac-A-Mug" (Clifford & Davies, 1989). Additionally, children may be asked to leaf through *mug books* containing photographs of as many as several hundred potential offenders (Ellis et al., 1989).

In the event of police inquiries turning up a potential suspect, the child may be called upon to make an identification. In Britain, such identifications are likely to be tested by the child's attendance at a live *line-up* or identification parade, where the accused will stand alongside 8 (as few as 5 in Scotland) innocent stand-ins and the child will be asked to chose the person they saw. They will be explicitly warned that the person may not be present and that they should only select someone if they are quite certain (see Shepherd, Ellis, & Davies, 1982, for the full British rules for the conduct of parades). Normally, identification by a child will be conducted from behind a one-way viewing screen. A second and legally less preferred alternative is *identification from photographs.* Here again, police procedure is prescribed by rules; these demand that the accused's portrait be placed beside 11 others, similar in age, build, and appearance. Occasionally and controversially, identification from photographs may precede attendance at a live line-up (Devlin, 1976). It is the latter process of photographic ID that is most satisfactorily simulated by the bulk of the child literature. Before turning to such studies, developmental research on the other phases of the identification process is briefly surveyed.

Verbal Recall

All investigations involving unknown suspects will include an initial attempt to establish basic appearance information to narrow the range of potential suspects. Memory studies of children's eyewitness testimony normally include a questioning or face report phase designed to test children's verbal recall, though many do not focus directly on recall of physical appearance as distinct from recall of events in general.

The classic finding, dating from the days of Binet (1900) and Sterne (1910, 1939) is that while the totality of information furnished by witnesses increases with age, the proportion of error remains remarkably constant. In an early study, Marin, Holmes, Guth, and Kovac (1979) contrived to have subjects aged from 6 years to adulthood observe a brief staged argument between 2 adults. The proportion of error in free reports (less than 10%) remained constant across age. A very similar finding was reported by Goodman and Read in a study involving 3-year-olds, 6-year-olds, and adults who played a participatory game with a stranger.

However, two reservations are necessary concerning such findings. First, the amount of information furnished by older children and adults is markedly greater than that of youngsters. In the Marin et al. study for instance, the adults recalled between five and six times as much information as the 6-year-olds whereas in the Goodman and Read study, the youngest group averaged less than one item of clothing or appearance information correct. Second, the actual type of information furnished changes at different ages. For the youngest children, spontaneous accounts tend to dwell upon action details (King & Yuille, 1986) and ignore all but the most striking physical characteristics of the actors (Dent & Stephenson, 1979a). Older children and adults, on the other hand, offer much more spontaneous information. In the study of Yuille, Cutshall, and King (1986) in which children observed the simulated theft of a bicycle, 10-year-olds spontaneously recalled nearly 90% more information relating to the appearance of the thief than did 8-year-olds.

It is possible to see here the operation of two developmental factors. On the one hand, it may reflect improvements in retrieval routines for episodic events which has been charted in a variety of laboratory tasks (Kail, 1990). On the other, there may be a growing metamnemonic awareness of the role of the witness and the societal demands of this task (Flin, Stevenson, & Davis, 1989).

When recall has focused on descriptive information alone, then a less positive picture emerges. Davies, Tarrant, and Flin (1989) conducted a simulated health inspection for children aged 6–7 and 10–11 years-of-age. The subsequent spontaneous comments of the children revealed a paucity of information about the inspector and the proportion of error among the younger group was significantly higher than for the older children. Where descriptive information was offered, hair was most frequently mentioned and accounted for over half the responses of the younger children. Other features mentioned in descending order of frequency included eyes (20%), freckles and spots (15%), and the nose (14%).

Action details by contrast were recalled much more readily and altogether more accurately: No errors occurred for either group in spontaneous accounts of the events they had experienced. These results are strikingly similar to those reported earlier by Yuille et al. (1986) in their bicycle theft study, where a similar pattern of minimal and inaccurate reporting of appearance information in the youngest children was combined with effective recall of events.

In order to build on such limited information it is necessary for researcher or police officer alike to probe further through the use of questions. Questioning can be open ended ("Tell me more about what he looked like"), focused ("Do you remember anything about his eyes?"), or closed ("Were his eyes close together or far apart?"). All such procedures appear to increase the amount of appearance detail provided, though at the cost of increased error. Moreover, such error rates are normally higher in younger children (Goetze, 1980; King & Yuille, 1986; List, 1986; Parker, Haverfield, & Baker-Thomas, 1986; Yuille et al., 1986). Different styles of questioning may offer different compromises between error and increased information (Dent & Stephenson, 1979a) but studies have failed to sample a wide enough age range or to focus questioning sufficiently on the person to provide guidance on the best method for eliciting identity information.

Information on height, weight, and age is frequently sought by investigators and appears to be a source of particular difficulty for children. In one study conducted by Davies, Stevenson-Robb, & Flin (1988) groups of children aged 7–8, 9–10 or 11–12 years interacted with an actor before being invited to estimate height, weight, and age. The proportion of children volunteering this information rose from 81% to 94% for the 11–12 year-olds. Children were most ready to estimate age (89%) followed by weight (59%) and height (51%). Accuracy on all three measures improved with age but was nevertheless not impressive: Accuracy was within acceptable limits on 27 to 33% of occasions amongst the oldest group. Comparable data have been reported by Goetz (1980), Brigham, Van Verst, and Bothwell (1986) and by Dent (1982). Ellis (in press) has provided convincing evidence that children below 10 years of age are simply less aware of age cues; they experience major difficulty in ordering a set of photographs of the same person at different ages, a task on which adults experience no difficulty.

Dent (1982) suggested that the problem of absolute judgment might be reduced if children were able to make judgments relative to a known figure such as a teacher or the experimenter. Davies et al. (1988) reported that such procedures did improve accuracy particularly for weight estimates, though there was still considerable variability. All studies to date lack adult controls, an important consideration, given the latter also find absolute judgments of height, weight, and age difficult (Flin & Shepherd, 1986).

Composite Production

The difficulties young children experience in furnishing accurate verbal descriptions of facial features has clear implications for composite production. All methods of composite production involve a preliminary phase in which a detailed verbal description is elicited in order to guide the technicians in their selection of relevant features. A photofit kit, for instance, contains 195 possible hairstyles and information on hair length, straightness and thickness is essential for effective selection.

Flin, Markham, and Davies (1989) asked children aged 8 and 11 years and adults to construct Photofit faces from a photograph that had been observed immediately prior to test. Under these laboratory conditions, the preliminary verbal descriptions of the adults proved a superior guide to likeness compared to those provided by the 11-year-olds which in turn were better than the 8-year-olds. This superiority in description also translated into quality of finished composites with accuracy improving with age. Overall quality of composites for both adults and children was not particularly high, with just over 50% of Photofits being accurately identified. Such limited accuracy is not uncommon with composite systems (Davies, 1981), a fact underlined by the consistent superiority of preliminary verbal descriptions as a guide to likeness compared to the composites they generated! A later, more forensically realistic study of Davies et al. (1989) also found a difference in quality of preliminary descriptions depending on the age of the subject, though on this occasion such differences did not translate into a significant superiority in overall composite quality.

Age and Preidentification Processes

In summary, existing studies of children's ability to recall facial and bodily information present a picture of steadily improving competence with age. This improvement is reflected both in terms of free and cued verbal recall of facial and bodily detail and estimates of height, weight, and age. Improvement in these skills seems particularly marked in the 6–11 year age group. In the case of faces, it extends not merely to verbal descriptive ability but also to the selection of facial components, which accurately reflect the appearance of the individual concerned. Moreover, there is evidence that inaccuracies are not only disproportionately higher among younger subjects in response to questioning about person detail but also extend to spontaneous statements about physical appearance. The latter finding deviates from the traditional view that younger subjects are less complete in their free recall of events but no less accurate than their older peers.

However, before fully accepting this somewhat gloomy prognosis, it is as well to invoke one of the lessons of contemporary developmental research: The danger of judging tasks from too adult a perspective. Widespread generalizations about the competencies (and incompetencies) of children have foundered on the fact that small changes in procedure or instructions may produce radically different patterns of response (Donaldson, 1978). There are at least some indications that the performance of younger children can be improved appreciably by the provision of social support. Moston and Engleberg (1992) studied the recall of 7- and 10-year-old children for a classroom incident. The 10-year-olds recalled more information and resisted leading questions better than the 7-year-olds. However, when the 7-year-olds were given the opportunity to discuss the event with a friend and the friend accompanied them at interview, the age difference was sharply attenuated. Likewise Goodman, Bottoms, and Schwartz-Kenney (1991a) interviewed 3–4 and 5–7 year-old children about their memories of a visit to a health clinic for inoculations. Children were either interviewed in a cool, detached way or in a warmer, more empathic and encouraging manner. The usual superiority of recall of the older over younger subjects was found under the impersonal style of interrogation. However, the introduction of nonspecific reinforcement increased accuracy for both age groups and in the case of leading questions, actually eliminated the age effect entirely.

In such findings, there are indications that age effects in orthodox experiments may not entirely reflect real differences in encoding competence. Further research is required that focuses specifically on person recall rather than recall for the event in general. Moreover, it needs to be clarified whether such socially facilitative effects cause equivalent increments to subjects of all ages or whether these effects are disproportionately greater among very young children. Clearly, exploration of such effects are not merely of theoretical interest but also practical utility in developing facilitative interviewing procedures.

EYEWITNESS IDENTIFICATION STUDIES

Three types of study have contributed to knowledge of children's competency at eyewitness identification. As the aims and sometimes the results of these studies are different, each is reviewed in turn.

Staged Incidents: Target Present Arrays

The first and historically oldest group of studies are those that use a staged incident and which subsequently require the child to identify the perpetrator from a photographic array containing the latter's picture and a number of foils. A listing of these studies is shown in Table 7.1.

As can be observed, the range of incidents has varied from the totally passive (observation of a sequence of slides; Parker, Haverfield, & Baker-Thomas, 1986) to the active and involving (games with an adult; Goodman & Reed, 1986). Likewise the nature of the incident has ranged from the innocuous (observing a man tending seedlings; King & Yuille, 1986) to the convincingly frightening (a staged theft where children were only debriefed subsequent to the photo task; Brigham, Van Verst, & Bothwell, 1986). Length of observation and duration of delay prior to test have also varied, though all studies have used relatively small arrays of between 5 and 7 photographs. Surprisingly, in these circumstances, there has been a marked absence of effects due to age of witness.

Two studies that incorporated adult controls failed to find an effect for age with children as young as 5 years (Marin, Holmes, Guth, & Kovac, 1979) and 8 years (Parker et al., 1986). Studies by Goetze (1980) and Soppe (1986) which used representative groups of subjects between 8 and 13 years found no simple relationship between age and competence. In Goetze's study, poorest perfor-

TABLE 7.1
Summary of Studies of Children's Eyewitness Competency Using Contrived Incidents and
"Target Present" Arrays Only

Experimenters	Subjects	Incident	Delay	Array	Result	Comment
1. Marin et al. (1979)	5 yrs, 8 yrs, 11 yrs & adults (n = 96)	Argument between 2 adults (15 sec)	10 min or 30 min	6 person array	5 yrs (54%), 8 yrs (45%), 11 yrs (75%), adults (54%)	No sig. age effect. No "not present" option
2. Goetze (1980)	8 yrs, 11 yrs, 13 yrs (n = 72)	Staged purse snatch (12 min, 45 sec	20 min	6 person array	8 yrs (42%) 11 yrs (25%) 12 yrs (17%)	No significant age effect
3. Goodman & Reed (1988)	3 yrs, 6 yrs, and adults (n = 48)	Copy movement made by adults (5 min)	4/5 days	5 person array	3 yrs (38%) 6 yrs (95%) adults (74%)	3 yr olds. Sig. worse. No effect of simultaneous vs. sequential presentation
4. King & Yuille (1986)	6 yrs, 10, yrs, 12 yrs and 17 yrs (n = 80)	Observed stranger who spoke briefly (2 min)	10 min	8 person array	6 yrs (45%); other groups (82-100%)	6 yr olds sig. worse. Otherwise no sig. age effect
5. Parker, Haverfield & Baker-Thomas (1986)	"children" (Mean age 8 yrs) & adults (n = 96)	Slide sequence of picnic incident (15 sec)	immediate testing	6 person array	50% correct identification	No sig. age effect. Child and adult targets employed
6. Soppe (1986)	8 yrs, 9 yrs, 10 yrs, 11 yrs, 12 yrs and 13 yrs (n = 283)	2 men talked to class (2 min)	3 days	8 person array	Target 1 : 12 yr olds (59%) sig. worse than others (68-84%) no difference target 2 : (31-38%)	Big variation between targets. No sig. age effect except "dip" at 12 for Target 1. No "not present" option
7. Brigham, Van Verst & Bothwell (1986)	9 yrs, 10 yrs & 16 yrs (n = 120)	Staged theft of tape recorder (30 sec)	10-15 min	6 person array	9 yrs (68%), 14 yrs (93%) 16 yrs (88%)	9 yr olds sig. worse. No effect for authority of interrogator. "Not present" explicit

mance was found in the 13-year group while the 12-year-olds of Soppe were significantly poorer in recognition of one of two targets than all other age groups, both findings reminiscent of the "dip" effects found in face processing studies.

The one study to use children as young as 3 years did report significantly poorer performance relative to 6-year-olds, but the latter performed on a par with adults (Goodman & Reid, 1986). The equivalence of 6-year-old and adult performance was not repeated by King and Yuille (1986) who found them inferior in accuracy to all older age groups who again did not differ. It could be argued that Goodman and Reed's incident was more involving for the child and included a longer and stronger interaction with the stranger, though the delay period was much shorter (10 minutes versus 4–5 days). The only other study to find younger children inferior was Brigham et al (1986) who, uniquely, reported that 9-year-olds were inferior to 14- or 16-year-olds. Significantly, perhaps, this study was probably the most stressful for all subjects with the belief that they had observed a real crime extending to the point of choosing from the array. Brigham et al. (1986) do not report any observational data on perceived stress levels, but clearly a replication of this study with debriefing being given before or after photo choice might shed light on this intriguing but otherwise aberrant finding. Overall, however, in contrast to the recall data, there is little evidence from these studies of a strong and consistent age effect.

Staged Incidents: Target Present and Absent Arrays

However, as potential guides to the performance of actual witnesses in line-up tasks, studies in this first category contain a major flaw: the photographic arrays always contain the target. As Wells (1988) and others have pointed out, such an assumption that the perpetrator is present cannot be made in real eyewitness contexts. In order to develop representative assessments of the competencies of witnesses of different ages at eyewitness tasks it is necessary to include test arrays from which the target is absent as well as those where he or she is present. These latter studies form the second and more recent group of experiments on children's witnessing capacities.

These studies in Table 7.2 present the same range of realism and degree of involvement as those from Table 7.1 and equally there is some variability in outcome. Once again, however, the results from the target present conditions show little indication of any consistent age effect. Although some researchers report a nonsignificant trend for older children to be more accurate (Davies et al., 1989; Yarmey, 1988), these are countered by at least one which found an inverse pattern (Parker & Carranza, 1989) and others where no clear age trend emerged (Davies et al., 1988; Leippe, Romanczyk, & Manion, 1991; Yuille, Cutshall, & King, 1986). However, these studies are noticeable for the lack of identified groups of very young (3–5 year-old) children, though the absence of age effect beyond 6 years is again impressive. Once more, there seems no consistent relationship between outcome, delay or the nature of the incident, though unlike Brigham et al., there are no studies that include stress at the time of choosing.

However, it is the target absent data that provides the most insightful findings. Studies with adults demonstrate that error rates on such arrays, where any choice must by definition be incorrect, tend to be higher than on target present pho-

TABLE 7.2
Summary of Studies of Children's Eyewitness Competency Using Contrived Incidents and "Target Present" and "Target Absent" Arrays

Experimenters	Subjects	Incident	Delay	Array	Result	Comment
8. Yuile, Cutshall & King (1979)	8/9 yrs, 10/11 yrs & 12/14 yrs (n = 139 across 2 studies)	Simulated bicycle theft (1 min)	Immediate testing	8 person array	Present: 8/9 yrs (64%) 10/11 yrs (70%) 12/14 yrs (68%) Absent: 8/9 yrs (15%) 10/12 yrs (39%0 12/14 yrs (58%)	No age effect (Data collapsed across studies) V. significant age effect High false alarm rates
9. Yarmey (1988)	4/8 yrs, 9/12 yrs, 20/37 yrs & 25/47 yrs (n = 154)	Video of simulated abduction	1 day	6 person array	Present: 4/8 yrs (59%) 9/12 yrs (76%) 20/37 yrs (72%) Absent: no difference across age	4/8 yr olds more confident on both subject present and absent arrays 4/8 yrs more lax in choosing
10. Davies, Stevenson-Robb & Flin (1988)	7/8 yrs, 8/10 yrs & 11/12 yrs (n = 96)	Assist adult with demonstration (5 min)	2 weeks	12 person array	Present: 7/8 yrs (63%) 9/10 yrs (63%) 11/12 yrs (69%) Absent: 7/8 yrs (13%) 9/10 yrs (50%) 11/12 yrs (44%)	No age effect Sig. age effect No modeling effect (low n)

	Subjects	Task (time)	Delay	Array	Results	Conclusions
11. Parker & Carranza (1989)	"children" (mean age = 9 yrs) and adults (n = 96)	Slide sequence of picnic incident (15 sec)	Immediate testing	6 person array	Present: children (42%) adults (25%) Absent: children (25%) adults (46%)	No age effect on either array Overall, children more likely to choose
12. Davies, Tarrant & Flin (1989)	6/7 yrs, 10/11 yrs (n = 128)	Simulated health inspection (5 min)	1 week	8 person array	Present: 6/7 yrs (47%) 10/11 yrs (72%) Absent: 6/7 yrs (78%) 10/11 yrs (81%)	No sig. age effect on either array. Choosing control ineffective.
13. Leippe, Romanczyk & Manion (1991)	5/6 yrs, 9/10 yrs and adults (n = 84)	Touching test (6 min)	Immediate	6 person array	Present: 5/6 yrs (79%) 9/10 yrs (63%) adults (93%) Absent: 5/6 yrs (67%) 9/10 yrs (87%) adults (92%)	No sig. age effect on either array. No greater rate of choosing by younger children
14. Peters (1991)	3/6 yrs (n = 68)	Simulated health check (2 min)	1 week	5 person array	Present: 56% Absent: 34%	Sig. relationship anxiety X correct choosing (.27) No age effect reported
15. Peters (1991)	6/9 yrs (n = 64)	Fire alert by adult (1 min)	Immediate	6 person array	Present: 52% (alarm) 71% (no alarm) Absent: 36% (alarm) 60% (no alarm)	No age data reported. Alarm disrupted performance sig. relative to no alarm

tospreads (Malpass & Devine, 1981). With the occasional exception (Davies et al., 1989), this is the general finding with child witnesses (Peters, 1991). However, a number of studies have reported that younger children experience particular difficulties in rejecting such arrays. Yuille et al. (1986) were the first to report a consistent and significant relationship between age and rate of choosing from the blank array, a result that has been subsequently replicated by Davies et al. (1988) and Parker and Carranza (1989). A similar trend was observed by Leippe et al. (1991), but on this occasion it fell short of significance. While occasional failures to replicate have been reported (Davies et al., 1989; Yarmey, 1988), there seems little doubt that this is a real effect.

Why should younger children be particularly vulnerable to target absent arrays? Potentially, the effect could be derived from differences in encoding, storage or retrieval processes at different ages, or some combination of these. However, most interpretations have focused on retrieval as the major source of difficulty for the younger witness. High false alarm rates reflect sociocognitive pressures ("suggestibility"): The presence of the array creating a setting where there is a strong demand characteristic to choose. There is an implicit assumption that the array contains the target, which is immune to the formal instructions that normally include an admonition that the target may not be present.

What evidence is there that age and frequency of choosing are positively correlated? Certainly a number of researchers have reported significantly higher rates of rejection of arrays, irrespective of whether the target is present or not, among older subjects (Parker & Carranza, 1989; Yarmey, 1988; Yuille et al., 1986), but this result is by no means invariable (Davies et al., 1989; Leippe et al., 1991). To sustain the demand characteristic explanation it is necessary to demonstrate that higher rates of choosing extend to target present as well as absent arrays and the data are as yet unconvincing on this point.

Given the ubiquity with which this explanation has been proposed, one might expect to find more support from studies that have tested directly its prediction. Authority figures who in other contexts increased children's *suggestibility* effects (Ceci, Ross, & Toglia, 1987) did not have any impact on rates of choosing in the one published study to manipulate the status of the interviewer (Brigham et al., 1986). Likewise, manipulation of the way in which the array is presented (simultaneous versus successive viewing) again had no effect upon choosing rates (Goodman & Reed, 1986).

Efforts to reduce the demand characteristics of arrays for younger children have also not met with great success. Yuille et al. (1986) suggested that children might be trained to search for the experimenter's face in target present and absent arrays prior to the crucial array. Davies et al. (1988) provided training arrays of this type to half their subjects but it failed to have any significant impact on their pattern of choosing from both target present and absent arrays. However, cell size for this comparison was quite small and statistical power attenuated. A subsequent study by Goodman et al. (1991a) used a more elaborate training routine and reported a significant facilitation for their 5–6 year group but not the 3–4 year-olds.

A rather different approach was adopted by Davies et al. (1989) which focused on the need of children to make a choice from the array. Half of their children received an orthodox array while the remainder had an array including an additional "Mr. Nobody" cartoon face incorporating a question mark. Children who received the latter array were invited to select Mr. Nobody in addition to the usual instructions about rejecting the array if the target was not present. Mr. Nobody had no impact on overall accuracy though there was a general shift to greater caution on both target present and absent arrays.

An alternative explanation might lie in terms of defective encoding: A failure of attention at the time of observation among younger children. This could arise simply through youngsters looking less at the target during the initial confrontation than youths or adults, though Goodman and Reed (1986) found no simple relation between looking time and accuracy of identification. As has been noted, there are similar equivocal results in the face processing literature. If the looking hypothesis were correct, one might expect to find some relation between the degree of personal involvement of the initial contact and subsequent performance on target present and absent arrays. Scrutinizing Table 7.2 suggests some tentative support for this view: those contexts where there is physical interaction between target and perceiver (Davies et al. 1989; Leippe et al. 1991) show less of a target absent effect than those where the child is a bystander (Davies et al. 1988; Yuille et al. 1986) or passive observer (Parker & Carranza, 1989). Clearly, there is scope for more studies that address issues of involvement and looking in a direct way through the participant/bystander paradigm (Goodman, Rudy, Bottoms, & Aman, 1991).

Another hypothesis worthy of exploration is that the presentation and storage of facial information does not receive high priority by young children; more attention is given to the activities that accompany the interaction rather than the actors (Leippe et al., 1991). Some support for this view comes from Yarmey's study of "street proofing": A lecture designed to emphasize the importance of observation and "stranger-danger" to young children. Such training induced the 9–12 year age group (but not the 4–8 years) to adapt a stricter criterion in making choices, but there was no indication of any improved accuracy of recognition, though an effect was found for recall of identity information (cf. Yuille et al., 1986).

If storage procedures were defective in younger children a disproportionate effect of delay might be expected on performance with age. Such an effect has recently been reported by Flin, Boon, Knox, and Bull (1992) for verbal recall of the details of an event; 6 and 9 year olds were disproportionately effected compared to adults by a delay of 5 months relative to an immediate test. However, the latter study did not include an identification task. Published studies in the literature that have included delay as a variable have failed so far to find on age/delay interaction though only relatively short delays have been employed (Goodman et al., 1991b; Marin et al., 1979; Peters, 1987, 1991).

However, all explanations that permit an encoding or storage deficit have to explain why there are so few examples of target present arrays inducing a consistent and significant effect for age of observer. Odd findings of equivalence might be explained by ceiling or basement effects but overall accuracy levels rarely confirm this possibility. On the other hand a retrieval-based suggestibility explanation seems insufficient in itself to explain all current data. There is a need for more studies that address directly such hypotheses rather than having them invoked in a post-hoc manner.

Such incident studies would also benefit from improvements in design to ensure that results enjoyed a degree of generality. One improvement would be to use a number of different actors to play the target rather than a single individual. Again, studies based on performance with one or two targets inevitably run the risk of low generalizability being equivalent to 1- or 2-item tests (Shavelson & Webb, 1981). A second concern would be the inclusion of more adult controls with whom the performance of children could be compared. The use of adolescents as the oldest group always run the risk of embracing a Carey/Flin regression in performance that would hamper comparability. If adults are employed, comparability in terms of ability range and social background is essential. Yarmey (1988) found a 20% difference in identification rate between a sample of parents of the children he tested (a very good control) and a college sample. A third consideration is that instructions should always emphasize the possibility that the target is not present. Some influential studies (Marin et al., 1979; Soppe, 1966) have not done so, making it difficult to partial out effects of accuracy and readiness to choose.

Such design problems are readily resolved, but other limitations such as the low levels of arousal and affect typical of contrived incidents are less easily overcome in an ethical science. However, the ingenuity of researchers has produced new ways of exploring such factors by exploiting naturally occurring stress and affect in children's lives. Such studies, triggered by the pioneering research of Goodman, Aman, and Hirschman (1987) have broken new ground but also raised new controversies over the competencies of child witnesses.

Memory and Affect

Recent years have seen a change in the style of research on identification by children; from child as bystander to child as victim. It is reflected in the gap between Marin et al.'s pioneering study where the child is an onlooker to a dispute between adults and the more recent studies where children physically interact with a stranger (Davies et al., 1989; Leippe et al., 1991; Peters, 1991). This in turn reflects a change in the target behavior that the experiment is designed to model: from child witness to child victim, most commonly of sexual abuse.

This concern with child witnesses as victims has gone hand in hand with a growing interest in the role of stress and arousal on performance. The relation of emotion to memory has a long research tradition (Rapaport, 1942); the problem has always been one of ethically inducing significant amounts of stress within an effectively controlled experimental paradigm. Goodman et al. (1987) introduced the idea of using potentially painful medical events from the child's life as source material for stress and testimony studies.

In their initial study Goodman et al. contrasted the impact of stressful and nonstressful versions of the same event on subsequent recall and recognition. A group of 9 children attended a clinic to have blood extracted for medical screening. After a delay of 3–4 days, they were tested on their recall of events and participants and asked to select a photograph of the technician involved from a 6 person, target-present array. Performance was compared to a group of matched controls who attended the clinic to have a transfer smoothed on their arm by the technician. Parental ratings confirmed the expected differences in perceived levels of overall stress between the two groups. When tested 3–4 days later, the groups did not differ in their recall of personal details of the technician nor in their ability to select that person from a target-present array. Age was unrelated to identification accuracy.

A second, larger-scale study compared the performance of children aged 3–4 years and 5–6 years in their ability to remember a visit to a clinic for a number of inoculations. Separate groups of children were tested after delays of 3–4 and 5–6 days. Description accuracy was unaffected by delay but 3–4 year-olds were less accurate than the 5–6 year-olds. Both age groups performed equivalently at the shorter delay though the 5–6 year-olds did better at the longer delay, the 3–4 year-olds performing at chance. Children's overall stress levels were rated from videofilm of the incident and compared to their ability to identify the technician: No simple relation emerged between stress ratings and identification accuracy, although the recall data showed a trend for the highest levels of stress to be associated with superior recall. Around half the sample were reinterviewed 1 year later and again asked to select the target from an array; on this occasion only 14% of children were able to identify the technician correctly (Goodman et al., 1991b).

Goodman et al. (1987, 1991b) interpret their data as demonstrating that high levels of emotional arousal at the time of an incident do not preclude effective recall and recognition. On the contrary, following Easterbrook (1959), Goodman argues that the impact of stress may be to channel attention onto the central features of an event at the expense of more peripheral aspects. According to this view, amount of attentional capacity is finite under all conditions, but high arousal induces a tradeoff between central and peripheral detail.

This position has been the subject of a sustained critique by Peters (1987, 1991) and others who argue that the impact of stress on performance in children, as in adults, is to disrupt rather than facilitate retention. Peters (1991) summarizes the results of a number of studies using a variety of paradigms that he has conducted using child witnesses. Two studies involved the use of stressful events from the children's own lives in the manner of Goodman. In the first (Peters, 1987) a large group of children aged 3–8 years on their first or second visit to the dentist were assessed for their memory of the experience after delays of 1–2 days or 3–4 weeks. A series of target present and target absent recognition tests assessed memory for the dentist, the dental nurse, and the room used for treatment. Peters manipulated stress by (a) taking ratings of the child's behavior at the time of treatment and comparing these with later performance, (b) by comparing the ability of children to recognize their dentist with their subsequent ability after a comparable delay to recognize the researcher who had tested them.

Peters reported little support for Goodman's contention that stress preserves or improves memory. Rated stress levels during treatment were negatively correlated with subsequent ability to recognize both the dentist (−.32) and dental nurse (−.21) but only for target present arrays. Recognition of the dentist (71% accuracy) was significantly better than for the researcher (43%). Age of witness significantly influenced performance on only one of the set of recognition tests (for the researcher, target present) and delay too had no consistent effects upon performance. As with the more orthodox experiments summarized in Table 7.2, target present arrays produced fewer errors than those from which the target was absent.

Peters (1987) concluded that, contrary to Goodman, stress impairs the performance of children. Certainly, there was little evidence for a focusing effect: recognition of treatment rooms was not consistently lower than for the main participants. However, there are design weaknesses, even in this ingenious study. The stress comparison suffers from the fact that average ratings of stress in the treatment condition were relatively low (only 1 child actually received treatment) while the rated stress at time of interview was relatively high (a stranger in the home) (Cole & Loftus, 1987). Moreover, the use of different target persons for the high and low stress conditions potentially confounds stress with target distinctiveness; the children may not have looked at the dentist and focused instead on the nurse (nurses received highest ratings overall for recognition accuracy).

A second study reported by Peters (1991) used an inoculation paradigm similar to Goodman et al. (1987). Children aged 3–9 years were assessed for their perceived level of anxiety while being given shots and then interviewed either 1 day or 10–14 days later. A parallel group of children attended the clinic to hear a lecture on immunization from the same nurse before being interviewed after similar delays. The interview covered the nurse's appearance and offered the opportunity to select the nurse from either a target present or target absent array.

Much larger between-group differences in overall levels of perceived stress were obtained by this manipulation but few differences in memory performance. The two groups did not differ either in accuracy of description of the nurse's appearance or in the ability to select the nurse from either type of array. An effect was, however, found for recognition of the rooms, where the high anxiety group were significantly poorer (38% accuracy) compared to the low (94%) on a target present array. Partitioning the subjects into three age groups revealed significant effects for both identification and description with performance improving with age.

This second study appears to offer more comfort to Goodman than Peters. To the extent that the room details can be regarded as peripheral, the data are consistent with a channeling effect. The children in the low stress condition, however, were taking part as a class rather than an individual encounter. Perhaps the inoculation lecture, however well delivered, might have caused the attention of the low stress subjects to wander.

What of other researchers, less committed to the stress debate, who have reported immunization studies? These and other findings from such 'natural' experiments are summarized in Table 7.3.

Steward (1989) studied the reports of 130 children aged 3–7 years who attended a pediatric outpatient clinic for examination. As part of a complex design that included different styles of interviewing and the use of aids such as dolls, children provided information on the appearance of medical staff and attempted to select those mentioned from target present arrays. Testing occurred immediately following the visit and again at 1 month and 6 months for those children who agreed to participate.

The procedure of only testing identification for those persons mentioned by the child is forensically realistic but makes an objective comparison across delays difficult. The accuracy rates reported (in excess of 80%) do underlie the fact, however, that children were accurate on those persons they claimed to remember. In line with Peters (1991), accuracy of recognition of the room was consistently lower than for key medical personnel. Repeated testing led to no significant change in recognition accuracy over time, nor was age a significant determinant of performance on the photo arrays. Children were also asked to give ratings of pain experienced and 47 children indicated that at least part of the examination had been extremely painful. However, Steward reported no differences in the identification performance of these subjects relative to others who had experienced no pain.

Steward's report that repeated testing had little or no impact on recognition accuracy was also found by Tucker, Merton, and Luszcz (1990) who interviewed 4–5 year-old children 1 day and 7 days after an inoculation. Unlike Steward, all children were tested for recognition of the nurse who gave the shots and a control group was included who were tested only at 7 days. Repeated testing improved recognition, through as in the Steward study, no target absent arrays were employed. Levels of stress, as rated by the nurse, were not related to performance, though average ratings indicated only mild stress (2.1 on a 5 point scale).

Another study by the same group (Merton, 1989) focused on the effect of age on memory accuracy for the inoculation session. Groups of 40 subjects aged 4–5 years, 13 years, and adults attempted to select the nurse involved from a target

TABLE 7.3
Summary of Studies of Children's Eyewitness Competency Using Naturally Occurring Stressful Events

Experimenters	Subjects	Incident	Delay	Array	Result	Comment
14. Goodman, Aman & Hirschman	3/4 yrs & 5/6 yrs (n = 48)	Innoculation (3/4 min)	3/4 or 7/9 days	6 person array (target present)	3/4 days: 3/4 yrs (50%) 5/6 yrs (54%) 7/9 days: 3/4 yrs (17%) 5/6 yrs (53%)	No effect for age at 3/4 days 3/4 yrs at chance at 7/9 days 1 yr test + 14% (sig. fall)
15. Peters (1987)	3–8 yrs (all levels combined for analysis) (n = 71)	Visit to dentist (13 min)	1/2 days or 3/4 weeks	5 person array Present and absent	Present: 43% (dentist) 64% (assistant) Absent: 28% (dentist) 22% (assistant)	No sig. effect of delay Anxiety negatively effect ID for dentist (-.32) and assistant (-.21)
16. Steward (1989)	3–7 yrs (all levels combined) (n = 130)	Visit to clinic	Immediate, 1 month old & 6 mos	6 person array (target present)	Immediate: 83% 1 month: 85% 6 months: 93%	Part of multiple interview format. No effect on accuracy when partitioned by age
17. Merton (1989)	4/5 yrs; 13 yrs & adults (n = 120)	Innoculation (4/5 yrs) (3 min) Test for TB (13 yrs & adults)	3 days	6 person array (target present)	4/5 yrs (60%); 13 yrs (67%) Adults (94%)	Potential confound: incident x age x stress level
18. Tucker, Merton & Luszcz (1990)	4/5 yrs (n = 67)	Innoculation (3 min)	1 day or 1 week	6 person array (target present)	1 day (73%); 1 week (79%); Controls (1 week only) (48%)	Children consistent in choosing over 1 week. Delay effect sig.
19. Oates & Shrimpton (1991)	4–9 yrs (all levels combined (n = 17)	Blood test	4–10 days or 3–6 weeks	13 person array (target present)	Collapsed across delay and age (-0.71)	"Not present" not explicit. Low n precludes further analysis
20. Goodman et al. (1991a)	3/4 yrs; 5/6 yrs (n = 70)	Innoculation	2 weeks or 4 weeks	6 person array (target absent)	3/4 yrs (11%) 5/6 yrs (30%)	No effect of delay or repeated interview. Modeling assisted older children. Sig. age effect
21. Peters (1991)	3–9 yrs (all levels combined) (n = 64)	Innoculation or talk by nurse	1 day or 10–14 days	5 person array	Present: 38% (Innoc.) 94% (talk) Absent: 50% (Innoc.) 31% (talk)	No effect of dalay. Low stress controls did better on target present but different task and setting

present array. Adults outperformed both child groups, though no data are provided on levels of stress or their relationship to identification accuracy.

Oates & Shrimpton (1991) attempted, like Peters (1991), to vary levels of stress between subjects. They compared a group of 17 children aged 4–9 years who had a blood sample taken at a clinic with controls who talked to a friendly stranger at school. Children's memory for these events was tested by means of directed questions and a target-present photo array. Levels of stress reported by the children differed significantly for the two events, but once again, no detectable differences were found in either quality of description or accuracy of identification for the person concerned. Irrespective of stress levels, 7–9 year-olds were more accurate in their descriptions of the nurse than the 4–6 year-old group but did not differ in recognition accuracy.

In sum, these four studies show little impact, either positive or negative, of stress on memory. In fairness one would need to point to various design failings: low power (Oates & Shrimpton, 1991), only moderate degrees of stress (Steward, 1989 excepted), potential confounding due to procedural differences (Merton, 1989; Oates & Shrimpton 1991) and the uniform use of target present arrays. On the other hand, several of the findings are also consistent with Goodman's recently published study of memory for inoculation experiences (Goodman et al., 1991a). In this latter study, children aged 3–4 or 5–6 years were interviewed after 2 and 4 weeks. A second group of children were tested only at four weeks. The range of tasks always included a target absent array. Consistent with Steward, Tucker, et al. and Oates and Shrimpton, no consistent relation emerged between parental ratings of stress and subsequent memory performance and repeated testing did not influence accuracy on the photo array. Consistent with the earlier study of Goodman et al. (1987), 5–6 year-olds outperformed 3–4 year-olds on the identification task.

What may be concluded from these studies of *natural* stress? What emerges most consistently is the lack of impact of perceived stress on descriptive ability or choosing behavior from arrays. With the exception of Peters (1987), there have been few meaningful or consistent effects of stress on behavior. Perhaps only in the presence of stronger and more consistent age effects do the natural data differ from their *contrived* counterparts. To the extent that performance remains undisrupted by stress, the data offer little support for Peter's position. To the extent that higher ratings of stress do not enhance recognition of the target person, the findings are equally contrary to Goodman's position, though the generally poorer recognition of rooms could be interpreted as offering some support.

Natural experiments are a significant advance in our study of children's (or indeed adult's) testimony in that potentially they allow ranges of stress to be explored which lie outside the boundaries of normal research. However, they are not a complete answer and carry with them implicit constraints in terms of design and analysis that are not shared by their more artificial counterparts.

Given that research is inevitably piggy-backed onto medical or dental practice, subject factors cannot be controlled leading to allegations that results may reflect idiosyncrasies of the particular subgroup involved (Peters, 1991). Where identification is a factor, there is no control over the distinctiveness or otherwise of the *targets* or the conditions or length of observation (Davies et al., 1989). Where a *low stress* control condition is involved, there is inevitably debates over its equivalence in terms of setting and rationale (Goodman, 1991; Peters, 1991). Where stress is measured as a within-group effect, there are difficulties in ensuring an adequate distribution of participants across the full range of the stress scale (Goodman et al., 1991b). These limitations have ensured that researchers have continued to explore the impact of stress, as indeed other variables, in contrived as well as naturalistic paradigms.

Peters (1991) describes two such studies, one involving a within group, the other a between group manipulation of stress. In the first experiment children aged 3–6 years interacted with a stranger culminating in the child's head being rubbed vigorously to the point of distress. The whole interaction was videotaped and scored for symptoms of stress. One week following the incident, all subjects took part in either a target present or absent photo selection task for the stranger. Levels of stress influenced performance on the target present but not the target absent array, which also produced a very high rate of false positive responding. Observed anxiety correlated .27 with accuracy on the photo task. However, as Goodman (1991) has pointed out, age and developmental level were not controlled or partialled out, so it is difficult unequivocally to conclude that stress alone influenced the pattern of performance.

In the second experiment, children aged 6–9 years had their blood pressure and pulse rate measured by a stranger. The procedure was interrupted by the sounding of an alarm and the arrival of a confederate who claimed to smell smoke (high stress condition) or by the turning on of a radio coinciding with the appearance of a confederate on an innocent errand (low stress condition). The use of pulse and blood pressure measures confirmed the success of the manipulation (parents were present for all child subjects). When interviewed about the incident immediately afterward, high stress subjects were less accurate overall compared to low stress on a photo identification task for the confederate, the effect being particularly marked on the target absent array. This ingenious experiment which, in this author's view skirts the limits of ethically acceptable experimentation, is probably the best evidence available for the proposition that stress at encoding disrupts subsequent memory performance.

If stress is to have an affect whether benign (Goodman) or disruptive (Peters) where is the locus of the effect? Both Goodman and Peters place the main emphasis upon activity at the time of encoding. However, an effect of stress upon storage is equally possible. Stressful memories might be subject to greater (rumination) or lesser (repression) rehearsal than more benign events. Thus a poorly encoded initial experience might be better represented over time than one which was more effectively encoded initially but was not subject to the same process of periodic review. Such *cross-over* effects of arousal on performance are not unknown in the literature (Kleinsmith & Kaplan, 1964).

The final possibility is that stress at encoding might influence performance at retrieval. The possibility of such a delayed effect seems unlikely, unless there were some form of state dependent learning (Eich, 1980) such that material encoded under conditions of high stress could only be retrieved under similar circumstances.

Peters (1991) has recently reported a study that provides a test of such a conception. Individual children at a summer camp aged between 5 and 10 years carried out a card sorting task with an experimenter before being left alone with a cigar tin of money. Half (the low encoding stress group) were told a research assistant might return to pick up the cash, which he did. The remainder (the high encoding stress group) were not so briefed and had the money ostentatiously stolen by the same assistant. Directly the assistant left the room, the experimenter re-entered with the child's parent and the child was asked either to pick out the assistant from a photo array (low retrieval stress) or from a live lineup (high retrieval stress). For those who had experienced the theft, the identification was introduced as essential to locating the suspect while for the remaining subjects it was represented as a memory game.

The results provided no support for a state-dependent interpretation, although perceived levels of stress varied consistently in the expected direction at encoding and retrieval. The major finding was the very low rates of identification (33%) in the condition involving a perceived theft and a live lineup. Over half the children in this group failed to make any identification. Several of the nonchoosing children told their parents that they did recognize the assistant but had been afraid to choose him. Clearly stress at retrieval through the use of an ostensible crime and a live lineup disrupts children's identification performance. But this form of stress and its mode of operation seems independent of stress at encoding. Stress at retrieval owes more to social and affective factors than any more general cognitive impairment associated with encoding. It is perhaps best tackled in those legislatures which insist on *live* identification, by the use of one-way screens or other protective devices, though their impact with children has yet to be demonstrated (Dent & Stephenson, 1979b). There is clearly a need for greater precision in analyzing the different mechanisms mediating stress and for more sophisticated designs which permit the isolation of its diverse effects.

The impact of stress could also vary depending upon its intensity. For ethical reasons levels of stress in contrived situations are inevitably low. Moreover, thanks to modern science, the length of such procedures as inoculations or dental inspections is fleeting and they are not unduly painful for the majority of children. It is possible that the general failure to find an impact of stress in naturalistic studies lies in the levels of stress experienced; perhaps medical procedures such as those explored by Steward are a more appropriate arena for such research.

The idea that arousal may have inconsistent effects depending upon its intensity is embodied in the Yerkes-Dodson law (Yerkes & Dodson, 1908), invoked by Deffenbacher (1983) in his explanation of the equally contrary findings of the impact of stress and affect on adult's identification performance. The concept of an inverted-U shaped relationship between stress and accuracy has attractions, but difficulties of application in practice (Warren-Leubecker, 1991). One needs at least three levels of stress within the same experiment in order to confirm the effect: precision rarely achieved in practice. Objectively, particularly in developmental studies, there is no way of knowing where on the arousal continuum the subjects status should be plotted. Moreover, the Yerkes-Dodson law does not in itself constitute an explanation of any findings, but rather, it is a higher-order rule which in turn demands a theoretical rationale. While the occasional positive finding tantalizes (Goodman et al., in press), the absence of independent measures seems to leave the inverted-U function in the category of panaceas that contain the Bermuda Triangle and their like.

In conclusion, *natural* experiments have yet to resolve the issue of whether stress and arousal influence retention. Debate has focused almost exclusively on methodology and questions of ecological validity at the expense of any but the most perfunctory considerations of theory. While in most respects the results from real and contrived experiments are similar in their impact of delay and target absent arrays, age effects seem much more pronounced and occur even on target present arrays. Yet, few researchers have sought to use this as a basis for theorizing or formulating predictions that can be tested by experiment. It is difficult to see how the current debate on the impact of stress on testimony can be resolved without embedding the dispute into some kind of theory that will provide a degree of integration and generality for these isolated pinpoints of empirical fact.

Conclusions

The three literatures on children's face memory abilities have now been reviewed. It is evident that the story they tell is not entirely consistent and several controversies remain unresolved. Nevertheless, a general picture of the growth of ability with age does emerge. Improvements with age seem strongest on verbal recall tasks which demand both detailed knowledge of a face, and equally importantly, an appreciation of the demands of the interviewer. Age effects seem least likely to be present when a task demands recognition of a single person who had previously taken part in some direct interaction with the child which has harnessed the witness' attention. Age effects are more likely to occur where the target's picture is not present in the array. The impact of stress and heightened affect at the time of encoding is not yet clear, but there does appear to be a tendency for stress at encoding to increase age differences in performance, whether stress is artificially contrived (Brigham et al., 1986) or the result of some medical intervention, though convincing between-group manipulations of stress have yet to be published. There is still a major gulf in aims and thinking between those who chose to study the face recognition process in the strictly controlled conditions of the laboratory and those who chose the school hall or medical clinic as their arena. Cross talk between these two research traditions can only benefit theory and practice.

Face processing researchers have already uncovered a number of interesting factors that are worthy of study in a wider and more realistic context. These include such factors as the impact of disguise, cross-racial recognition and physical distinctiveness on identification rates. The latter is particularly interesting in the light of a recent study by Ellis (1992) that examined the ability of children aged 6–14 years to recognize a sequence of faces that were either physiognomically distinctive or typical. Typical faces showed no improvement in recognition with age, a finding reminiscent of the eyewitness testimony literature. Distinctive faces on the other hand showed a typical increase in accuracy with age. Given that stooges in eyewitness studies are generally selected for their mundane appearance this deserves to be followed up, though the usual caveats about the use of multiple actors to play the stooge in order to avoid generalization problems clearly applies.

The face processing literature is also endowed with a wealth of models and theoretical ideas that might usefully be raided to sharpen conceptual models of eyewitnessing. As has been shown in discussions of choosing behavior and stress, experimental research tends to focus on one particular phase (whether encoding, storage or retrieval) and not examine or consider other possibilities. It would be a useful exercise for researchers of both disciplines to take contemporary theories of face processing and ask like Carey (1981) "What develops?".

Equally, researchers in the eyewitness testimony tradition have much to offer their colleagues in the face processing industry. Like verbal learning researchers of an earlier generation, they tend to treat the result from their paradigms as reflecting the workings of basic mechanisms immune from subject or procedure influences. As has been noted, quite trifling changes in procedure appear to produce marked effects on the relative performance of children of different ages. There is perhaps a need for face processing studies to go through the same learning experience as Piagetian researchers have undergone in terms of widening their data base and looking at tasks from a child's perspective before talking confidently of universal rules which can readily be generalized to the real world.

Likewise, most models of face processing treat it as a purely cognitive process divorced from social and affective influences (Bull & Rumsey, 1988). Yet, as has been observed, the influence of these factors appears to be pervasive in the real world: the influence of interviewing style and social support on face recall; suggestibility effects in target absent arrays; the impact of stress on encoding, and the performance of children on live line-ups to name but a few. Theories need to take account of such factors in their basic building blocks; a peripheral box marked 'affective and social influences' just will not do!

What are the implications of these two research traditions for the reception of children's evidence on identification? First, the fact that face processing studies show an improvement with age is not a reason for excluding a child's testimony. Developmental studies are designed to reflect age differences, that is their goal. At the heart of the laws of evidence lies the concept of competence: Is the witness sufficiently reliable that the court should hear their testimony? In recent years, a number of judicial systems including those in Britain and parts of the United States have moved to a more liberal definition of competence. Is the evidence so unreliable that the court should *not* hear it? In all the studies surveyed in this review, there have been few where chance identification has occurred, even in the target absent arrays and several where very high rates of accurate identification have occurred. Moreover, within any one age group there will be witnesses who perform well or badly; it would be instructive to calculate the amount of variance accounted for by age in those studies that have found significant effects for this variable.

Thus, to use the results of studies that have simply found significant developmental effects as a reason for excluding children from giving testimony would be quite wrong. It would be tantamount to the argument that just because children's overall spelling skills improve with age, it is necessary automatically to discard the child's version of a word and always embrace the adult's; adult competencies are not so well developed nor children's so uniformly inferior that this tactic could be adopted. It would exclude such effective witnesses as Julie, whose story began this paper and the 3-year-old described by Jones and Krugman (1986), from legal redress for the appalling suffering they endured.

In conclusion, critics such as Benaji and Crowder (1989) have called for a return to basic laboratory research as the only source of reliable and generalizable data and a rejection of so called everyday memory studies. The pure and applied studies described in this chapter illustrate, to this author's satisfaction, what a regressive step this would be. Laboratory and applied research do not in themselves individually hold the key to understanding human behavior. Rather the most fruitful way forward lies in this, as in other less controversial areas, in continuing dialogue and respect for the different goals and sensitivities of these distinct research traditions.

REFERENCES

Banks, W. P. (1970). Signal detection theory and human memory. *Psychological Bulletin, 74*, 81–99.

Benaji, M., & Crowder, R. (1989). The bankruptcy of everyday memory. *American Psychologist, 44*, 1185–1193.

Binet, A. (1900). *La suggestibilité*. Paris: Schleicher Freres.

Brigham, J. C., Van Verst, M., & Bothwell, R. K. (1986). Accuracy of children's eyewitness identifications in a field setting. *Basic & Applied Social Psychology, 7*, 295–306.

Bruce, V., & Young, A. (1986). Understanding face recognition. *British Journal of Psychology, 77,* 305–327.

Bull, R. H., & Rumsey, N. (1988). *The social psychology of facial appearance.* New York: Springer Verlag.

Carey, S. (1978). A case study: Face recognition. In E. Walker (Ed.), *Explorations in the biology of language* (pp. 175–201). Vermont: Bradford Books.

Carey, S. (1981). The development of face perception. In G. Davies, H. Ellis, & J. Shepherd (Eds.), *Perceiving and remembering faces* (pp. 9–38). London: Academic Press.

Carey S. (1992). Becoming a face expert. *Philosophical Transactions of the Royal Society of London: Series B, 335,* 95–103.

Carey, S., Diamond, R., & Woods, B. (1980). Development of face recognition: A maturational component? *Developmental Psychology, 16,* 257–269.

Ceci, S. J., Ross, D. F., & Toglia, M. P. (1987). Suggestibility in children's memory: Psychological implications. *Journal of Experimental Psychology: General, 116,* 38–49.

Chance, J. E., & Goldstein, A. G. (1987). Face recognition memory: Implications for children's eyewitness testimony. *Journal of Social Issues, 40,* 69–85.

Chance, J. E., Turner, A. L., & Goldstein, A. (1982). Development of differential recognition for own and other race faces. *Journal of Psychology, 112,* 29–37.

Chi, M. (1978). Knowledge structures and memory development. In R. S. Siegler (Ed.), *Children's thinking: What develops?* (pp. 73–96). Hillsdale, NJ: Lawrence Erlbaum Associates.

Clifford, B. R., & Davies, G. M. (1989). Procedures for obtaining identification evidence. In D. Raskin (Ed.), *Psychological methods in investigation and evidence* (pp. 47–95). New York: Springer Verlag.

Cole, C. B., & Loftus, E. F. (1987). The memory of children. In S. J. Ceci, M. P. Toglia, & D. F. Ross (Eds.), *Children's eyewitness memory* (pp. 178–208). New York: Springer Verlag.

Cross, J. F., Cross, J., & Daly, J. (1971). Sex, race, age and beauty as factors in recognition of faces. *Perception and Psychophysics, 10,* 393–396.

Davies, G. M. (1981). Face recall systems. In G. Davies, H. Ellis, & J. Shepherd (Eds.), *Perceiving and remembering faces* (pp. 227–250). London: Academic Press.

Davies, G. M. (1989). On the applicability of facial memory research. In A. Young & H. Ellis (Eds.), *Handbook of research on face processing* (pp. 557–562). Amsterdam: North Holland.

Davies, G. M. (in press). Influencing public policy on eyewitness testimony: Problems and possibilities. In F. Loesel, D. Bender, & T. Bliesener (Eds.), *Psychology and law: International perspectives.* Berlin: De Gruyter.

Davies, G. M., & Christie, D. (1982). Face recall: An examination of some factors limiting accuracy for facial recall. *Journal of Applied Psychology, 67,* 103–107.

Davies, G. M., & Milne, A. (1982). Recognizing faces in and out of context. *Current Psychological Research, 2,* 235–246.

Davies, G. M., & Noon, E. (1991). *An evaluation of the live link system for child witnesses.* London: Home Office Research and Planning Unit.

Davies, G. M., & Robertson, N. (in press). Recognition accuracy for motor cars: A developmental study. *Bulletin of the Psychonomic Society.*

Davies, G. M., Stevenson-Robb, & Flin, R. (1988). Tales out of school: Children's memory for an unexpected incident. In M. Gruneberg, P. Morris, & R. Sykes (Eds.), *Practical aspects of memory: Vol. 1* (pp. 122–127). Chichester: Wiley.

Davies, G. M., Tarrant, A., & Flin, R. (1989). Close encounters of a witness kind: Children's memory for a simulated health inspection. *British Journal of Psychology, 80,* 415–429.

Deffenbacher, K. (1983). The influence of arousal on reliability of testimony. In B. R. Clifford & S. Lloyd-Bostock (Eds.), *Evaluating witness evidence* (pp. 235–251). Chichester: Wiley.

Dent, H. (1982). The effects of interviewing strategies on the results of interviews with child witnesses. In A. Trankell (Ed.), *Reconstructing the past* (pp. 279–298). Stockholm: Norstedt.

Dent, H., & Stephenson, G. (1979a). An experimental study of the effectiveness of different techniques of questioning child witnesses. *British Journal of Social and Clinical Psychology, 18*, 41–51.

Dent, H. R., & Stephenson, G. M. (1979b). Identification evidence: Experimental investigations of factors affecting the reliability of juvenile and adult witnesses. In D. P. Farrington, K. Hawkins, & S. M. Lloyd-Bostock (Eds.), *Psychology, law and legal processes* (pp. 195–206). Atlantic Highlands, NJ: Humanities Press.

Devlin, Lord P. (1976). *Report to the secretary of state for the Home Department of the departmental committee on evidence of identification in criminal cases.* London: Her Majesty's Stationery Office.

Diamond, R., & Carey, S. (1977). Developmental changes in the representation of faces. *Journal of Experimental Child Psychology, 23*, 1–22.

Donaldson, M. (1978). *Children's minds.* Glasgow: Fontana.

Doris, J. (Ed.). (1991). *The suggestibility of children's recollections.* Washington: American Psychological Association.

Easterbrook, J. A. (1959). The effect of emotion on the utilization and organization of behavior. *Psychological Review, 66*, 183–201.

Eich, E. (1980). The cue-dependent nature of state-dependent retrieval. *Memory and Cognition, 8*, 157–173.

Ellis, H. D. (1990). Developmental trends in face recognition. *The Psychologist, 3*, 114–119.

Ellis, H. D. (1992). The development of face processing skills. *Philosophical Transactions of the Royal Society of London, Series B, 335*, 105–111.

Ellis, H. D., & Deregowski, J. B. (1991). Within-race and between-race recognition of transformed and untransformed faces. *American Journal of Psychology, 94*, 27.

Ellis, H. D., & Flin, R. H. (1990). Encoding and storage effects in 7 year olds' and 10 year olds' memory for faces. *British Journal of Developmental Psychology, 8*, 77–92.

Ellis, H. D., Jeaves, M., Newcomb, F., & Young, A. (Eds.). (1986). *Aspects of face processing.* Dordrecht, Holland: Nijhoff.

Ellis, H. D., Shepherd, J. W., & Bruce, A. (1973). The effect of age and sex upon adolescents' recognition of faces. *Journal of Genetic Psychology, 123*, 173–174.

Ellis, H. D., Shepherd, J. W., Shepherd, J., Flin, R., & Davies, G. (1989). Identification from a computer driven retrieval system compared with a traditional mugshot album search: A new tool for police investigations. *Ergonomics, 32*, 167–177.

Feinman, S., & Entwisle, D. R. (1976). Children's ability to recognize other children's faces. *Child Development, 47*, 506–510.

Finkelhon, D. (1979). *Child sexual assault.* New York: Free Press.

Flin, R. H. (1980). Age effects in children's memory for unfamiliar faces. *Developmental Psychology, 16*, 373–374.

Flin, R. H. (1985a). Development of face recognition: An encoding switch? *British Journal of Psychology, 76*, 123–134.

Flin, R. H. (1985b). Development of visual memory: An early adolescent regression. *Journal of Early Adolescence, 5*, 259–266.

Flin, R. H., Boon, J. W., Knox, A., & Bull, R. (1992). Children's memories following a five-month delay. *British Journal of Psychology, 83*, 323–336.

Flin, R., Bull, R., Boon, J., & Knox, A. (1990). *Child witnesses in Scottish criminal prosecutions. Final report to the Scottish Home and Health Department.* Glasgow: Glasgow College.

Flin, R., & Dziurawiec, S. (1989). Developmental factors in face processing. In A. Young & H. Ellis (Eds.), *Handbook of research on face processing* (pp. 335–378). Amsterdam, The Netherlands: North Holland.

Flin, R. H., Markham, R., & Davies, G. M. (1989). Making faces: Developmental trends in the construction of face composites. *Journal of Applied Developmental Psychology, 10*, 123–137.

Flin, R. H., & Shepherd, J. W. (1986). Tall stories: Eyewitness ability to judge height and weight characteristics. *Human Learning, 5,* 29–38.

Flin, R., Stevenson, Y., & Davies, G. (1989). Children's knowledge of court proceedings. *British Journal of Psychology, 80,* 285–297.

Goetze, H. J. (1980). *The effect of age and method of interview on the accuracy and completeness of eyewitness accounts.* Unpublished Doctoral dissertation, Hofstra University.

Goldstein, A. G., & Chance, J. E. (1964). Recognition of children's faces. *Child Development, 35,* 129–136.

Goldstein, A. G., & Chance, J. E. (1965). Recognition of children's faces: II. *Perceptual and Motor Skills, 20,* 547–548.

Goldstein, A. G., & Mackenberg, E. J. (1966). Recognition of human faces from isolated facial features: A developmental study. *Psychonomic Science, 6,* 149–150.

Goodman, G. S. (1991). Commentary: On stress and accuracy in research on children's testimony. In J. Doris (Ed.), *The suggestibility of children's recollections* (pp. 77–82). Washington: American Psychological Association.

Goodman, G. S., Aman, C., & Hirschman, J. (1987). Child sexual and physical abuse: Children's testimony. In S. J. Ceci, M. P. Toglia, & D. F. Ross (Eds.), *Children's eyewitness memory* (pp. 1–23). New York: Springer Verlag.

Goodman, G. S., Bottoms, B. L., Schwartz-Kenney, B. M., & Rudy, L. (1991a). Children's memory for a stressful event: Improving children's reports. *Journal of Narrative and Life History, 1,* 69–99.

Goodman, G., & Reed, R. (1986). Age difference in eyewitness testimony. *Law and Human Behavior, 10,* 317–332.

Goodman, G. S., Rudy, L., Bottoms, B., & Aman, C. (1991b). Children's concerns and memory: Issues of ecological validity in the study of children's eyewitness testimony. In R. Fivush & J. Hudson (Eds.), *Knowing and remembering in young children* (pp. 249–284). New York: Cambridge University Press.

Goulet, L. R. (1968). Verbal learning in children: Implications for developmental research. *Psychological Bulletin, 60,* 359–376.

Jones, D. P. H., & Krugman, R. D. (1986). Can a three year old child bear witness to her sexual assault and attempted murder? *Child Abuse and Neglect, 10,* 253–258.

Kail, R. (1990). *The development of memory in children* (3rd Ed.). San Francisco: Freeman.

King, M. A., & Yuille, J. C. (1986). *An investigation of the eyewitness abilities of children.* Unpublished manuscript, University of British Columbia.

Kleinsmith, L. J., & Kaplan, S. (1964). Interaction of arousal and recall interval in nonsense syllable paired associate learning. *Journal of Experimental Psychology, 67,* 124–126.

Leippe, M. L., Romonczyk, A., & Manion, A. P. (1991). Eyewitness memory for a touching experience: Accuracy differences between child and adult witnesses. *Journal of Applied Psychology, 76,* 367–379.

List, J. A. (1986). Age and schematic differences in the reliability of eyewitness testimony. *Developmental Psychology, 22,* 50–57.

Malpass, R., & Devine, P. G. (1981). Eyewitness identification: Lineup instructions and the absence of the offender. *Journal of Applied Psychology, 66,* 482–489.

Marin, B. V., Holmes, D. L., Guth, M., & Kovac, P. (1979). The potential of children as eyewitnesses. *Law and Human Behavior, 3,* 295–305.

Markham, R., Ellis, D. M., & Ellis, H. D. (1991). The effect of context changes on children's recognition of unfamiliar faces. *British Journal of Developmental Psychology, 9,* 513–520.

Merton, P. (1989). The memory of young children for eyewitness events. *Australian Journal of Social Issues, 24,* 23–32.

Moston, S., & Engelberg, T. (1992). The effect of social support on children's eyewitness testimony. *Applied Cognitive Psychology, 6,* 61–76.

Nelson, C. A., & Ludemann, P. (1989). Past, current and future trends in infant perception research. *Canadian Journal of Psychology, 43,* 183–198.

Oates, K., & Shrimpton, S. (1991). Children's memories for stressful and non-stressful events. *Medicine, Science and the Law, 31,* 4–10.

Parker, J. F., & Carranza, L. E. (1989). Eyewitness testimony of children in target-present and target-absent lineups. *Law and Human Behavior, 13,* 133–149.

Parker, J. F., Haverfield, E., & Baker-Thomas, S. (1986). Eyewitness testimony of children. *Journal of Applied Social Psychology, 16,* 287–302.

Pedelty, L., Levine, S. C., & Shevell, S. K. (1985). Developmental changes in face processing: Results from multidimensional scaling. *Journal of Experimental Child Psychology, 39,* 421–436.

Peters, D. P. (1987). The impact of naturally occurring stress on children's memory. In S. J. Ceci, M. P. Toglia, & D. F. Ross (Eds.), *Children's eyewitness memory* (pp. 122–141). New York: Springer Verlag.

Peters, D. P. (1991). The influence of stress and arousal on the child sitness. In J. Doris (Ed.), *The suggestibility of children's recollections* (pp. 60–76). Washington: American Psychological Association.

Rapaport, D. (1942). *Emotions and memory.* Baltimore: Williams and Wilkins.

Shavelson, R. J., & Webb, N. M. (1981). Generalizibility theory: 1973–1980. *British Journal of Mathematical and Statistical Psychology, 34,* 133–166.

Shepherd, J. W. (1981). The face and social attribution. In A. Young & H. Ellis (Eds.), *Handbook of face processing* (pp. 289–320). Amsterdam: North Holland.

Shepherd, J. W., Davies, G. M., & Ellis, H. D. (1981). Studies in cue saliency. In G. Davies, H. D. Ellis, & J. W. Shepherd (Eds.), *Perceiving and remembering faces* (pp. 105–132). London: Academic Press.

Shepherd, J. W., Ellis, H. D., & Davies, G. M. (1982). *Identification evidence: A psychological evaluation.* Aberdeen: Aberdeen University Press.

Soppe, H. J. G. (1986). Children's recognition of unfamiliar faces: Development and determinants. *International Journal of Behavioural Development, 9,* 219–233.

Spencer, J., & Flin, R. (1990). *The evidence of children: The law and the psychology.* London: Blackstone.

Sterne, L. W. (1910). Abstracts of lectures on the psychology of testimony and the study of individuality. *American Journal of Psychology, 21,* 270–282.

Sterne, L. W. (1939). The psychology of testimony. *Journal of Abstract and Social Psychology, 34,* 3–20.

Steward, M. S. (1989). *The development of a model interview for young child victims of sexual abuse: Comparing the effectiveness of anatomical dolls, drawings and video graphics* (Grant 90 CA1332). Washington, D.C.: National Center on Child Abuse & Neglect, Department of Health and Human Sciences.

Thomson, D. M. (1984, May). *Context effects on recognition memory: A developmental study.* Paper presented at the Experimental Psychology Society Conference, Geelong, Australia.

Tucker, A., Merton, P., & Luszcz, M. (1990). The effect of repeated interviews on young children's eyewitness memory. *Australian & New Zealand Journal of Criminology, 23,* 117–124.

Valentine, T. (1991). A unified account of the effects of distinctiveness, inversion and race on face recognition. *Quarterly Journal of Experimental Psychology, 43A,* 162–204.

Warren-Leubecher, A. (1991). Commentary: The influence of stress and arousal on the child witness. In J. Doris (Ed.), *The suggestibility of children's recollections* (pp. 83–85). Washington: American Psychological Association.

Wells, G. L. (1988). *Eyewitness identification.* Toronto: Carswell.

Yarmey, A. D. (1988). Streetproofing and bystander's memory for a child abduction. In M. Gruneberg, P. E. Morris, & M. Sykes (Eds.), *Practical aspects of memory, Vol. 1* (pp. 112–116). Chichester, England: Wiley.

Yerkes, R. M., & Dodson, J. D. (1908). The relation of strength of stimulus to rapidity of habit formation. *Journal of Comparative Neurology and Psychology, 68,* 347–362.

Young, A., Hay, D., & Ellis, A. (1985). The faces that launched a thousand slips: Everyday difficulties and errors in recognizing people. *British Journal of Psychology, 76,* 495–524.

Yuille, J. C., Cutshall, J. L., & King, M. A. (1986). *Age related changes in eyewitness accounts and photo-identification.* Unpublished manuscript, University of British Columbia.

8 The Child Witness, the Courts, and Psychological Research

Steven Penrod
University of Minnesota Law School

A friend who is a public defender and from time to time defends cases in which children appear as witnesses tells me that in his closing arguments he calls the jury's attention to a closing argument made by a prosecutor in one of the Salem witch trials 300 years ago. As you may recall, those trials resulted in the hanging of 19 women and the pressing to death of a 20th who refused to make a plea at her trial. The witnesses at these trials testified that they had seen the defendants engage in variety of bizarre supernatural behaviors. According to my friend, the prosecutor in one of these cases referred to two girls who had testified against one defendant and rhetorically asked what possible reason the two girls had to lie about the supernatural behaviors they had witnessed.

The story, whether true or not, underscores the point that children do serve as witnesses in legal proceedings, and as a consequence, the reliability of the testimony they offer is worthy of investigation. Indeed, in recent years it seems that not a week goes by in which the media fails to call our attention to yet another case, typically a sexual abuse case, in which children appear as witnesses. As noted shortly, recent changes in the law virtually assure that children and their evidence will appear with increasing frequency in the courts. Furthermore, recent case law indicates that the courts are solicitous of child-generated evidence and at the same time are interested in and even receptive to research on child witness reliability.

Critics have argued that in some ways the courts have been entirely too eager to receive child witness evidence and entirely too eager to employ *scientific* evidence from behavioral scientists eager to bolster child testimony. Law Professor Robert Levy (1989) has, in particular, been an outspoken critic of the courts' use of what he terms "pseudoscientific nostrums" in cases involving child witnesses, particularly in sexual abuse (and divorce) cases. Levy's criticisms apply broadly to cases in which children testify and they underscore both the importance and the need for research such as that Graham Davies reviews in this volume.

Levy tellingly skewers psychologists and psychiatrists who, over a period of many years, regularly testified in court proceedings that "children never lie." He regards this as one of the earliest examples of the court over reaching with child testimony. He gives an example from a 1985 trial transcript.

> *Question by County Attorney to a psychologist:* "In your capacity as a child psychologist do you have occasion to do research in the field, talk to other psychologists who have dealt with such issues, read treatises in the matter?" *Answer:* "I've done reading in the field of sexual abuse. There are books and articles out in that field. I've talked with other people in the field, particularly in this area, and heard people talk at workshops discussing that subject." *Question:* "What's the general consensus about young people's capacity to fabricate stories of sexual abuse?" *Answer:* "I've not in my readings and in my studies read a minority opinion that children do fabricate such things. The opinion that I have both read and encountered in talking with other experts, is that young children do not fabricate stories of sexual abuse."

Levy raises questions about the scientific foundations for such a proposition and cites favorably admonitions from within those professions that "Such overstatement invites criticism of efforts to protect children, and skepticism of professional knowledge and motives" (Meyers et al., 1989, p. 110).

Clinicians who drew upon Roland Summit's (1983) impressionistic article about "child sexual abuse syndrome" and purported symptoms such as delayed reporting and retraction of accusations also draw Levy's fire. Summit, a California psychiatrist, originally formulated this syndrome in a paper, the purpose of which, as Summit noted, was not to provide a sexual abuse test, but to improve therapy and advocacy for kids. The original article provided some impressionistic clinical findings, but no data of any kind. Nonetheless, Levy points out Summit's syndrome was turned into a perverse testimonial tool.

Child abuse syndrome evidence could be and was used to prove sexual abuse when the child made an accusation in an unconvincing fashion. Summit indicated that unconvincing accusations were characteristic of what he saw in victims of sexual abuse. It was used because the experts asserted that sexually abused children, suffering from the syndrome, retract their accusations. Hence, sexual abuse could be proven even when the child him or herself claimed the accusation was untrue, because this retraction was consistent with the syndrome spelled out by Summit. Levy observes that Summit's original analysis, intended as a therapeutic tool, was quickly converted into an adversarial courtroom tool as prosecutors elicited testimony from *experts* prepared to say that late reporting and retractions were symptoms of the syndrome and therefore evidence of abuse.

Unfortunately, the growth in such expert testimony was not accompanied by scientific testing or validation of Summit's impressions. Levy notes that the courts have grown more savvy in their willingness to accept this kind of evidence; nonetheless, their overeagerness opened the door to evidence of questionable validity.

Levy's third attack on misbegotten judicial overreceptivity to behavioral scientist's testimony about child witnesses targets child abuse experts who use anatomically correct dolls in interview sessions designed to determine whether young children have been the victims of abuse. As Levy (1989) caustically notes: "Dolls were 'discovered' in 1976 and first manufactured for general use in child sexual abuse investigations in 1980, and the first appellate decision following a trial in which an expert testified about anatomically correct dolls occurred in 1982" (p. 400).

Unfortunately, this rapid dissemination of the technique and accompanying testimony was not supported by scientific research. By Levy's count, 129 civil and criminal appellate cases were reported prior to the publication of the first empirical study of the efficacy of anatomically correct doll procedures. Of course, these reported appellate cases may be a fraction of the total number of trials in which such evidence was admitted. Furthermore, on the basis of the few studies presently available, it is still possible to support Levy's conclusion that such testimony should simply be inadmissible.

The eagerness of the courts to accept this kind of testimony stands in contrast to their reluctance to receive expert testimony about eyewitness identification issues in adult cases. It is quite clear that the literature with regard to adult witnesses is much better developed than the body of literature on any of the three techniques involving child witnesses and better developed than the literature on child witnesses reviewed by Graham Davies.

The point in reiterating Levy's arguments about such testimony is not so much that behavioral scientists may sometimes overstep their science (though that is clearly a problem that must be reckoned with). Rather, the point is that courts are eager—probably much too eager—to receive scientific and pseudoscientific testimony that might bolster evidence provided by children. Clearly, the better the evidence that can be provided about child witnesses, the sounder the decisions courts will make with regard to what kind of testimony is admitted from children.

A recent United State Supreme Court decision in *Craig v. Maryland* (110 S.Ct. 3157, 1990) further underscores the solicitous attitude toward child witnesses that is characteristic of our time. In *Craig,* a 5–4 decision, the majority ruled that the Confrontation Clause of the Constitution does not guarantee a defendant the absolute right to a face-to-face confrontation with the witnesses against them. Rather, when the witness in question is a child, the state's interest in protecting the child's physical and psychological well-being outweighs the defendant's confrontation rights and permits the state, as in this case, to elicit testimony from a child witness via a closed circuit television system in which the child is never confronted by the accused. In part this decision drew support from arguments advanced in an amicus brief prepared by the American Psychological Association—indeed, the majority cite the brief and its authorities for the proposition that there is a body of literature documenting psychological trauma to children who must testify in court.

Justice Scalia, unpersuaded by APA and other arguments in support of the majority opinion, concluded in his dissent that a significant Constitutional guarantee had been swept away in a "tide of public opinion." Indeed, critics within the psychological community have argued that even APA overstepped the scientific research in its apparent haste to support the interests of children who might be traumatized by in-court confrontation (Goodman, Levine, Melton, & Ogden, 1991; Underwager & Wakefield, 1992).

The courts' interest in child evidence and their eagerness to receive even pseudoscientific evidence about children reflects something of a reversal in the fortunes of children as witnesses. Under the traditional common law—the prevailing form of law until about the last 20 years—a variety of witnesses were deemed incompetent to testify. These included the insane, those who did not believe in a supreme being, those with an interest in the outcome of a case (including defendants), felons, and young children. Most of these exclusions were based on a concern with unreliable or perjured testimony.

Over the past century incompetencies have been gradually abolished by statue. Among the first to go was the incompetency to testify for defendants, but in more recent times, most specific barriers to testimony have largely been erased and the traditional grounds for incompetency have been turned into grounds for impeaching a witness—thus, a previous conviction, bias, or youth can be used to challenge the reliability, credibility, and veracity of a witness. Indeed, the Federal Rules of Evidence (which have been widely adopted by the states), Rule 601 specifies, in part: Every person is competent to be a witness except as otherwise provided in these rules.

Although there is clearly a presumption that witnesses are competent to testify, judges still retain broad power to exclude some or all of a witness's testimony on the ground that no one could believe the witness or that the witness's testimony will not be helpful to the jury, or that the evidence is not worth the time required to develop the testimony.

The prevailing view of competency is that it is a matter to be assessed on a case by case basis and it is not uncommon for the court to find that young children are not competent to testify. In fact, in two significant cases discussed next, the children whose evidence was offered in court were themselves not permitted to testify. That is, they were deemed to be incompetent to testify as witnesses, but the statements they had made to examining physicians or parents outside the courtroom were deemed to be sufficiently reliable to merit the reporting of those statements through testimony of adult witnesses who received the children's communications.

The children in these two cases were very young—2½ to 3 years-old—and when assessing the competency of a child to testify the principal determination made by the court is whether a child is able to understand and respond to questions in a sensible way when he or she is testifying on the stand. Many would argue that is it logically inconsistent to maintain that a child is not competent to testify in court but is competent to make out-of-court statements to third persons and then let those third persons repeat the statements in the courtroom.

The courts that have addressed the question are persuaded that the ability to respond to questions in the courtroom is a different type of competency than is required when relating events to *someone*—other than the district attorney on direct examination, or the defense attorney on cross examination—such as the child's mother, father, and other individuals. Whether these competencies are different is an empirical question—on which there is presently no direct evidence. Courts are certainly prepared to make a distinction between the two types of competency and it is clear that with the removal of general barriers to child testimony, not only do children now appear on the stand more often, but the statements that they make out of court may be admissible during trial, even though the child may not be testifying.

In addition to the general increase in receptivity to child witnesses, other legal developments also make the need for child witness research imperative, and, at the same time, identify some possible avenues for future research. A recent and important child witness case underscores this point. The case is *Idaho v. Wright* (110 S.Ct. 3139) decided by the U.S. Supreme Court in June of 1990. This case involved a defendant who was charged with lewd conduct with her 5½ and 2½ year-old daughters. The 2½ year-old had made statements out of court to a Dr. Jambora who had interviewed the child. The child was declared not competent to appear as a witness, and therefore was not permitted to testify. Nonetheless the statements made to the physician were ruled admissible by the trial court—despite the fact many of the statements were obviously hearsay.

The Supreme Court of Idaho held that the admission of the out-of-court statements was an error because the statement was unreliable and violated the defendant's Constitutional Right to confrontation. The U.S. Supreme Court—in another 5–4 decision—also concluded that the testimony was inadmissible. One of the more interesting aspects of the decision—an aspect that has important implications for experimental psychological research on child witnesses—concerned the criteria and standards that were to be used when testing whether these types of out-of-court statements could be placed before the jury. Justice O'Connor, speaking for the majority, noted that where the state seeks to introduce evidence presumptively barred by the Confrontation Clause and the rule against hearsay, the state has the burden of establishing that the out-of-court statements bear sufficient "indicia of reliability" to overcome those traditional barriers.

The Court considered three possible sources of indicia of reliability. It first considered the procedural safeguards that might be employed during interviews with children (e.g., videotaping of interview sessions and minimizing the use of leading questions), but concluded it would not erect a set of procedural criteria as the basis for rejecting the testimony because such procedures may be inappropriate or unnecessary in some cases. The court also rejected the presence or absence of other corroborating evidence (such as medical tests) as a basis for determining whether out-of-court statements were sufficiently reliable to merit admission. Essentially, the evidence would have to stand or fall on its own merits.

Instead, the Court said that only the circumstances surrounding the making of the statements should be used as the basis for determining the admissibility of the statements. In this particular case the Court identified several factors that the trial court had examined: whether the child had a motive to make up such a story; whether the statements made by the child were of a type that a child of that age might fabricate; the spontaneity of the statements (in light of any previous interviews); and changes in demeanor accompanying the statements. Examination of the record convinced the Court that the statements in question did not possess sufficient reliability and affirmed the decision of the Idaho Supreme Court, which had ruled that the out-of-court statements were inadmissible.

The Minnesota Supreme Court confronted a similar case in *State of Minnesota v. Lanam,* also decided in the summer of 1990. This was another situation in which a 3-year-old was deemed not competent to testify as a witness, but out-of-court statements made to the child's mother were admitted at trial. The court followed the U.S. Supreme Court decision in *Idaho v. Wright* and looked at such factors as the spontaneity with which the statement was made, whether the interviewer had preconceived notions concerning what the child should say, the consistency with which the story was told, motives to fabricate, the use of leading or nonleading questions, and whether or not the statement by the child was of a variety that one might expect children to fabricate.

It thus appears that the courts are going to fasten upon aspects of the situation in which a child renders a story. Now it is clear that although some of the research reviewed by Graham Davies in this volume relates to some of the circumstantial factors that can bear upon the reliability of child statements, overall there is very little such research. There is much more comparable research with adults (Penrod, Bull, & Lengnick, 1989). There is substantial adult research on leading questions, but there is not much research with children with regard to leading questions. There is very little research on the extent to which adult expectations can modify the reports made by children. There is virtually no research with regard to whether or to what extent children's stories change or whether that is a reliable indication of whether the child is telling the truth. We know little about the extent to which spontaneity serves as a guarantee of reliability for child statements. Clearly, these are areas and questions where research can dwell. Given the direction of recent cases such as *Idaho v. Wright* and *Minnesota v. Lanam,* one has to expect that these issues will increasingly be the focus of disputes about the reliability of children's testimony and that additional research in these areas may play a profound role in shaping the receptivity of the courts to testimony from children.

In sum, it is clear that courts are and are going to remain receptive to child testimony—particularly in situations where children are victimized. It is also clear that the courts are concerned about the reliability of child testimony and have identified the circumstances surrounding the generation of statements made by children as the critical factors in assessing the reliability of those statements. Experimental researchers interested in affecting policy and improving court scrutiny of child testimony have a clear research mandate.

Researchers who are not especially inclined to tackle child witness issues using experimental methods also have a useful role to play in helping courts to assess the state of scientific knowledge about child witnesses. By analogy to work with adult witnesses, there are at least two important types of research that can be conducted. The first concerns research directed to child witness researchers that assesses their judgments about the reliability, validity, and practical implications of child witness research findings. An excellent model of this type of research is a study by Kassin, Ellsworth, and Smith (1989) who report the results of a survey of 63 psychologists with research expertise on eyewitness reliability issues. The experts were surveyed about the reliability of research findings in 21 different eyewitness research domains including weapon focus, lineup instructions, cross-racial identification, and postevent information.

Kassin et al. found that for 13 of the topics more than 70% of the respondents believed that research findings were sufficiently reliable to merit expert testimony based on that research—though, in fact, only 54% of the respondents had ever given expert testimony. On only one topic (sex differences) did fewer than one-third believe the findings were not sufficiently reliable to merit such testimony. Given the rapid recent growth in child witness research, a similar survey of experts would provide an interesting and informative overview of experts perceptions of the strengths and weaknesses of the child witness research.

A second useful, though nonexperimental, approach to the research literature would be a meta-analysis of research findings—a quantitative summary of the reliability and magnitude of effects obtained in the experimental literature. A major task in a meta-analysis is to identify those studies in which a common independent variable has been manipulated and, across studies, specify the strength of the relationship between the manipulated variable and a common dependent variable. In eyewitness identification and facial recognition studies, the obvious dependent variable is identification accuracy.

One model for such an approach is a study by Shapiro and Penrod (1986) in which we coded 128 studies, involving 960 experimental conditions and 16,950 subjects. We were interested in testing the reliability of the effects that had been tested in the experimental research on more than 25 different topics. The results are reproduced in Table 8.1. The Table is divided to reflect performance in

TABLE 8.1
Manipulated Variables

				Hits			
Variable	N	n	d	SD	D	Z	p
1. Individual differences	103	9699	.13	.27	.13	7.34	***
2. Encoding instructions (hi vs. low)	29	1868	.97	1.32	.63	9.87	***
3. Context reinstatement (yes vs. no)	23	1684	1.91	1.87	1.39	17.54	***
4. Target distinctiveness (hi vs. low)	22	2174	.76	.79	.67	12.53	***
5. Sex of target (male vs. female)	19	2052	.02	.38	-.08	1.88	n.s.
6. Transformation (none vs. disguise)	19	2682	1.05	.83	.67	13.46	***
7. Race of target (White vs. minority–Black or Oriental)	18	1894	.24	.55	.10	2.05	*
8. Retention interval (short vs. long)	18	1980	.43	.61	.27	8.03	***
9. Same vs. cross race identification	17	1571	.53	.56	.40	6.99	***
10. Same vs. cross sex identification	13	1197	.14	.19	.23	3.18	***
11. Mode of presentation at recognition phase (live or videotape vs. still)	13	1807	.07	.28	.14	3.13	*
12. Face was associated with rich vs. poor elaboration at exposure time	10	362	1.00	.67	.98	8.15	***
13. Pose at study (3/4 vs. front or profile)	10	1266	.53	.87	.30	5.37	***
14. Subject age (young vs. old)	9	603	1.10	.68	.78	13.34	***
15. Training in facial recognitions yes vs. no)	8	534	.18	.58	.08	.54	n.s.
16. Exposure time at study time (long vs. short)	8	990	.61	.74	.38	4.48	***
17. Mode of presentation at study time (live or videotape vs. still)	5	896	.50	.80	.18	3.92	**
18. Knowledge of recognition task	5	703	.10	.12	.05	.42	n.s.
Grand means for entire data set	443	44301	.47	.85	.32	25.57	

(Continued)

studies that have examined hit rates, that is, accuracy in identify target individuals when they are present in arrays. The bottom half concerns studies that have looked at false alarms. Most of those studies measure false alarms of individuals in arrays where the target is present—a much smaller number of studies use target absent procedures that can give rise to a somewhat different and forensically more meaningful kind of false alarm.

The results can be explained with an example that examines research in a domain where a relatively large number of studies had been conducted is same versus cross-race identification, number 9. We found 17 studies in which cross-race identification was an experimentally manipulated independent variable. Those studies involved nearly 1600 subjects. The average effect size—that is, the number of standard deviations difference between the means for same versus cross-racial identifications was a little over a half a standard deviation (that average effect size declines to .40 when studies are weighted by sample size. It is quite clear from the table that when you cumulate across these studies and look at the cumulative Z, that there is a significant cross-race effect. The reliability of

TABLE 8.1
(*Continued*)

| | | | | *False Alarms* | | | |
Variable	*N*	*n*	*d*	*SD*	*D*	*Z*	*p*
1. Individual differences	70	6941	.08	.25	.06	2.23	*
2. Encoding instructions (hi vs. low)	19	1733	.38	.48	.21	2.07	*
3. Context reinstatement (yes vs. no)	18	1982	-.44	.40	-.26	-2.75	*
4. Target distinctiveness (hi vs. low)	18	1957	.78	.96	.55	7.89	***
5. Sex of target (male vs. female)	12	1690	-.07	.34	-.13	-3.40	***
6. Transformation (none vs. disguise)	6	1494	.40	.30	.32	5.64	***
7. Race of target (White vs. minority—Black or Oriental)	15	1626	.18	.39	.06	.23	n.s.
8. Retention interval (short vs. long)	14	1868	.33	.45	.20	2.02	***
9. Same vs. cross race identification	14	1432	.44	.55	.44	7.43	***
10. Same vs. cross sex identification	5	784	.02	.17	.07	.06	n.s.
11. Mode of presentation at recognition phase (live or videotape vs. still)	10	1407	.17	.36	.07	.14	n.s.
12. Face was associated with rich vs. poor elaboration at exposure time	2	72	-.06	.09	-.07	-.27	n.s.
13. Pose at study (3/4 vs. front or profile)	4	1027	0	0	0	0	n.s.
14. Subject age (young vs. old)	5	408	.66	.68	.86	13.33	***
15. Training in facial recognitions yes vs. no)	5	371	-.04	.06	-.04	-.15	n.s.
16. Exposure time at study time long vs. short)	8	1389	.22	.31	.08	.67	n.s.
17. Mode of presentation at study time (live or videotape vs. still)	2	280	.27	.68	.05	.27	n.s.
	5	1100	.27	.21	-.06	-1.03	n.s.
18. Knowledge of recognition task							
19. Target present/absent lineup	12	1694	.65	.50	.63	12.35	***
Grand means	282	28232	.18	.49	.21	7.95	***

Note. *N* = number of experimental manipulations studies. *n* = number of subjects. *d* = unweighted effect size. *SD* = standard deviation of unweighted effect sizes. *D* = weighted average effect size.
*p < .05; **p < .001; ***p < .0001. Based on Shapiro and Penrod (1986).

other effects examined in the experimental literature are similarly summarized in the table.

By way of note, the large numbers of individual difference studies were analyzed separately because most individual difference variables had been examined in very few studies. The individual difference that had received the greatest attention was gender of subject, for which differences were reported in 48 studies. In contrast to the opinions expressed in the Kassin et al. (1989) study, there were reliable relationships between gender and both hit and false alarm rates— though the effect sizes were rather small: d = .10 for hits and d = .08 for false alarms. Women produced higher hit rates, but also higher false alarm rates.

Topic 14 in Table 8.1 is subject age and the results reported there (in contrast to most other domains) are quite dated. At the time the meta-analysis was being prepared there very few studies that had looked at subject age. Only two child studies were available when data for this meta-analysis were compiled in late

1984 and 1985. Most of the research that Graham Davies covers (this volume) in his review is very new research. In fact, the subject age results reported in Table 8.1 are based on studies that predominately look at young adult versus older adult performance.

It should be clear from the sheer quantity of studies reviewed by Graham Davies that the body of child witness research is now large enough to merit meta-analyses that can provide us with similar insights into the reliability of the experimental findings and permit comparisons with the adult literature.

One other set of Shapiro and Penrod analyses are relevant to the external validity issues raised by Graham Davies. There can be a very sharp distinction between laboratory studies and field studies, and although eyewitness identification studies are becoming richer, more life-like, and higher in ecological validity, the vast majority of studies are weak in characteristics normally associated with high external validity. Do research methods affect outcomes in a manner that should cause us concern about external validity?

To explore this question Shapiro and Penrod undertook an exploratory analysis in which we made the documentably erroneous assumption that the 960 experimental conditions we examined were independent observations and looked at the possible impact on eyewitness accuracy of not only the experimental manipulations employed in the studies but also the experimental techniques used by the researchers in those studies. We used a hierarchical regression analysis designed largely to parallel the temporal processes of making an identification.

In the analyses we entered blocks of variables measuring the extent to which attention was directed to targets, the numbers of targets and foils presented to subjects, variables reflecting individual differences in target and subjects, retention interval, etc. To illustrate the process, we first entered attentional factors—including a judgment made by a blind rater of the degree to which the procedure used in the study would direct the attention of the subject to the target face. Irrespective of whether a study is conducted in a laboratory or in the field, you can make judgments about the extent to which procedures call the attention of the witness/subject to the perpetrator. Though it is unlikely, one can imagine field studies that call the attention of the witness to the perpetrator as strongly as any laboratory study that would request subjects to scrutinize the faces because they are going to be making an identification later on. We entered variables reflecting the mode of presentation of target faces—that is, whether subjects were looking at pictures or they were looking at live individuals. We coded whether the subjects knew that they were later going to be called upon to make an identification or not.

The last variable we entered in the analysis was a variable that reflected whether the study was a field experiment or a laboratory study. One of the things we were interested in was the question of what differences in performance do we observe between studies that use laboratory versus field techniques? We knew that the zero-order correlation between the field versus laboratory study variable and performance was fairly high for both hit rates ($r = .59$) and false alarm rates ($r = .55$)—with performance on both measures much higher in laboratory studies. On the other hand, we wanted to know what would happen to those relationships when (through hierarchical regression) we took account of the systematic differences that exist between laboratory and field settings (e.g., differences in where attention was being directed, subjects' knowledge about the identification test, the number of targets being studied, target of race, target gender, retention interval, the load that was imposed on subjects at recognition, etc).

What we found is that by the time you partial out the effects of all these other systematic differences, you are left with a partial r of .17 for hits and .14 for false alarms. In effect, one can systematically account for differences in performance that occur in laboratories as opposed to field studies, once one recognizes that they vary in systematic ways and take account of that systematicity. This suggests that it is possible to generalize from laboratory studies to the real world. Given the explosion in child witness research, there is now a body of findings that is susceptible to such analysis and that can provide some insights into the external validity and the ecological validity of these studies and the implications that they have for the real world.

The problems confronting a child witness meta-analyst are in some ways more complex than the ones Shapiro and Penrod confronted. In developmental studies, one must expect there are going to be developmental trends—age differences require testing for interactions between subject age and all of the independent variables that might bear upon the accuracy of identifications made by child witnesses. This imposes another order of magnitude of complexity on the enterprise. Nonetheless it is a desirable enterprise to undertake—not only because it can provide a summary of the state of the research, but because it will be of assistance in identifying where research needs to be expanded, where the effects are clear and consistent, and where they are not clear and consistent. Such analyses will also have the effect of underscoring, for those who wish to apply research findings to the courtroom and to the real world, which findings are robust, which are reliable, and which are worthy of presentation in the courtroom.

In sum, the child witness has come of age—at least in the sense that there has been a recent dovetailing of legal and psychological interest in child witnesses. Issues concerning child witnesses have featured prominently in a number of important appellate and United States Supreme Court decisions at the same time there has been a rapid growth in the number of experimental studies of child witnesses. As detailed earlier, the courts have, at times, been overenthusiastic in their use of psychological and psychiatric expertise—particularly clinical expertise thought relevant to the evaluation of child witness reliability. Only recently have appellate decisions given clear recognition to the importance of the insights that experimental research on child witnesses can yield.

Although the courts have not explicitly called upon the research community to answer the questions posed in appellate litigation, recent opinions clearly constitute an implicit invitation for relevant research. In particular, the courts have identified aspects of child witnessing—especially the circumstances under which child statements are elicited—that will be critical to judicial evaluation and admission of child evidence. Identification and explanation of the effects that interviewing and reporting conditions can have on the reliability of child witness reports will be of great interest to the courts. Authoritative summary statements of conclusions based upon this research will be particularly helpful to courts seeking to determine the conditions under which child witnesses will be allowed to testify and the conditions under which their reports to adult witnesses will be independently admissible. Researchers interested in guiding this evaluation process are likely to find their studies are eagerly received by the courts.

REFERENCES

Goodman, G. S., Levine, M., Melton, G. B., & Ogden, D. W. (1991). Child witnesses and the confrontation clause: The American Psychological Association brief in *Maryland v. Craig*. *Law and Human Behavior, 15,* 13–29.

Kassin, S. M., Ellsworth, P. C., & Smith, V. L. (1989). The "general acceptance" of psychological research on eyewitness testimony. *America Psychologist, 44,* 1089–1098.

Levy, R. J. (1989). Using "scientific" testimony to prove child sexual abuse. *Journal of Family Law, XXIII,* 383–409.

Myers, J. E. B., Bays, J., Becker, J., Berliner, L., Corwin, D. L., & Saywitz, K. J. (1989). Expert testimony in child sexual abuse case litigation. *Nebraska Law Review, 68,* 1–145.

Penrod, S., Bull, M., & Lengnick, S. (1989). Children as observers and witnesses: The empirical data. *Journal of Family Law, XXIII,* 412–431.

Shapiro, P., & Penrod, S. (1986). A meta-analysis of facial identification studies. *Psychological Bulletin, 100,* 139–156.

Summit, R. (1983). The child sexual abuse accommodation syndrome. *Child Abuse & Neglect, 7,* 177–193.

Underwager, R., & Wakefield, H. (1992). Poor psychology makes poor law. *Law and Human Behavior, 16,* 233–243.

Understanding Children's Memories of Medical Procedures: "He Didn't Touch Me and It Didn't Hurt!"

Margaret S. Steward
University of California, Davis

MEDICAL PROCEDURES: A CONTEXT FOR STUDYING MEMORY AND EMOTION

All children in our society are subject to medical procedures sometime during the period from birth through 6 years-of-age to assess health status, prevent disease, or to diagnose and treat illness. Most healthy infants and young children experience annually body touch and handling by medical staff using a stethoscope, an otoscope, a thermometer, a tongue depressor, and a hammer during routine pediatric examinations. Nearly every child will have experienced "the needle" prior to entrance in public school programs, as we strive for our national health goal that all young children be inoculated against common childhood diseases. During periods of acute illness or following accidental injury, a young child may be introduced to additional medical procedures if, for example, she or he is required to give a urine or blood sample or have an X-ray taken. Approximately 10 to 15% of the children in our society, cutting across all ethnic and socioeconomic groups, have a chronic, sometimes life-threatening, disease that requires vigorous, repeated, and often very painful medical procedures (Hobbs, Perrin, & Ireys, 1985).

Whether healthy or ill, a child's encounter with a medical procedure presents a complex set of stimuli which may compel a child's attention, elicit strong emotions, and evoke a broad range of coping strategies. A richly textured, highly personal event or scenario such as this is likely to remembered. To date there are few research studies on children's memory of medical procedures, and even fewer that explore the impact of the affective experience of medical procedures on a child's subsequent memory of the event (Peterson, Harbeck, Farmer, &

Zink, 1991). However, there are research data in three related fields that can be drawn upon for the design and interpretation of studies of children's memory of medical procedures. First, there are clinical vignettes and case studies in the pediatric literature reporting children's experience with illness, medical procedures, and hospitalization extending back at least 50 years (Bergmann & Freud, 1965; Jackson, 1942; Jessner, Blom, & Waldfogel, 1952; Levy, 1945; Pearson, 1941; Plank, 1971). The majority of this work has focused on unique defensive or protective functions of children's emotional responses to illness and is based on observations of individual children made by pediatric or psychiatric staff members in hospital settings. One particularly rich report in this genre is based on a diary kept by Joyce Robertson of her daughter's 3-day hospitalization for a tonsillectomy (Robertson & Freud, 1956). Details of Robertson's report will be reviewed later in this chapter as it describes the child's anticipation and memory of medical and surgical procedures over a 6-month time frame.

Second, investigators interested in children's memory of medical procedures may benefit from the findings of studies on the development of children's understanding of the causes of illness. Research was initiated in the early 50s by Nagy, a Hungarian psychologist, who documented what healthy and hospitalized children knew about body contents, function and dysfunction. Initially chronological age differences were sought (Gellert, 1962; Nagy, 1953; Williams, 1979); then children's explanations of illness causation and treatment were framed by the structural differences of Piagetian cognitive stages (Bibace & Walsh, 1980, 1981; Brewster, 1982; Carandang, Folkins, Hines, & Steward, 1979; Myers-Vando, Steward, Folkins, & Hines, 1979; Neuhauser, Amsterdam, Hines, & Steward, 1978; Perrin & Gerrity, 1981; Perrin, Sayer, & Willett, 1991; Potter & Roberts, 1984; Steward & Regalbuto, 1975; Sussman, Dorn, & Fletcher, 1987; Whitt, Dykstra, & Taylor, 1979). Currently, emphasis on a child's domain specific knowledge including unique expertise with illness (Bearison, 1990; Eiser, 1989; Siegal, Patty, & Eiser, 1990) children's self-attributions with regard to their illness/injury (Moss, Steward, & Racusin, 1992), and attention to the beneficial effects of illness on social, emotional, and cognitive development (Nelms, 1989; Parmalee, 1986) are augmenting the age/stage-based developmental hypotheses.

Third, research on children's experience of pain, though lagging far behind research on adult pain (Bush & Harkins, 1991; Ross & Ross, 1988), is important, for pain may play a critical role in mediating children's memory of medical procedures. Pain has been defined by the International Association for the Study of Pain as "an unpleasant sensory and emotional experience associated with actual or potential tissue damage, or described in terms of such damage" (Merskey, 1979). Ross and Ross (1982), in their interviews with nearly 1000 children, have demonstrated that children think about and remember their own painful experiences. The initial work on the clinical assessment of children's pain was conducted by pediatric nurses because of their concern about undermedication of postsurgical and burn patients (Eland, 1974; Eland & Anderson, 1977). Nursing research also evolved from the pragmatic need to determine when to administer analgesic medication ambiguously ordered "PRN" (pro re nata) by children's physicians (Zeltzer, 1991). A wide variety of tools have been developed to assess the quality (Wilkie, Holzemer, Tesler, Ward, Paul, & Savedra, 1990) and quantity (Beyer & Wells, 1990; Kuttner & Lepage, 1989; Lollar, Smits, & Patterson, 1982; McGrath, 1987) of young children's self-report of pain and to code the behavioral (Jay, Ozolins, Elliott, & Caldwell, 1983) and biochemical distress that pain evokes (Gunner, Hertsgaard, Larson, & Rigatuso, 1992).

Careful studies of children's memory of medical procedures may contribute to three quite distinctive endeavors. First, children's memory of necessary but painful medical procedures can contribute to the growing research literature on children's event memory (Bearison & Pacifici, 1989). Second, the documentation of children's memory of medical procedures may enhance the clinical care of ill children as the information will enable medical staff who must administer necessary procedures to do a better job of preparation and follow-up with individual children (Jay, 1988; Melamed, 1991b). Third, the results of research on children's experience of medical procedures may provide an ecologically valid empirical data base from which to interpret reports from investigative or therapeutic interviews of children's memory of other emotionally charged events centered on the body such as their observation of domestic violence or their direct experience as victims of child physical and sexual abuse (Goodman, 1984; Melton, 1981).

In the next section I offer an operational definition of medical procedures and the relation of such procedures to stress. Then, I discuss characteristics of young children's memories and, finally, three models of the impact of distress on memory.

What Are Medical Procedures?

We have defined a medical procedure as "any procedure conducted or supervised by medical personnel for the purpose of evaluating or modifying health status" (Steward & Steward, 1981). This definition includes three essential components—the what, the who, and the why. These components incorporate an inherent developmental perspective. The first component in our definition of medical procedure—"any procedure"—focuses on the child's sensorimotor experience of just what is happening as the medical equipment required for the procedure is brought into juxtaposition to his or her body. Medical procedures range widely and from the child's perspective include such activities as standing in stocking feet on the doctor's scales to be weighed and measured, feeling the cold stethoscope pressing on one's chest or back as the doctor listens to the heart and lungs, experiencing the prick of a needle and watching the bubble begin to develop just below the skin when a TB test is administered, or being physically restrained by tape and belts on an X-ray table as a big metal plate is lowered overhead. Attention to the sensorimotor information predominates, regardless of the age of the individual receiving the procedure. The sight, sound, smell of the procedure and all kinesthetic, proprioceptive, and nocioceptive (painful) experiences are often vivid, rarely verbalized, yet apparently rarely forgotten.

The second component of our definition of medical procedure—"conducted or supervised by medical personnel"—focuses on who is administering the procedure. For young children it is nearly always a medical staff member or a parent under medical staff direction who is responsible for administering a procedure, but increasingly for children as young as six, the child may self-administer a procedure under the direction of medical staff. For most children there are increasing choices, as they become developmentally appropriate, in the process of administration. For example, a child may be asked in which arm she or he prefers to receive an injection. This shift in the child's role from a passive to a collaborative or active participant is seen as contributing differentially to the child's cognitive and emotional experience of the procedure and may impact the child's memory of the experience as well. (Note that home remedies, such as a parental "kiss-to-make-it-well," or the kindergarten teacher's placement of an ice cube "between the pain and the brain" are not included in this definition. Nor is children's unsupervised self-medication, although these events merit study.)

The third component of our definition of medical procedure—"for the purpose of evaluating or modifying health status"—focuses on the reason for the procedure. In Piagetian terms, we believe that it isn't until an individual is a concrete operational thinker that medical procedures can be categorized accurately as diagnostic or treatment procedures. Young children, regardless of what they are told, sometimes confuse the two different purposes, believing that every procedure will "get me better." Adults who are poorly informed, or whose cognitive faculties are compromised by anxiety, illness, or both often confuse the purpose of medical procedures as well, giving rise to curative placebo effects following procedures that are solely diagnostic. Regardless of the mandate for informed consent, it is probably only the person able to mobilize formal operational thinking who can evaluate the probable physical and psychological impact of diagnostic or treatment procedures on their health status and subsequent quality of life.

Are All Medical Procedures Stressful?

This question is not as simple to answer as it might first seem—and it is one that must ultimately be answered by the child who experiences the procedure, a point to which we return. I have developed a three dimensional, intersecting matrix in order to describe the relative distress that a child might experience with any particular medical procedure (Steward, 1988). The dimensions include the following: (a) the relative painfulness of a procedure (this may range from no pain to excrutiating pain); (b) proximity of the equipment used in the procedure to the body (this may range from diagnostic or treatment procedures that do not touch the body to those that penetrate body boundaries, e.g., breaking the skin or penetrating a body orafice); and (c) the cognitive congruence with the child's understanding of the need for the procedure (ranging from the procedure being consonant with the child's understanding to being totally incongruent and incomprehensible to the child). These dimensions have been drawn from the clinical literature and our own clinical observations of ill or injured children.

Our clinical observations suggest that it is likely that any procedure that falls at the upper extreme of any of the three dimensions will be experienced by a child as distressing. Of course, any procedure that hurts is distressing, and when the procedure needs to be repeated frequently, anticipatory fear and anxiety increase the stressfulness of the experience—even if a child understands why it is necessary. Invasive procedures that break body boundaries or place Q-tips, hands, tubes, or instruments into body orifices are stressful for they are experienced by children as unwanted, and aptly described as invasive. Procedures that children don't understand, even if they are described as noninvasive and painless, can be very distressing to children. For example, if an X-ray of an arm can reveal a broken bone, and results in a cast being placed on the broken arm, it all makes good sense to the child. But shift the target of the X-ray or CT scan to the same child's head, and the child may become very agitated believing that the doctor is trying to read the bad thoughts in her mind.

Procedures that fall in the three dimensional space defined as painful, invasive, and incomprehensible appear to be cognitively and emotionally the most distressing for children. All procedures that involve a needle as the most salient feature, for example where it is used to take something out of the body (e.g., blood or spinal fluid) or to put something into the body (e.g., medication, live virus, etc.), fit that description. Further research is needed to determine if the contributions of the three variables are additive or multiplicative.

YOUNG CHILDREN'S MEMORIES

Most of our work is with young children, ranging from infancy to 6 years-of-age, and therefore we have become particularly interested in the characteristics of early childhood memory. Nelson (1989), a pioneer in the study of event memory of young children, has identified the following features. First, a young child's memory is rarely deliberate. Second, the content of early childhood memories consists primarily of events that were directly experienced by the child. Third, most of the content of the young child's memory is inaccessible to retrieval later in life. Fourth, memory can be manifested in a variety of intentional behaviors, including verbal response. She notes, in addition, that the child may remember more than he or she can tell.

We have found it useful to place Nelson's characteristics of young children's memory within a dual memory system, a developmental framework proposed by Pillemer and White (1989). The authors have described the first memory system, which is present at birth and continues to predominate into early childhood, as containing the memories that are organized and evoked by an infant's experiences of persons, location, and emotion. Situational and affective cues access these memories that are experienced through images, behaviors, or emotions. The first memory system is not verbally mediated, nor are the memories easily *transported* outside the original experiential stimulus context. The second, language-based memory system posited by Pillemer and White begins to develop in early childhood. Memories are accessible in this socially connected system through intentional retrieval efforts in contexts other than the original learning environment. Event representations are encoded in narrative form or processed into verbal symbolizations, and are brought into *socialized memory*.

The model of the dual memory system suggests that young children who experience medical procedures may store different facets of the experience in each of the two systems, depending on their cognitive development, language skill, and/or emotional distress. It may also be that even after the language-based memory system is well established, some facets of the memory of older children, adolescents, and adults for a specific medical procedure that evokes strong emotional responses will also be stored in the first memory system. Pillemer and White posit that the two systems function separately but both may continue to operate throughout the life span. The theory suggests that even after the language-based memory system is established, some experiences are powerful enough to leave a person speechless, and memories stored in the first system will not be easily retrieved by a simple verbal interview.

Models of Memory and Distress

What is the impact of distressing emotional experiences on children's memories? There are two models that might be posited to predict differential memory of the event utilizing the variable of the relative distress of a medical procedure and a third model that factors self-evaluation of one's role in a stressful experience and the frequency of occurrence into the model. First, a simple linear model suggests that the more distressing the experience, the more a child would be able to remember it. Earlier, I identified three potential sources of stress from our clinical work with ill children (painfulness, invasiveness, and incongruence of a medical procedure with the child's understanding of his or her needs). This model predicts that children who experience more distress as a result of pain, invasiveness, and/or incongruence, also experience increased arousal and alertness which accompanies distress and thus are able to remember more about the events of a medical procedure than can children who were less distressed (Gold, 1987).

A second model suggests a cubic relationship such as the inverted U-shaped curve. The cubic model predicts that if an experience is either of neutral valence (eustress) or extremely distressing it will be remembered less well than if the emotional experience is mid-range. Many link this model back to the work of Yerkes and Dodson (1908) in which they tested the relationship between the strength of the negative reinforcement and the number of trials needed by the dancer mouse to learn a visual discrimination task.[1] On the extreme left hand side of the curve fall experiences that are not experienced as sufficiently distressing for an individual to enlist perceptual or cognitive skills to appraise or cope. There is little to remember about the event. On the extreme right hand side of the curve there are intense emotional experiences. Easterbrook (1959) demonstrated experimentally that intense emotional experience limits the range of perceptual cues that an individual is able to process, a mechanism that inhibits an individual's performance and subsequently the ability to recall an event.

There are at least two data sets, one from adults in dangerous environments (Baddeley, 1972; Broadbent, Reason, & Baddeley, 1991), and another from traumatized children (Terr, 1991), which suggest that both the linear and the cubic models are too simple to be useful to explain the relationship between distress and children's memory of medical procedures. Research by Baddeley acknowledges the impact of perceptual narrowing on performance in dangerous environments described by Easterbrook, but suggests that an individual's performance in a dangerous situation will improve if she or he believes that performance on the task is important. Performance will deteriorate, as predicted by the cubic model, only if the task is deemed by the individual to be peripheral. A child's evaluation of the relative importance of his role during medical procedures—regardless of the specific assignment—may be dependent on the skill of parents and medical staff during the preparation phase to convey not only what the child is expected to do during the medical procedure (e.g., to hold the left arm very still), but why it is important that the child do it just that way (e.g., so the procedure can be done quickly, won't have to be repeated, will hurt less, etc.). Baddeley further predicts that with repeated experience in dangerous situations individuals inhibit anxiety, judge the experience as less dangerous and thereby reduce the amount of impairment to performance of peripheral tasks, and may remember peripheral tasks better.

Terr (1979, 1983, 1988, 1990, 1991) has focused on children's memory of extremely stressful, traumatic experiences in which, by definition, children are helpless. She has hypothesized that under these conditions it is the relative frequency of occurrence of a stressful event that differentially impacts a child's memory. Childhood trauma is defined as ". . . the mental result of one sudden,

---

[1] It should be noted that in the original data set published by Yerkes and Dodson the U-shaped curve described the relationship between stress and performance when the discrimination tasks were moderately or very difficult, while a linear model described the relationship of stress to learning when the task was easy.

external blow or a series of blows, render ng the young person temporarily helpless and breaking past ordinary coping and defensive operations. . . . All childhood traumas originate from the outside. . . . Once the events take place, a number of internal changes occur" (p. 11). Terr (1991) has described two categories of trauma: (a) Type 1 disorders result from a one time occurrence, an unanticipated "single-blow," while (b) Type II disorders result from repeated exposure to extreme external events. Terr asserts that children's memories to Type I trauma are reported in "amazingly clear and detailed fashion" whereas memories of children suffering Type II trauma "appear to be retained in spots rather than in clear, complete wholes." Children's reports of events causing Type II trauma are characterized by a number of defensive strategies which might interrupt the memory such as denial and self-numbing, self-hypnosis and dissociation, and rage (which paradoxically is dealt with by extreme passivity).

A third model of the link between relative distress and memory, incorporating the work of Baddeley and Terr, resembles a graphic overlay of the linear and cubic models. The linear prediction of high memory performance about a highly stressful experience holds for a single traumatic event and/or one in which the child perceives him or herself to play an important role; repeated traumatic experiences that render the child helpless depress memory with the y axis dropping theoretically to total amnesia at the zero point. Terr typifies the child who has experienced a Type I trauma as repetitively reviewing the traumatic experience mulling the question, "How could I have avoided it?" This psychologically driven rehearsal of the child's behavior before and during the event may serve ego defensive purposes and suggests à la Baddeley a child's post hoc attempt to assign a significant role in the event to herself. The third model of stress and memory predicts that both rehearsal and role reassignment processes contribute to strengthen a child's memory of the event. The child who has experienced Type II traumas is existentially alert asking, "How will I avoid it next time?" The process of drawing attention away from the past event limits rehearsal and fails to assign a child an important role in the past traumatic event. The third model predicts that these experiences lead to a deterioration of memory about a past event. The current pediatric population offers a potential resource for testing empirically the usefulness of each of the three models for predicting or describing the link between experiences that are emotionally stressful and memory.

Anna Freud (1952) asserted that it is not the severity of the injury or illness that is important in determining the relative stressfulness of that experience for a child, but rather the meaning of the illness to the child. Research results support Miss Freud's caution by documenting that parents share a common judgment about the relative stressfulness of specific medical procedures (Watt-Watson, Evernden, & Lawson, 1991), but children do not (Beyer, Berde, & Bournaki, 1991; Lehmann, Bendebba, & DeAngelis, 1990). Terr (1991) has extended that discussion by identifying some of the "internal changes" that a child must invoke to cope with repeated events that he judges to be traumatic, which interfere with subsequent recall of the events. In order to test any of the models of the link between memory and emotion in the context of medical procedures, the assessment of a child's distress and judgments about the importance of the child's role in medical procedures must be made by the child. Of course, children's assessments may change over time. It is possible, for example, that with experience a child's judgment about the relative *dangerousness* of a particular medical procedure may diminish and future encounters may become less memorable. With maturity the judgment of the relative importance of his or her role is likely to be proportional to the child's participation in the administration of a procedure (such as when a diabetic child takes over the role of testing her own blood glucose). Memory may be enhanced with increased responsibility. It may be useful, both theoretically and clinically to collect judgments from adult observers (e.g., parents, medical staff, research assistants) about the child's distress, for discrepancies between adult and child judgment can provide another independent variable which may contribute to the predictive power of any of the models. However, adult judgments of child distress or importance should never be substituted for the child's judgment.

The biochemistry of distress and memory in children has not been studied extensively but clearly offers another set of variables anchored in the child's body. Stress can be measured most easily by assessing changes in cortisol levels in a child's blood or saliva. The stress system plays a critical role in setting the level of arousal, and interacts with other central nervous system elements that influence the retrievability and analysis of information, the initiation of specific action and the setting of the emotional tone (Chrousos & Gold, 1991). Jay and her colleagues (Jay & Elliott, 1990; Jay, Elliott, Katz, & Siegel, 1987) have explored simultaneously multiple measures of children's distress (e.g., self-report estimates of distress, behavioral observations of a child's distress, and cortisol levels) during medical procedures, but to my knowledge there has been no research on the incorporation of biochemical measures of stress into an optimal set of child stress variables to predict memory.

Finally, it should be noted that research on memory and emotion in the context of medical procedures can shed light on only a limited range of emotional experiences from neutral to negative at the time of encoding. Early versions of coding systems used to record children's behavior during invasive medical procedures included such categories as laughing and smiling. Those have been deleted in later versions because of infrequent use. Ross (1989, personal communication) reported that when children are asked to give advice to doctors, one of their common requests is that the doctors "don't be too jokey!" In a new study that is currently underway (Steward, Reinhart, Joye, & Steward, 1992), a colleague urged us to include the question, "Did you do anything fun with the doctor today?"—no child has yet answered "Yes." In addition, professional ethics preclude experimental manipulation of mood at postevent interviews, although note could be made of the child's mood by the interviewer.

DOING RESEARCH ON CHILDREN'S MEMORY IN MEDICAL SETTINGS

The Laboratory versus the Natural Setting

There is a lively debate occurring among memory researchers about the relative merits of the study of memory within the confines of the laboratory versus memory study in the setting of the "everyday" (Banaji & Crowder, 1989; Loftus, 1991). This is a discussion that was initiated more than a decade ago by Neisser (1978) and by Bronfenbrenner (1979). The discussion is not only about the relative amount of experimental control; it is, as Neisser (1991) pointed out, also about the interaction between research subjects and the setting. Neisser (1988) asserts that a person is always nested in an environment that contributes to and extends the complexity of the phenomena to be studied. For those interested in children's memory, research in the natural setting is important, for it has been documented that the capacities of children to perform and remember are often underestimated in a laboratory situation (Ceci & Bronfenbrenner, 1991).

Schneider and Pressley (1989), reviewing research on children's memory, observed that most researchers accept a memory model in which contextual and motivational variables are presumed to be important determinants of memory. But for the most part, these same researchers continue to study memory without regard to naturalistic situational or motivational states. Schneider and Pressley call for work on interindividual differences and intraindividual differences in children's memory performances in order to understand consistency across situations. For those of us who are interested more specifically in the impact of traumatic events on children's memories, research in the natural setting becomes even more compelling. Fabes and his colleagues (Fabes, Eisenberg, McCormick, & Wilson, 1988; Fabes, Eisenberg, Nyman, & Michealieu, 1991) assert that it is possible to study a range of children's emotion and experience in the natural setting, the circumstances of which would never pass a human Subject Review Committee, nor receive parental approval were they proposed for a laboratory setting. And unlike a child's participation in a laboratory setting, in a medical setting if a procedure is deemed necessary, a child may not refuse to participate.

OBSERVATIONS ABOUT MEMORY IN THE MEDICAL SETTING

The medical setting offers more diversity than do laboratory settings. For example, the physical and psychosocial settings in which children experience a medical procedure may range from a calm, child-friendly private office of a beloved pediatrician to a chaotic, impersonal emergency room of a large metropolitan hospital or even to a child's hospital bed. A child may be surrounded by a three generational delegation of family members, sit on a parent's lap throughout a procedure or be handed over to a medical staff person by a transportation worker of half hour's acquaintance to cope with the experience alone.

Many of us who have worked with children in medical settings have been impressed with what we believe to be the detailed and uncanny accuracy of children's memories of specific medical experiences. Children's memories of who, what, where, and when seem to be particularly vivid in the medical setting. For example, children can describe, and often name, the nurse who "doesn't do the shots good," the size of the needle used in a blood draw, exactly where a little girl was when her broken arm was set, and whether a boy's surgery was before or after Halloween. Children sometimes remember what happened to them in the hospital more accurately than their parents or their doctors (Beuf, 1979). Furthermore, many adults retain clear memories of their childhood accidents, injuries, and illnesses (Massie, 1985).

It is now possible to test hypotheses developed from the rich clinical vignettes of children's experience in medical settings: to document their experiences and subsequently to determine just how accurate, complete, and consistent their memories are. From a methodological perspective, by placing videocameras in pediatric settings, one can insure an objective record, an atheoretical flow, if you will, of events, actions, and language against which to compare children's later reports of events. It has been our experience that there has been little objection to making the video recordings when cameras are inobtrusively mounted (for example in one corner of the room) and when they don't take floor space or interrupt swift, but unpredictable movement of children, parents, or staff.

We have found that access to medical records (increasingly computerized) may still be necessary to clarify events that children experience and later report, but that are not shown on camera. Sometimes in our work a doctor's body filled the screen and we would have miscoded a child's description of "the pump and the ribbon thing" if we had not found notation of a child's blood pressure in the medical record. We have found, however, that, as a rule, a child's medical record is far sparser than the video record. For example, medical staff rarely note in a child's medical record how many "tries" or persons were required to start an I.V. successfully, or the names of medical students or staff who were present for part or all of a medical or surgical procedure. Never does the medical record reflect the often subtle communication between medical staff and parent, or any but the most extreme expressions of emotional behavior of a parent or child.

The earliest work in the pediatric literature that speaks to the issue of children's memory of medical procedures can be found in clinical vignettes and case studies. For developmental psychologists, the carefully documented case study is the oldest method of collecting data on child behavior (Achenbach, 1978). There is renewed interest in the case study method for generating and testing hypotheses about mechanisms that, for example, contribute to cognitive development (Siegler & Crowley, 1991) and for tracking individual response to pediatric human immunodeficiency viruses (Fletcher, Francis, Pequegnat, Raudenbush, Bornstein, Schmitt, Brouwers, & Stover, 1991). The limitations to generalizability of the findings of an observational study of an individual child are balanced by the opportunity to review a child behavior's longitudinally, usually in natural settings.

The observations reported next were selected from the diary that Joyce Robertson (Robertson & Freud, 1956) kept over a 26-week period about her daughter's tonsillectomy. These data are presented in the best tradition of the "baby biographies" written by parents such as Charles Darwin (1877) and Jean Piaget (1952, 1954). Robertson's piece provides an introduction (or reminder) to the reader who may be unfamiliar with young children's medical experiences and will serve as a template to identify some thematic issues with respect to children's anticipation, experience, and memory of the events and people surrounding medical and surgical procedures.

The classic theoretical paper on children's response to illness, "The role of bodily illness in the mental life of children," was written by Anna Freud in 1952. Robertson's work provided an important translation from theory to a clinical data base, and Anna Freud wrote an appreciative interpretive piece that was published along with the diary. Although neither Anna Freud nor Joyce Robertson focused explicitly on memory, each author had something to say about the link between the illness experience and the child's memory of those experiences.

An Early Case Study

Joyce Robertson's (Robertson & Freud, 1956) diary about her 4-year-old daughter Jean's trip to the hospital for a routine tonsillectomy was begun 6 weeks before hospitalization. It includes daily entries until 3 weeks after the return home, and a brief addendum to summarize events from the 11th to the 20th weeks home. The results suggest that the anticipation and memory of the events of a 3-day hospitalization, which included brief medical and surgical procedures deemed successful and unremarkable from a medical perspective, filled Jean's life for 6 months.

It should be noted that this was no ordinary vignette. It is interesting and important for historical and psychodynamic reasons. First, just prior to Jean's hospitalization, her father, James Robertson (1953a), had completed an astonishingly poignant black and white, silent film entitled, "A Two Year Old Goes to the Hospital." The film, by documenting the surprise, terror, and subsequent depression of a toddler "abandoned" by parents to medical staff, challenged the wisdom of the then current practice in Great Britain and the United States of separating the young patient from the parent during hospitalization. Jean's father not only had begun a revolution that would impact a number of decisions about hospital care of young children (a revolution that is unfortunately not yet complete today), he also created some of the first materials to prepare children for hospitalization (Connell, 1953; Robertson, 1953b). Thus Jean had easy access to the hospital stories of two children she named "Tonsil Boy" and "Laura."

Second, Jean had the benefit of an unusually sensitive, patient, and observant mother. Joyce Robertson faithfully recorded Jean's words and deeds reflecting her daughter's anticipatory distress, her behavior during the course of hospitalization and posthospital recovery. Mrs. Robertson was a participant-observer, for she was her daughter's fulltime and primary parental caretaker at home. In addition she stayed in her daughter's room throughout the hospitalization and arranged to provide all but the most technical of nursing care during her daughter's hospital stay. All of this occurred during a period of time when parents were typically allowed to visit their children in hospital *one hour a week!* Third, Anna Freud was a family friend. Miss Freud was so impressed by Joyce Robertson's diary notes that she changed her stance on the potential scientific contribution which could be gleaned from mothers as observers of their own children.

In spite of all these extraordinary features, 4-year-old Jean still had a rocky time. I rehearse briefly Jean's experience during three periods—the preparatory phase, the in-hospital phase and the posthospitalization phase at home.

Preparation.   Even though Joyce Robertson had planned to wait to prepare Jean until a week before the surgery—recommendations that we still give today to mothers of preschoolers—Jean overheard during an outpatient visit her doctor's decision to schedule a tonsillectomy for 6 weeks hence. The very next day she began to give clues that she had some understanding of what might lie ahead for her and that she didn't like the idea at all! Her protest included a refusal to eat, then a refusal to use silverware, linking eating with the planned assault on her throat; initiation of knife play on herself, her mother, furniture; separation anxiety—taunting her sister that mother would stay in hospital with her, but requesting that Daddy stay too; the definition of operation as punishment and equation of medical staff with policemen and the hospital with prison; repeated discussion of, then rejection of, other children's illness/death and increased accident-prone behavior. Jean's troublesome behavior not only signaled the need for repeated clarification and expansion by her mother of up-coming events, she initiated preparatory activities herself by rummaging through her father's papers to find the stories of "Tonsil Boy" and "Laura," asking that they be read to her many times each day.

Postsurgery.   Apparently Jean was fascinated by her lack of memory for an event that occurred in which her body was not only touched and handled, but actually had a piece cut out. She repeatedly marveled at her absence of memory. She had been well-prepared for the special sleep, for some pain following the surgery, and even for the experience of "not remembering." Postsurgery she verballized again and again, "You were quite right, Mummy. My throat does hurt a lot—but I didn't feel them come out." She repeatedly asked her mother to rehearse the scenario beginning with the preparatory pills and injection through the trolley trip, the funny smell, the surgery, the return to her room, and finally mother beside her reading a story. Following each rehearsal, Jean had many questions—sometimes about the doctor, other times about the special room, or the exact location of her tonsils ("were my tonsils in my nose too?")—which allowed her mother to elaborate the story.

My favorite episode in the story came when Jean demonstrated her accurate memory for a presurgery injection 3 days after surgery by speaking in "a friendly way to her Big Nurse, but then {she} shot a flying toy which hit the Big Nurse's leg." Six days postsurgery, while bouncing her head on and off a pillow, she asked her mother "Was it yesterday you kept telling me to lay my head on the pillow? I didn't want to—I wanted to sit up." The interchange to which Jean was referring between herself and her mother had occurred just half an hour after the surgery—a period most believed she would not remember.

Posthospitalization.   Three features stand out in Joyce Robertson's rich description of the posthospital period. First, although Jean's memory for the exact spot on her leg where she received an injection continued to be accurate, she changed temporarily the identity of the medical staff member who administered the procedure, first claiming it was a student nurse. Two weeks later she spontaneously announced, "It was my Big Nurse who pricked my leg. I didn't like it. Why did she?" On the 15th day home she told her sister with "impish laughter" about the time she hit the Big Nurse's leg with the flying toy—"She hit me, so I hit her." On the 16th day she was playing doctors and said, "We must have a doctor, and you be the doctor. You must hurt her leg and then you must make her quite better." On the 18th day home she reported "I didn't like the Big Nurse pricking my leg. Which leg did she prick? Did she make a hole?"

Second, although Jean was spared the anxiety of being separated from her mother during hospitalization and commented both before and after her hospitalization on the sadness of children whose mothers did not visit or did not stay the night, she demonstrated marked ambivalence toward her mother. Mother had been a warm and comforting presence, yet at the same time she had delivered Jean to the hospital and did not protect Jean from the necessary painful procedures, the surgery and resulting sore throat. She could not protect her child from vomiting blood, or a bloody nose. And though the Robertsons had sufficient clout to insure mother's presence in the hospital, Jean wanted a bed for daddy as well. The first evening home Jean slapped her mother. In fact Joyce Robertson reported that "she slapped me hard saying, 'I don't like you because you took me to the hospital.' " The heightened ambivalence did not resolve immediately, as is seen on the 8th day home when Jean asked for 4 bedtime stories. Her mother began with Jean's own story and the child said, "Yes, I am cross with you for taking me to the hospital. I didn't want to go." Five minutes later she cuddled round her mother's neck saying "I do like you Mummy. I do like you."

Third, Jean demonstrated a long distance vulnerability reflecting her continuing access to many detailed, but distressing memories of her illness experience. During the 11th week home, Jean's behavior suddenly deteriorated into temper tantrums, weepy and dependent demands for parental attention, etc. Her mother identified a series of external events which triggered her memories: the anticipated tonsillectomy of a friend, a trip away from her children by a mother whom Jean knew, and the arrangements for a Robertson family holiday. The occurrence most parallel to her own tonsillectomy was the tonsillectomy of a friend. Unfortunately, there were medical complications and the friend's return home from the hospital was delayed by a week. When the child finally was able to play again, Jean announced, "I thought you were dead." Robertson believed that the activities preholiday cued Jean's anxious prehospital memories, while the mother's absence raised Jean's worries again about being abandoned in the hospital. Jean's behavioral upset played itself out, with sensitive intervention by Robertson, by 20 weeks post hospitalization.

Anna Freud (Robertson & Freud, 1956), commenting on Jean's experience, said,

> ". . . it is not the external danger, real and serious as it may be, which accounts for the traumatic value of an experience. Injections, loss of blood, surgical interventions, etc., are shown to remain manageable events unless they touch on and merge with id material which transforms them into experiences of being assaulted, emptied out, castrated or condemned . . . I believe in a sliding scale between external and internal threats and fears . . . Mrs. Robertson helped her child . . . meet the operation on the level of reality, to keep the external danger in consciousness to be dealt with by a reasonable ego instead of letting it slip to those depths in which the rational powers of the ego become ineffective and primitive methods of defense are brought into action." (p. 436)

Clinical observation and research has been done to help children who must undergo medical procedures. Little of this work has been linked to memory research. The administration of medical procedures provides a temporal framework and many variables which memory researchers can use to develop their own theories and to enhance the medical care of children.

THE CURRENT SCENE IN PEDIATRIC MEDICINE

Jean's story, written nearly 40 years ago, still has coinage today. It offers some nice examples of linkages between reality, affect, and memory for the young child and of a young child's fascination with her own metacognitive processes. Information given to a child in anticipation of a medical procedure is still rehearsed, supported, or challenged by actual experiences. A child's memory for a medical procedure as simple as an injection may be a mixed blessing. Memory may burden a child with fragments of negative affect as a result of sensory pain and loss of control. Anxious rehearsal of the event is easily triggered for months and sometimes years to come. Children whose lives are interrupted by negative memories may require sensitive parental or therapeutic intervention in order to lay the past experience down.

What has changed since Jean was hospitalized for a tonsillectomy? The patterns of pediatric illness have changed, as have the models of health care delivery, the team of health care professionals with whom the child and parents work, the constellation of the family, and advancing medical technology. I review these features of the current pediatric scene in the next section.

Patterns of Illness

Haggerty (1986) asserts that the face of pediatrics has changed dramatically during the past 4 decades, with marked decreases in the numbers and percentages of children suffering from common infectious disease agents such as polio, measles, rubella, and mumps. The bulk of hospital pediatric care has shifted during the past decade to emergency treatment of accident/injury/abuse, and to the episodic readmissions of children with chronic, life threatening diseases such as asthma, congenital heart disease, diabetes, sickle cell anemia, etc. (Hobbs et al., 1985). It is a different group of children, with far more serious injury or severe physical disease, who are seen in medical centers today. The frequency of surgery to remove the tonsils and adenoids, which reached nearly ritualistic proportions for children of Jean Robertson's generation, has decreased dramatically. If that surgery were deemed necessary today it would probably be handled on an outpatient or 1-day surgery basis (Starfield, 1991). Paradoxically, nearly 80% of the children seen by the private pediatrician are brought by their parents with requests for the pediatrician's help with their children's school problems, parental divorce, sibling relationship or moving; not for medical reasons. In short, the children in the hospital are sicker, and the children in the private pediatricians office are more healthy than ever before in our history.

The Biopsychosocial Model of Health Care Delivery

The model of health care delivery has changed. In most medical settings the biopsychosocial model of illness now dominates the delivery of children's medical care. The biopsychosocial model was introduced by Engel (1977) to supplant the biomedical model of illness, prevalent when Jean Robertson was a youngster, which argued that the physician's major effort should focus on the biologic aspects of physical illness. Engel proposed that biological, psychological, and social variables all contribute to the predisposition, onset, course, and outcome of most illnesses. The biopsychosocial model increases the responsibility of the individual for health maintainance, emphasizes the link between health-risk behaviors and illness, and increases the possibility of participation by the patient with medical staff in diagnostic and treatment decisions during illness. Developmental variables fit nicely within this new model as do such concepts as locus of control, coping, and self-efficacy.

The biopsychosocial model differentiates *disease* from *illness*. Disease is defined as the biological pathophysiology that results in symptoms and signs that are commonly recognizable in everyone, everywhere, at any age, who is diagnosed with the disease. Disease belongs to the medical system. In contrast, illness refers to the experience of the individual, and thus belongs to the personal, family, and social systems. Parmalee (1986), who has been interested in the beneficial effects of illness on children's cognitive and affective development, pointed out that one can have a disease without feeling ill, or can feel ill without having a disease.

Professionals Who Care for Children in Pediatric Settings

The introduction of the biopsychosocial model was accompanied by a parallel development of subspecialty training in pediatrics and psychology (Davidson, 1988). Developmental and behavioral pediatrics and pediatric psychology programs focus on the psychosocial health care needs of infants, children, and adolescents. There are new opportunities for training, consultation, and collaboration (and competition, as Davidson notes) between pediatricians and psychologists in the full range of health care delivery.

Until very recently most pediatric research has been on children's disease rather than on children's illness. The biopsychosocial model and the professionals who practice within that framework insure that in the future we will see clinical and research attention to both the pathophysiology of children's disease and to children's experiences of illness. Professionals from both developmental pediatrics and pediatric psychology may serve as excellent collaborators on teams interested in studying childhood memory and other related developmental phenomena within the context of the medical setting.

There are many participants in the delivery of contemporary pediatric medicine, especially in a university medical complex. As an outpatient, a child may meet an assortment of medical and graduate students, interns, residents, and faculty during a visit to a pediatric specialty clinic. A typical child who is an inpatient in our teaching hospital is visited by more than 50 "strangers" who come in their room in a 24-hour period (e.g., medical, psychological, and nursing staff and trainees, TV repair men, maintenance staff, relatives of other pediatric patients, etc.). Studies of children's memory of experiences and events that occur in a medical setting could benefit from analysis of the interaction of these persons with the child and with one another.

The Role of the Family

The contemporary American family is changing. Family constellations are now such that many children don't have a daddy with a big car to drive them to the hospital, or a full-time mother, as Jean Robertson did. Even though the bio-psychosocial model envisions a much more active and responsible role for parents in the care of their sick children, and hospital policy has been liberalized so that a parent may stay in the hospital with his or her child, many children today must face medical and surgical procedures alone. Many of today's working mothers can't take the time off to meet the preventive health care needs of their young children, let alone stay full-time with their hospitalized children. In addition, the medical care of many children today is compromised by economic, ethnic, and language barriers between parents and medical staff. These changing demographic and relational features of the child's family potentially contribute to children's medical experience and to their memory. I describe next research on the involvement of parents as coaches in preparation for medical procedures, and the research on parent-staff-child interaction during medical procedures.

New Technology

Advances in medical science and medical technology, while enormously important for the health care of children, mean that children are subjected to a new array of aggressive, invasive, radical, and repeated diagnostic and treatment procedures (Pruitt & Strickland, 1987). For young children with chronic diseases such as cancer these medical procedures are painful. Multiple procedures are administered during one outpatient clinic visit. Yet the routine use of potent analgesia/anesthesia is often medically contraindicated. At our medical center the typical child with acute lymphoctyic leukemia receives approximately 2–4 bone marrow aspirations, 15–20 spinal taps, and countless venipunctures during diagnosis and treatment—a painful process that may last 12 to 36 months (C. Abildgaard, personal communication, December 28, 1991).

In contemporary pediatric care memory plays a very important role. Young pediatric patients are awake to experience and remember; unfortunately their memories often contribute to anticipatory anxiety before return visits—which can in turn elicit unpleasant experiences for the child such as nausea and vomiting, compounding the distress further. Misperceptions and misconceptions may also be woven into child's memory and unnecessarily traumatize or emotionally burden the child, making it even more difficult for a child to tolerate/cope with repeated procedures.

The interaction of the biopsychosocial model and modern technology plays out for children and adolescents as a double-edged sword. Some multistep pediatric treatment regimens involving data collection and analysis, judgment and subsequent behavior, are likely to be administered at home thereby increasing the importance of the role of the child and the family in the child's care. The emotional burden for the child may also be increased if she or he is made to feel responsible for the illness or given charge of the testing or treatment too early. Some believe that we have gone from the myth of the vulnerable child to the myth of excessive resilience. For example, children as young as 6 years diagnosed with Type I, insulin dependent diabetes mellitus, are now trained to monitor their own blood glucose (ideally 4 times/day) with small portable devices. For elementary aged children, parents supervise the administration of blood testing. Communication skills may be a mediating factor in joint control determining which "diabetic tasks" shift from the parent to the child as the child matures (Anderson, Auslander, Jung, Miller, & Santiago, 1990). Gudas, Koocher, and Wypij (1991) have studied compliance with children and adolescents who have cystic fibrosis. They remind us that increasing autonomy—particularly with regard to medical compliance—may be the wrong goal even for the chronically ill adolescent.

LaGreca (1990) has written about the growing interest in techniques for documenting the reliability of reports of pediatric compliance with medical regimen administered at home—a problem of double memory: (a) Did the child remember to do X? and (b) Did the child remember that he remembered? Memory errors at either point can compromise a child's health status with, for example, diabetic patients. Memory errors can be life-threatening if, for example, pediatric seizure patients or renal transplant patients forget a necessary medication or administer it twice. It is estimated that the overall adherence rate for pediatric regimens is approximately 50% (Litt & Cuskey, 1980), although that estimate masks differences between short-term vs. long-term regimens. Adherence is considerably higher for the former than the latter, and includes only patients willing to participate in compliance studies, biasing the data towards overestimation. LaGreca notes that verification of the double memory process is complex because of the long chain of command involved in instructions for the administration of a procedure (physician to parent to child). Parents may depend on a child's report and physicians may depend on a parent's report, with no independent source of information to confirm that the procedure was indeed remembered. A recent study that utilized independent parent and child reports assumed that a behavior in a diabetic regimen sequence had occurred if either parent or child remembered it (Freund, Johnson, Silverstein, & Thomas, 1991). Clearly it is strategically difficult to place observers in a child's home and school environment inobtrusively enough so that the observation process does not influence the child's behavior. I report shortly a study that employed independent observers in a camp setting to establish the accuracy of children's memory of self-administered glucose/ketone testing and insulin injections.

In the next section I review clinical and research work focused specifically on the three temporal stages of medical procedures: (a) the preparation of children for medical/surgical procedures, (b) the "in vivo" experience of the procedure, and (c) the debriefing period. Next, I review a set of studies that report what children remember from a medical experience about body touch, persons and location. Finally, I identify several subject populations who might be of special interest to researchers curious about the long-term impact of childhood experience of medical procedures on adult memory.

USING MEDICAL PROCEDURES TO STUDY CHILDREN'S MEMORY

The administration of contemporary medical procedures provides an opportunity to study children's memory of complex, personal events in natural settings such as hospitals, outpatient clinics, physicians private offices, and children's homes. The role that memory plays in the child's exposure to complex medical procedures can be studied, as suggested by the clinical case study of Jean Robertson, by linking the three temporal stages of the experience: preparation, experience, and debriefing. Preparation strategies can be understood as a seeding of the short-term memory for the event to come. Debriefing after a procedure provides an opportunity to seed long-term memory by assessing (and correcting or clarifying if necessary) the perceptions, cognitions, and emotions a child associates with the experience of medical procedures that he has just completed.

Measures of memory of medical procedures can include behavioral, verbal, and biochemical indices. For example, one can study children's memory of their preparation for medical procedures in the short range by observing how children cope during the administration of the procedure, and in the long range by observing their behavior at one or several points in time after the procedure is completed. Children can also be asked, postprocedure, to reflect on the correspondence or discrepancies between their preparation for and their experience of medical procedures. Those verbally mediated memories can be analyzed for accuracy, completeness, and consistency. In addition to observational and self-report measures of memory, it may be possible to document adequacy or lack of preparation, insufficient or inaccurate preparation by studying changes in biochemical/neuroendocrine stress responses, such as salivary or blood cortisol levels. Gunnar, Marvinney, Isensee, and Fisch (1989) identified "significant changes in demands that the organism is not immediately prepared to meet" as the basic stimulus to the neuroendocrine system. A rise in a child's cortisol level following the experience of a medical procedure signals the distress of an unprepared child. The magnitude of the change can be related to memory.

Multiple methods of assessing memory for medical procedures are necessary because children's willingness to verbally report their memories of medical procedures may be negatively influenced by self-conscious emotions such as embarrassment, shame, and guilt (Lewis, Sullivan, Stanger, & Weiss, 1989). Negative self-evaluations may be activated when medical procedures require relative states of dress/undress to expose sensitive or "private parts" of a child's body for careful examination, or when body touch and manipulation occur against a child's will (Beuf, 1979). Careful interview techniques need to be crafted to elicit memories of medical procedures if coersion, bribery, or threat was invoked to elicit a child's cooperation (Bussey, 1990).

There is little research on children's memory of medical procedures. The bulk of the clinical and research literature available on the topic of medical procedures with children is devoted to the preparation of children for a future event. There is relatively less information about the interaction of children, parents, and staff during medical and surgical procedures, and very little literature that reports the results of talking with children about what happened to them after their medical experience. Until very recently, there has not been much interest in children's perceptions of their medical experience. (However, see Bearison, 1990, for a new, powerful set of verbatim interviews with childhood cancer patients.) We believe that parents and medical staff (for very different reasons) have decided not to discuss with children their past medical experiences. This is quite striking in light of K. Nelson's (this volume) observation that most researchers studying event memories in young children have analyzed parent-child rehearsals of past events, but have done little with parent-child discussions of future events. Research in the pediatric setting inverts this emphasis. Students of childhood memory in medical and nonmedical settings need to be in conversation.

Preparation and Memory

What is the impact of preparation for medical procedures on children's memory? Although there is a vast clinical literature on preparing children for hospitalization and medical procedures (Beuf, 1979; Peterson & Mori, 1988; Petrillo & Sanger, 1980; Plank, 1971; Steward & Steward, 1981), there has been very little test of the impact of that preparation on children's memory. Melamed (1991b) has called for more research on the role of children's memories in anticipating, preparing for, and forgetting painful experiences in order to improve the delivery of medical care for children. The clinical research literature on preparation of children for medical procedures can serve as a source for the identification of variables which the memory researcher can use to organize studies of children's memory of medical procedures. Variables prominent in the preparation literature that may impact both the efficacy of the preparation experience and memory of the child include children's cognitive level of development (Perrin et al., 1991; Rasnake & Linscheid, 1989), past medical experience (Eiser, 1989; Melamed,

1991a; Siegel et al., 1990), preferred coping styles (Fanurik & Zeltzer, 1991; Peterson, 1989; Smith, Ackerson, & Blotcky, 1989), choice of timing (Burstein & Meichenbaum, 1979; Melamed, Robbins, & Graves, 1982; S. A. Ross, 1984), sequencing of information (Peterson & Toler, 1986), and parental presence (Bauchner, Waring, & Vinci, 1989; Gonzalez, Routh, Saab, Armstrong, Shifman, Guerra, & Fawcett, 1989; Pinto & Hollandsworth, 1989; Shaw & Routh, 1982; Ross & Ross, 1988).

Three sets of clinical studies are reported here in some detail to highlight the potential impact on memory of differential preparation. None of these studies addresses the question of children's memory of medical procedures squarely, but each suggests a critical facet which could be studied. The first set of studies focuses on content of preparation; the second set looks at the source of preparation; and the third set presents the tailoring of preparation to enhance a child's natural coping strategies.

Content of Preparation.   Claflin and Barbarin (1991) have done a small study on children's memory of preparation for medical procedures. They reverse the question about how memory is influenced by preparation, asking instead about children's memory of the preparation itself. Claflin and Barbarin interviewed a group of 43 children with cancer, ranging in age from 3 years to 18 at the time of diagnosis, about explicit information which the children remembered receiving about diagnosis, treatment, and prognosis. Children were clustered in 3 groups for the purpose of data analysis: (a) the youngest group included 18 children whose average age was 5.4 years at diagnosis and 7.4 years when interviewed, (b) the middle group included 15 children whose average age was 11.3 years at diagnosis and 12.1 years when interviewed, and (c) the oldest group included 10 children whose average age was 16.1 years at diagnosis and 17.3 years when interviewed. The authors were testing the hypothesis that if children received less information about the diagnosis and treatment of cancer— if the children were less well-prepared—the children would be "protected" from some of the negative impact of having cancer (e.g., they would experience fewer negative side effects of the chemotherapy, be less aware of parental worry, etc). Seventy-two percent of the children remembered having medical procedures explained to them. Differences in the quality and quantity of explanation were identified as a function of the age of the child, and as a function of the source of the information (parent vs. medical staff).

Children in the two younger groups remembered receiving less information, and less specific information than the oldest group. With one exception no child in the younger two groups remembered being given a rationale for the procedures, while 56% of the oldest group remembered receiving detailed information and rationales about treatment procedures. The age differences found in these children's memory of their preparation may have resulted from confounding the age of the child with source of information. Children in the younger two groups were more likely to be prepared by parents, while the oldest group was more likely to be prepared by medical staff. In spite of differential preparation across all age groups children rated their experience of medical procedures as the most stressful of seven domains of illness-related stress about which they were questioned. No age differences were found in the number or kind of symptoms or treatment side effects, or children's awareness of parental distress related to the children's disease. Claflin and Barbarin concluded that withholding preparation information did not *protect* children with cancer from negative consequences of the treatment or disease process.

Unfortunately, there was no independent corroboration for any discrepancies between what the children were actually told by parents or medical staff and what children reported remembering. The authors noted further that all of the families studied had volunteered, and that these families and their children may have differed along a number of dimensions (adjustment of individuals within the family, severity of the course of the disease, and symptoms at the time of contact) from those who refused, including families who never told their children that they had been diagnosed and treated for cancer.

A study by Fernald and Corry (1981) links the impact of differential information given by medical staff to children during preparation to their subsequent thoughts and feelings. Staff prepared children for venipuncture or finger stick with one of two strategies: empathetic preparation—"I'll bet the alcohol feels cold. In a moment I'm going to stick you. You're probably feeling scared. You can cry if you want."—and directive preparation—"Act big and brave. Remain very still." Children prepared empathetically demonstrated fewer distress behaviors such as crying, wincing, and refusing to comply during the administration of the procedure. Even more important, after the procedure was completed children who were prepared emphatically had fewer negative self-reports. For example, only 5% felt angry after the venipuncture and only 5% felt the technician had tried to hurt them, whereas in the group of directively prepared children 58% were angry and 47% believed the lab technician had tried deliberately to hurt them.

Even this very brief differential preparation influenced the stress children experienced during the procedure and also influenced the amount of distress they felt subsequently—as reflected in at least two measures: anger and sense of victimization. It is likely that the memories that the two groups of children hold of a technically similar medical procedure differ. This difference may influence subsequent interactions with medical staff. K. Nelson (1989) suggested that young children's memory can be manifested in a variety of intentional behaviors, nonverbally as well as verbally. Children in the empathetically prepared group will be more likely to approach subsequent medical experiences with confidence and to trust new medical staff, while children who were directively prepared— fearful of revictimization—may act on their anger and behave aggressively toward medical staff, retaliating as Jean Robertson did against "big Nurse." Unfortunately, a recent study by Stern, Ross, and Bielass (1991) demonstrated a belief bias, or stereotype, by 4th-year medical student clerks about children described as being "in remission from cancer," such that they are more likely than healthy children to receive a less sensitive, more time-expedient approach when administered an injection. Such behavior by medical staff reinforces negative memories of an event which could contribute to a child's escalating cycle of anger and mistrust.

My colleagues and I are conducting currently a content analysis of mothers' preparation of their 3 to 6 year-old children for a wide variety of outpatient procedures. Seventy mothers completed a parental preparation questionnaire in the waiting room prior to a medical visit. Their children were interviewed after the medical visit. We found a striking discrepancy between the number of mothers who claimed that they prepared their children for a medical procedure (95%), and the number of children who confirmed after the procedure that they had been forewarned (33%). Why did two-thirds of the children *forget* that they had been prepared? And what was it that their mothers told them that they forgot? In order to investigate differences in the content of the information given the group of children who remembered being prepared and those who forgot, the mothers responses are being analyzed within a 3 × 3 matrix. The cells of the matrix represent the interaction of three components of medical procedures—the what, the who, and the why—which we have identified from the clinical literature (Steward & Steward, 1981), and an adaptation of three attributional features that Seligman and his colleagues (Peterson & Seligman, 1984) find that people use to explain a negative event: (a) whether the self or another initiated the event, (b) the uniqueness of the event, and (c) the sensory and descriptive specificity of the experience. The third component parallels information from the empathetic preparation of Fernald and Corry. Although the study is limited to second order data—what the mothers told us they told their children, we will be able to triangulate the content of the mothers' reports of preparation, the children's memory of having been prepared, and the accuracy and completeness of children's memory of the procedures. Some of the things that mothers tell their children may not lead to memories of preparation per se, but the information given may alert the child so that his or her memories of the procedures are enhanced.

Finally, the selection and use of props is a critical feature of the content of most preparation programs designed for young children, and provides an interesting variable that may impact children's memory of medical procedures differentially. In the medical setting staff, who are not aware of the specific cognitive gifts and limitations which young children bring, often make mistakes in their use of props. One frequent mistake is the use of model, rather than real medical equipment. Models may be charmingly designed but they are ineffective or irrelevant to the preparation of young children for an upcoming medical or surgical event. DeLoache and her colleagues (DeLoache, 1987, 1990; De-

Loache, Kolstad, & Anderson, 1991) have demonstrated that for very young children it is difficult to make the connection between the model and the real thing. The model, rather than serving as a symbol for another thing, is seen and understood as an object in its own right. Thus toy models of hospital rooms with beautifully polished minature wooden X-ray machines won't prepare a child for the icy cold sensation of the table, or the fact that everyone will scurry out of the room and leave them, naked and alone, while a huge piece of metal is slowly lowered over their body. I know of no empirical studies that test the impact on a child's memory of use of toy models vs. real medical equipment during medical preparation. As Fernald and Corry (1981) demonstrated, children report feeling tricked and angry when they are not well-prepared—emotions that are likely to enhance memory of the event and the person who prepared them.

When Parents are the Source of Preparation Information.   Persons who prepare the child may influence differentially what a child will remember about a procedure. In the Claflin and Barbarin study reported earlier the age of the child and source of information were confounded. When parents serve as sources of information, younger children may remember less about the preparation period—not only because they have more cognitive and language limitations than older children—but also because the information from parents, while emotionally supportive, may contain less detail about process or equipment than information that a medical staff person might have given. In addition the authority of the informer may play a role in determining a child's willingness to accept preparation information. To date there have been no experimental studies that examine the differential influence of the source of preparation on children's memory. Results of such studies would contribute to the event memory literature, and would prove very useful in the design of preparation events for young children.

Parental preparation of their children for an examination that includes the use of a colposcope highlights a problem shared by many parents, who do not know exactly what their child is about to experience. Some parents wrongly assume that the colposcope is merely another name for the pelvic examination performed on adolescent and adult women that includes both digital penetration of the vagina and anus, the introduction into the vagina of a cold metal instrument, a speculum, to open the area for visual inspection, and the collection of tissue for a pap smear. In contrast, the colposcope is an instrument that provides a source of light and magnification, and includes a camera for the collection of evidentiary data for subsequent legal proceedings. The instrument stands about one foot away from the child and never touches the child's body. Even adults who understand the operation of a colposcope often withhold full information about the genital examination from children on the premise that they do not want to retraumatize an allegedly abused child—a premise tested and challenged by the Claflin and Barbarin study reported earlier. Children may be told only about the spotlight and the camera. One mother reported to us that she told her child that the doctor would "look at her eyes, her nose, and her pretty face." After the medical examination was completed the child announced to our interviewer with considerable surprise and irritation in her voice that "the doctor looked at my peepee!" We hunch that a poorly prepared child is likely to remember and be forced to rework an event that a well-prepared child may be able to forget.

My colleagues and I are conducting currently a clinical interview study with allegedly abused children about the source and accuracy of their information prior to undergoing an examination using a colposcope. Immediately following the examination and again 1 week later the children are asked what information another child who is their same age and gender should be given about the procedure, and who should give them that information. The purpose of the study is to improve the preparation of children for this unusual procedure, and to lessen children's surprise and distress.

A second problem parents face as they prepare their children for medical procedures is that they may not anticipate the pain that their child will experience as a result of the procedure. A recent study by Watt-Watson et al. (1991) in a Canadian hospital focused on parents' perceptions of children's acute pain experience. Seventy-one parents of 62 children (92% < 6 years-of-age) hospitalized on short-term pediatrics wards rated their children's most painful procedures. They rated blood work (M = 46), intravenous therapy (M = 74) and lumbar punctures (M = 79) as the most painful procedures. Fifty-eight percent of the parents claim that they were not told the procedure would be painful and 70% claimed that they were not told of any way they could alleviate the pain! Parents as well as their children may be surprised. Parents may transform their surprise into anger and frustration, which may fuel their own and their children's memory of the event in synergistic ways.

The behavioral interaction of parents and their children prior to medical procedures may contribute to a child's level of distress, which in turn will impact both the child's coping strategies during the procedure and their memory afterwards. Bush, Melamed, Sheras, and Greenbaum (1986) observed 50 mother-child dyads during a 5-minute period before medical procedures were administered to the children. They found that maternal agitation and maternal reassurance were each associated with increases in child distress. Distraction techniques, information giving, and low rates of ignoring by the mother were associated with low rates of child distress. Melamed and her colleagues (1991a) are studying crisis-parenting by examining cues that mothers give their children during the waiting period (e.g., anticipatory restraining and agitated maternal behavior) which might signal the child that a dangerous situation is about to occur, and maternal personality traits (e.g., especially state and trait anxiety) that may lead the child to develop anxiety rather than coping skills.

Preparation and Children's Natural Coping Strategies.   One of the most controversial new research endeavors with respect to preparation of children for medical procedures involves the pretesting of a child's natural coping strategies. If a child must endure repeated, painful medical procedures, what kind of help can that child be given? Two different research teams (Fanurik & Zeltzer, 1991; Siegel, 1991) have shown that by pretesting a child's strategies for withstanding pain, preparation for necessary medial procedures can be tailored so that the child's strategies can be enhanced. As a result medical procedures can be experienced as less painful. Fanurik and Zeltzer employed a "cold pressor" technique in which children were asked to lower one arm into a vat of very cold water and leave it there as long as they could tolerate it. After the child quit, each was interviewed to determine what they had done in order to keep their arm in so long.

The children's spontaneous strategies were categorized into two general groups. One group of children, *distractors,* used a strategy that involved mental distraction or escape. The other group of children, *attenders,* focused directly on the sensory experience—monitoring how cold it was, whether or not their arm was changing color, etc. Then each group was divided in half, creating a 2×2 design in which half of the distractors and half of the attenders were taught mental distraction techniques. The remaining children, half distractors and half attenders, were instructed to focus directly on the sensations they experienced. The purpose was to see if children would benefit from learning other strategies, broadening their coping repertoire.

The results revealed that instruction in distraction techniques benefited the children who already spontaneously used that strategy by significantly increasing their cold pain tolerance, but did not improve the cold pain tolerance of the children who initially used the sensory focusing technique. The instructions to focus on the sensory input did not improve the performance of either group.

Siegel (1991) trained children in a laboratory with a sensory pressure/pain stimulus, which he believed paralleled the sensation that children would experience in a bone marrow or spinal tap procedure. His strategy was to seek to enhance the child's self-efficacy while their hand was placed under a bar that exerted variable pressure on their fingers.

The debate about pretesting children's coping strategies to handle painful sensory stimulation is not limited to the cold pressor or variable pressure bar techniques, for there are other techniques that could be designed. The debate is an ethical one. Although pretesting provides useful sensory information about an upcoming medical procedure, and increases the clarity and importance of a child's role assignment, does painful pretesting increase to an unacceptable level the *pain burden* the ill child already has to carry? The debate might be framed differently, by asserting that when necessary painful experiences can be made less traumatic, then haunting memories of the necessary event may be less disruptive in young children's lives. A well-designed study could determine if children, pretested to determine natural coping strategies and prepared with skill training to enhance those strategies, remember fewer details about the medical procedure, and if those memories are less negatively toned than those of children left to cope with medical procedures on their own.

There are two notes of caution for the memory researcher who plans to focus on the impact of preparation on memory for medical procedures. The first has to do with the characteristics of children who experience medical procedures. The second has to do with the difficulty of keeping experimental groups *pure* in a clinical setting. The population of children available for study in medical settings is limited and rather uniquely defined. Preparation of children for medical procedures which occur during outpatient, well-child check-ups is usually done, if at all, by parents prior to arrival and thus may not be available for research observation. For those children attending specialty clinics, one should anticipate an interaction between the child's previous medical experience and preparation offered. We know clinically that it is very, very difficult to prepare a child a second time. Their memories of previous negative medical experiences interrupt and challenge a presentation that is made too simple or too true (Dahlquist et al., 1989; Melamed, 1991b).

The pediatric inpatient population is bimodal with respect to preparation at our medical center. The majority of children are not planned, scheduled admissions; rather children come into our hospital as a result of accident, injury, or poisoning. In fact, less than 25% of the children in our inpatient pediatric units have been prepared prior to admission for the experience of hospitalization or for the medical procedures that they will experience. Preparation, if it does occur, may be provided at any point in the 24-hour day, by one or several staff. For the researcher the problems of variable timing and the potential of multiple, overlapping (or conflicting) information offer significant problems. Another smaller group of children in our hospital are returning because of chronic illness, and previous negative experiences with medical staff, medical procedures experience and the constraints of hospitalization interact with attempts to prepare those children.

The second caution is a result of the fact that in front-line clinical settings the pragmatist often wins over the scientist. That is particularly true in medical settings where clinical trials are aborted if one diagnostic or treatment strategy appears to be superior to others. An example of that is found in research by Kuttner, Bowman, and Teasdale, (1988), who reported that there appeared to be "some contamination in the control group" between the beginning and end of a study in which different kinds of cognitive/behavioral strategies were taught during a preparation period to enhance a child's coping with painful medical procedures. This meant that children and their parents assigned to the control group were learning from children and their parents in the experimental group how to handle better the distress of medical procedures.

In sum, there are a number of factors from the preparation period that may impact both the experience and memory of the child. These include content and sources of the preparation, and informational and strategic preparation of the child for coping with pain. Research to date reveals that some children don't even remember being prepared. Studies are underway to determine how memory for preparation is related to memory for the subsequent medical events. There is no *protective* advantage to withholding preparation information from children. Children may be forced to remember painful medical procedures if they are given incomplete, directive preparation as opposed to empathetic preparation (which allows children to anticipate both sensory and emotional contingencies) because children are likely to feel angry at and victimized by medical staff. Children may also be more distressed and thus remember more when they are prepared by parents who have limited information about the equipment that will be used, the relative painfulness of the experience, or are agitated and distressed themselves. On the other hand enhancing the skills of children who naturally use distraction/imagery may impact memory by shifting the perceptual and cognitive focus of the child away from the procedure and lowering the distress. The result should be that these children will remember less about the procedures.

Experience of Medical Procedures and Memory

During medical and surgical procedures children's bodies are touched, handled, and sometimes, when necessary, hurt by medical staff in the process of diagnosis or treatment. There are two sets of variables that can be measured during the administration of medical procedures that enhance or interfere with memory: the child's experience of pain, and the psychosocial interaction amongst parent, child, and staff. There is vigorous new clinical research interest in both areas. Pain is a personal experience, with no simple physiological, neurological, or biochemical marker independent of the judgment of the individual (McGrath, 1987). Investigators who have studied childhood pain understand that the "unpleasant set of sensory and emotional experiences" (Merksey, 1979) may include feelings of fear, anxiety, loneliness, anger, and sadness. The fact that the experience of pain is associated with "actual or potential tissue damage" highlights the dynamic role of memory in the assessment of previous experience with medical procedures and of cognitive appraisal informed by that memory in anticipation of subsequent procedures (Merskey, 1979). Jay et al. (1985) believe that the complex set of sensory, emotional, and cognitive variables that are included in the childhood experience of pain is more parsimoniously conceptualized as *distress* (Jay et al., 1985).

A wide variety of pain scales has been developed to assess children's self-report of pain, including visual analogue scales, face scales, verbal scales often used with adults, as well as a range of physiological measures (Beyer & Wells, 1990; Bush, 1987; McGrath, 1987; Ross & Ross, 1988). Two recent studies have asked children to remember and rate the intensity of past painful episodes, and a third contrasted memories of two groups of children who differed on the organic vs. functional cause of their pain.

Beyer, Berde, and Bournaki (1991) asked 46 3–7 year-olds "Can you remember a time when you had a hurt?" Children identified a total of 143 incidents and rated them on a 0 to 5 photographic Oucher scale. Approximately half of the incidents (52%) were recalled spontaneously, the remaining incidents were prompted by parents or the interviewer. Thirty-eight percent of the children had previously experienced surgery, but none of those children spontaneously mentioned painful medical or surgical experiences associated with their surgery. Although pain scores varied widely for similar incidents (e.g., falls and needles both received ratings across the full range from 0 to 5), in general, less traumatic incidents were given lower pain scores than more traumatic incidents. Children remembered incidents that had occurred from a few minutes to 4 years prior to the interview.

Lehmann, Bendebba and DeAngelis (1990) interviewed 91 3–8 year-olds asking them to remember two recent painful events. Children were interviewed on two occasions 7 days apart in order to estimate the consistency with which children would rank order the two experiences of pain they remembered and four others identified by the authors (shot, stomachache, cut, and a bump). Five scaling procedures were employed, including the simple question, "Which hurt more?" The 7 and 8 year-olds were more consistent than were the younger children, yet the authors cautioned against the use in clinical settings of past painful experiences as anchors for current pain estimates. Using an 80% agreement as their definition of consistency, they found that children over the age of 5 remembered pain intensity consistently in response to the verbal question, but the other scaling procedures created by the authors (which combined various directional, color and/or face cues) did not elicit consistent responses. The inconsistent responses to the multidimensional pain scales may be a reflection of a methodological problem, not a developmental one. Both the study by Beyer and her colleagues and the study by Lehmann and his colleagues suffer from the lack of independent confirmation from parents, medical staff, or medical records about actual occurrence of the painful events children reported.

Geist (1991) compared the descriptions of pain from the medical records of a group of 30 school-aged children diagnosed with an organic etiology for their stomach pain (inflamed bowel syndrome) and a group of 32 children diagnosed with "functional pain" (no known etiology for chronic abdominal pain). She identified a series of differences between the two groups of children in their memories about several dimensions of the pain and how children coped with it. For example, children with an organic cause for their pain had only vague memories about the onset of the pain, reported the pain to be of variable, unpredictable intensity, and complained that it awoke them from sleep. In contrast, the children with functional pain remembered exactly when the pain began, reported constant intensity and complained of problems falling asleep. The children with functional pain also reported, rather suspiciously, that exercise aggrevated the pain, rest alleviated it, and they avoided going to school when in pain. The active role that the children with functional pain had in the construction of their description of the event, and the secondary gain which apparently resulted from the functional pain may have contributed to sharper, clearer memories when they reported the pain to their physicians. The provocative findings from this retrospective study call for replication.

There is a link between children's experience of pain and how they cope with it. The observation of coping strategies that children actually use during brief but repeated painful treatment for chronic or life-threatening diseases suggests that even very young children can use modeling, "thought-stopping" techniques, and coping skills training to reduce their anxiety (Jay et al., 1987; Koocher, 1985; Peterson & Mori, 1988; D. M. Ross, 1984; Zeltzer, Jay, & Fisher, 1989; Zeltzer & LeBaron, 1986). However, it is rare for young children to initiate stress-reducing strategies unless they are specifically cued by supportive adult coaches. This phenomenon will be very familiar to those who conduct research on the role of retrieval cues in young children's memory (Ritter, Kaprive, Fitch, & Flavell, 1973; Smith, Ratner, & Hobart, 1987).

A child may exhibit behavioral distress at different points in the process of administration of a medical procedure. For example, our (Steward, Steward, Joye, & Reinhart, 1991) research with 79 3–6 year-olds, and work by Blount and his colleagues (Blount, Sturges, & Powers, 1990) reveal that children may manifest more distress behavior in anticipation of the insertion of the needle in a bone marrow, spinal tap, or venipuncture than after the needle is in. Blount and his colleagues found that children exhibited an increase in demonstrative distress (crying, screaming, etc.) and a decrease in apprehensive distress (request for emotional support, verbal fear etc.) from the prepainful to the painful phase. We have found that different procedures elicit different profiles of behavioral distress. In our study children's memories of their distress behavior did not match the behavior we observed. For example, 66% of the 36 children who cried did remember, but 17% of the 43 children who did not cry also reported crying; only 5% of the 25 children who asked for help or emotional support remembered and reported that while 4% falsely reported the same behavior.

Several research teams are now focusing on the psychosocial interaction between the child patient, the medical staff and the parent during the process of medical procedures. Blount and his colleagues (Blount, Corbin, Sturges, Wolfe, Prater, & James, 1989) studied audiotape recordings of 23 pediatric oncology patients prior to, during, and after bone marrow aspiration and lumbar puncture procedures with the primary goal of establishing which adult vocalizations most often preceded or followed child distress and coping. They found that children's coping with necessary medical procedure has been enhanced by adult commands to cope, humor, and nonprocedural talk.

The pride felt by both the child and the parent when the child-parent team *handles* a painful session better this time than last time, with less overt distress and more sense of control, may well contribute to enhancement of positive memories of their teamwork, and concomittant decrease in memories of the painful procedures. On the other hand, memories of the painful procedures may be enhanced when children's distress is escalated by parental agitation (Bush, Melamed, & Cockrell, 1989), criticism, adult apologies, inappropriate giving over of control to the child—or even well-intended adult reassurance (Blount et al., 1989). In fact 7 of 8 child distress behaviors observed in the Blount study were preceded most often by adult's reassuring comments. A further analysis of these data revealed that it did not matter whether the adult giving the reassurance was the parent or a medical staff person (Blount, Landolf-Fritsche, Powers, & Sturges, 1991).

Parents often find it difficult and confusing to be present with their children during painful medical procedures. Unfortunately, what parents do may exacerbate the child's distress as well as what they say. Even the parent who accompanies a child for necessary medical procedures with the best of intentions to provide emotional support for their child may "join the opposition" by, for example, helping medical staff hold down a child whose defensive bodily movements may jeopardize a procedure and result in injury to the child. Sometimes parents become angry at a child's verbal protest or uncooperative behavior (Blount et al., 1989). Some children experience harsh parental coercion, threats, or even temporary abandonment in the clinic (Bush et al., 1989). Parents in the pediatric setting can develop feelings of shame and embarrassment that distance them from their troubled child at the very time that they are most needed, and wanted (Gonzalez et al., 1989).

It has been found that parents and medical staff often underestimate children's experience of pain and distress (Lollar, Smits, & Patterson, 1982; Schechter, 1989; Steward, Steward, Joye, & Reinhart, 1991). For example, Watt-Watson et al. (1991) found that 9% of the parents of children who had received painful, invasive medical procedures denied that their child had experienced pain. Another parent, confusing pain with coping, stated, "He took it like a man!" The denial by a significant adult that a child has been hurt may challenge the child's experience of the reality of the painful body touch, or inhibit a child's willingness to talk about that touch with another adult for fear that she or he may not be believed. However, Lumley, Abeles, Melamed, Pistone, and Johnson (1990) found mothers' ratings of the negative overall quality of their children's previous medical experience was predictive of their children's behavioral distress and cooperation during subsequent anesthesia induction.

In sum there are a number of factors that occur during the administration of medical procedure that may impact a child's experience of those procedures and subsequently their memory of those procedures. These factors include the child's experience of pain and distress, the coping strategies used by the child, and interaction of the child with parents and staff. Research studies document that children can remember and rate past painful experiences, and that consistency of ratings improves with age; but these studies lack independent confirmation of the occurrence of the painful event. Children's clear, sharp memories of functional pain—in contrast to the vaguer memories of children with organically caused pain—may be related to the constructive role that the children played in describing the pain, and in the secondary gain that children achieved with that pain report. Studies on the psychosocial interaction of children and adults during medical procedures reveal that adult behavior, language, and judgments can effectively cue a child's memory for previously mastered coping skills, enhance a child's coping ability, and probably a child's positive memory of a job well done. It is likely that the child's memory of the specific details of the procedure would be diminished. However, adults can increase the child's distress in an already stressful situation, heightening subsequent memory of painful procedures.

Debriefing and Memory

The task of debriefing a child following medical and surgical procedures is a critical one. The purpose of having the medical staff debrief a child after a procedure is to review the events, processes, and procedures that have been administered; report any findings that the child should know; and answer any questions that a child may have about the event. In the past debriefing was rarely done routinely by medical staff. Even today memories based on a young child's misperception and miscognition are most often observed only by the nonmedical staff in the pediatric play room (Chan, 1980; Plank, 1971). Most postprocedural/ postsurgical conversations are between medical staff and parents. They focus on the schedule and administration of necessary medications, dietary, or behavioral restrictions. In general the focus is on the healing process. Until recently, the child was not necessarily even addressed, let alone interviewed about his understanding (Beuf, 1979). Children, feeling powerless and frightened, often inhibit their thoughts and feelings when medical staff do inquire. A 6-year-old girl describing her experience of a spinal tap to a nonmedical staff member reported: "I had three tests and I was mad. When they do one I feel too much. I get mad. I say, 'Don't do more!' They say they're gonna do one more . . . they do one more and they do one more again and they do three times that." (Lewis, 1978). This was all reported in a hushed voice, for she was fearful that her doctors might hear her.

Some parents interrupt the conversations between medical staff and their young patients at debriefing time, even as they do prior to administration of procedures, on the false assumption that this will *protect* the child (Claflin & Barbarin, 1991). Koocher and O'Malley (1981) found a dramatic instance of that when they recontacted patients who were on the cancer registry because they were survivors of childhood cancer. They invited the children and their families back for interviews. They found one family unwilling to participate in the follow-up study because they had never told their daughter that she had been diagnosed and successfully treated for cancer as a very young child. In addition, 24% of the siblings of cancer victims interviewed by Koocher and his team reported that they never knew that their sibling had been diagnosed with cancer. Some children carried unnecessary guilt, blaming themselves for causing a mysterious period of ill-health when in fact the etiology was cancer. More recently a review of 1928 adults who survived childhood cancer found that 14% of the survivors of malignancies at sites other than the central nervous system reported at follow-up that they had not had cancer (Byrne, Lewis, Halamek, Connelly, & Mulvihill, 1989).

Piaget has characterized the preoperational thinker as one who is bound to believe what he sees and hears. For the hospitalized child, this can be quite a fascinating and sometimes terrifying experience. During bedside medical rounds children hear and remember words which they interpret literally so that edema—a swelling—becomes "a demon in my belly," the order to stop a medication, e.g., "Cut out the gentomyacin," is understood as a demand for surgery, and the diagnosis of diabetes is heard as the death sentence = die-a-betes! There are also misperceptions and miscognitions about medical experiences that have developed because the child is a competent preoperational thinker at the time of initial diagnosis (Gudas et al., 1991). One very disturbing set of reports about the long-term impact of young children's remembered misperception of repeated, necessary genital examinations is reported by Money and Lamacz (1987). They identified three girls who inaccurately understood the examinations as sexually abusive, and who experienced negative sequelae on into adulthood.

Unfortunately some children hold on to their misperceptions or misunderstandings and are never debriefed, so they grow to middle childhood, adolescence or young adulthood "remembering," for example, that their exploratory abdominal surgery resulted in the removal of "2 kidneys." Many of our preschoolers, victimized by sexual abuse, believe that they have been "all broken inside," while some sexually abused girls (Asher, 1988) and boys recovered from Hodgkins disease (Wasserman, Thompson, Williams, & Fairclough, 1987) grow into adolescence remembering/believing that they are sterile.

In sum, the debriefing period is a natural time to determine the relative accuracy of children's perceptions and cognitions of recently completed medical procedures. There is a biochemistry to support the perspective from developmental psychology that debriefing is a critical time for making any necessary clarifications or corrections for young children before the experience is stored into long-term memory (Gold, 1984, 1987; McGaugh, 1983).

RESEARCH ON WHAT CHILDREN REMEMBER ABOUT MEDICAL PROCEDURES

Seven empirical research studies of children's experience of medical procedures that deal explicitly with and directly assess what children remember are reviewed next. In these studies children's reports have been validated by an independent observer, audio or videotape, and/or medical record so that reliable estimates of memory can be derived. Estimates of children's distress in these studies range from very minimal to very high. Interviewing strategies and measures of memory differ. Two studies (Bearison & Pacifici, 1989; Reynolds, Johnson, & Silverstein, 1990) focus on children's memory for complex, sequential events. Four studies, designed as analogues to child court testimony, focus on children's capacity to remember and describe or identify the persons and location, as well as to report their experience of body touch and handling (Davies, Tarrant, & Flin, 1989; Goodman, Hirschman, Hepps, & Rudy, 1991; Peters, 1987; Saywitz, Goodman, Nicholas & Moan, 1991). Our own study (Steward, 1989; Steward, Steward, Farquhar, Reinhart, Joye, Myers, & Welker, 1992) was designed both as a court analogue study and to improve our own teaching and delivery of health care to children.

Memory of Complex Medical Events

Jacoby (1989) identified two distinctive functions of memory. It allows one to "be aware of and communicate with others about one's personal past." It also sets the stage "for perception and the interpretation of later events." Nelson's (1989) functional understanding of memory would support Jaccoby's view. Bjorklund (1985, 1987) has championed the importance of the knowledge base that the child has acquired prior to an event about which child is being interrogated. Chi (1978) has documented the novice/expert distinction by demonstrating that children with "expertise" can remember more than adults new to an experience. Nelson and Hudson (1988) have found through the study of children's scripts an effective way to tap into children's expertise. Children can tell us about their knowledge of familiar, routine events. Their narratives usually contain information about causal-temporal sequences, people, and props, and bear a strong relation to underlying event representations from which reports are generated. Nelson and Hudson have found that although the narrative may be somewhat incomplete or skeletal, the content is rarely misrepresented.

If the event a child is asked to remember is affectively charged, then there may be an additional anticipatory lens with which to perceive a repeated event. Nelms (1989) has documented that chronically ill children express significantly more empathy and emotional responsiveness to stories evoking pride, happiness, anger, fear, and sadness than do healthy children. She suggests that because chronically ill children undergo intense experiences, and are repeatedly asked how they are feeling, they develop a heightened awareness of both positive and negative inner states. New theoretical work on the linkages between cognitive and emotional systems (Case, Hayward, Lewis, & Hurst, 1988; Fischer, Shaver, & Carnochan, 1990) suggests that changes in the development of each system has concommitant or subsequent influence on the other.

We have observed clinically that when children remember highly stressful events, the causal-temporal sequence that appears in scripts of neutrally-toned events is interrupted. Children returning to our medical center after hospitalization that included medical and surgical procedures have drawn us pictures of "leaving the hospital with mom" as the event that they remember *first*. Although the sequence is not reported, two of the four story cards Jean Robertson selected pictured the child, "Laura," putting on shoes in preparation for going home, and then leaving the hospital with her mother.

Bearison and Pacifici (1989), were the first research team to study empirically children's scripts of medical procedures. They interviewed a group of 4- to 7-year-old children with cancer twice to elicit narratives about "experimental" scripts for "What happens when you come to the oncology clinic?" vs. "control" scripts for eating at a restaurant or going to a birthday party. The youngest children in their study, the 4- to 6-year-olds, recalled significantly fewer event representations and were less consistent in representing the same event from the first to the second interview. There were no content errors in any of the scripts, but there were sequencing errors. As the younger children described a typical visit to the outpatient hematology/oncology clinic, they reported leaving the clinic before they reported some of the medical procedures that they experienced regularly during a treatment visit. They made significantly more sequencing errors in the clinic script than in the scripts of the other two events. The authors suggested that although none of the children showed signs of distress when producing the narrative about the clinic visit, the clinic experience was more highly affectively valenced than the restaurant or party events. Bearison and Pacifici speculated that the sequencing errors reflected the apprehension that the youngest children had about the clinic routines, and the children's desire to leave the situation.

The authors found no differences in clinic script knowledge based on length of time in treatment, prognosis, order of interview, or gender. They assert that clinic scripts are well established early in treatment and parallel findings of children's general knowledge of other social routines (Nelson, 1986). Clinic scripts may provide an important method for assessing differences in individual children's level of understanding and adjustment across time to necessary but painful medical treatment.

Reynolds et al. (1990) were the first to employ independent observers to investigate the accuracy of diabetic children's 24-hour recall of the self-administration of medical procedures. They observed two procedures that cause children mild stress—glucose/ketone testing and insulin injection—as well as their memory for exercise and dietary behaviors, events related in important ways to blood glucose levels. Seventy-five 7–12-year-old children, attending a special camp for diabetic children were observed. Twelve observers each monitored 3 or 4 children from the same cabin from the time the campers got up in the morning until after they finished the dinner meal. A 13th observer collected observer reliability data throughout the study. All children were observed on 3 randomly selected days over the course of 2 weeks, with 24 recall interviews conducted the day after each observation. Unfortunately the interview format was limited to direct questions, so that accuracy of the content but not sequence of children's memory could be assessed. In general, the children's memory was demonstrated to be highly accurate for the occurrence of events across the whole day, but less so for specific timing and quality of activities remembered. Children's memory was highly accurate (above 90%) on 9 out of 10 measures related to insulin injection (the observers reported that the injections occurred later than did the children). Children were judged to be "reasonably accurate" (above 70%) in reporting the occurrence of glucose/ketone tests, exercise, and meals, but they underestimated duration and strenuousness of exercise and their food intake—especially their intake of sweets (60%), bread (34%), and fat (17%). The 7 and 8 year-olds were less accurate than were the older children on details of exercise and diet. Age differences in remembering may have been dependent upon differences in the fine-tuning of initial categories, such as dietary exchange units, that children used to monitor and code their experiences as well as on differential capacities in the storage or retrieval of remembered events. Subtle but critical differences in memory for the sequences of eating, exercise, testing, administration of insulin might be revealed if an event memory methodology were utilized with this population of children and adolescents.

Analogue Studies: Children's Memory of Touch, Persons and Place

Davies, Tarrant, and Flin (1989) created a simulated health inspection for 128 children, half 6–7 year-olds and half 10–11 year-olds. The medical procedures were painless, simple, and noninvasive. Children were asked to remove their shoes. Then they were individually weighed, measured, and eye color checked by a "health survey visitor." Each child was touched only once by the health survey visitor: either on the arm or on the shoulder. One week later children were asked to describe the health visitor and what had occurred. Following free recall, children were asked direct questions about the health visitor's appearance including several details of the hair, face, eye, nose, mouth, and lips. They were also asked the health visitor's name, whether or not the child had clothing removed, if they had been touched, and location of touch. There were no gender differences and few age differences found in the accuracy of children's memory of the events. Older children did report more information than younger children on free and prompted recall of events and appearance and made fewer errors on recall of appearance. In free recall the younger group remembered only 23% of the 12 key events in the sequence, while the older group remembered 36% of the events. No child in either group mentioned an event that had not occurred. There were no differences between the two age groups on identification of the health visitor from photographic array or the goodness of children's construction of a composite pictures. The confidence that children had in their own judgments was not related to accuracy/error of their memories. Children from both age groups were able to report more of what they remembered when cued with direct questions. The errors in cued recall were more frequent for descriptions of the health visitor than for information about the event in which the children participated.

Saywitz and her colleagues (Saywitz, et al., 1991) interviewed 36 5-year-old and 36 7-year-old girls 1 week or 1 month following a special physical examination. Half of the girls in each age group received a vaginal and anal examination and half received a checkup for scoliosis incorporated into the examination. The focus of the study was to explore how best to elicit a girl's memory of genital contact. A sequence of three interview strategies was employed. Memory for body touch was elicited first by free recall. Then a child was asked to demonstrate touch with dolls. Finally the examiner pointed to body location on the dolls as the child was asked directly about touch to the genitalia and back. Accuracy for free recall was 93% and for demonstration was 87%. Both the 5- and 7-year-old girls reported nearly twice as much information when given the opportunity to demonstrate the event they experienced. Yet reports of body touch were sparse when free recall (10%) or demonstration techniques were employed (29%). When the information from free recall and demonstration are combined 27% of the girls reported vaginal touch and 19% reported anal touch at least once, while 92% reported vaginal touch and 82% reported anal touch when asked directly. Only one of the girls reported spinal touch in free recall and none in demonstration. When asked directly, 60% reported spinal touch accurately, but that rate does not differ significantly from chance. The difference in reporting rates for touch to different body parts may be a function of the fact that genital touch may be more stressful from a socioemotional perspective and therefore more memorable than back touch to little girls. In response to direct inquiry, errors increased, but errors of omission were more frequent than errors of commission and no child in the back touch condition falsely reported genital touch. In this study specific interview strategies were correlated with order, so that question repetition as well as question format may have contributed to reporting differences.

Peters (1987) studied the impact of moderate stress on memory. He observed 3- to 8-year-old children undergoing dental visits. The focus of his study was on children's ability to remember persons and settings, not on children's memory of the dental experience (96% were for dental check-ups or teeth-cleaning, only one child had cavities filled). Stress was defined by rating the child's anxiety during the dental visit, based on a combination of judgments made by the parent and the dentist. Two additional anxiety ratings were made by the parent and different research interviewers following two home visits. Children were judged to be more anxious in the dental visit than at home. Peters suggested that this higher level of anxiety functioned to inhibit children's subsequent photo identification of the dentist (43% accuracy) in contrast to the research interviewer whom the children met at home (71% accuracy). The more anxious the child, the less accurate she or he was in identifying the dentist or his assistant, and the greater the likelihood of false identification in photo recognition tasks. There were no effects of stress on relative accuracy of photo identification of the setting, or the voice recognition (earwitness).

Goodman and her colleagues (Goodman et al., 1991) conducted a series of studies with 3- to 7-year-old children about their memories of a venipuncture or an injection in the arm or thigh. In two studies—one with 9 children, and another with 17 children—reports by the subjects were contrasted with reports of control children. The controls were carefully matched so that they were seen in the same clinic by the same staff for a painless application of a stencil on the same body location where the experimental child received a needle. Children's distress was judged on a 6-point scale by parents and research assistants who observed the event. Goodman and her colleagues found no impact on accuracy or suggestibility as a result of stress. In a third study 5 of 48 children were rated as being "extremely frightened or upset." These highly distressed children recalled significantly more correct information about their experience with an injection and were significantly more resistant to suggestion than children rated as less stressed. Unfortunately none of the children who were rated as highly stressed were available for the 1 year follow-up so the long-term impact of distress on their memory could not be determined. In neither the Goodman nor the Peters study was stress rated by the children who experienced the procedures.

The Child Memory Study

We (Steward, 1989; Steward et al., 1992) have just completed a study of 130 young children's memory of the experience of a visit to one of seven outpatient clinics at our medical center. The children in our study were touched typically on a dozen different places on their bodies and they experienced a very wide range of potentially stressful medical procedures. Children rated their own distress on a face scale originally designed by children (Bieri, Reeve, Champion, Addicoat, & Ziegler, 1990) and the medical staff person who administered the procedure to a child rated the child's distress on a 6-point Likert scale. The pediatric visits and interviews of the children were all videotaped so that we could study three different measures of memory—the accuracy, completeness, and consistency of children's reports—over a 6-month period. We were interested in what children could tell us about touch and handling of their bodies, and how well they could describe the persons present during the clinic visit, and the place it occurred. Four experimental interview strategies were designed: a core verbal interview, and three interviews enhanced with drawings, dolls and equipment, or computer graphics. In addition to assessing the differential efficacy of the interview strategies to elicit children's memories, the predictive power of twelve covariates was assessed in four blocks, organized according to the ease/expense of acquiring the information: (a) child's age, gender, and ethnicity, (b) parental report of child's health history, family stress, and parental education, (c) child's experiences during the pediatric visit including the number of invasive medical procedures, medical staff rating of child's health status and of children's distress, the child's pain judgments, and (d) the number of outpatient and inpatient visits that occurred between the original clinic visit and follow-up interviews at 1 and 6 months.

The analysis of the data from our study is complex and the reader is invited to review our report for a more detailed discussion of the results. In brief, 5 of the covariates entered significantly into the predictions of accuracy, completeness, and consistency (age, distress, maternal education, medical experience, and the number of medial procedures a child experienced); 7 of the covariates never came into play (gender, ethnicity, family stress, health status, medical staff judgment of distress, number of intervening outpatient or inpatient visits). There were very few consistent errors and none of the variables contributed to prediction of the error scores.

At the initial interview the data revealed that 3–6 year-old children were highly accurate in their spontaneous recall of the locations on their bodies where they were touched by medical staff (94%), but they reported only 25% of the touch they experienced. The accuracy of their descriptions of what they were touched with (72%), the persons who touched them (86%), and the place where the event occurred (86%) were also high, but lower than body touch. When children repeated information at follow-up interviews their reports were more consistently accurate than consistently in error. When directly questioned about touch to four body locations, their errors of omission were 5 times higher than their errors of commission. Over time accuracy of report of body touch dropped to 70%; yet some children offered new accurate information about body touch at the 1 and even at the 6-month follow-up interviews. Children who received enhanced interviews were able to provide more complete reports of their experience than were those in the verbal interview. The reports of very young children (3 and 4 year-olds) in the verbal interview were especially sparse. Age contributed to the predictions of both completeness and consistency, but never to the accuracy of children's reports.

Children's rating of distress was significantly correlated with the completeness, but not accuracy of a child's spontaneous recall of body touch during the initial and 1 month follow-up interview. Distress became a significant predictor of both accuracy and completeness of children's reports of body touch at the 6 month follow-up interviews. Distress was never related to scores of consistent accuracy or consistent error at 1 or 6 months. There was no relationship between the children's rating of distress and the ratings given by physicians or nurses, nor were medical staff ratings significantly related to any of the three measures of children's memory.

Our own work employing medical equipment, which had been used during medical procedures, to elicit memory of what children were touched with offers a complex, not a simple picture—at least in the case of young children. In one of the four interview protocols the children had access to medical equipment. These children were able to provide a more complete report by demonstrating their experience of body touch immediately after the event, than were children in the verbal interview. But at 1- and 6-month follow-up interviews children who had access to the equipment received lower accuracy scores, well below that of children who gave verbal reports. Review of the videotapes revealed that children did not use the medical equipment as toys in fantasy play, as might be suggested by DeLoache. Rather the medical equipment stimulated event memories so that children used the medical equipment to demonstrate procedures they had experienced on other pediatric visits—though not the one that we had videotaped. This interpretation was supported by the finding at the 1-month follow-up of a low, but significant negative correlation between the accuracy of children's memory of body touch and the parent's report of the child's past medical experience, suggesting the intrusion of previous medical scripts into their memory (Nelson & Hudson, 1988).

Because we are interested in the role of trauma on memory there were two groups of children who particularly caught our eye: those who reported high distress and those who denied not only the distress, but even the body touch. There were 47 children who rated at least one of the body touches they received as extremely painful. They did not differ from the rest of the children on scores of medical experience, language skills, or family stress. These children did, however, disclose more information on all three interviews. And the accuracy of their report about body touch dropped only to 81% by the 6-month interview.

There were 43 children who did not rate any of the body touches by our medical staff as being painful. When we took a closer look at the videotapes, it was apparent that 23 of the children had experienced a routine pediatric examination. There was little reason to judge any of the touches as painful. The videotapes of the remaining 20 children revealed that they had all received invasive medical procedures that were judged by the medical personnel who administered them as having been at least somewhat painful, and several received touches judged even by our medical staff (who tended to rate children's distress quite conservatively) as extremely painful. This group of children, whom we characterized by the report of one child that "He didn't touch me and it didn't hurt!", did not differ from the "no pain/no reason" group on language skills or family stress. They did differ on two other characteristics: gender and medical experience. There were 11 boys and 12 girls in the "no pain/no reason" group, while there were 14 boys and 6 girls in the "He didn't touch me" group. The "no pain/no reason" group also had significantly less medical experience than did the "He didn't touch me" group.

It is too simple to label either the "He didn't touch me" group or their psychodynamic strategy as denial. These children do not fit the expectations of memory deficit seen in the repeatedly traumatized group defined by Terr (1991). In contrast to the "no pain/no reason" group, they were more accurate in their descriptions of both the persons present and the clinic room. Joey, the 4-year-old boy who told us that "He didn't touch me and it didn't hurt!", is one of the children from this group. He was interviewed after he had experienced a spinal tap. Rather than providing a spontaneous and detailed report of his experience as might be expected from the clinical literature, he boldly told us nothing. This child's report of his visit to our medical center was challenged by one of my pediatric colleagues who confirmed that he had administered the medical procedure and who judged it to have been painful for the child. We reviewed the videotape of the child's clinic visit and coded his behavioral protest which included crying, a physical struggle with the nurse who had a firm grip on his head and upper torso, and a plea to his mother to "Help me!".

We don't know why Joey didn't tell us what happened to him, but we do have some hunches that we are currently testing. Joey, a strong, sassy, competent child had been frightened, physically hurt, and had his body restrained. Why would anyone want to rehearse such a terrible, helpless scene? For a child medical procedures are nested not only in the personal but also in interpersonal and environmental contexts. As Neisser (1988) observed, each context may contribute variables that independently and in interactive ways synergize to modify both memory and reporting processes. When Joey called for help, his angry and embarrassed mother shouted back at him, "If you don't shut up, I'm going to leave you!" We surmise that she imagined the medical staff was judging her parenting skills rather harshly since she was unable to control her noncompliant son. Her threat to abandon him may have been her last ace in the hole. In the telescoping scenario Joey was in trouble with himself and with his mom, and his mom was in trouble with the medical staff.

As a result of this work we have become interested not only in children's remembering, but also in children's reporting. We have begun to focus not only on what children tell us about past events, but also what they choose not to tell us. There may be little or no discrepancy between children's memories and what they report when the experience in focus has been an emotionally neutral one. Strong negative emotions appear to drive a wedge between remembering and reporting and result in what we have begun to term the "narrative of omission." Joey was able to tell us who was present, and to describe where the medical procedures took place—items that fit Terr's (1991) description of a child thinking about how to protect himself from those particular people and that particular setting next time. What he omitted from his report was just what had happened to him.

We have begun a careful analysis of the events that occurred during the pediatric visit to determine just what variables/experiences/persons might have contributed to this narrative of omission. We are examining the adult-child and adult-adult conversations during the procedures to determine if either the informational or affective content challenged the child's experience. Were any of these children told that they "would NOT get the needle today," and/or were any of them told that "it won't/doesn't/didn't hurt?" We are also examining the interview tapes for clues to children's self-conscious emotions which Lewis, Sullivan, Stanger, and Weiss (1989) have identified, such as being ashamed of their behavior during the painful procedure. In other words is the child's silence the result of a self-instruction not to tell us, due to the fact that it would be embarrassing or shameful, not "grown-up" or would do no good (i.e., a child's protest may not be able to prohibit effectively "uncontrollable events") (Altshuler & Ruble, 1989).

What do our research results suggest about the shape of the relationship between memory and emotion? First, it is not a straightforward linear one. More memory is not necessarily elicited from children who were more distressed. There is some support for a cubic (inverted U-shaped) relationship. At the far left, we found that children who had experienced only the benign pediatric touch of a well-child visit remembered/reported little about the who, what, or where of the event. At the far right, it is possible to believe that with highly distressing experiences a child's coping mechanisms can be overwhelmed (Type II trauma, Terr, 1991) resulting in a narrowing of the perceptual field of relevant stimuli (Easterbrook, 1959) such that a child's memory for the event is impaired. A second mechanism may be operating in another group of children who underreport very distressing experiences. We believe some children may underreport in response to stimulation by parent, medical staff, or self of negative self-evaluative emotional experiences (Lewis et al., 1989). These negative stimuli may inhibit reporting but not memory. Anna Freud's (1952) valuing of the child's meaning of the event over some absolute or objective judgment by another, is strongly supported by our data. In fact, our data fit an inverted U-shaped curve only if the child, as opposed to an observer, makes the judgment about just where on the curve the experience lies.

FUTURE DIRECTIONS IN RESEARCH

Adults Who Remember Childhood Illness

The upsurge of studies in autobiographical memory is of interest to many researchers focusing on the link between childhood and adult memory. However, some may be troubled by the lack of requirement for veridicality of the material produced (Brewer, 1986). There is no doubt that memory reconstructed in adulthood about childhood events may influence meaningfully a person's beliefs, decisions, and behaviors—whether it is true or not. However, as is shown by the work of Loftus and her colleagues (1979; Loftus & Davies, 1984; Loftus & Ketcham, 1991) on the suggestibility of adult eyewitness memory, we should be cautious in evaluating the accuracy of adult memories of childhood events where there is little or no corroboration.

There are two groups of adults who experienced illness as children and one group of adults who were eyewitnesses to childhood illness that might be of particular interest to researchers who wish to understand the interplay of the development of affect and cognition on the accuracy of childhood memories: Adults who were diagnosed with polio as children, those diagnosed with childhood cancer, and siblings of persons chronically ill in childhood. For both groups of former child patients there is the likelihood that their medical records are still available to enable accuracy checks on current memories; access to sibling data may require cooperation and corroboration of a number of family members.

Most post-polio adults are currently in their 50s and 60s. These adults experienced dramatic medical intervention, and vigorous encouragement from medical staff and parents to invest in recovery. Many endured excruciating pain and distress during physical therapy on their way to regaining mobility. The story of their physical health status continues to change. Unfortunately for many in midlife there is a swift deterioration of the muscles originally affected by the disease process and strengthened so painfully by physical therapy. My informal conversations with adults from this group reveal considerable negative affect and disillusionment at this turn of events.

Given the potential confounding influence of current depressed mood on memory retrieval, an investigator would need to struggle with the identification of an appropriate control group. It might still be possible to identify a healthy cohort within the group of post-polio adults, although that appears increasingly unlikely. Self-reported ratings by individuals of their emotional status at several points throughout the life cycle might provide an interesting covariate. These reports could include the period of active disease status, the period of stable health and current deteriorating health status. Reports for the first two periods would be, of course, retrospective.

The second group of adults with childhood experiences of medical procedures are now in their 20s and 30s. They are the first wave of adult survivors of childhood cancer. The change in treatment which occurred in the early 1960s has transformed the survival rates from 5–10% to upwards of 80%. Research on this group has focused primarily on cognitive and educational strength/vulnerabilities during the school years; and on marital status, employment, insurance issues in adulthood (Koocher & O'Malley, 1981). For these young adults, there has often been a veil of silence and sometimes even secrecy about their early medical experiences. There is a counter-phobic defensive maneuver that supports the silence of the adult survivor—if one doesn't discuss cancer, maybe it will not recur. The discussion of cancer elicits fearful responses from some listeners. Some believe that it is strategically unwise to inform a potential employer of one's childhood cancer as one's job, and more importantly, job-related benefits such as medical and life insurance may be negatively impacted. For both the polio and cancer groups there is a wealth of potentially verifiable information that could be elicited about their childhood experiences.

Siblings constitute a generally forgotten subpopulation within the constellation of families who have a child with chronic illness. As a group, they are once removed from medical procedures. Their memories of medical procedures are built on a different data set—absent the proprioceptive, kinesthetic, and nocioceptive cues that are components in the experience of the child patient. Pynoos and Nadar (1989) used a semistructured interview technique to study children's memory of a schoolyard shooting. They found that the *distance* a child was from a traumatic experience influenced the amount and kind of accurate information a child remembered and also the pattern of distortions found in a child's memory. It would be very instructive to apply their research techniques and compare their findings when siblings of chronically ill children are interviewed about medical procedures. Distance variables might include sibling presence/absence during procedures, participation in the procedure (e.g., as a donor of blood, bone marrow, etc.), actual or perceived responsibility for the ill sibling, etc. Other variables that might impact sibling memory of medical procedures include birth order of the chronically ill child vs. the sibling, and intense feelings such as jealousy, or fear. Koocher and O'Malley (1981) found that 25% of the siblings of childhood cancer in their study did not even know that their brother or sister had been diagnosed with cancer. Earlier follow-up of sibling memories might contribute not only to the memory literature, but also to the mental health of these children.

METHODOLOGICAL ISSUES FOR FUTURE RESEARCH ON MEMORY AND EMOTIONS IN PEDIATRIC SETTINGS

There are four issues about memory and emotions which have become clearer from this review of clinical and experimental research in pediatric settings, and from examining our own work in this context.

1. Remembering and reporting are not identical phenomena. K. Nelson (1989) noted that young children often remember more than they can tell. When the focus is memory of medical procedures there are several variables that should be tested to determine how they serve as moderator variables between remembering and reporting. One set of variables is related to the fact that the child is being asked to report body touch and handling—sensory, kinesthetic, and proprioceptive stimuli for which a child may not have developed adequate expressive language. A second set of variables is related to the fact that the child is being asked to report a neutral to negatively valenced experience over which she had no control, and from which she could not escape.

2. For young children remembering/reporting of important past experiences can be communicated nonverbally as well as verbally. This is compatible with

the dual memory model of Pillemer and White (1989). Many of the research data collected thus far on children's memory have been dependent on audiotape technology. By definition there has not been access to nonverbal cues. We believe that much has been missed, or will be missed, if the analysis of verbalized memories is not augmented (or even contradicted) by information from the face, from body gesture, and from the opportunity to demonstrate with props. In our own videotaped study of 3- to 6-year-olds children's memories of medical procedures only 17% of their responses were purely verbal, 58% included both verbal and nonverbal gesture, and 25% of their responses were exclusively nonverbal (Steward, 1989).

3. There is a complex relationship between remembering, reporting, and emotion. This complexity challenged our belief, based on clinical vignettes, that all children had an uncanny ability to report the details of painful medical and surgical procedures. We found not one but two clusters of response when children were asked to remember and report experiences that were judged to be very distressing. For the majority of children, the more negatively toned the experiences were judged, the more complete the report. But for a second group of children, their report became a narrative of omission as they told us who was there and where it happened, but not what had happened to them—an experience that was guarded from the interviewer but was clearly not forgotten by the child.

4. The veridicality of an individual's memory of childhood events is critical to the assessment of their physical and mental health in adolescence and adulthood. Although there is renewed interest in autobiographical memory, the findings from those data sets do not serve children well because there is no test of veridicality built into the methodology. Self-care and accurate diagnosis of physical symptoms of individuals in adolescence and adulthood are dependent on accurate information about childhood illness, injury and disease (Byrne et al., 1989). The psychotherapist, like the physician, needs accurate information about past childhood physical and sexual abuse in order to work therapeutically with the troubled adolescent or young adult (Lyons, 1987).

SUMMARY

The pediatric setting is rich with action, players and experiences. For those researchers interested in the accuracy and consistency of either short- or long-term memory of children's early experiences, the pediatric setting is especially attractive. There is access to an independent source in the medical records to corroborate children's narratives and reports. The pediatric setting also has much to offer those researchers interested in children's memory of highly emotionally charged experiences, particularly highly negatively charged emotional events, and in the impact of parents and medical staff behavior on children's experiences and memories.

Review of research on children's memory of medical procedures to date reveals that even very young children can report many facets of that complex experience with high degrees of accuracy, but in conditions of little or no stress they spontaneously report only a small fraction of what they remember. With skillful interviewing, including direct questioning, it is possible to elicit a more complete report of what they remember. Children's distress when defined in terms of physically painful, invasive procedures has been shown to interrupt the sequence, but not the accuracy of children's reports. When defined by observers, extreme distress appears to increase free recall and resistance to suggestion. When defined by children, highly stressful experiences of body touch and handling increase the completeness and accuracy of their reports over at least a 6-month period.

In many facets of children's lives memories of past events are deemed a good thing. Yet when an event is very stressful, memory may haunt a child with compulsive rehearsal or immobilize a child with fear. Such memories may interrupt rather than facilitate a child's normal growth and development. There is need for longitudinal study. Joyce Robertson's diary of her daughter's 3-day hospitalization, nested in 6 months of observation, is still the most detailed event record available on children's memory of medical procedures. The diary highlights the active role of the child in anticipation of the event and in rehearsal following the event—with both anticipation and rehearsal contributing to the working memory of the event. There is no parallel in the research literature to document and verify a child's memory of repeated, complex, multistep medical regimens where the sequencing of events is critical. The results of such studies could contribute to professionals who work in the health, mental health, and legal communities.

In sum, the pediatric setting provides a context where a stressful event can be studied with attention to preparation and debriefing; with attention to the interaction of biological, psychological and social variables on memory; with attention to the character of memories of painful events and their impact on future experiences; and with attention in research design to the documentation of the event to be remembered later.

REFERENCES

Achenbach, T. M. (1978). *Research in developmental psychology: Concepts, strategies, methods.* New York: The Free Press.

Altshuler, J. L., & Ruble, D. N. (1989). Developmental changes in children's awareness of strategies for coping with uncontrollable stress. *Child Development, 60,* 1337–1349.

Anderson, B. J., Auslander, W. F., Jung, K. C., Miller, J. P., & Santiago, J. V. (1990). Assessing family sharing of diabetes responsibilities. *Journal of Pediatric Psychology, 15,* 477–492.

Asher, S. J. (1988). The effects of childhood sexual abuse: A review of the issues and evidence. In L. E. A. Walker (Ed.), *Handbook on sexual abuse.* New York: Springer.

Baddeley, A. D. (1972). Selective attention and performance in dangerous environments. *British Journal of Psychology, 63,* 537–546.

Banaji, M. R., & Crowder, R. G. (1989). The bankruptcy of everyday memory. *American Psychologist, 44,* 1185–1193.

Bauchner, H., Waring, C., & Vinci, R. (1989). Parental presence during procedures in an emergency room: Results from 50 observations. *Pediatrics, 87,* 544–548.

Bearison, D. J. (1990). *They never want to tell you.* Cambridge, MA: Harvard University Press.

Bearison, D. J., & Pacifici, C. (1989). Children's event knowledge of cancer treatment. *Journal of Applied and Developmental Psychology, 10,* 469–486.

Bergmann, T., & Freud, A. (1965). *Children in the Hospital.* New York: International Universities Press.

Beuf, A. H. (1979). *Biting off the bracelet: A study of children in hospitals.* Philadelphia, PA: University of Pennsylvania Press.

Beyer, J. E., Berde, C. B., & Bournaki, M. C. (1991). Memories of pain in three to seven-year old children. *Journal of Pain and Symptom Management, 6,* 174.

Beyer, J. E., & Wells, N. (1990). The assessment of pain in children. *Pediatric Clinics of North America: Acute Pain in Children, 36,* 837–854.

Bibace, R., & Walsh, M. E. (1980). Development of children's concepts of illness. *Pediatrics, 66,* 912–917.

Bibace, R., & Walsh, M. E. (1981). Children's conceptions of illness. In R. Bibace & M. E. Walsh (Eds.), *New directions for child development: Children's conceptions of health, illness and bodily functions. Number 14,* San Francisco: Jossey-Bass.

Bieri, D., Reeve, R. A., Champion, G. D., Addicoat, L., & Ziegler, J. B. (1990). The faces pain scale for the self-assessment of the severity of pain experienced by children: Development, initial validation, and preliminary investigation for ratio scales properties. *Pain, 41,* 139–150.

Bjorklund, D. F. (1985). The role of conceptual knowledge in the development of organization in children's memory. In C. J. Brainerd & M. Pressley (Eds.), *Basic processes in memory development: Progress in cognitive development research.* New York: Springer-Verlag.

Bjorklund, D. F. (1987). How age changes in knowledge base contribute to the development of children's memory: An interpretive review. *Developmental Review, 7,* 93–130.

Blount, R. L., Corbin, S. M., Sturges, J. W., Wolfe, V. V., Prater, J. M., & James, L. D. (1989). The relationship between adults' behavior and child coping and distress during BMA/LP procedures: A sequential analysis. *Behavior Therapy, 20,* 585–601.

Blount, R. L., Landolf-Fritsche, B., Powers, S. W., & Sturges, J. W. (1991). Differences between high and low coping children and between parent and staff behaviors during painful medical procedures. *Journal of Pediatric Psychology, 16,* 793–807.

Blount, R. L., Sturges, J. W., & Powers, S. W. (1990). Analysis of child and adult behavioral variations by phase of medical procedure. *Behavioral Therapy, 21,* 33–48.

Brewer, W. F. (1986). What is autobiographical memory? In D. Rubin, *Autobiographical Memory.* Cambridge, England: Cambridge University Press.

Brewster, A. B. (1982). Chronically ill hospitalized children's conceptions of their illness. *Pediatrics, 69,* 355–362.

Broadbent, D. E., Reason, J. T., & Baddeley, A. (Eds.). (1991). *Human Factors in Hazardous Situations.* New York: Oxford University Press.

Bronfenbrenner, U. (1979). *The ecology of human development.* Cambridge, MA: Harvard University Press.

Burstein, S., & Meichenbaum, D. (1979). The work of worrying in children undergoing surgery. *Journal of Abnormal Child Psychology, 7,* 121–132.

Bush, J. P. (1987). Pain in children: A review of the literature from a developmental perspective. *Psychology and Health, 1,* 215–236.

Bush, J. P., & Harkins, S. W. (Eds.). (1991). *Children in pain: Clinical and research issues from a developmental perspective.* New York: Springer-Verlag.

Bush, J. P., Melamed, B. G., & Cockrell, C. S. (1989). Parenting children in a stressful medical situation. In T. W. Miller (Ed.), *Stressful life events*. Madison, CT: International Universities Press.

Bush, J. P., Melamed, B. G., Sheras, P. L., & Greenbaum, P. E. (1986). Mother-child patterns of coping with anticipatory medical stress. *Health Psychology, 5,* 137–157.

Bussey, K. (1990, March). *Adult influence on children's eyewitness reporting.* Paper presented at the biennial meeting of the American Psychology and Law Society, Williamsburg, VA.

Byrne, J., Lewis, S., Halamek, L., Connelly, R. R., & Mulvihill, J. J. (1989). Childhood cancer survivors' knowledge of their diagnosis and treatment. *Annals of Internal Medicine, 110,* 400–403.

Carandang, M. L. A., Folkins, C. H., Hines, P. A., & Steward, M. S. (1979). The role of cognitive level and sibling illness in children's conceptualizations of illness. *American Journal of Orthopsychiatry, 49,* 474–481.

Case, R., Hayward, S., Lewis, M., & Hurst, P. (1988). Toward a neo-Piagetian theory of cognitive and emotional development. *Developmental Review, 8,* 1–51.

Ceci, S. J., & Bronfenbrenner, U. (1991). On the demise of everyday memory: "The rumors of my death are much exaggerated" (Mark Twain). *American Psychologist, 46,* 27–31.

Chan, J. M. (1980). Preparation for procedures and surgery through play. *Paediatrician, 9,* 210–219.

Chi, M. (1978). Knowledge structures and memory development. In R. Siegler (Ed.) *Children's thinking: What develops?.* Hillsdale, NJ: Lawrence Erlbaum Associates.

Chrousos, G. P., & Gold, P. W. (1991). *The concepts of stress and stress system disorders: Overview of behavioral and physical homeostasis.* National Institutes of Health, Bethesda, MD.

Claflin, C. J., & Barbarin, O. A. (1991). Does "telling" less protect more? Relationships among age, information disclosure, and what children with cancer see and feel. *Journal of Pediatric Psychology, 16,* 169–191.

Connell, L. F. (1953). Tonsils: In or out? *Parents Magazine, 28,* 40–44.

Dahlquist, L. M., Gil, K. M., Armstrong, F. D., DeLawyer, D. D., Greene, P., & Wuori, D. (1989). Preparing children for medical examinations: The importance of previous medical experience. *Health Psychology, 5,* 249–259.

Darwin, C. R. (1877). A biographical sketch of an infant. *Mind, 2,* 286–94.

Davidson, C. V. (1988). Training the pediatric psychologist and the developmental-behavioral pediatrician. In D. K. Routh (Ed.), *Handbook of Pediatric Psychology.* New York: Guilford.

Davies, G. M., Tarrant, A., & Flin, R. (1989). Close encounters of the witness kind: Children's memories for a simulated health visit. *British Journal of Psychology, 80,* 415–429.

DeLoache, J. (1987). Rapid change in the symbolic functioning of very young children. *Science, 238,* 1556–1557.

DeLoache, J. (1990). Young children's understanding of models. In R. Fivush & J. Hudson (Eds.), *What young children remember and know.* New York: Cambridge University Press.

DeLoache, J. S., Kolstad, V., & Anderson, K. N. (1991). Physical similarity and young children's understanding of scale models. *Child Development, 62,* 111–126.

Easterbrook, J. A. (1959). The effect of emotion on cue utilization and the organization of behavior. *Psychological Review, 66,* 183–201.

Eiser, C. (1989). Children's concepts of illness: Towards an alternative to the "stage" approach. *Psychology and Health, 3,* 93–101.

Eland, J. M. (1974). *Children's communication of pain.* Unpublished master's thesis. University of Iowa.

Eland, J. M., & Anderson, J. E. (1977). The experience of pain in children. In A. K. Jacox (Ed.), *Pain: A source book for nurses and other health professionals.* Boston: Little Brown.

Engel, G. (1977). The need for a new medical model: A challenge for biomedicine. *Science, 196,* 129–136.

Fabes, R. A., Eisenberg, N., McCormick, S. E., & Wilson, M. S. (1988). Preschooler's attributions of the situational determinants of others' naturally occurring emotions. *Developmental Psychology, 24*: 376–385.

Fabes, R. A., Eisenberg, N., Nyman, M., & Michealieu, Q. (1991). Young children's appraisals of others' spontaneous emotional reactions. *Developmental Psychology, 27*, 858–866.

Fanurik, D., & Zeltzer, L. (1991). The relationship between children's coping styles and psychological intervention for cold pressor pain. *Journal of Pain and Symptom Management, 6*, 145.

Fernald, B. F., & Corry, J. J. (1981). Empathetic versus directive preparation of children for needles. *Journals of the Association for the Care of Children's Health, 10*, 44–47.

Fischer, K. W., Shaver, P. R., & Carnochan, P. (1990). How emotions develop and how they organize development. *Cognition and Emotion, 4*, 81–127.

Fletcher, J. M., Francis, D. J., Pequegnat, W., Raudenbush, S. W., Bornstein, M. H., Schmitt, F., Brouwers, O., & Stover, E. (1991). Neurobehavioral outcomes in diseases of childhood: Individual change models for pediatric human immunodeficiency viruses. *American Psychologist, 46*, 1267–1277.

Freud, A. (1952). The role of bodily illness in the mental life of children. *Psychoanalytic Study of the Child, 7*, 69–80.

Freund, A., Johnson, S. B., Silverstein, J., & Thomas, J. (1991). Assessing daily management of childhood diabetes using 24-hour recall interviews: Reliability and stability. *Health Psychology, 10*, 200–208.

Geist, R. (1991, April). *Use of imagery to describe functional abdominal pain: An aid to diagnosis in a pediatric population.* Paper presented at the Second International Symposium on Pediatric Pain, Montreal, Canada.

Gellert, E. (1962). Children's conceptions of the content and functions of the human body. *Genetic Psychology Monographs, 65*, 293–405.

Gold, P. E. (1984). Memory modulation: Neurobiological contexts. In G. Lynch, J. L. McGaugh, & N. M. Weinberger (Eds.), *Neurobiology of Learning and Memory*. New York: Guilford.

Gold, P. E. (1987). Sweet memories. *American Scientist, 75*, 151–155.

Gonzalez, J. C., Routh, D. K., Saab, P. G., Armstrong, F. D., Shifman, L., Guerra, E., & Fawcett, N. (1989). Effects of parent presence on children's reactions to injections: Behavioral, physiological and subjective aspects. *Journal of Pediatric Psychology, 14*, 449–462.

Goodman, G. (1984). The child witness: Conclusions and future directions. *Journal of Social Issues, 40*(2), 157–175.

Goodman, G. S., Hirschman, J. E., Hepps, D., & Rudy, L. (1991). Children's memory for stressful events. *Merrill-Palmer Quarterly, 37*, 109–158.

Gudas, L. J., Koocher, G. P., & Wypij, D. (1991). Perceptions of medical compliance in children and adolescents with cystic fibrosis. *Developmental and Behavioral Pediatrics, 12*, 236–242.

Gunnar, M. R., Hertsgaard, L., Larson, M., & Rigatuso, J. (1992). Cortisol and behavioral responses to repeated stressors in the human newborn. *Developmental Psychobiology, 24*(7), 487–506.

Gunnar, M., Marvinney, D., Isensee, J., & Fisch, R. O. (1989). Coping with uncertainty: New models of the relations between hormonal, behavioral and cognitive processes. In D. S. Palermo (Ed.), *Coping with uncertainty: Behavioral and developmental perspectives*. Hillsdale, NJ: Lawrence Erlbaum Associates.

Haggerty, R. J. (1986). In N. A. Krasnegor, J. D. Arasteh, & M. F. Cataldo (Eds.), *Child health behavior*. New York: Wiley.

Hobbes, N., Perrin, J. M., & Ireys, H. T. (1985). *Chronically ill children and their families*. San Francisco: Jossey-Bass.

Jackson, E. B. (1942). Treatment of the young child in the hospital. *American Journal of Orthopsychiatry, 12*, 56–68.

Jacoby, L. L. (1989). Memory observed and memory unobserved. In U. Neisser & E. Winograd (Eds.), *Remembering reconsidered: Ecological and traditional approaches to the study of memory*. New York: Cambridge University Press.

Jay, S. (1988). Invasive medical procedures: Psychological intervention and assessment. In D. K. Routh (Ed.), *Handbook of Pediatric Psychology*. New York: Guilford Press.

Jay, S. M., & Elliott, C. H. (1990). A stress inoculation program for parents whose children are undergoing painful medical procedures. *Journal of Consulting and Clinical Psychology, 58,* 799–804.

Jay, S. M., Elliott, C. H., Katz, E., & Siegel, S. E. (1987). Cognitive-behavioral and pharmacologic interventions for children's distress during painful medical procedures. *Journal of Consulting and Clinical Psychology, 55,* 860–865.

Jay, S. M., Elliott, C. H., Ozolins, M., Olson, R. A., & Pruitt, S. D. (1985). Behavioral management of children's distress during painful medical procedures. *Behavior Research and Therapy, 23,* 513–520.

Jay, S. M., Ozolins, M., Elliott, C. H., & Caldwell, S. (1983). Assessment of children's distress during painful medical procedures. *Health Psychology, 2,* 133–147.

Jessner, L., Blom, G. E., & Waldfogel, S. (1952). Emotional implications of tonsillectomy and adenoidectomy on children. *Psychoanalytic Study of the Child, 7,* 126–169.

Koocher, G. P. (1985). Promoting coping with illness in childhood. In J. C. Rosen & L. J. Solomon (Eds.), *Prevention in health psychology*. Hanover, VT: University Press of New England.

Koocher, G. P., & O'Malley, J. E. (1981). *The Damocles syndrome: Psychosocial consequences of surviving childhood cancer*. New York: McGraw-Hill.

Kuttner, L., Bowman, M., & Teasdale, M. (1988). Psychological treatment of distress, pain and anxiety for young children with cancer. *Journal of Developmental and Behavioral Pediatrics, 9,* 374–381.

Kuttner, L., & Lepage, T. (1989). Faces scales for the assessment of pediatric pain: A critical review. *Canadian Journal of Behavioral Science/Review of Canadian Science Comp., 21,* 198–209.

LaGreca, A. M. (1990). Issues in adherence with pediatric regimens. *Journal of Pediatric Psychology, 15,* 423–436.

Lehmann, H. P., Bendebba, M., & DeAngelis, C. (1990). The consistency of young children's assessment of remembered painful events. *Developmental and Behavioral Pediatrics, 11,* 128–134.

Levy, D. (1945). Psychic trauma of operations in children. *American Journal of Diseases of Childhood, 69,* 7–25.

Lewis, M., Sullivan, M. W., Stanger, C., & Weiss, M. (1989). Self development and self-conscious emotions. *Child development, 60,* 146–156.

Lewis, N. (1978). The needle is like an animal. *Children Today,* January-February, pp. 18–21.

Litt, I. F., & Cuskey, W. R. (1980). Compliance with medical regimens during adolescence. *Pediatric Clinics of North America, 27,* 3–15.

Loftus, E. F. (1979). *Eyewitness testimony*. Cambridge, MA: Harvard University Press.

Loftus, E. F. (1991). The glitter of everyday memory . . . and the gold. *American Psychologist, 46,* 16–18.

Loftus, E. F., & Davies, G. M. (1984). Distortions in the memory of children. *Journal of Social Issues, 40,* 51–68.

Loftus, E. F., & Ketcham, K. (1991). *Witness for the defense: The accused, the eyewitness, and the expert who puts memory on trial*. New York: St. Martin's Press.

Lollar, D. J., Smits, S. J., & Patterson, D. L. (1982). Assessment of pediatric pain: An empirical perspective. *Journal of Pediatric Psychology, 7,* 267–277.

Lumley, M., Abeles, L., Melamed, B. G., Pistone, L., & Johnson, J. H. (1990). Coping outcomes in children undergoing stressful medical procedures: The role of child-environment variables. *Behavioral Assessment, 12,* 223–238.

Lyons, J. A. (1987). Posttraumatic stress disorder in children and adolescents: A review of the literature. *Developmental and Behavioral Pediatrics, 8,* 349–356.

Massie, R. K., Jr. (1985). The constant shadow: Reflections on the life of a chronically ill child. In

N. Hobbs, & J. M. Perrin (Eds.), *Issues in the care of children with chronic disease*. San Francisco: Jossey-Bass.

McGaugh, J. L. (1983). Hormonal influences on memory. *Annual Review of Psychology, 34*, 297–323.

McGrath, P. A. (1987). An assessment of children's pain: A review of behavioral, physiological and direct scaling techniques. *Pain, 31*, 147–176.

Melamed, B. G. (1991a). Future pain horizons. In J. P. Bush & S. W. Harkins (Eds.), *Children in pain: Clinical and research issues from a developmental perspective*. New York: Springer-Verlag.

Melamed, B. G. (1991b). Putting the cart before the horse: Anxiety and coping in hospitalized children. *Psychological Science Agenda,* November/December, 10–12.

Melamed, B. G., Robbins, R. L., & Graves, S. (1982). Preparation for surgery and medical procedures. In D. C. Russo & J. W. Varni (Eds.), *Behavioral pediatrics*. New York: Plenum Press.

Melton, G. B. (1981). Children's competency to testify. *Law and Human Behavior, 5*, 73–85.

Merskey, H. (1979). Pain terms: A list with definitions and notes on usage. Recommended by the International Association for the Study of Pain (IASP) Subcommittee on Taxonomy. *Pain, 6*, 249–252.

Money, J., & Lamacz, M. (1987). Genital examination and exposure experience as nosocomial sexual abuse in childhood. *Journal of Nervous and Mental Disease, 175*, 713–721.

Moss, N., Steward, M. S., & Racusin, G. (1992). *The influence of causal attribution and severity of injury on children's recovery from accidental injury*. Unpublished manuscript.

Myers-Vando, R., Steward, M. S., Folkins, C. H., & Hines, P. A. (1979). The effects of congenital heart disease on cognitive development, illness, causality concepts, and vulnerability. *American Journal of Orthopsychiatry, 49*, 617–625.

Nagy, M. (1953). Children's concepts of some bodily functions. *Journal of Genetic Psychology, 83*, 199–216.

Neisser, U. (1978). Memory: What are the important questions? In M. M. Gruneberg, P. E. Morris, & R. N. Sykes (Eds.), *Practical aspects of memory*. London: Academic Press.

Neisser, U. (1988). New vistas in the study of memory. In U. Neisser & E. Winograd (Eds.), *Remembering reconsidered: Ecological and traditional approaches to the study of memory*. New York: Cambridge University Press.

Neisser, U. (1991). A case of misplaced nostalgia. *American Psychologist, 46*, 34–36.

Nelms, B. C. (1989). Emotional behaviors in chronically ill children. *Journal of Abnormal Child Psychology, 17*, 657–668.

Nelson, K. (1986). *Event Knowledge: A functional approach to cognitive development*. Hillsdale, NJ: Lawrence Erlbaum Associates.

Nelson, K. (1989). Remembering: A functional developmental perspective. In P. R. Solomon, G. R. Goethals, C. M. Kelley, & B. R. Stephens (Eds.), *Memory: Interdisciplinary approaches* (pp. 127–150). New York: Springer-Verlag.

Nelson, K., & Hudson, J. A. (1988). Scripts and memory: Functional relationships in development. In F. E. Weinert & M. Perlmutter (Eds.), *Memory development: Universal changes and individual differences* (pp. 147–167). Hillsdale, NJ: Lawrence Erlbaum Associates.

Neuhauser, C., Amsterdam, B., Hines, P., & Steward, M. S. (1978). Children's concepts of healing: Cognitive development and locus of control. *American Journal of Orthopsychiatry, 448*, 325–341.

Parmalee, A. H. (1986). Children's illness: Their beneficial effects on behavioral development. *Child Development, 57*, 1–10.

Pearson, G. H. J. (1941). Effective operative procedures on the emotional life of the child. *American Journal of Diseases of Children, 62*, 716–729.

Perrin, E. C., & Gerrity, P. S. (1981). There's a demon in your belly: Children's understanding of illness. *Pediatrics, 67*, 841–849.

Perrin, E. C., Sayer, A. G., & Willett, J. B. (1991). Sticks and stones may break my bones . . . reasoning about illness causality and body functioning in children who have a chronic illness. *Pediatrics, 88,* 608–619.

Peters, D. P. (1987). The impact of naturally occurring stress on children's memory. In S. J. Ceci, M. P. Toglia, & D. F. Ross (Eds.), *Children's eyewitness memory.* New York: Springer-Verlag.

Peterson, C., & Seligman, M. E. P. (1984). Causal expectations as a risk factor for depression: Theory and evidence. *Psychological Review, 91,* 347–374.

Peterson, L. (1989). Coping by children undergoing stressful medical procedures: Some conceptual, methodological and therapeutic issues. *Journal of Consulting and Clinical Psychology, 57,* 380–387.

Peterson, L., Harbeck, C., Farmer, J., & Zink, M. (1991). Developmental contributions to the assessment of children's pain: Conceptual and methodological implications. In J. P. Bush & S. W. Harkins (Eds.), *Children in pain: Clinical and research issues from a developmental perspective.* New York: Springer-Verlag.

Peterson, L. J., & Mori, L. (1988). Preparation for hospitalization. In D. K. Routh (Eds.), *Handbook of pediatric psychology.* New York: Guilford Press.

Peterson, L., & Toler, S. M. (1986). An information seeking disposition in child surgery patients. *Health Psychology, 5,* 343–358.

Petrillo, M., & Sanger, S. (1980). *Emotional care of the hospitalized child* (2nd ed.). Philadelphia, PA: J. B. Lippincott.

Piaget, J. (1952). The origins of intelligence in children (M. Cook, Trans.). New York: International Universities Press. (Originally published, 1936).

Piaget, J. (1954). The construction of reality in the child (M. Cook, Trans.). New York: Basic Books. (Originally published in 1937).

Pillemer, D. B., & White, S. H. (1989). Childhood events recalled by children and adults. In H. W. Reese (Ed.), *Advances in child development and behavior* (pp. 297–340). New York: Academic Press.

Pinto, R. P., & Hollandsworth, J. G. (1989). Using videotape modeling to prepare children psychologically for surgery: Influence of parents and costs versus benefits of providing preparation services. *Health Psychology, 8,* 79–95.

Plank, E. (1971). *Working with children in hospitals: A guide for the professional team* (2nd edition). Cleveland: Press of Case Western Reserve University.

Potter, P. C., & Roberts, M. C. (1984). Children's perceptions of chronic illness: The roles of disease symptoms, cognitive development, and information. *Journal of Pediatric Psychology, 9,* 13–27.

Pruitt, D. B., & Strickland, M. (1987). Psychological factors affecting children's response to medical procedures: A guideline for clinicians. *Psychiatric Medicine, 5,* 199–209.

Pynoos, R. S., & Nadar, K. (1989). Children's memory and proximity to violence. *Journal of the American Academy of Child and Adolescent Psychiatry, 28,* 236–241.

Rasnake, L. K., & Linscheid, T. R. (1989). Anxiety reduction in children receiving medical care: Developmental considerations. *Journal of Developmental and Behavioral Pediatrics, 10,* 169–75.

Reynolds, L. A., Johnson, S. B., & Silverstein, J. (1990). Assessing daily diabetes management by 24-hour recall interview: The validity of children's reports. *Journal of Pediatric Psychology, 15,* 493–509.

Ritter, K., Kaprove, B. H., Fitch, J. P., & Flavell, J. H. (1973). The development of retrieval strategies in young children. *Cognitive Psychology, 5,* 310–321.

Robertson, J. (Director). (1953a). *A two year old goes to the hospital* (Film). London: Tavistock Clinic; New York: New York University Library.

Robertson, J. (1953b). A two year old goes to the hospital. *Nursing Times, 49,* 388–393.

Robertson, J., & Freud, A. (1956). A mother's observation on the tonsillectomy of her four-year-old daughter. *Psychoanalytic Study of the Child, 11,* 410–436.

Ross, D. M. (1984). Thought-stopping: A coping strategy for impending feared events. *Issues in Comprehensive Pediatric Nursing, 7,* 83–89.

Ross, D. M., & Ross, S. A. (1982). *A study of the pain experience in children.* Final report (Ref. No. 1 ROI HD 13672-01). Bethesda, MD: National Institute of Child Health and Human Development.

Ross, D. M., & Ross, S. A. (1988). *Childhood pain: Current issues, research and management.* Baltimore: Urban & Schwarzberg.

Ross, S. A. (1984). Impending hospitalization: Timing of preparation for the school-aged child. *Children's Health Care, 12,* 187–189.

Saywitz, K. J., Goodman, G. S., Nicholas, E., & Moan, S. (1991). Children's memories of a physical examination involving genital touch: Implications for reports of child sexual abuse. *Journal of Consulting and Clinical Psychology, 59,* 682–691.

Schechter, N. L. (1989). The undertreatment of pain in children: An overview. *Pediatric Clinics of North America, 36,* 781–794.

Schneider, W., & Pressley, M. (1989). *Memory development between 2 and 20.* New York: Springer-Verlag.

Shaw, E. G., & Routh, D. K. (1982). Effect of mother presence on children's reaction to aversive procedures. *Journal of Pediatric Psychology, 7,* 33–42.

Siegel, L. J. (1991). Increasing pain tolerance through self-efficacy training. *Journal of Pain and Symptom Management, 6,* 174.

Siegal, M., Patty, J., & Eiser, C. (1990). A re-examination of children's conceptions of contagion. *Psychology and Health, 4,* 159–165.

Siegler, R. S., & Crowley, K. (1991). The microgentetic method: A direct means for studying cognitive development. *American Psychologist, 46,* 606–611.

Smith, K. E., Ackerson, J. D., & Blotcky, A. D. (1989). Reducing stress during invasive medical procedures: Relating behavioral interventions to preferred coping style in pediatric cancer patients. *Journal of Pediatric Psychology, 14,* 405–418.

Smith, B. S., Ratner, H. H., & Hobart, C. J. (1987). The role of cuing and organization in children's memory for events. *Journal of Experimental Child Psychology, 44,* 1–24.

Starfield, B. (1991). Childhood morbidity: Comparisons, clusters and trends. *Pediatrics, 88,* 519–526.

Stern, M., Ross, S., & Bielass, M. (1991). Impact of health status label on medical students' expectations for children's coping style and choice of approach. *Journal of Social and Clinical Psychology, 10,* 91–101.

Steward, M. S. (1988). Illness: A crisis for children. In J. Sandoval (Ed.), *Crisis counseling, intervention and prevention in the schools.* Hillsdale, NJ: Lawrence Erlbaum Associates.

Steward, M. S. (1989). *The development of a model interview for young child victims of sexual abuse: Comparing the effectiveness of anatomical dolls, drawings and video graphics.* Final Report of grant # 90CA1332 for the National Center on Child Abuse and Neglect, U.S. Office of Health and Human Services, Washington, D.C., Nov 30, 1989.

Steward, M. S., & Regalbuto, G. (1975). Do doctors know what children know? *American Journal of Orthopsychiatry, 45,* 146–149.

Steward, M. S., Reinhart, M., Joye, N., & Steward, D. S. (1992). *Evaluation of children's behavioral distress during the colposcope examination in contrast to two other medical procedures.* Manuscript submitted for publication.

Steward, M. S., & Steward, D. S. (1981). Children's concepts of medical procedures. In R. Bibace & M. Walsh (Eds.), *The Development of children's conceptions of health and related phenomena.* San Francisco: Jossey-Bass.

Steward, M. S., Steward, D. S., Farquhar, L., Joye, N., Reinhart, M., Myers, J. E. B., & Welker, J. (1992). *A visit to the doctor: The accuracy, completeness and consistency of children's memory.* Manuscript submitted for publication.

Steward, M. S., Steward, D. S., Joye, N., & Reinhart, M. (1991). Pain judgements by young children and medical staff. *Journal of Pain and Symptom Management, 6,* 202.

Sussman, E. J., Dorn, L. D., & Fletcher, J. C. (1987). Reasoning about illness in ill and healthy children and adolescents: Cognitive and emotional developmental aspects. *Developmental and Behavioral Pediatrics, 8,* 266–273.

Terr, L. (1979). Children of Chowchilla: A study of psychic trauma. *Psychoanalytic Study of the Child, 34,* 547–623.

Terr, L. (1983). Chowchilla revisited: The effects of psychic trauma four years after a schoolbus kidnapping. *American Journal of Psychiatry, 140,* 1543–1550.

Terr, L. (1988). What happens to the memories of early childhood trauma? *Journal of the American Academy of Child and Adolescent Psychiatry, 27,* 96–104.

Terr, L. (1990). Children's responses to the Challenger disaster. *New Research Programs and Abstracts,* American Psychiatric Association 143rd Annual Meeting, Washington, D.C.

Terr, L. (1991). Childhood traumas: An outline and overview. *American Journal of Psychiatry, 148,* 10–20.

Wasserman, A. L., Thompson, E. I., Williams, J. A., & Fairclough, D. L. (1987). The psychological status of survivors of childhood/adolescent Hodgkin's disease. *American Journal of Diseases of Children, 141,* 626–631.

Watt-Watson, J., Evernden, C., & Lawson, C. (1991). Parents' perceptions of children's acute pain experience. *Journal of Pain and Symptom Management, 6,* 149.

Whitt, J. K., Dykstra, W., & Taylor, C. A. (1979). Children's conceptions of illness and cognitive development. *Clinical Pediatrics, 18,* 327–339.

Wilkie, D. J., Holzemer, W. L., Tesler, M. D., Ward, J. A., Paul, S. M., & Savedra, M. C. (1990). Measuring pain quality: Validity and reliability of children's and adolescents' pain language. *Pain, 41,* 151–159.

Williams, P. D. (1979). Children's concepts of illness and internal body parts. *Maternal and Child Nursing Journal, 8,* 115–123.

Yerkes, R. M., & Dodson, J. D. (1908). The relation of strength of stimulus to rapidity of habit formation. *Journal of Comparative Neurological Psychology, 18,* 459–482.

Zeltzer, L. K. (1991). Forward. In J. P. Bush & S. W. Harkins (Eds.), *Children in pain: Clinical and research issues from a developmental perspective.* New York: Springer-Verlag.

Zeltzer, L. K., Jay, S. M., & Fisher, D. M. (1989). The management of pain associated with pediatric procedures. *Pediatric Clinics of North America, 36,* 941–964.

Zeltzer, L. K., & LeBaron, S. (1986). Fantasy in children and adolescents with chronic illness. *Developmental and Behavioral Pediatrics, 7,* 195–198.

A Case Example of Clinically Relevant Research: Commentary on Steward

Susan Phipps-Yonas

I came to the task of discussing Steward's chapter (this volume) as a clinical psychologist who works primarily in the area of sexual abuse. I approached it, as well as the other chapters that constitute this volume, from the perspective of one who believes that the field of psychology, indeed all of the disciplines that contribute to the study of mental health, has been grossly negligent, at least until very recently, in terms of considering the impact of such trauma on development. Like most of my colleagues, I was trained at a time when there was virtually no mention of sexual abuse. Freud had long since thrown out his poorly termed "seduction theory," and psychiatry textbooks in use at that point (20 years ago) reported the incidence of incest as 1 in a million (e.g., Freedman, Kaplan, & Sadock, 1975). Although developmental psychopathology was emerging within the academic world, there was no attention given to what would have been deemed an extremely rare problem had psychology professors even considered such a possibility. Nor did clinical supervisors appear to know any better. As a psychology intern in 1975, I was assigned a child patient who had been sodomized by her stepfather and consequently placed in foster care. In my ignorance, I asked my supervisor what to do with such a freakish situation. He advised me, as likely would most of his peers, not to bring up the subject in the therapy sessions that I had with this youngster. Because she remained silent—as we now understand most victims do (see Berliner & Conte, 1991; Briere & Conte, 1989; Briere & Zaidi, in press; Finkelhor, 1984; Jones & McQuiston, 1988), we never talked about what had happened to her nor what it meant in terms of her mental health status. While I was thankful at the time for that fact, current experts (e.g., Friedrich, 1990, 1991; James, 1989) would deem such a practice incompetent.

A number of authors (e.g., Butler, 1978; Crewdson, 1988; Money, 1985; Reiss, 1990; Rush, 1980; Summit, 1988) have offered varied and interesting speculations as to the source of our earlier ignorance. It seems that as a society, we have relied upon repression and denial of a problem of immense proportion (see Peters, Wyatt, & Finkelhor, 1986; Russell, 1988 for discussions of incidence and prevalence). The taboo and resulting silence attached to the subject of sexual abuse, remain with us, in large part. However, by the early 1980s, the situation had changed somewhat in that many mental health professionals recognized first, that sexual abuse was a common problem within the populations with which we worked and second, that it had significant developmental implications for our patients, as well as for our theories of human behavior. There was very little, nevertheless, in the psychological literature on the topic. It was relatively easy at that point to read all that was written, treat a few victim/survivors and become a so-called "expert."

Over the past decade more and more books and articles have appeared that address questions regarding the prevalence and historical or cultural significance of sexual abuse or outline evaluation, treatment, and prevention strategies; however very little that has been written offers any type of developmental perspective on the subject. This has troubled (and puzzled) me because there are seemingly endless questions that developmental researchers could explore that could aid the clinical work of therapists who work with child victims as well as provide empirical data that could be employed to educate judges and jurors about children who give, or are the subject of, often difficult and confusing courtroom testimony.

Regardless of the particular domain of their research, be it in the area of cognitive or social or personality development, most child psychologists are in a position to advance the state of knowledge relevant to sexual abuse. The value of basic research notwithstanding, it is important that scientists appreciate the kinds of questions that need answers in the real world. Consider, for example, that when James Gibson, one of the premier theorists and researchers in perception, was called upon in World War II to apply what was known in his field to selecting pilots who could land airplanes successfully and teaching them how to be more skilled, he concluded that virtually nothing that was known about perception at that point was helpful for that task. As distressing as that conclusion may have been at the time, it directed him to study action in the real world, and thus came to guide his work and that of many of his students in the decades that followed the war.

In my view, basic research that is relevant to problems that individuals face in day-to-day living and that can therefore inform practitioners is superior to research which is not. The data presented at the 1991 Minnesota Symposium invite a number of potential (and exciting) applications for those of us who work directly with young patients and their families. Along with other recent efforts such as the 1989 Cornell Conference on the Suggestibility of Children's Recollections (Doris, 1991), this volume constitutes a significant step in an important direction.

SOME CHALLENGES OF APPLIED RESEARCH

The above stated enthusiasm notwithstanding, several cautions are indicated. The first follows upon the issues raised by Davies (this volume). As he has noted, courts in this country and, in fact, around the world, are seeking information about children so as to make better decisions about what certain behaviors and/or statements may mean or what youngsters can and cannot be expected to do. Unfortunately, many of the data that find their way into legal proceedings are, at best, quasi-scientific in nature. In part, this may be due to the fact that our system of justice functions in many ways that are antithetical to those of science. While both enterprises may seek an ever elusive "truth" about the world, our courts go about doing so in an adversarial manner wherein observations and conclusions are, by necessity, absolute. In such an arena of "good guys" and "bad guys" there is very little room for ambiguities or for complexities. Yet all competent students of human behavior, be they researchers or clinicians, know that our subject areas are extremely complicated. Almost nothing is black or white, and only rarely can we make statements that do not require some qualification. Furthermore, we strive to distance what we say from our values. The way that psychologists typically talk and write is an anathema to attorneys.

Thus, it is often difficult to maintain any semblance of scientific neutrality when one is drawn into a courtroom. The scene there often elicits adversarial posturing. This is what apparently happened at the Cornell Conference; sides have been drawn up and now some researchers seemingly seek ammunition for their "cause." The need for balance is critical, yet difficult to achieve. As Bull (1991), one of the Cornell conferees, so aptly framed the question: What should psychologists being asked to testify in court do if there is good reason to believe that the court or jury holds views, or a lawyer presents arguments, for which (a) there exists no support from psychological research or (b) the research that does exist suggests an opposing view?

Davies (1991, and this volume) provides an excellent model as to how to maintain a scientific balance that can be useful to a court. His approach deserves to be emulated. As he has advised, scientists should be thoughtful both in framing research questions and in interpreting the findings. Although researchers need not be advocates themselves, they should be mindful of what is done with their work.

The following excerpt provides an example of how, all too often, so-called scientific results are presented to courts of law. It is taken verbatim from a report submitted to a judge in a child custody trial by a Minnesota psychologist.

> . . . questionable prceedure (sic) is having two therapists with the children and parents for all interviews. This clearly establishes the liklihood (sic) of undue influence being exerted upon the children by the biases and prejudces (sic) of the interviewers. There are at least six absolutly (sic) well established and irrefutable areas of the science of Psychology that show the power, subtley, (sic) and extent of influence in such situations. . . . interviewers bias, expectancy effect, experimenter bias, over-obedience, verbal conditioning psychotherapy research, and the Asch or majority effect. The latter clearly shows that two or more people present with children will ellicit (sic) whatever statments (sic) are desired . . .

In a typical case, the author of the above commentary uses this type of reasoning to discredit a child's testimony, and if necessary in the course of a hearing, he cites specific references to support his contentions. One seemingly favorite claim of this "expert" is that the sole basis for memories reported by young children is verbal conditioning. He likely would argue that Tesler's findings as reported by Nelson (this volume), wherein young children failed to recall information regarding an experience they had with their mothers unless the latter had talked about such, *proves* his point. He has, in a similar vein, testified on many occasions that Piaget *proved* that preadolescents cannot tell the difference between fact and fiction. As preposterous as this may seem to psychologists, it can be conveyed very convincingly to judges and jurors who are ignorant of cognitive development. Obviously, the results may be disastrous for a child when that happens.

Another note of caution pertains to what might happen to data that are incorporated in a meta-analysis of the sort advocated by Penrod (Shapiro & Penrod, 1986) for child witness studies. Consider, for example, Peters' (1991) finding that 58% of the 5- to 10-year-olds who witnessed a staged theft stated incorrectly that the thief was not present in the live, line-up they saw (i.e., most of his subjects made false nonidentifications). He went on, however, to report that among that group of presumably poor witnesses, over half later disclosed to their parents that they had failed to acknowledge the presence of the thief out of fear. It was clear that they knew who the thief was, that is, their memory was correct, but they were inhibited about reporting such. What would happen to those numbers in a meta-analysis?

The same finding of Peters' invites another concern in that the researcher characterized his data as "encouraging." While the conclusion that many children perform poorly as witnesses may delight the guilty defendant, it is hardly encouraging for a victimized child. The laudable call for caution in applying research findings often appears to be directed towards assisting adults who are accused of perpetrating abuse much more than towards protecting possibly victimized children. It seems that the taboo regarding sexual abuse remains strong within the scientific community.

A COUNTER EXAMPLE—OR HOW TO DO THIS WORK

Steward's research (this volume) appears to be generated out of a context and set of assumptions similar to that which I have endorsed. I see it as an important contribution in several regards. Clearly, her work is a prime example of a natural study. While inherently high on ecological validity, her methodology nevertheless affords an opportunity to tease apart a number of variables in a manner more characteristic of laboratory research.

As an exploration of children's experiences with various medical procedures per se, Steward's data constitute significant basic knowledge along with a wealth of information for medical practitioners who want to better serve their young patients. The children's accounts can inform adults about how to prepare young patients more satisfactorily, about what to attend to during a given procedure, and about what should be incorporated into debriefing sessions.

Steward's findings also should alert medical personnel to the importance of certain individual differences in ascertaining the meaning of their interventions to children. Especially intriguing are the implications of this work for studying the use of dissociation as a coping strategy. Experts on multiple personality disorder (Dean, Giem, Guerro, & Leark, 1989; Peterson, 1989; Putnam, 1989; Ross, 1989) have found that the rare individual with multiple personality disorder who has not experienced severe early abuse almost always has a history of early hospitalization with extensive invasive medical procedures. Medical professionals may be able to apply the lessons from Steward's work in efforts to reduce, if not eliminate, the iatrogenesis of such defensive processes.

Equally important as the above mentioned applications is the relevance of the Steward data to the understanding of children's reports of sexual and other physical abuse. The finding that high levels of pain are associated with more accurate and complete recall of touch experiences supports the view of Goodman (1991) that stress facilitates memory, as well as the more general belief that children remember what is salient for them, especially when it involves them in action (Ceci, Toglia, & Ross, 1987; Garbarino & Stott, 1989). It is hardly remarkable in this regard that Steward's subjects are more accurate about events involving their genitals than they are about those pertaining to their ears. Nor is it surprising in the context in which these painful touches occurred that children remember the "what happened" to their bodies better than the "who did it." Knowing the latter, that is "the who," would have little functional value, given that for most youngsters medical professionals are interchangeable. (A doctor is a doctor is a doctor. . . .) What is important to attend to is whether the treating individual uses a needle or intends to make an alternatively painless intervention. For the same reason it seems silly to think that children should remember the color of the sweater of a woman who alerts them to a phony fire after they have been taken, likely by a trusted adult, to a laboratory room where they receive an injection (Peters, 1991).

The fact that accurate as they were, Steward's subjects reported only 30% of what happened is consistent with the finding (Berliner & Conte, 1991) that when later confirmed child sexual abuse victims first disclose what happened to them, they typically fail to tell everything. Indeed, the Berliner–Conte data revealed that less than half of their sample (wherein sexual abuse was clearly validated) admitted to the abuse when first questioned.

It is significant that most children in the "he-didn't-touch-me-and-it-didn't-hurt" group were male. Many child therapists have disregarded the incidence data on sexual abuse (Peters, Wyatt, & Finkelhor, 1986), which suggest that females are victimized more commonly than males. Furthermore, the proportion of little boy victims has been rising as more abuse is uncovered. Steward's "he-didn't-touch-me-and-it-didn't-hurt" patient offers one possible explanation as to why male victims are underreported. It may well be that gender role socialization, perhaps of the sort possibly reflected in Fivush's study (this volume) influences disclosure. Simply put, it may be too shameful for young boys to admit that they have not had control over what has happened to their bodies or that they would allow themselves to be hurt. Expressing emotion, especially pain or fear, is still proscribed for many males in our society. I would point again to the fact that this group provides considerable evidence that dissociation, as helpful as it may be at the time of stress, interferes significantly and predictively with individuals' ability to report their experiences.

A CALL TO DEVELOPMENTAL RESEARCHERS

The contents of this volume provide a number of leads for the direction in which developmental research on memory and affect should, in my view, head. They reaffirm for me a sense of how extraordinarily capable very young children are, along with the conclusion that the problems that we adults, as researchers or as parents, have in communicating with toddlers is due as much to our limitations as to theirs (see Garbarino & Stott, 1989; Melton & Thompson, 1987 for more elaborate discussions of this point). It thus behooves us to understand how we can facilitate youngsters' ability to tell us what they know and feel. There are many ways beyond those proposed herein that this can be accomplished.

One claim often voiced by attorneys who represent defendants in cases involving sexual abuse allegations is that very young children cannot tell the difference between what has happened to them and what they have been coached to say, or in a perhaps less deviantly adversarial sense, may have been suggested to them. Studies of toddlers' crib talk or of their dialogues with significant others regarding interactions that they actually have had, relative to interactions about which they have been told, could provide data relevant to such defense claims. Obviously, it would be important in such work to vary the nature of the interactions studied as well as the circumstances of and players involved in the subsequent discussions.

Another area that should beckon cognitive psychologists is developmentally sensitive work along the lines of studies conducted by Raskin and his colleagues involving statement reality analysis (Raskin & Esplin, 1991; Raskin & Yuille, 1989). What are the factors that differentiate accounts that children provide of real life events versus their fabrications? As a clinician, I can recall two children, among others, who offered allegations of sexual abuse that I found unconvincing. In one case the preschooler told a story about what her father allegedly had done to her on multiple occasions. When I tried to question her about her statements, I learned that she could not respond credibly if I interrupted her account. She could not talk about anything midway through the "incident"; instead she had to begin at the beginning of her story which she then repeated verbatim, as one would do with a memorized script. I was not persuaded, nor, fortunately I would add, both for her sake as well as her father's, did the family court judge, who instead awarded custody of the little girl to this man.

The second youngster was 5-years-old. At our first session, she gave me a reasonable description of abuse allegedly perpetrated by her father, with "facts" that corroborated those provided by a second victim who was a year younger and who was seeing a different therapist. My client continued to speak about what had happened at our next session, during which, I would note, her mother, who was conflicted about what to believe, watched the videotape that I had made of the earlier interview. The following week this girl, who was in her mother's custody, retracted her previous claims. In response to my direct questions at that point, she would only say "Mommy said to say that daddy didn't do it." However, when I made indirect inquiries which assumed that the abuse had occurred, she answered in a confirmatory manner and provided more details about what had happened. Needless to say, I found the recantation unconvincing. Nevertheless, the child refused to budge, and the prosecutor found it impossible to persuade the jury beyond a reasonable doubt that a crime had been committed.

Of course, neither I nor any other psychological evaluator, no matter how well trained, experienced, or competent (see APSAC guidelines), can ever be absolutely positive of our conclusions. We are however, and will continue to be, called upon to offer our views, and as cases like those described earlier demonstrate, it is critical that developmental researchers enter this arena as well. Thus, in conclusion, I would plead for assistance in educating judges and jurors as to the likely meaning of children's statements and behaviors by providing relevant empirical data.

REFERENCES

American Professional Society on the Abuse of Children. (1990). *Guidelines for psychosocial evaluation of suspected sexual abuse in young children.*

Berliner, L., & Conte, J. (1991, November). *Workshop: Child sexual abuse.* Presented at the Midwest Conference on Child Sexual Abuse and Incest, Madison, Wisconsin.

Briere, J., & Conte, J. (1989). *Amnesia in adults molested as children: Testing theories of repres-*

sion. Paper presented at the American Psychological Association Annual Convention, New Orleans.

Briere, J., & Zaidi, L. Y. (in press). Sexual abuse histories and sequelae in female psychiatric emergency room patients. *American journal of psychiatry*.

Bull, R. (1991). Commentary: The issue of relevance. In J. Doris (Ed.), *The suggestibility of children's recollections* (pp. 134–137). Washington, D.C.: American Psychological Association.

Butler, S. (1978). *Conspiracy of silence: The trauma of incest*. San Francisco: Volcano Press.

Ceci, S. J., Toglia, M. P., & Ross, D. F. (1987). *Children's eyewitness memory*. New York: Springer-Verlag.

Crewdson, J. (1988). *By silence betrayed: Sexual abuse of children in America*. Boston: Little, Brown.

Davies, G. (1991). Concluding comments. In J. Doris (Ed.), *The suggestibility of children's recollections* (pp. 177–187). Washington, D.C.: American Psychological Association.

Dean, G., Giem, D., Guerro, J., & Leark, R. (1989, November). *Comparison of incipient MPD and MPD predictors and disorders commonly diagnosed in children and adolescents*. Paper presented at the Proceedings of the Sixth International Conference on Multiple Personality/Dissociative States, Chicago.

Doris, J. (Ed.). (1991). *The suggestibility of children's recollections*. Washington, D.C.: American Psychological Association.

Finkelhor, D. (1984). *Child sexual abuse*. New York: The Free Press.

Freedman, A. M., Kaplan, H. I., & Sadock, B. J. (Eds.). (1975). *Comprehensive textbook of psychiatry* (2nd edition). Baltimore: Williams and Wilkins.

Friedrich, W. N. (1990). *Psychotherapy of sexually abused children and their families*. New York: W. W. Norton.

Friedrich, W. N. (Ed.). (1991). *Casebook of sexual abuse treatment*. New York: W. W. Norton.

Garbarino, J., & Stott, F. (1989). *What children can tell us*. San Francisco: Jossey-Bass.

Goodman, G. (1991). Commentary on stress and accuracy in research on children's testimony. In J. Doris (Ed.), *The suggestibility of children's recollections* (pp. 77–82). Washington, D.C.: American Psychological Association.

Goodman, G., Rudy, L., Bottom, B., & Aman, C. (1989). Children's concerns and memory: Ecological issues in the study of children's eyewitness memory. In R. Fivush & J. Hudson (Eds.), *What young children remember and why* (pp. 189–206). Cambridge, England: Cambridge University Press.

James, B. (1989). *Treating traumatized children*. Lexington, MA: D.C. Heath.

Jones, D. P. H., & McQuiston, M. G. (1988). *Interviewing the sexually abused child* (3rd edition). Oxford, England: Alden Press.

Melton, G. B., & Thompson, R. A. (1987). Detours to less traveled paths in child-witness research. In S. J. Ceci, M. P. Toglia, & D. F. Ross (Eds.) *Children's eyewitness memory* (pp. 209–229). New York: Springer-Verlag.

Money, J. (1985). *The destroying angel*. Buffalo, NY: Prometheus Books.

Peters, D. P. (1991). The influence of stress and arousal on the child witness and Commentary responsive to Goodman. In J. Doris (Ed.), *The suggestibility of children's recollections* (pp. 60–76; 86–91). Washington, D.C.: American Psychological Association.

Peters, S. D., Wyatt, G. E., & Finkelhor, D. (1986). Prevalence. In D. Finkelhor (Ed.), *A sourcebook on child sexual abuse* (pp. 15–59). Newbury Park, CA: Sage Publications.

Peterson, G. (1989, November). *Assessment and diagnosis of child and adolescent multiple personality disorder: Issues and procedures*. Paper presented at the Proceedings of the Sixth International Conference on Multiple Personality/Dissociative States, Chicago.

Putnam, F. W. (1989). *Diagnosis and treatment of multiple personality disorder*. New York: Guilford Press.

Raskin, D. C., & Esplin, P. W. (1991). Assessment of children's statements of sexual abuse. In J.

Doris (Ed.), *The suggestibility of children's recollections* (pp. 153–164). Washington, D.C.: American Psychological Association.

Raskin, D. C., & Yuille, J. C. (1989). Problems in evaluation interviews of children in sexual abuse cases. In S. J. Ceci, D. F. Ross, & M. P. Toglia (Eds.), *Perspectives on children's testimony* (pp. 184–207). New York: Springer-Verlag.

Reiss, I. L. (1990). *An end to shame: Shaping our next sexual revolution.* Buffalo, NY: Prometheus Books.

Ross, C. A. (1989). *Multiple personality disorder: Diagnosis, clinical features and treatment.* New York: Wiley.

Rush, F. (1980). *The best kept secret: Sexual abuse of children.* New York: McGraw-Hill.

Russell, D. E. (1988). The incidence and prevalence of intrafamilial and extrafamilial sexual abuse of female children. In L. E. A. Walker (Ed.), *Handbook on sexual abuse of children* (pp. 19–36). New York: Springer.

Shapiro, P. N., & Penrod, S. (1986). Meta-analysis of facial identification studies. *Psychological Bulletin, 100,* 139–156.

Summit, R. C. (1988). Hidden victims, hidden pain: Societal avoidance of child sexual abuse. In G. E. Wyatt & G. L. Powell (Eds.), *Lasting effects of child sexual abuse* (pp. 39–60). Newbury Park, CA: Sage Publications.

11 From Dialogue to Internal Working Models: The Co-Construction of Self in Relationships

Inge Bretherton
University of Wisconsin-Madison

Psychoanalytic thinkers and developmental psychologists interested in the social construction of reality have long focused on mental representation as the mediating link between parental behavior and child personality. However, until recently their research enterprises have proceeded somewhat independently of each other. Within the psychoanalytic tradition (including attachment theory) the emphasis has been on internalized childhood experiences with parents as they affect later mental health and the capacity to form close relationships. Researchers interested in the social construction of reality, by contrast, have focused on the parentally guided internalization of diverse cultural, ethnic, and social class values. A third line of relevant research consists of investigations into children's short-term and long-term memories of traumatic experiences.

This chapter represents an attempt to integrate these separate theoretical and research strands. After a brief review of the psychoanalytic perspective on representation as a person's "inner world," I summarize Bowlby's (1969, 1973, 1980) reformulation of these ideas, inspired by Craik's (1943) concept of representation as "internal working models" of self and parent as they originate in patterns of nonverbal and verbal communication or miscommunication. I then present empirical studies of attachment in support of these ideas and flesh out the notion of working models of self and other in attachment relationship by applying theories and empirical studies of event representation to attachment theory. Next, I discuss research on the co-constructive origins of memory organization and memory content in parent-child discussions of experienced events and stories as related to the development of different self-identities. Finally, I consider the impact of highly traumatic experiences on the development and transformation of children's internal working models of the world and the self, emphasizing the need for long-term interpretive support from parents and other adults. I also discuss how the mental health and enculturation approaches to parental influences on the child's growing self might cross-fertilize each other.

THE PSYCHOANALYTIC TRADITION WITH AN EMPHASIS ON ATTACHMENT THEORY

Classical Views

Freud (1940) proposed that thinking is experimental mental action based on an internal copy of the outer world that individuals build up from a store of memories of earlier perceptions. Along similar lines, Hartmann (1958) suggested that thinking is trial activity, displaced into the interior of the organism as motor action directed toward the external world is suppressed.

In accord with this general approach to mental representation as internal simulation, psychoanalysts interested in interpersonal relatedness viewed the concepts of self and other as internalized chunks of relationship patterns. For example, Sullivan (1953) spoke of me–you patterns acquired in the mother-child relationship that are later imposed like templates on close relationships with friends and sexual partners while Fairbairn (1952) proposed the notion of internal (love) objects and associated portions of the ego.

Freud and other psychoanalysts after him not only assumed an "inner world" but also posited a variety of information processing systems that enable an individual to operate on this inner world (primary and secondary process, reality testing, and defense mechanisms). Unfortunately, the then current academic research on memory for nonsense word lists could not shed much light upon these phenomena. A notable exception was Bartlett's (1933) work suggesting that memory schemas affect and distort the processing of new information. Another exception were experiments on perceptual defense which have remained somewhat controversial.

Attachment Theory

In the late 1960s, the psychoanalytic concept of "inner world" was further elaborated by John Bowlby (1969) in the context of formulating attachment theory. In doing so, he drew on Craik's (1943) concept of representation as an "internal working model." Craik, a British psychologist interested in the development of intelligent rocket guidance systems, conceived of working models in terms of *mental structures* that conserve salient aspects of the temporal and causal configuration (or relation-structure) of real world phenomena. Internal working models enable individuals to mentally entertain and evaluate a variety of possible actions in the world.

Bowlby favored Craik's term "internal working model" over other related metaphors such as "image," "map," or "inner world," because both "working" and "model" suggest a dynamic representational system on which an individual can operate in order to engage in planning, decision-making, and interpretation. Bowlby went beyond Craik, however, in elucidating the intergenerational and developmental processes involved in a child's construction of internal working models of the world, attachment figures, and the self.

Internal working models of self and attachment figure(s) as defined by Bowlby (1969, 1973) are dynamic representations that serve to predict and interpret the partner's behavior, as well as to plan one's own behavior in response to the partner. Building on Piaget's theory of sensorimotor development, Bowlby speculated that internal working models of self and caregiver are constructed out of the actual transaction patterns between the partners, and are, for that reason, complementary. If the caregiver has fairly consistently acknowledged the infant's needs for comfort and protection, and respected the infant's need for independent exploration of the environment, the child is likely to develop an internal working model of self as valued and self-reliant. Conversely, if the parent has frequently rejected the infant's bids for comfort or for exploration, the child is likely to construct an internal working model of self as unworthy or incompetent.

Clinical studies reviewed by Bowlby (1973) further suggest that, in nonsupportive attachment relationships, the child is likely to develop at least two mutually inconsistent working models of the caregiver and self. One working model—accessible to awareness and discussion—represents the parent as good and the parent's rejecting behavior as due to the "badness" of the child. The other model—defensively excluded from awareness—represents the hated or disappointing side of the parent. Bowlby (1985, citing Cain & Fast, 1972) maintained that such splits in working models occur as a result of intrapsychic conflict between what a child remembers and subsequent innocuous or contradictory interpretations of the event by parents, accompanied by a taboo on further discussion.

To help him shed further light on defensive processes involved in the development of dissociated and inconsistent working models, Bowlby (1980) introduced Tulving's (1972) distinction between semantic and episodic memory. Episodic memory, in Tulving's framework, refers to experienced (autobiographical) events whereas semantic memory refers to general knowledge which may be abstracted from a variety of direct experiences or acquired through instruction by others. Bowlby suggested that some children may repress their autobiographical memories of a traumatic event, and retain conscious access only to verbally conveyed parental interpretations stored in semantic memory. Unfortunately, as Crittenden (1990) aptly noted, a set of dissociated working models is not likely to work well in helping an individual adapt to reality.

To explain the process of repression (Bowlby calls it *defensive exclusion* of information from awareness), Bowlby drew on information-processing theory.

Defensive exclusion, he maintained, is merely a special case of the ubiquitous and well confirmed process of *selective exclusion* which helps humans to focus attention on the most salient stimuli. Such processes have been well documented in dichotic listening experiments which demonstrate that incoming information of which an individual is completely unaware can nevertheless undergo high level processing. For example, individuals who are concurrently exposed to two different verbal messages via headphones, are able to monitor one message while remaining oblivious to the other until their personal name is mentioned (see reviews of this literature by Dixon, 1971).

In discussing the development of internal working models, Bowlby (1969) contends that their construction precedes the acquisition of language:

> Starting, we may suppose, toward the end of the first year, and probably especially actively during his second and third year when he acquires the powerful and extraordinary gift of language, a child is busy constructing working models of how his mother and other significant persons may be expected to behave, how he himself may be expected to behave, and of how each interacts with all the others. Within the framework of these working models he evaluates his situation and makes his plans. And within the framework of the working models of his mother and himself he evaluates special aspects of his situation and makes his attachment plans. (p. 354)

To account for the development of working models, Bowlby had to rely on Piaget's (1951, 1954) theory of sensorimotor development, governed by the twin processes of assimilation and accommodation. By acting on the world the infant was said to develop schemas into which relevant experiences could subsequently be assimilated, but which could also be refined or accommodated so as to better fit external reality. These schemas were later said to become "interiorized" allowing the child to engage in mental trial and error. However, the schemas in which Piaget was interested were precursors of logico-mathematical operations, and much of his theory is therefore not particularly useful in clarifying the concept of internal working model of self and other in attachment relationships. Other more helpful ideas that since emerged from the domain of cognitive psychology are discussed later. First, I present evidence from empirical studies that supports many of Bowlby's notions regarding the emergence of internal working models of self through communication with attachment figures.

This research suggests that communicative failures between infants and parents can engender distortions in internal working models, even when they do not involve severe trauma. A caregiver's systematic disavowal or discounting of infant signals results in the elimination of specific topics from reciprocal, mutually validating communication. It appears that the resulting partial, biased, and distorted communication patterns can in and of themselves lead to a disassociation between conscious and unconscious internal working models of self and attachment figure (see also the review of Stern, 1985, for similar ideas). To put it differently, lack of open communication between attachment partners may be associated with a restricted flow of information about attachment issues not only *between* partners, but *within* each partners' representational system (Bowlby, 1988).

Empirical Studies of Attachment: Communication and Representation

Mary Ainsworth's painstaking observational work with mothers and infants in naturalistic settings, first in Uganda (1967) and later in Baltimore (Ainsworth, Blehar, Waters, & Wall, 1978), points to the pathway whereby parent-child communication patterns are translated into internal working models.

Together with her colleagues, Ainsworth discovered that mothers who, during the first 3 months of the infants' life, were relatively insensitive to their infant's signals during feeding (Ainsworth & Bell, 1969), face-to-face interaction (Blehar, Lieberman, & Ainsworth, 1977), physical contact (Ainsworth, Bell, Blehar, & Main, 1971), separation-reunion (Stayton & Ainsworth, 1973), and distress episodes (Bell & Ainsworth, 1972), had infants who—during the last quarter of the first year—had less harmonious relationships with their mothers. Not only did these infants cry more, and demand close bodily contact more often without particularly enjoying it, they also behaved differently from sensitively mothered infants in a laboratory procedure known as the Strange Situation (Ainsworth, Bell, & Stayton, 1974; Ainsworth et al., 1978).

The Strange Situation (Ainsworth et al., 1978) consists of a standard sequence of 3-minute episodes in a laboratory playroom where mother and baby are joined by an unfamiliar woman. Of special importance are two sequences during which the mother leaves the room and then returns. Infants whose mothers had responded sensitively to their signals during feeding, crying, holding, and face-to-face episodes at home during the first 3 months of life, welcomed their mother's return after a brief separation in the Strange Situation. They approached her readily, sought interaction or close contact, were relatively quickly soothed and then returned to play. These infants were labeled secure (group B).

Insensitively mothered infants either avoided the returning mother in the Strange Situation by snubbing her, looking, turning, walking away, or refusing interaction bids (insecure-avoidant or group A), or responded ambivalently when the mother came back, seeking close bodily contact, but also showing angry, resistant behavior. Infants assigned to this insecure–ambivalent group (C) wanted to be held, but showed tantrumy behavior in addition to contact-seeking. At home, the mothers of the avoidant babies provided less affectionate holding during the first 3 months and frequently rejected bids for close bodily contact during the last quarter of the first year. These mothers also talked about their dislike of bodily contact in conversations with the observer. Mothers of ambivalent babies, by contrast, were inconsistently sensitive at home. Although they frequently ignored their babies' signals, they did not reject close bodily contact.

These findings suggest that a mother's sensitivity plays a major role in setting the initial tone of the relationship. However, as memory and information-processing abilities increase, infants become better able to assume an active reciprocal role in upholding the emerging transactional patterns. The latter has been documented in several micro-analytic studies of parent-child interactions undertaken in Germany. Escher-Graeub and Grossmann (1983) observed mothers and infants in a laboratory play situation, separate from the Strange Situation. They noticed that mothers of infants who had been avoidant of the parent in the Strange Situation reunions were eager to join their infants in play while the infants were cheerfully exploring the toys. However, these very same parents withdrew from interaction when their infants signaled negative feelings. Parents of secure infants, on the other hand, watched quietly from the sidelines as long as the infants did not signal a need for support or interaction. They joined in supportively, however, when their infants showed signs of stress or distress. A study of communication patterns in the Strange Situation itself revealed a complementary infant strategy. Infants classified as avoidant tend not to communicate with parents after reunion, as if expecting that attachment behaviors will be rejected (Grossmann, Grossmann, & Schwan, 1986).

Studies by Matas, Arend, and Sroufe (1978) corroborate these findings. Matas et al. noted that mother-infant pairs classified as secure or insecure in the Strange Situation communicated differently with each other when the children were 24 months old. Faced with a difficult problem-solving task, secure toddlers initially worked on their own but asked for mother's assistance when necessary. Their mothers, in turn, intervened effectively and supportively. Insecure toddlers, by contrast, tended to give up easily and whine, while their mothers tended not to offer help. In clinical samples (Radke-Yarrow, Cummings, Kuczynsky, & Chapman, 1985; Lieberman & Pawl, 1990) such mutually maladaptive communication patterns are even more apparent.

Not only do these findings support Bowlby's theoretical claims that communication patterns become relationship patterns, they are also consonant with other process-oriented studies that have documented infants' negative responses to a noncontingent, misattuned parent (e.g., Brazelton, Kozlowski, & Main, 1974; Stern, Beebe, Jaffe, & Bennett, 1977; Stern, 1985; Tronick, Ricks, & Cohn, 1982) though these studies have not documented longitudinal effects.

At the verbal level, empirical studies of preschoolers and their parents document an interesting connection between attachment partners' ability to communicate openly and sensitively *with* each other and their ability to communicate coherently *about* attachment relationships with third persons. In attachment-theoretic terms, one may infer that the functioning of internal working models of self in relation to attachment figures manifests itself in both types of communication (see also Bretherton, 1990, 1991). This is true for parents as well as children.

For example, how a parent discusses attachment relations in his or her family of origin with an interviewer is strikingly correlated with how the same parent communicates with his or her child (Main, Kaplan, & Cassidy, 1985). Main et al. used a structured, open-ended interview to probe for parental recollections of childhood attachment figures, and for thoughts about the significance of attachment relations in general, including their influence on the parent's own development.

In evaluating the interview transcripts, Main et al. (1985) discovered that parents of 6-year-olds who were classified as securely attached to them in the Strange Situation in infancy valued both attachment and autonomy, and were at ease when discussing the influence of attachment-related issues upon their own development (whether or not they recalled a secure childhood). Parents of children who were classified as insecure-avoidant with them in infancy, on the other hand, dismissed and devalued attachment, maintaining that early attachment experiences had little effect on their own development. They frequently claimed not to remember any incidents from childhood, and specific memories that emerged despite this denial were likely not to support the generalized (often highly idealized) descriptions of parents.

Parents of children previously classified as insecure-resistant seemed preoccupied with earlier family attachments, recalling many specific, often conflict-ridden incidents about their childhood attachments. However, these parents could not integrate these conflictual memories into a coherent overall picture. In sum, both the dismissing and preoccupied groups found it difficult to discuss attachment relationships in an integrated way. By inference, these parents operated with internally inconsistent working models, a situation of which they seemed to be unaware.

Finally, parents of children classified as insecure-disorganized in infancy (a new classification suggested by Main and Solomon, 1990) seemed to be struggling with unresolved issues concerning loss of a parent before maturity (see Main & Hesse, 1990). Since 1985, these results have been replicated in several other samples (Eichberg, 1987; Grossmann, Fremmer-Bombik, Rudolph, & Grossmann, 1988; Fonagy, Steele, & Steele, 1991; Ward, Carlson, Altman, Levine, Greenberg, & Kessler, 1990); for related findings see Bretherton, Biringen, Ridgeway, Maslin, & Sherman, 1989, and Kobak & Sceery, 1988).

One could, of course, argue that correlations between infant-parent attachment and the parents' accounts of their own childhood attachments derive from selective recall, cued by current experiences with a particular child. However, some recent studies have reported that response styles in the adult attachment interview predicted later parent-infant attachment even when the interviews were given before the infant's birth (Fonagy et al., 1991; Ward et al., 1990). Selective recall is unlikely, therefore, to explain these findings.

Correlations between communication style *within* attachment relations and *about* attachment relations were also obtained for children. In her longitudinal study Main et al. (1985) discovered that 6-year-old children classified as secure with mother in the Strange Situation in infancy gave coherent, elaborated, and open responses to drawings of parent-child separation scenes. In contrast, children earlier judged insecure-avoidant with mother described the pictured children as sad, but could not say what they could have done in response to separation. Children classified as disorganized/disoriented (Main & Hesse, 1990) were often completely silent or gave irrational or bizarre responses (Main et al., 1985; for similar findings see Cassidy, 1988; Slough & Greenberg, 1990).

Inspired by Main et al.'s (1985) findings, Bretherton, Ridgeway, and Cassidy (1990) undertook a study of even younger children. In their study, 37-month-olds were asked to complete attachment doll story stems. If children addressed the story-issues with little hesitation, and invented benign resolutions, they were classified as secure. If, on the other hand, they produced irrelevant or very bizarre story resolutions (e.g., after a separated family is reunited, they have a car-crash) or if they had to be prompted for a response many times, the children were classified as insecure. Secure-insecure classifications of doll-story responses were highly concordant with classifications of an actual separation-reunion procedure. They were also correlated with maternal responses to a structured open-ended interview, modeled on the Adult Attachment Interview (Bretherton et al., 1989), but probing maternal representations about her own child.

I argue that these findings reflect intergenerational processes in the transmission of internal working models. Even before an infant is born, parents have anticipatory working models of themselves as parents, and of the unborn infant (Brazelton & Cramer, 1990; Heinicke, Diskin, Ramsey-Klee, & Given, 1983; Zeanah, Keener, Stewart, & Anders, 1985). After the infant's birth, these anticipatory working models must be corrected and fine-tuned to fit the particular baby's temperament and needs (see also Stern, 1985), a task that will be relatively easy if the new parents' internal working models are coherent and well organized, and not deeply affected by defensive distortions. It will be much more difficult if the parent's internal working models of self and infant are pervasively affected by defensive exclusion. In this case, a parent is likely to communicate with his or her infant in such a way as to interfere with the infant's ability to construct adequate internal working models of interpersonal relations.

Under this view, the converse happens for secure parents whose internal working model of attachment figures and of self is reasonably consistent and well adapted to reality. Such parents are likely to give the infant helpful and informative feedback, hence facilitating flexible adaptation to new relationships. Furthermore, both partners' internal working models will be easier to update, because there are few defensive impediments to information processing.

Bowlby (1973) phrased it thus:

Because in all these respects children tend unwittingly to identify with parents and therefore to adopt, when they become parents, the same patterns of behaviour

> towards children that they themselves have experienced during their own childhood, patterns of interaction are transmitted, more or less faithfully, from one generation to another. Thus the inheritance of mental health and of mental ill health through the medium of family microculture is certainly no less important, and may well be far more important, than is their inheritance through the medium of genes. (p. 323)

The major new insight Main et al. (1985) brought to this discussion is that the intergenerational transmission of relationship patterns, while common, need not occur. In Main et al.'s study, most parents who described secure childhoods had children who related to them securely. However, there were some parents with secure children who reported abusive or rejecting relationships in their family of origin. What distinguished these parents was their ability to discuss adverse childhood experiences with emotional openness and coherence. They seemed to have come to terms with what had happened to them, and had come to understand why their parents had behaved as they did. Unfortunately, we do not know what specific conditions enabled these individuals to break a vicious intergenerational cycle by reconstructing earlier working models, though having a supportive spouse may be helpful (Ricks, 1985).

The Concept of Working Model in Light of Theories of Event Representation

As previously noted, the concept of internal working model of self and attachment figures implies an ability to simulate relationship patterns at the mental level. This in turn implies a representational system that operates with dynamic event- or agent-action-object structures. When Bowlby (1969) first incorporated the concept of internal working models into his writings, no existing theory of mental representation explicitly dealt with thinking as internal simulation of events and experiences.

In some contexts it may be sufficient to regard representations of self and other as "inner persons" with whom an individual can engage in imaginary interactions. However, in my view, much is to be gained by updating our theorizing about internal working models with findings and insights from the study of representation.

Recent developments in cognitive science have provided some useful conceptual clarifications. These suggest that the internal simulation of reality is a complex multileveled process. This work has also highlighted the fact that the term internal working model can be used in two senses: to refer to working models of past experiences that are stored in *long-term memory* and to new models that are "composed" afresh in short-term or *working* memory to understand current reality or to extrapolate to possible realities. In short, in considering the operation of working models we need to discuss the encoding, retrieval, operation, and reconstruction of working models in long-term and working memory.

No memory researchers have paid attention to all aspects of the operation and structure of internal working models. Some have primarily focused on the structure of long-term memory, while others have studied the construction of working models in short-term memory.

Inspired by Bartlett's (1933) work on remembering, Mandler (1979), Neisser (1987), and Schank and Abelson (1977) proposed hypothetical entities, termed *event schemas* or *scripts,* that were defined as sequentially organized representational structures with "slots" for specific agent-roles, for action sequences motivated by specific goals and emotions, for recipients of actions, and for locales. Schank and Abelson argued that, in processing recurrences of familiar events individuals, "instantiate" the relevant stored script or event schema to help predict what might happen next. These researchers do not, however, specify what internal processes enable the instantiation of relevant event schemas.

Nor does script theory, as originally formulated, tell us much about our undoubted ability to extrapolate extant schemas or scripts to hypothetical situations, to understand stories about never-before-encountered events, or to think of the same situation at several levels of abstraction (Neisser, 1987). Fortunately, Schank's (1982) reformulation of script theory provides some relevant suggestions. In his book on *Dynamic Memory,* Schank argued that each episodic or autobiographical memory is reprocessed, partitioned into smaller components, cross-indexed, and summarized into a variety of different schema categories each of which simulate some aspect of the spatio-temporal-causal-affective-motivational structure of experience. Only some of these schemas organize mini-event representations into coordinated, longer event sequences (such as the *scripts* of going to a restaurant or putting a baby to bed), others summarize information derived from similar mini-events (e.g., all infant-mother feeding situations regardless of context), and yet others generalize across different event sequences (e.g., all caregiving routines). Note that Schank's new conceptualization blurs the distinction between episodic (autobiographical) and semantic memory (the generic knowledge base) as originally proposed by Tulving (1972, 1983), and substitutes instead a set or web of multiply interconnected hierarchies composed of schemas that range from being very experience-near to being very general and abstract. These hierarchies are constructed and continually revised and refined on the basis of new input (for related ideas see Nelson, 1986), and could therefore provide the building blocks for the recombination of old elements into new mental models.

Johnson-Laird (1983) implicitly assumes such a system when he infers that humans can combine old part-schemas, drawn from long-term memory, to form new ones in short-term memory. His research shows that individuals find it much easier to solve a logical problem when it is presented in terms of a concrete situation of which they can construct a mental model. Performance suffers, however, when the same problem is presented in terms of highly abstract concepts (Wason & Johnson-Laird, 1972).

There remains the question how these ideas from cognitive science help us conceptualize internal working models of self and other, especially in light of the fact that theories of event representation were, for the most part, designed to explain an individual's understanding of routine and somewhat unemotional experiences with generic partners, rather the representation of highly charged transactional patterns with particular individuals.

Notwithstanding the fact that they were developed with a different aim in mind, I suggest that theories of event representation are entirely consonant with the idea that individuals may develop mental models of relationships with *specific partners*. Indeed, from Schank's (1982) theory of dynamic memory we can infer that schemas of interaction with particular partners may be the building blocks from which an individual derives a general conception of people. Note that such schemas must include affect and motivation, a fact for which Schank's theory explicitly makes provision.

Theories of event representation also do not specify that all schemas be directly accessible to conscious reflection. They are hence compatible with the notion that some transactional schemas may only be available as procedural or sensorimotor knowledge (i.e., manifested only in action). Such hypothesized procedural schemas of interpersonal interaction may form the most experience-near level in a working model consisting of hierarchically organized affective-cognitive schema systems with an unknown but finite number of levels of abstraction, with information possibly encoded in different ways at different levels. I would also like to emphasize that, in such a representational system, it is unlikely that an individual's working models of self, other, and world are neatly segregated from each other, because all schemas (i.e., of the physical environment, of "human nature," of attachment relationships in general, and of specific relationships) are presumed to feed back into each other. Hence those individuals who do not feel secure in interpersonal relationships may find the world as a whole a dangerous place (Guidano & Liotti, 1983).

Importantly, Schank's theory can also provide some conceptual tools for rethinking the operation of defensive phenomena in the construction of working models. If portions of an individual's autobiographical memories enter into cross-referenced schemas at many levels in a variety of schema hierarchies, it is possible to see how defensive processes might selectively interfere in this cross-referencing. For example, one might speculate that material that has been defensively excluded from recall as an autobiographical memory might still influence schema formation at other levels (i.e., general schemas about parenting), thus making the model internally inconsistent and contradictory. The converse might also occur. Autobiographical episodes may be accessible to consciousness, but may be prevented from further processing, and thereby from proper integration into the individual's working model of the world. Once the lines of communication within the representational system (working model of the world) are partially or completely severed, later input will not be adequately processed because distorted or dissociated schemas now guide the processing of new experience (Erdelyi, 1985).

I therefore favor the view that insecure individuals have working models of self and attachment figure in which relevant schemas or schema networks may be dissociated from one another across and within hierarchical levels, giving rise to contradictory communication with others. In a working model with internal organizational impediments, updating of information may occur at one level of the hierarchy, but may then not propagate to others; or schemas of feared or hoped for events may not be clearly tagged as such and hence treated as schemas of actual circumstances. The possible confusions, contradictions and distortions in the interpretation and conduct of attachment relations that such malfunctioning and hence inflexible internal working models could generate are endless. Further research on defensive processes will, of course, be necessary to clarify these ideas. It is particularly important to specify the various organizational levels at which biased processing, storage and retrieval of information is taking place, and to elucidate how biased processing affects communicative processes and vice versa.

Event Representation and the Development of Internal Working Models

It is now time to place research and theorizing on event representation into a developmental framework. That infants remember events as early as 3 months-of-age has been documented in a number of studies that attempted to reelicit previously learned behavior by reinstating the original learning context (e.g., Rovee-Collier & Fagen, 1981; Rovee-Collier & Lipsitt, 1981; Hayne, Rovee-Collier, & Perry, 1987). By 8 months, infants give quite unambiguous indications that they remember the sequential structure of past events. For example, Izard (1978) reported that by 8 months infants with prior experiences in a doctor's office cringe in fear while their arm is being prepared for an injection and subsequently refuse to interact with the nurse responsible for the unpleasant experience. At this age infants also display anticipatory smiles during peek-a-boo games *before* a playmate reappears from behind a cloth (Sroufe & Wunsch, 1972) and anticipatory distress when an attachment figure prepares for departure (Piaget, 1954). Based on these and similar findings as well as Schank's (1982) writings, Stern (1985) postulated that infants may register routine interaction sequences with a caregiver as generalized episodes that store *small coherent chunks of lived experience including not only actions, but sensations, goals, and affects of self and other in a temporal-physical-causal relationship*. Stern called these generalized memory structures RIGs, (Representations of Interactions that have been Generalized). Note, however, that Stern's use of the term representation with respect to RIGs is nontraditional. It implies recognition in context, not a capacity for free recall.

With the onset of representation in the traditional sense (indexed by recall memory not cued by actual events), toddlers demonstrate through engaging in pretend play that they have formed mental schemas of everyday events. In pretense, they reenact on familiar routines, beginning with single acts such as sleeping or eating and progressing to complex sequenced acts that include others (people or dolls) as actors and recipients (see Bretherton, 1984, for a review). The ability to encode simple events in language develops concurrently (e.g., Greenfield & Smith, 1976; Shore, O'Connell, & Bates, 1984).

By 3 years of age, children's growing conversational skills allow us to study their understanding of event schemas through simple interview procedures. Especially if aided by props, children of this age can capably describe routine events such as having dinner or attending a birthday party (Nelson & Gruendel, 1981). Young preschoolers, it turns out, have a good grasp of the order in which the action sequences of routine events take place, especially when these sequences are causally related to each other (see also, Fivush, Keubli, & Clubb, 1992). Furthermore, young children do not have to experience an event many times in order to construct a schema of it (Fivush, 1984; Price & Goodman, 1990). When they expect an event to recur (like going to school), they use the impersonal "you" and the timeless present tense usually reserved for event representations even to talk about the first day of school (". . and then you do reading or something"; Fivush, 1984).

Perhaps not surprisingly, both younger and older preschoolers can access many more details about an event when contextual support is available, either in the form of props (to stimulate reenactment) or in the form of specific verbal probes. In a study of 4- to 7-year-olds, Farrar and Goodman (1992) showed that contextual cues short of reenactment also help. This is true regardless of age. Interestingly, children recall action information about unique events much more accurately than details about the appearance of unfamiliar persons who participate in these events (see review by Davies, this volume; King & Yuille, 1986; Yuille, Cutshall, & King, 1986).

Researchers have also documented a number of age changes in young children's ability to remember events. Autobiographical memories of a specific event—such as eating dinner *last night*—are not easily produced by younger preschoolers (Nelson, 1986; this volume). When asked about a particular dinner episode, 3-year-olds tended to give a generic dinner description instead. At this early age, an event had to be truly extraordinary (going to the circus for the first time) to be recalled as an episodic or autobiographical memory. Older preschoolers not only tended to provide much more detail about routine and unique events, but were also much more likely to make more probabilistic statements about common events than younger preschoolers, reporting details about what might, but need not necessarily happen (Fivush, Kuebli, & Clubb, 1992; Fivush

& Slackman, 1986). Along the same lines, Farrar and Goodman (1992) established that young school children are better able to keep routines and unique events distinct in memory than are young school children. Finally, 3- to 4-year-olds benefit more than 5- to 7-year-olds from being interviewed in a warm, empathic style. Hence, impersonal methods of memory elicitation may give a misleading impression of what younger preschoolers can remember about a unique event (Goodman, Bottoms, Schwartz-Kenney, & Rudy, in press).

This rather brief review of the developmental literature on event representation suggests that, in charting the developmental course of memory, we need to examine important distinctions between *sensorimotor* memories dating from the preverbal period versus later event memories, between memories available to free recall versus memories that are only available in cued or contextually scaffolded recall, and memories for routine events versus autobiographical memories for specific episodes. Having made these distinctions, we need to attend in much greater depth to the role of parent-child dialogue in guiding the child's construction of internal working models of self, others and the world in general.

Studies of Children's Autobiographical Memory and the Social Construction of Reality

As I stated earlier, studies focusing on attachment at the representational level identified parent-child communication as the vehicle for the intergenerational transmission of optimal versus nonoptimal relationship patterns and the construction of self in attachment relationships. A related line of thinking, pioneered by Baldwin (1895), Mead (1934), and Vygotsky (1962), emphasized that a child's construction of reality is, in large part, dependent on social reality as presented by parents and other family members, and later by the larger social network. Although studies in this tradition also focused on intergenerational phenomena, they emphasize the transmission of implicit or explicit cultural content and values rather than issues of mental health.

In their provocative 1989 review on research about the vexing problem of childhood amnesia, Pillemer and White add to this discussion by proposing the existence of two functionally separate memory systems. The first, more primitive system, said to operate from birth, is "addressable" only by external cues and operates via visual and sensory images and affects. This kind of memory system resembles, but is not completely concordant, with the nonverbal memory systems proposed by Bowlby (1980) and Stern (1985) who, unlike Pillemer and White, emphasize that this earlier procedural system also has a social origin.

The second system suggested by Pillemer and White, is socially constructed during the preschool years, is encoded through narrative and can be accessed through deliberate internal retrieval efforts or through social demands. Pillemer and White do not suggest that, in the course of development, the second system comes to replace the first, nor that language can simply be superimposed on the first system. Rather, they posit that verbal communication makes the parallel creation of the second system possible as parents and other supportive adults teach the child how to remember the past through structuring dialogue and leading questions. Such supportive memory talk with adults, they say, will help children acquire a meta-script for deliberate recall and memory sharing. According to this view, individual differences in childhood memories are a product of variation in early patterns of discourse about the past. Only through becoming part of a shared memory system will past events become retrievable by purposeful, internally guided efforts. To use an analogy, only memories in the second system are located in an organized "library" that is organized for systematic memory retrieval, and become increasingly retrievable as the child learns through parental guidance to systematically query his or her memory. According to Pillemer and White, then, dialogue with parents and other supportive adults is important not only with respect to memory content (as suggested by Baldwin, Vygotsky, and Mead) but with respect to its very structure.

Nelson (this volume) reviews a series of important studies on parent-child dialogue that support the notion of parents as socializers of memory structure and content (and hence the child's internal working model of self). For example, Engel's (1986) report on mother-child talk about the past, identified "pragmatic" and "elaborative" maternal styles. Pragmatic mothers tended to discuss concrete events with their 18- to 24-month-olds whereas elaborative mothers presented their children with rich narratives that specified intentions and causes. Elaborative mothers additionally invited their children to help them co-construct the narrative. By 2 years-of-age, their children had begun to engage in more complex memory talk than the children of pragmatic mothers. In a similar study of mother-child conversations about the past, Fivush and Fromhoff (1988) discovered "elaborative" and "repetitive" maternal styles. Elaborative mothers provided their 2-year-olds with a story line, and invited the child's contributions, whereas repetitive mothers were more interested in extracting single items of *correct* information. At the end of the study, children of elaborative mothers produced better episodic memories, even when general language ability was controlled.

Tessler (1986) discovered analogous style differences in maternal talk about *ongoing* events, styles that affected children's later memories of these events. Hers was an experimental study in which mothers were given different instructions on how to behave during a museum visit with their 3.5 year-old children. One group of mothers was told to answer the children's questions, but not to volunteer any comments, while the second group was asked to behave as they normally would. One week later children of mothers behaving normally remembered significantly more about the museum visit than those whose mothers had been limited to answering questions. Interestingly, style differences between mothers in the "normal" group also affected children's recall. Following Bruner's (1986) classification of cognitive styles, Tessler designated these mothers "paradigmatic" versus "narrative." Paradigmatic mothers focused on naming and describing objects, in contradistinction to "narrative" mothers who, like the elaborative mothers mentioned earlier, talked about intentions, causes, and feelings. Narrative mothers also tended to create connections between the museum experience and the child's own life. Given the findings on mother-child conversations about the past, it is not surprising that children of narrative mothers later remembered more about the museum visit than children of paradigmatic mothers. Most notably, no child remembered objects or events that had not been part of a mother-child *dialogue*. In a second study, Tessler (1991) additionally found that quality of recall was not influenced by the style of questioning adopted by the experimenter. The performance of the children with pragmatic mothers did not improve when the researcher used a pragmatic style of memory elicitation. By contrast, children of elaborative mothers performed well, regardless of whether the tester used a pragmatic or elaborative elicitation style.

Unfortunately, there are no corresponding studies on how parents prepare their young children for future events, but Nelson (this volume) was able to draw on her well-known case study of Emily (Nelson, 1989) whose bedtime talk with parents and subsequent crib monologues were regularly audio-recorded beginning at 21 months. Nelson reports that, at bedtime, Emily's parents frequently commented on events that would happen the next day or a few days hence. In subsequent crib monologues Emily recalled these planning talks and often embellished them with simple inferences and speculations (e.g., who would bring a book to read at the babysitter's the next day).

This set of findings on mother-child talk about the present, past, and future suggests that parental styles of structuring and guiding conversation impact the general organization and structure of children's memories, although they do not directly test Pillemer and White's notions. It should also be remembered, as Nelson (this volume) emphasizes, that this process should not be viewed as one of indoctrination, but one of dialogic co-construction in which the child also takes an active role (though mothers appear to differ in the degree to which they encourage active dialogue).

In contrast to the studies reviewed by Nelson, Fivush's studies on parental talk about emotions (see this volume) focus on the *content* of maternal talk to children with respect to gender-specific cultural values. Not only did mothers, in conversing with their children about emotions, implicitly convey what responses are and are not considered appropriate or important in general, they also convey what responses are expected of each gender. Mothers of 2.5- to 3-year-olds who are asked to discuss a memorable event with their children, often chose emotionally charged events. In doing so they mentioned negative emotions to sons more frequently than to daughters, and more readily accepted statements about negative emotions from sons than from daughters. The same was true of fathers. Both fathers and mothers who were asked to discuss emotional situations with their children, attributed more positive emotions to daughters than sons. When distinct emotions were considered, both male and female parents talked more about sadness to daughters than to sons, and created resolutions involving adult comforting more often with daughters than sons. In a third study, mothers again talked more about anger to sons and happiness to daughters. Interestingly, when mothers did discuss anger with daughters, they more often resolved the angry situation through highlighting reestablishment of social ties. With sons, mothers more frequently accepted anger as an appropriate response, and did not object when sons mentioned retaliation (girls never did). Note that, in these studies, both male and female parents adopted strategies in their discussions of emotions that depended on the child's gender. This is concordant with an earlier study by Dunn, Bretherton, and Munn (1987) in which mothers conversed more about emotions with daughters than sons.

Fivush suggests that, as a result of dialogue with their parents, female children much more than male children will come to understand emotions as an integral part of social relationships. Boys and girls will therefore acquire a very different emotional self-concept, although they seem to acquire knowledge appropriate to the self-concept of both genders (otherwise parents would not be able to adopt socialization strategies appropriate to a child of the opposite gender). From a socialization standpoint, it is also noteworthy that the children tended to agree with most of their parents' emotional attributions.

Although Fivush's specific findings cannot be generalized beyond middle-class White families, the overall conclusion (that the content of parents' talk about emotions implicitly conveys messages about gender-related values) is supported by other studies. In an analysis of mother-daughter dialogue in working class families, Miller, Potts, Fung, Hoogstra, and Mintz (1990) showed that these mothers valued anger, self-assertion, and feistiness in their daughters, though we do not yet have data on how this related to the child's self-concept later.

More importantly for Fivush's hypotheses about the socialization of memory, Miller has been able to demonstrate that personal story telling is an important part of the everyday life of families from many cultural backgrounds, be they White working-class families in South Baltimore, low income African-American families in Chicago, or middle-class Chinese families in Taipei. In all three settings, children were exposed to personal stories. In addition to hearing and participating in stories about themselves, children also overheard stories told about other people. Miller et al. underscore that the experience and participation in personal stories may define or redefine the child's sense of relational self, or in the language I have used here, may contribute to the child's internal working model of self in relationships.

Miller, Hoogstra, Mintz, Fung, and Williams (this volume) also emphasize that, beyond talking to their children about personal experiences, parents bring children in contact with cultural products such as books. Dialogues structured around cultural products are a further avenue through which parents, as individuals and members of their cultural group, have an impact on their children's working model of self. Miller et al.'s chapter (this volume) illustrates how one 23-month-old child appropriates a well-known story, and through a series of retellings comes to terms with some of its disturbing implications. The story in question, the "Tale of Peter Rabbit" by Beatrix Potter, depicts Peter as disobeying his mother's injunctions, helping himself to forbidden food in Mr. McGregor's garden, encountering mortal danger (in the person of the fearsome Mr. McGregor), miraculously escaping, getting lost and finally finding his way home to mother and siblings. It is important to know that the child to whom the story was read (Kurt) had had many pleasant experiences in his grandparents' garden where he had also seen rabbits.

Over a period of several weeks, Kurt requested many readings of the story, and then used retellings to work through the various disturbing story issues that did not seem to accord with his own experience of families in gardens. In the course of these retellings, naughty Peter becomes an obedient child who lives in harmony with his mother, engages in reparative behavior such as planting seeds in the garden, and for whom the fearsome Mr. McGregor is no longer an enemy.

An especially noteworthy aspect of the retellings was a lessening of affect as threats to Kurt's world were gradually resolved. Once his personal concerns about the story were worked out (that Peter might disobey mother and destroy the garden, that he might experience danger alone and be scared, that bad things might happen to the family), the retellings ceased. Another important aspect of Kurt's retellings was Kurt's impressive ability to take the perspectives of Peter Rabbit, of Peter's mother, and of an involved narrator who sided first with Peter and then with Peter's mother. Kurt assimilated the story by taking on the role of other selves. Finally, it is notable that, in terms of constructing an internal working model of self, Kurt's mother accepted and supported his attempts to come to grips with the story's challenges to his world. We can imagine a different outcome for Kurt if his mother had insisted, instead, that he stick to the *facts* of the story.

This study of how one small child deals with upsetting story situations leads me to a discussion of how memories of actual traumatic experiences (as opposed to somewhat upsetting stories) are incorporated into a child's internal working model of self and the world. Although Bowlby (1980, 1985) dwelt on the importance of open parent-child communication about traumatic events for healthy development, he did not sufficiently consider the young child's inability to understand such events. There is always a danger, overlooked by most attachment researchers, that children may misinterpret what they are told because their background knowledge or level of cognitive understanding is insufficient. There is, of course, also a danger (already noted by Bowlby, 1973, 1980) that parents may find it unbearable to communicate about events that are painful or guilt-inducing to them.

Research on Memory of Traumatic Experiences

Steward (this volume) reports that amongst young children undergoing medical procedures misinterpretations are rampant. Children may misunderstand the motivations and abilities of medical staff ("they stole my blood" or "the doctor will be able to see the bad thoughts in my head"). Even when parents are very sensitive to a child's experience, painful, invasive, and incomprehensible procedures may lead the child to blame the parent for allowing such traumatic things to happen (Robertson & Freud, 1956).

What about long-lasting memories of traumatic experiences on a child's working model of self? Terr (1983; see also Terr, 1991) studied 23 children who were trapped by kidnappers in a buried van for over 24 hours, but were able to escape by their own efforts. At the time of this event, the children were between 5- and 14-years-old. Four years later, memories of the original event were still clearly etched in the children's minds as shown by their ability to visualize the experience in vivid detail. Rather than repressing the memory of the event itself, as expected on the basis of findings with adults, the children had suppressed/ repressed memories of their subsequent symptoms and behaviors. Panic attacks and nightmares, mentioned by many shortly after the kidnapping, seemed to have vanished from the children's memories. Most notably however, in terms of their internal working model of self, victims had acquired a frighteningly pessimistic outlook on life. Many felt that they would die young or that the world might soon come to an end. Furthermore, many had reinterpreted events prior to the kidnapping as omens that ought to have warned them or their parents of the impending disaster (choosing guilt and anxiety over helplessness). Dreams of the event were disguised or modified, and half of the children remembered dying in their dreams. In addition, many engaged in repetitive posttraumatic play of the kidnapping.

Although Terr reports that the children's parents downplayed the significance of the kidnapping event, it is not clear to what extent the children could have withstood this kind of assault to their internal working model of the world as a trustworthy place, even if parents could have been emotionally more available to them.

Because parents are guides and partners in a child's construction of internal working models of self and the world, findings on children's difficulties in processing traumatic memories have implications for helping parents (and other supportive adults) help the child (Steward, 1988), possibly over a long period of time. By making parents aware of what a child is likely to experience or (in the case of disasters) to have experienced, the parents will be better able to support and understand the child's coping attempts. In line with this argument, a study by Pinto and Hollandsworth (1989) shows that children's preoperative fears were significantly allayed when they were asked to view an informative videotape prior to the child's elective surgery. The parents' anxiety was also significantly allayed by this procedure. In addition, the recovery time was significantly shorter when video-preparation was provided. A less anxious, better informed parent, is better able to provide emotional support to the child, and a well-informed child is less anxious. By contrast, an ill-informed parent may either not be able to cooperate with the hospital staff, or may take sides against the child.

Steward (this volume) reports that parents who underestimate their child's pain often become angry when the child resists or complains and side with the medical staff, rather than offering comfort to their child. Other parents, wanting to protect their children from unpleasant reality, resist attempts by hospital staff to debrief children about medical procedures or their illness. Hence a number of child cancer victims grow up without much guidance on how to make sense of their early memories of hospital experiences. Unfortunately, however, ignoring these issues does not mean that the children will not think about the meaning of traumatic experiences. Steward reports that when either parents or medical staff fail to provide comprehensible preparation and debriefing, hospitalized children try to help each other. In doing so, they will often share their (perhaps horrifying) misconceptions with each other, misconceptions that may haunt them for many years.

In one recent study by Steward, Steward, Farquhar, Joyce, Reinhart, Myers, and Welker (1991) children were videotaped during a medical procedure and later interviewed about the touching and handling they received. Children's memories tended, on the whole, to be very accurate, even several months later, with two subgroups providing particularly interesting insights. One group reported extreme distress at some of the procedures and gave outstandingly accurate reports of their experiences, but neither the doctors nor the nurses were aware of the level of these children's distress (there was no correlation between the children's own ratings of distress and those by medical staff). A second group of children did not rate any of the touches or handling they had received as painful, even though they seemed to have perceived the quite invasive procedures (some involving body restraint) as painful at the time. Despite their denial of pain, children in this group were nevertheless able to quite accurately remember the clinic room as well as the persons present in it. In her preliminary analyses of these findings, Steward suggests links between this behavior and parental coping, citing the responses of one mother who countered her child's protest by: "If you don't shut up, I'm going to leave you." Steward wonders whether this child simply *chose* not to report his painful experiences because he was shamed for them, or whether he did not remember them at all. Investigators have tended not to distinguish between these possibilities. Nevertheless, whether the child chose not to mention pain, or had repressed his memories of pain, these circumstances deprived the child of the opportunity to come to terms with his experience through dialogue with supportive others.

The research on traumatic memories reminds me of Stern's (1985) contention that language can be a double-edged sword. On the one hand, it makes experience more sharable with others, but on the other hand it may drive a wedge between experience as lived and as narrated. Stern, like other psychoanalysts, posits that nonverbalized (sensorimotor-affective) experience continues to influence behavior. Bowlby, also, warned that unbearable mental conflict ensues when a child is not permitted to share his or her traumatic experiences with a supportive parent, leading to defensive exclusion of memories from awareness. Although perhaps not as damaging, refraining from sharing remembered events because they engender feelings of doubt and shame may also have a detrimental influence on a child's working model of self. First, because there is no opportunity to correct misconceptions, and second because the child's sense of self-worth will be affected.

CONCLUSION

Bowlby's notion that interaction patterns are translated into internal working models of self, other, and the world have significance beyond attachment theory, narrowly conceived. Attachment research teaches us that sensitive and emotionally open communication with parents results in working models of a self that is securely related to others. By inference, attachment research suggests that emotionally open child-parent communication patterns affect the very structure and organization of memory, not just its content. Memory structure, according to attachment theory, may become distorted by pervasive defensive processes as dissociative and repressive phenomena of greater or lesser pervasiveness interfere with the organization of internal working models and hence with an individual's ability to communicate and to adapt to reality. Although this process is bidirectional (both partner's working models are involved), attachment theory highlights the initial importance of the parent's ability to respond to positive and negative child signals with appropriate feedback.

Interestingly, Pillemer and White's (1989) theorizing on the development of a deliberately addressable narrative memory system also involves parental communication strategies in the child's emerging memory organization. By scaffolding their children's attempts at producing narrative accounts of the past, parents induce the development of a well-organized system that can be intentionally accessed. Nelson's review (this volume) corroborates this view of memory socialization, but also sheds light on the origin of individual differences by documenting that parents' narrative style comes to be reflected in the structure of child memories (elaborative or narrative versus repetitive, or pragmatic). We cannot yet make predictions about more long-lasting effects of elaborative and restricted narrative styles on adult memory structure, but some of these ideas mesh well with attachment theory.

Parents and other important social partners socialize not only the structure and organization of children's memory systems, but also influence the content of memory. According to attachment theory, a sensitively responsive parent helps a child develop an internal working model of self as worthy of support and love. Gender and cultural differences have not been emphasized by attachment researchers because their focus tends to be on cross-cultural similarity, rather than culture-specific differences. By contrast, social constructionists, who also regard working models of self as the joint product of parent-child interaction, focus on such issues as gender, ethnic, and class differences without overtly assigning a positive or negative value to individual differences. I suggest that two approaches could profitably cross-fertilize each other, with social constructionists paying attention to issues of defense and mental health (the chapter by Miller et al. is a step in this direction) and attachment theorists examining how different cultures socialize attachment and other interpersonal behaviors in relation to their adult ideal of mental health.

The research on memories of trauma, however, is a useful reminder that some experiences are exceedingly difficult to process, even when a supportive figure is available. Attachment theory suggests that their assimilation will be even more difficult if parents themselves engage in defensive exclusion of their children's pain, but we need to acknowledge that even a supportive parent may fail in this regard. We need to learn much more about healthy coping and unhealthy defensive processes in situations that shake a child's confidence in the trustworthiness of the world. We also need to know more about developmental differences in children's ability to cope with trauma.

In short, we have a long way to go before we can confidently chart memory development from the emergence of interpersonal schemas within early transactions with caregivers to the establishment of ever more complex internal working models of self and others, whether from the mental health or enculturation perspective. A yet more difficult task for the future (see also Nelson, this volume) is to examine internal working models from a historical perspective, that is, to provide a developmental account of how individuals socially construct autobiographical narratives, linking salient personal memories of the past to goals for and fears of the future. I surmise that this, too, begins much earlier than we have hitherto suspected.

REFERENCES

Ainsworth, M. D. S. (1967). *Infancy in Uganda: Child care and the growth of love.* Baltimore, MD: The Johns Hopkins University Press.

Ainsworth, M. D. S., & Bell, S. M. (1969). Some contemporary patterns in the feeding situation. In A. Ambrose (Ed.), *Stimulation in early infancy* (pp. 133–170). London: Academic Press.

Ainsworth, M. D. S., Bell, S. M., Blehar, M. C., & Main, M. (1971, April). *Physical contact: A study of infant responsiveness and its relation to maternal handling.* Paper presented at the biennial meeting of the Society for Research in Child Development, Minneapolis, Minnesota.

Ainsworth, M. D. S., Bell, S. M., & Stayton, D. (1974). Infant-mother attachment and social development. In M. P. Richards (Ed.), *The introduction of the child into a social world* (pp. 99–135). London: Cambridge University Press.

Ainsworth, M. D. S., Blehar, M. C., Waters, E., & Wall, S. (1978). *Patterns of attachment: A psychological study of the strange situation.* Hillsdale, NJ: Lawrence Erlbaum Associates.

Baldwin, J. M. (1895). *Mental development of the child and the race: Methods and processes.* New York: Macmillan.

Bartlett, F. C. (1933). *Remembering: A study in experimental and social psychology.* London: Cambridge University Press.

Bell, S. M., & Ainsworth, M. D. S. (1972). Infant crying and maternal responsiveness. *Child Development, 43,* 1171–1190.

Blehar, M. C., Lieberman, A. F., & Ainsworth, M. D. S. (1977). Early face-to-face interaction and its relation to later infant-mother attachment. *Child Development, 48,* 182–194.

Bowlby, J. (1969). *Attachment and loss. Vol. 1: Attachment.* New York: Basic Books (2nd revised edition, 1982).

Bowlby, J. (1973). *Attachment and loss. Vol. 2: Separation.* New York: Basic Books.

Bowlby, J. (1980). *Attachment and loss. Vol. 3: Loss, sadness and depression.* New York: Basic Books.

Bowlby, J. (1985). The role of childhood experience in cognitive disturbance. In M. J. Mahoney & A. Freeman (Eds.), *Cognition and psychotherapy* (pp. 181–200). New York: Plenum.

Brazelton, T. B., & Cramer, B. G. (1990). *The earliest relationship.* Reading, MA: Addison Wesley.

Brazelton, T. B., Kozlowski, B., & Main, M. (1974). The origins of reciprocity in mother-infant interactions. In M. Lewis & L. A. Rosenblum (Eds.), *The effect of the infant on its caregiver.* New York: Wiley.

Bretherton, I. (1980). Young children in stressful situations: The supporting role of attachment figures and unfamiliar caregivers. In G. V. Coelho & P. J. Ahmen (Eds.), *Uprooting and development.* New York: Plenum.

Bretherton, I. (1985). Attachment theory: Retrospect and prospect. In I. Bretherton & E. Waters (Eds.), Growing points of attachment theory and research. *Monographs of the Society for Research in Child Development, 50,* Serial No. 209 (1–2), 3–35.

Bretherton, I. (1987). New perspectives on attachment relations: Security, communication, and internal working models. In J. Osofsky (Ed.), *Handbook of infant development* (pp. 1061–1100). New York: Wiley.

Bretherton, I. (1990). Open communication and internal working models: their role in the development of attachment relationships. In R. A. Thompson (Ed.), *Socioemotional development. Nebraska symposium on motivation 1988* (pp. 59–113). Lincoln: University of Nebraska Press.

Bretherton, I. (1991). Pouring new wine into old bottles: the social self as internal working model. In M. Gunnar & L. A. Sroufe (Eds.), *Self processes in development.* Minnesota Symposia on child psychology (Vol. 23, pp. 1–41). Hillsdale, NJ: Lawrence Erlbaum Associates.

Bretherton, I., Biringen, Z., Ridgeway, D., Maslin, C., & Sherman, M. (1989). Attachment: The parental perspective. *Infant Mental Health Journal, 10,* 203–221.

Bretherton, I., Ridgeway, D., & Cassidy, J. (1990). Assessing internal working models of the attachment relationship: An attachment story completion task for 3-year-olds. In D. Cicchetti, M. Greenberg, & E. M. Cummings (Eds.), *Attachment during the preschool years* (pp. 272–308). Chicago: University of Chicago Press.

Bruner, J. S. (1986). *Actual minds, possible worlds.* Cambridge, MA: Harvard University Press.

Cain, A. C., & Fast, I. (1972). Children's disturbed reactions to parent suicide. In A. C. Cain (Ed.), *Survivors of suicide* (pp. 93–111). Springfield, IL: C. C. Thomas.

Cassidy, J. (1988). The self as related to child-mother attachment at six. *Child Development, 59,* 121–134.

Craik, K. (1943). *The nature of explanation.* London: Cambridge University Press.

Crittenden, P. (1990). Internal representational models of attachment relationships. *Infant Mental Health Journal.*

Dixon, N. F. (1971). *Subliminal perception: The nature of a controversy.* London: McGraw-Hill.

Dunn, J., Bretherton, I., & Munn, P. (1987). Conversations about feeling states between mothers and their young children. *Developmental Psychology, 23,* 132–139.

Eichberg, D. (1987, April). *Quality of infant-parent attachment: Related to mother's representation of her own relationship history.* Paper presented at the biennial meetings of the Society for Research in Child Development, Baltimore, MD.

Engel, S. (1986). *Learning to reminisce: A developmental study of how young children learn to talk about the past.* Unpublished doctoral dissertation, City University of New York, Graduate Center.

Erdelyi, H. M. (1985). *Psychoanalysis: Freud's cognitive psychology.* San Francisco: W. H. Freeman.

Escher-Graeub, D., & Grossmann, K. E. (1983). *Bindungssicherheit im zweiten Lebensjahr-die Regensburger Querschnittuntersuchung* [attachment security in the second year of life: The Regensburg cross-sectional study]. Research Report, University of Regensburg.

Fairbairn, W. R. D. (1952). *Psychoanalytic studies of the personality.* London: Tavistock Publications.

Farrar, M. J., & Goodman, G. S. (1992). Developmental changes in event memory. *Child Development, 63,* 173–187.

Fivush, R. (1984). Learning about school: The development of kindergartners' school scripts. *Child Development, 55,* 1697–1709.

Fivush, R., & Fromhoff, F. A. (1988). Style and structure in mother-child conversations about the past. *Discourse Processes, 8,* 177–204.

Fivush, R., Kuebli, J., & Clubb, P. A. (1992). The structure of events and event representations: A developmental analysis. *Child Development, 63,* 188–207.

Fivush, R., & Slackman, E. (1986). The acquisition and development of scripts. In K. Nelson, *Event knowledge: Structure and function in development* (pp. 71–96). Hillsdale, NJ: Lawrence Erlbaum Associates.

Fonagy, P., Steele, H., & Steele, M. (1991). Intergenerational patterns of attachment: Maternal representations during pregnancy and subsequent infant-mother attachments. *Child Development, 62,* 891–905.

Freud, S. (1940). An outline of psychoanalysis. In J. Strachey (Ed. and Trans.), *The standard edition of the complete psychological works of Sigmund Freud* (Vol. 23, pp. 137–207). London: Hogarth.

George, C., Kaplan, N., & Main, M. (1984). *Adult attachment interview for adults.* Unpublished manuscript, University of California, Berkeley.

Goodman, G. S., Bottoms, B. L., Schwartz-Kenney, B. M., & Rudy, L. (1991). Children's memory for a stressful event: Improving children's report. *Journal of Narrative and Life History, 1,* 69–99.

Greenfield, P. M., & Smith, J. (1976). *The structure of communication in early relationships.* New York: Academic Press.

Grossmann, K., Fremmer-Bombik, E., Rudolph, J., & Grossmann, K. E. (1988). Maternal attachment representations as related to patterns of infant-mother attachment and maternal care during the first year. In R. A. Hinde and J. Stevenson-Hinde (Eds.), *Relationships within families* (pp. 241–260). Oxford: Oxford University Press.

Grossmann, K. E., & Grossmann, K. (1990). The wider concept of attachment in cross-cultural research. *Human Development.*

Grossmann, K. E., Grossmann, K., & Schwan, A. (1986). Capturing the wider view of attachment: A reanalysis of Ainsworth's Strange Situation. In C. E. Izard & P. B. Read (Eds.), *Measuring emotions in infants and children* (vol. 2, pp. 124–171). New York: Cambridge University Press.

Guidano, V. F., & Liotti, G. (1983). *Cognitive processes and emotional disorders.* New York: The Guilford Press.

Hartmann, H. (1958). *Ego psychology and the problem of adaptation.* New York: International Universities Press.

Hayne, H., Rovee-Collier, C., & Perris, E. E. (1987). Categorization and memory-retrieval by 3-month-olds. *Child Development, 58,* 750–767.

Heinicke, C. M., Diskin, S. D., Ramsey-Klee, D., & Given, K. (1983). Pre-birth parent characteristics and family development in the first year of life. *Child Development, 54,* 194–208.

Izard, C. E. (1978). Emotions as motivations: An evolutionary-developmental perspective. In R. A. Dienstbier (Eds.), *Nebraska symposium on motivation* (pp. 163–200). Lincoln: University of Nebraska Press.

Johnson-Laird, P. N. (1983). *Mental models.* Cambridge, MA: Harvard University Press.

King, J. L., & Yuille, J. C. (1986). *An investigation of the eyewitness abilities of children.* Unpublished manuscript, University of British Columbia.

Kobak, R. R., & Sceery, A. (1988). Attachment in late adolescence: Working models, affect regulation, and perceptions of self and others. *Child Development, 59,* 135–146.

Lieberman, A. F., & Pawl, J. H. (1990). Disorders of attachment and secure base behavior in the second year of life: Conceptual issues and clinical intervention. In M. T. Greenberg, D. Cicchetti, & E. M. Cummings (Eds.), *Attachment in the preschool years* (pp. 375–397). Chicago: University of Chicago Press.

Main, M., & Goldwyn, R. (in press). Interview-based adult attachment classifications: Related to infant-mother and infant-father attachment. *Developmental Psychology.*

Main, M., & Hesse, E. (1990). The insecure disorganized/disoriented attachment pattern in infancy: Precursors and sequelae. In M. Greenberg, D. Cicchetti, & E. M. Cummings (Ed.), *Attachment during the preschool years: Theory, research, and interventions* (pp. 161–182). Chicago: University of Chicago Press.

Main, M., Kaplan, K., & Cassidy, J. (1985). Security in infancy, childhood and adulthood: A move to the level of representation. In I. Bretherton & E. Waters (Eds.), Growing points of attachment theory and research, *Monographs of the Society for Research in Child Development, 50,* Serial No. 209 (1–2), 66–104.

Main, M., & Solomon, J. (1990). Procedure for identifying infants as disorganized/disoriented during the Ainsworth Strange situation. In M. Greenberg, D. Cicchetti, & E. M. Cummings (Ed.), *Attachment during the preschool years: Theory, research, and intervention* (pp. 121–160). Chicago: University of Chicago Press.

Mandler, J. H. (1979). Categorical and schematic organization in memory. In C. R. Puff (Ed.), *Memory organization and structure* (pp. 259–299). New York: Academic Press.

Matas, L., Arend, R. A., & Sroufe, L. A. (1978). Continuity and adaptation in the second year: The relationship between quality of attachment and later competence. *Child Development, 49,* 547–556.

Mead, G. H. (1934). *Mind, self and society.* Chicago: University of Chicago Press.

Miller, P. J., Potts, R., Fung, H., Hoogstra, L., & Mintz, J. (1990). Narrative practices and the social construction of self in childhood. *American Ethnologist, 17,* 292–311.

Neisser, U. (1987). What is ordinary memory the memory of? In U. Neisser and E. Winograd (Eds.), *Remembering reconsidered* (pp. 356–373). New York: Cambridge University Press.

Nelson, K. (1986). *Event knowledge: Structure and function in development.* Hillsdale, NJ: Lawrence Erlbaum Associates.

Nelson, K., & Gruendel, J. (1981). Generalized event representations: Basic building blocks of cognitive development. In M. E. Lamb & A. Brown (Eds.), *Advances in developmental psychology* (vol. 1, pp. 131–158). Hillsdale, NJ: Lawrence Erlbaum Associates.

Pinto, R. P., & Hollandsworth, J. G. (1989). Using videotape modeling to prepare children psychologically for surgery: Influence of parents and cost versus benefits of providing preparation services. *Health Psychology, 8,* 79–95.

Piaget, J. (1951). *The origins of intelligence in children*. New York: Norton.

Piaget, J. (1954). *The construction of reality in the child*. New York: Basic Books.

Pillemer, D. B., & White, S. H. (1989). Childhood events recalled by children and adults. In H. W. Reese (Ed.), *Advances in child development and behavior* (pp. 297–340). New York: Academic Press.

Price, D. W. W., Goodman, G. S. (1990). Visiting the wizard: Children's memory for a recurring event. *Child Development, 61*, 664–680.

Radke-Yarrow, M., Cummings, E. M., Kuczynsky, L., & Chapman, M. (1985). Patterns of attachment in two- and three-year-olds in normal families and families with parental depression. *Child Development, 56*, 884–893.

Ricks, M. H. (1985). The social transmission of parenting: attachment across generations. In I. Bretherton & E. Waters (Eds.), Growing points of attachment theory and research, *Monographs of the Society for Research in Child Development, 50*, Serial No. 209 (1–2), 211–227.

Robertson, J., & Freud, A. (1956). A mother's observation on the tonsillectomy of her four-year-old daughter. *Psychoanalytic Study of the Child, 11*, 410–436.

Rovee-Collier, C. K., & Fagen, C. W. (1981). The retrieval of memory in early infancy. In L. P. Lipsitt (Ed.), *Advances in infancy research, Vol. 1* (pp. 225–254). Norwood, NJ: Ablex.

Rovee-Collier, C. K., & Lipsitt, L. P. (1981). Learning, adaptation, and memory. In P. M. Stratton (Ed.), *Psychobiology of the human newborn* (pp. 147–190). New York: Wiley.

Schank, R. C., & Abelson, R. P. (1977). *Scripts, plans, goals and understanding*. Hillsdale, NJ: Lawrence Erlbaum Associates.

Schank, R. C. (1982). *Dynamic memory: A theory of reminding and learning in computers and people*. London: Cambridge University Press.

Shore, C., O'Connell, B., & Bates, E. (1984). First sentences in language and symbolic play. *Developmental Psychology, 20*, 872–880.

Slough, N., & Greenberg, M. (1990). 5-year-olds representation of separation from parents: responses for self and a hypothetical child. In I. Bretherton & M. Watson (Eds.), *Children's perspectives on the family* (New Directions for Child Development, W. Damon, Series Editor). San Francisco: Jossey-Bass.

Sroufe, L. A., & Fleeson, J. (1986). Attachment and the construction of relationships. In W. Hartup & K. Rubin (Eds.), *Relationships and development* (pp. 51–71). Hillsdale, NJ: Lawrence Erlbaum Associates.

Sroufe, L. A., & Wunsch, J. P. (1972). The development of laughter in the first year of life. *Child Development, 43*, 1326–1344.

Stayton, D. J., & Ainsworth, M. D. S. (1973). Individual differences in infant responses to brief everyday separations as related to other infant and maternal behaviors. *Developmental Psychology, 9*, 226–235.

Stern, D. N. (1985). *The interpersonal world of the infant*. New York: Basic Books.

Stern, D. N., Beebe, B., Jaffe, J., & Bennett, S. (1977). The infant's stimulus world during social interaction. In H. R. Schaffer (Ed.), *Studies in mother-infant interaction*. London: Academic Press.

Steward, M. S. (1988). Illness: A crisis for children. In J. Sandoval (Ed.), *Crisis Counseling, intervention, and prevention in the schools* (pp. 109–129). Hillsdale, NJ: Lawrence Erlbaum Associates.

Steward, M. S., Steward, D. S., Farquhar, L., Joyce, N., Reinhart, M., Myers, J. E. B., & Welker, J. (1991). *A visit to the doctor: The accuracy, completeness, and consistency of children's memory*. Manuscript submitted for publication.

Sullivan, H. S. (1953). *The interpersonal theory of psychiatry*. New York: Norton.

Terr, L. (1983). Chowchilla revisited: The effects of psychic trauma four years after a school-bus kidnapping. *American Journal of Psychiatry, 140*, 1543–1550.

Terr, L. (1991). Childhood traumas: An outline and overview. *American Journal of Psychiatry, 148*, 10–20.

Tessler, M. (1986). *Mother-child talk in a museum: The socialization of a memory.* Unpublished manuscript, City University of New York Graduate Center.

Tessler, M. (1991). *Making memories together: The influence of mother-child joint encoding on the development of autobiographical memory style.* Unpublished doctoral dissertation, City University of New York Graduate Center.

Tronick, E. Z., Ricks, M., & Cohn, J. F. (1982). Maternal and infant affective exchanges: Patterns of adaptation. In T. Field & A. Fogel (Eds.), *Emotion and early interaction.* Hillsdale, NJ: Lawrence Erlbaum Associates.

Tulving, E. (1972). Episodic and semantic memory. In E. Tulving and W. Donaldson (Eds.), *Organization of memory* (pp. 382–403). New York: Academic Press.

Tulving, E. (1983). *Elements of episodic memory.* New York: Oxford University Press.

Vygotsky, L. (1962). *Thought and language.* Cambridge, MA: MIT Press.

Ward, M. J., Carlson, E. A., Altman, S., Levine, L., Greenberg, R. H., & Kessler, D. B. (1990, April). *Predicting infant-mother attachment from adolescents' prenatal working models of relationships.* Paper presented at the 7th International Conference on Infant Studies. Montreal, Canada.

Wason, P. C., & Johnson-Laird, P. N. (1972). *Psychology of reasoning: Structure and content.* Cambridge, MA: Harvard University Press.

Yuille, J. C., Cutshall, J. L., & King, M. A. (1986). *Age related changes in eyewitness accounts and photo-identification.* Unpublished manuscript, University of British Columbia.

Zeanah, C. H., Keener, M. A., Stewart, L., & Anders, T. F. (1985). Prenatal perception of infant personality: A preliminary investigation. *Journal of the American Academy of Child Psychiatry, 24,* 204–210.

Author Index

Subject Index